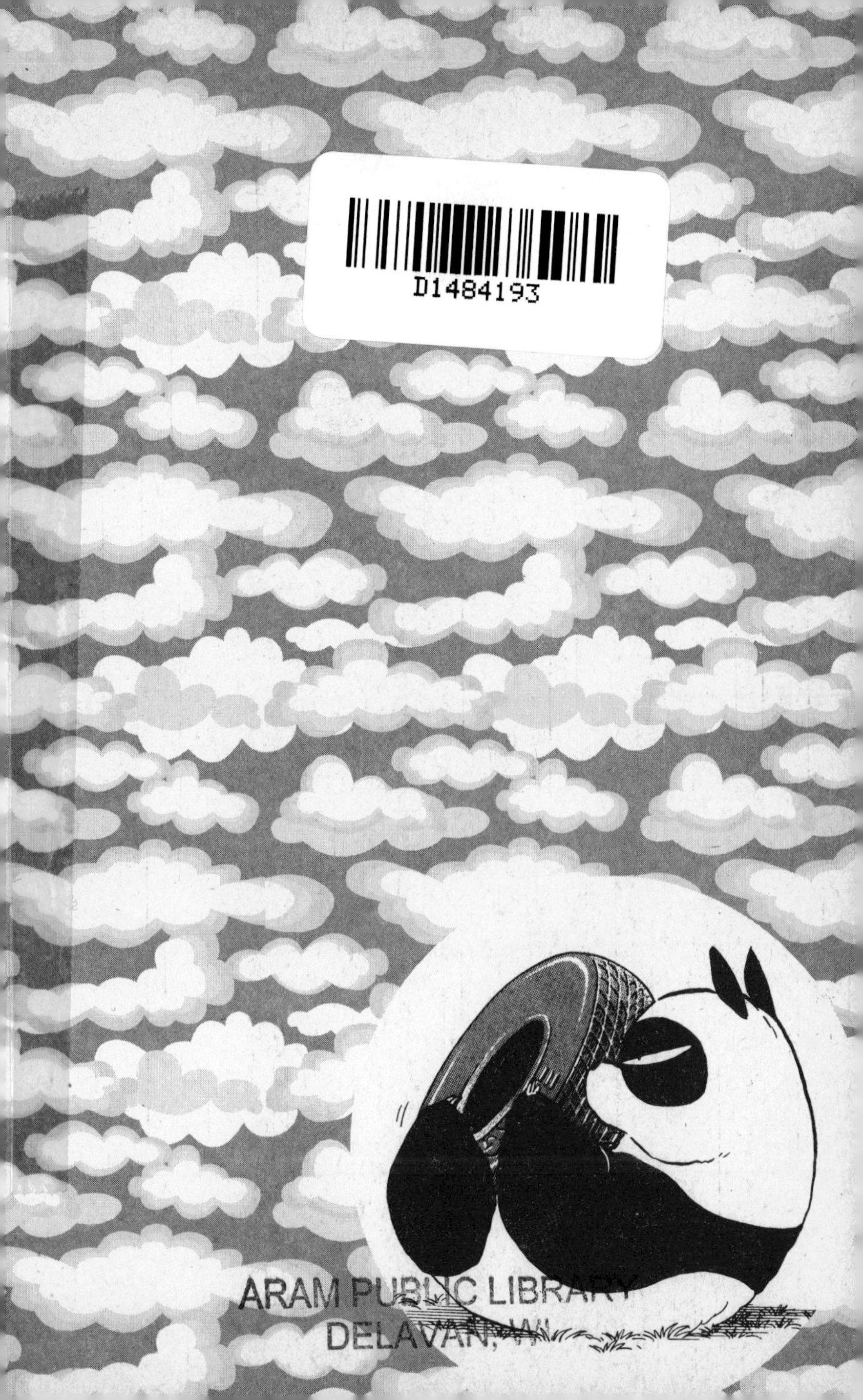

Ranma 1/2

VOL. 30
Action Edition

Story and Art by
RUMIKO TAKAHASHI

English Adaptation/Gerard Jones
Touch-Up Art & Lettering/Bill Schuch
Cover and Interior Design /Yuki Ameda
Editor (1st Edition)/Julie Davis
Editor (Action Edition)/Avery Gotoh
Supervising Editor (Action Edition)/Michelle Pangilinan

Managing Editor/Annette Roman
Director of Production/Noboru Watanabe
Editorial Director/Alvin Lu
Sr. Director of Acquisitions/Rika Inouye
Vice President of Sales & Marketing/Liza Coppola
Executive Vice President/Hyoe Narita
Publisher/Seiji Horibuchi

Printed in Canada.

Published by VIZ, LLC
P.O. Box 77010
San Francisco, CA 94107

Action Edition
10 9 8 7 6 5 4 3 2 1
First Printing, April 2005

www.viz.com

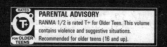

PARENTAL ADVISORY
RANMA 1/2 is rated T+ for Older Teen. This volume contains violence and suggestive situations. Recommended for older teens (16 and up).

store.viz.com

Ranma ½

VOL. 30   Action Edition

STORY & ART BY
RUMIKO TAKAHASHI

STORY THUS FAR

The Tendos are an average, run-of-the-mill Japanese family—on the surface, that is. Soun Tendo is the owner and proprietor of the Tendo Dojo, where "Anything Goes Martial Arts" is practiced. Like the name says, anything goes, and usually does.

When Soun's old friend Genma Saotome comes to visit, Soun's three lovely young daughters—Akane, Nabiki and Kasumi—are told that it's time for one of them to become the fiancée of Genma's teenage son, as per an agreement made between the two fathers years ago. Youngest daughter Akane—who says she hates boys—is quickly nominated for bridal duty by her sisters.

Unfortunately, Ranma and his father have suffered a strange accident. While training in China, both plunged into one of many "cursed" springs at the legendary martial arts training ground of Jusenkyo. These springs transform the unlucky dunkee into whoever—or whatever—drowned there hundreds of years ago.

From then on, a splash of cold water turns Ranma's father into a giant panda, and Ranma becomes a beautiful, busty young woman. Hot water reverses the effect...but only until next time. As it turns out, Ranma and Genma aren't the only ones who have taken the Jusenkyo plunge—and it isn't long before they meet several other members of the Jusenkyo "cursed."

Although their parents are still determined to see Ranma and Akane marry and assume ownership of the training hall, Ranma seems to have a strange talent for accumulating surplus fiancées...and Akane has a few stubbornly determined suitors of her own. Will the two ever work out their differences and get rid of all these "extra" people, or will they just call the whole thing off? What's a half-boy, half-girl (not to mention all-girl, angry girl) to do...?

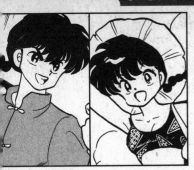

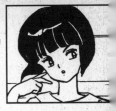

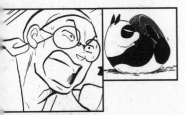

RANMA SAOTOME
Martial artist with far too many fiancées, and an ego that won't let him take defeat. Changes into a girl when splashed with cold water.

NABIKI TENDO
Always ready to "make a buck" off the suffering of others, cold-hearted capitalist Nabiki is the middle Tendo daughter.

KASUMI TENDO
Sweet-natured eldest Tendo daughter and substitute mother figure for the Tendo family.

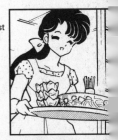

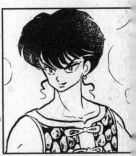

GENMA SAOTOME
Ranma's lazy father, who left his wife and home years ago with his young son (Ranma), to train in the martial arts. Changes into a panda.

PANTYHOSE TARO
Yet another victim of the Jusenkyo Plunge, he holds a wicked grudge against both Ranma and Happosai, whom he holds responsible for his unfortunate name.

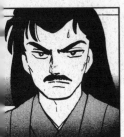

SOUN TENDO
Head of the Tendo household and owner of the Tendo Dojo. Father of three daughters.

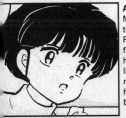

AKANE TENDO
Martial artist, tomboy, and Ranma's reluctant fiancée. Has no clue how much Ryoga likes her, or what relation he might have to her pet black pig, P-chan.

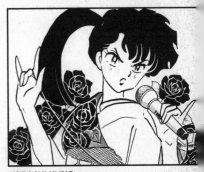

KODACHI KUNO
Twisted sister of Tatewaki. An expert in Martial Arts Rhythmic Gymnastics, she's determined to use her ribbon-whipping skills to tame Ranma.

CONTENTS

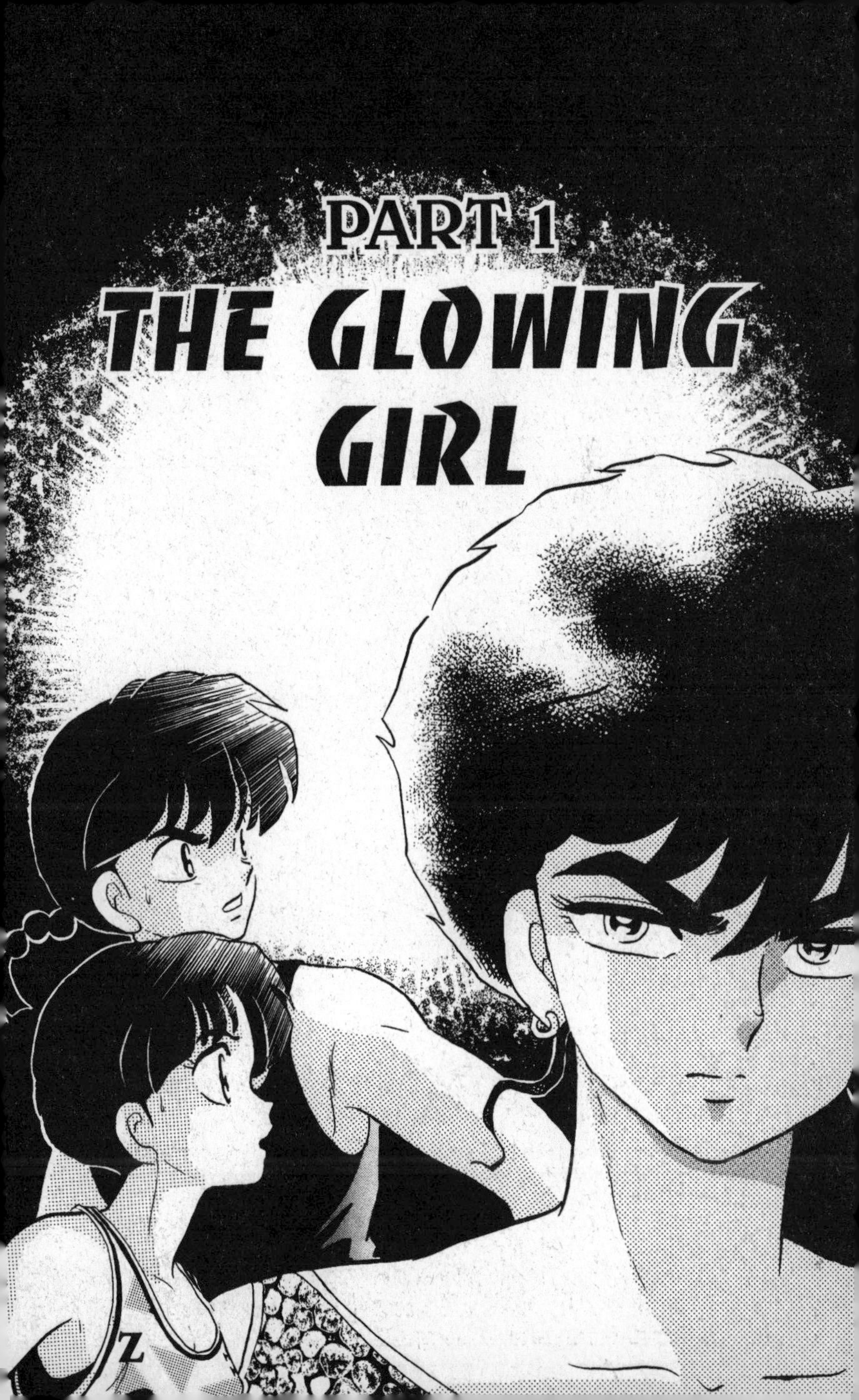
PART 1
THE GLOWING GIRL

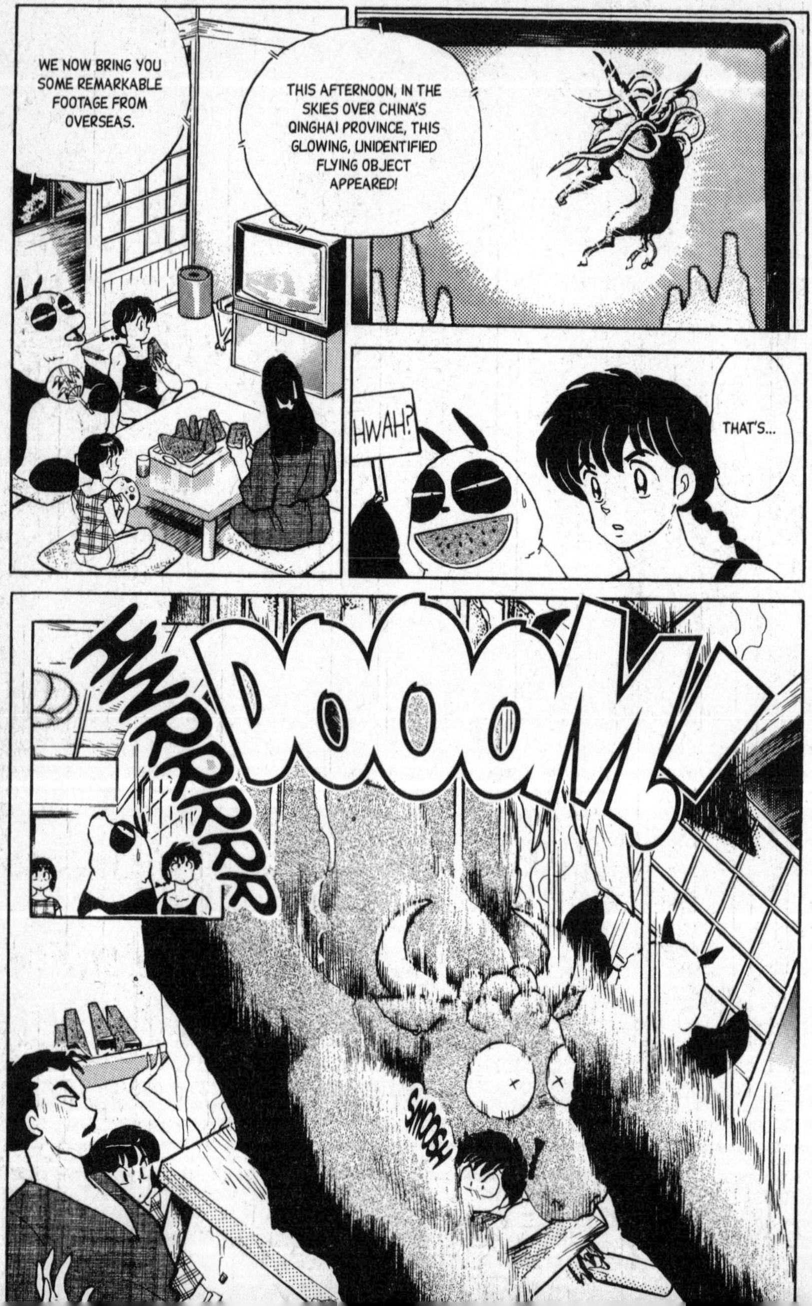
WE NOW BRING YOU SOME REMARKABLE FOOTAGE FROM OVERSEAS.
THIS AFTERNOON, IN THE SKIES OVER CHINA'S QINGHAI PROVINCE, THIS GLOWING, UNIDENTIFIED FLYING OBJECT APPEARED!
HWAH?
THAT'S...
HWRRRRRR
DOOOM!
SWOOSH

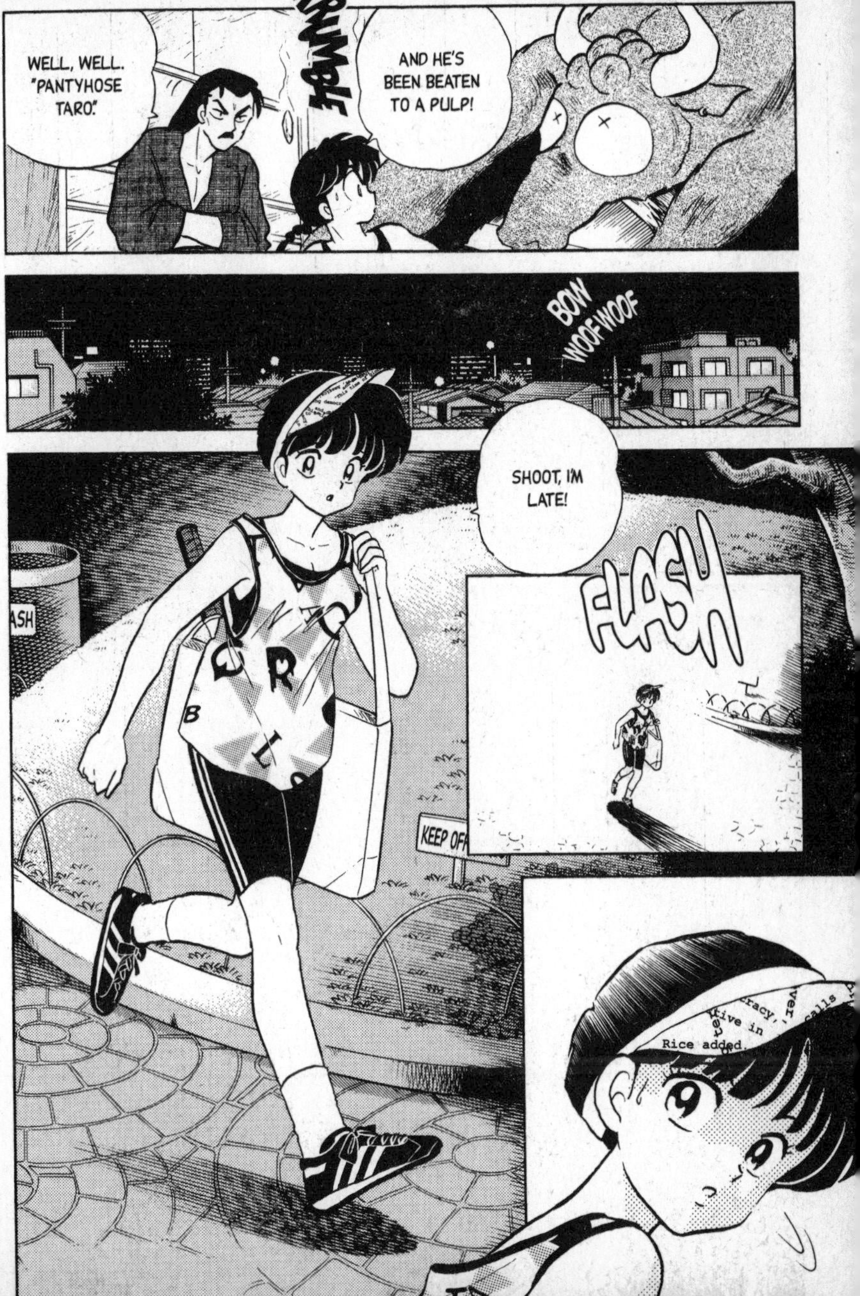
WELL, WELL. "PANTYHOSE TARO."
KRUMBLE
AND HE'S BEEN BEATEN TO A PULP!
BOW WOOF WOOF
SHOOT, I'M LATE!
FLASH
Rice added.

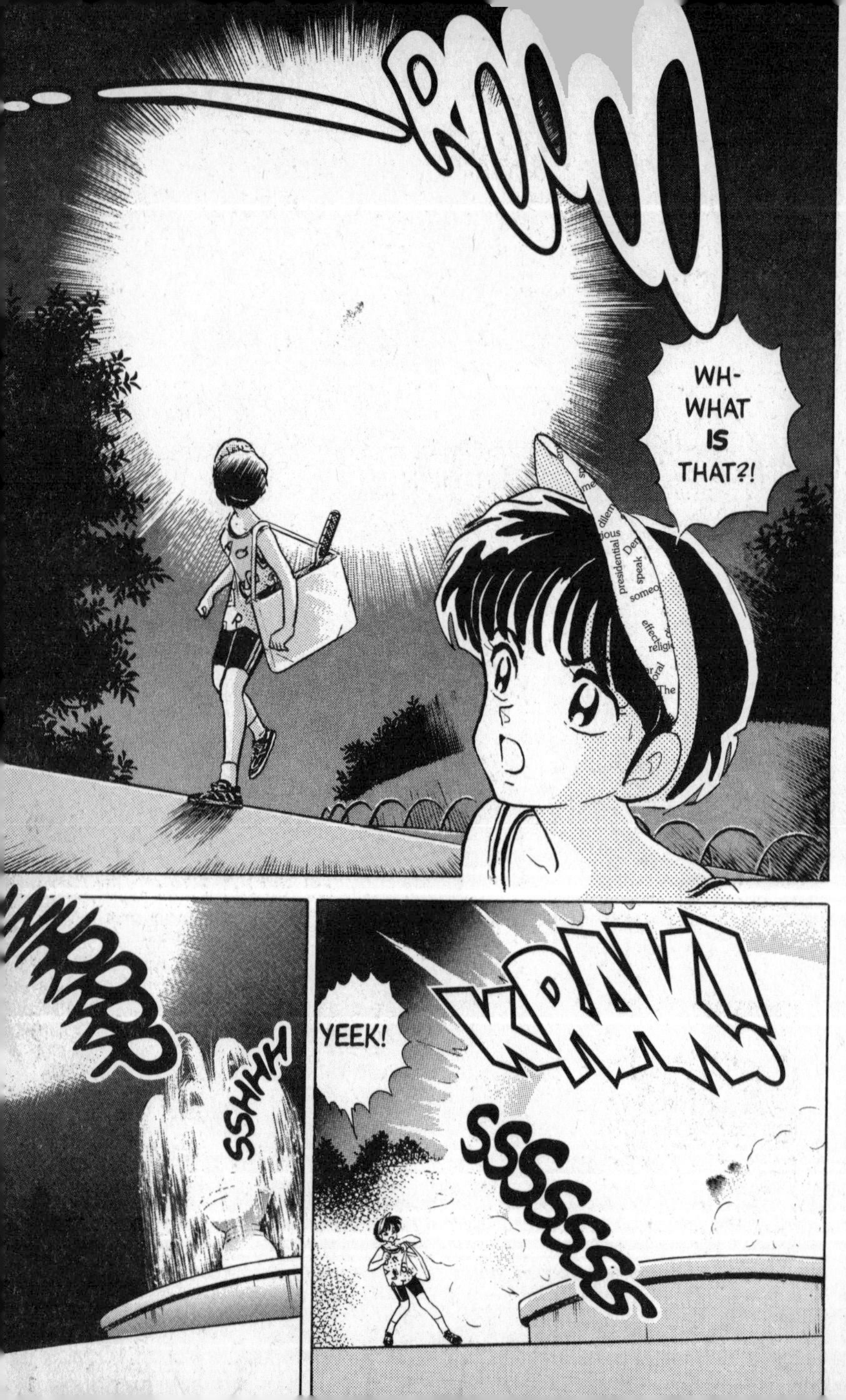
...ROOOO
WH- WHAT IS THAT?!
SSHHH
YEEK!
KRAK!
SSSSSSS

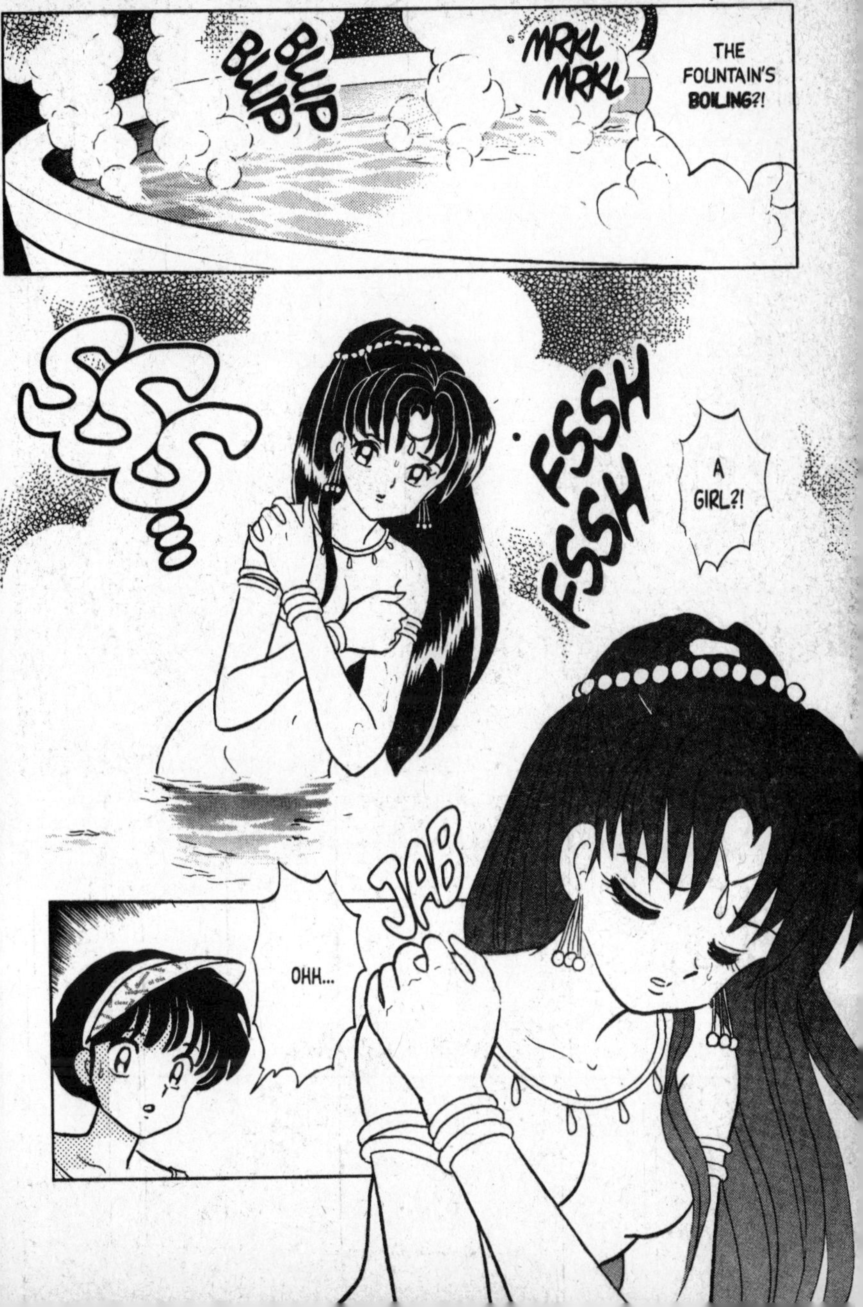
BLUP BLUP
MRKL MRKL
THE FOUNTAIN'S BOILING?!
SSSooo
FSSH FSSH
A GIRL?!
OHH...
JAB

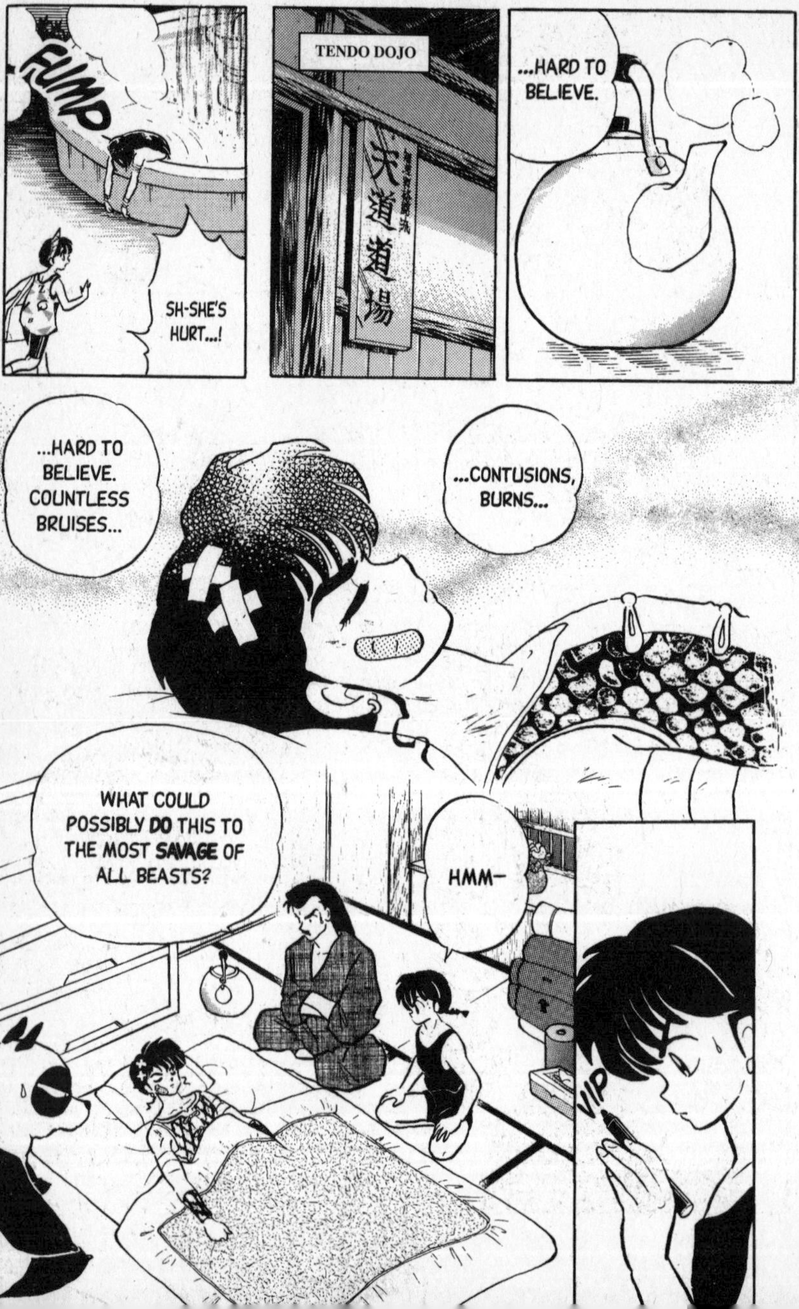
FUMP
SH-SHE'S HURT...!
TENDO DOJO
天道道場
...HARD TO BELIEVE.
...HARD TO BELIEVE. COUNTLESS BRUISES...
...CONTUSIONS, BURNS...
WHAT COULD POSSIBLY **DO** THIS TO THE MOST **SAVAGE** OF ALL BEASTS?
HMM-
VIP

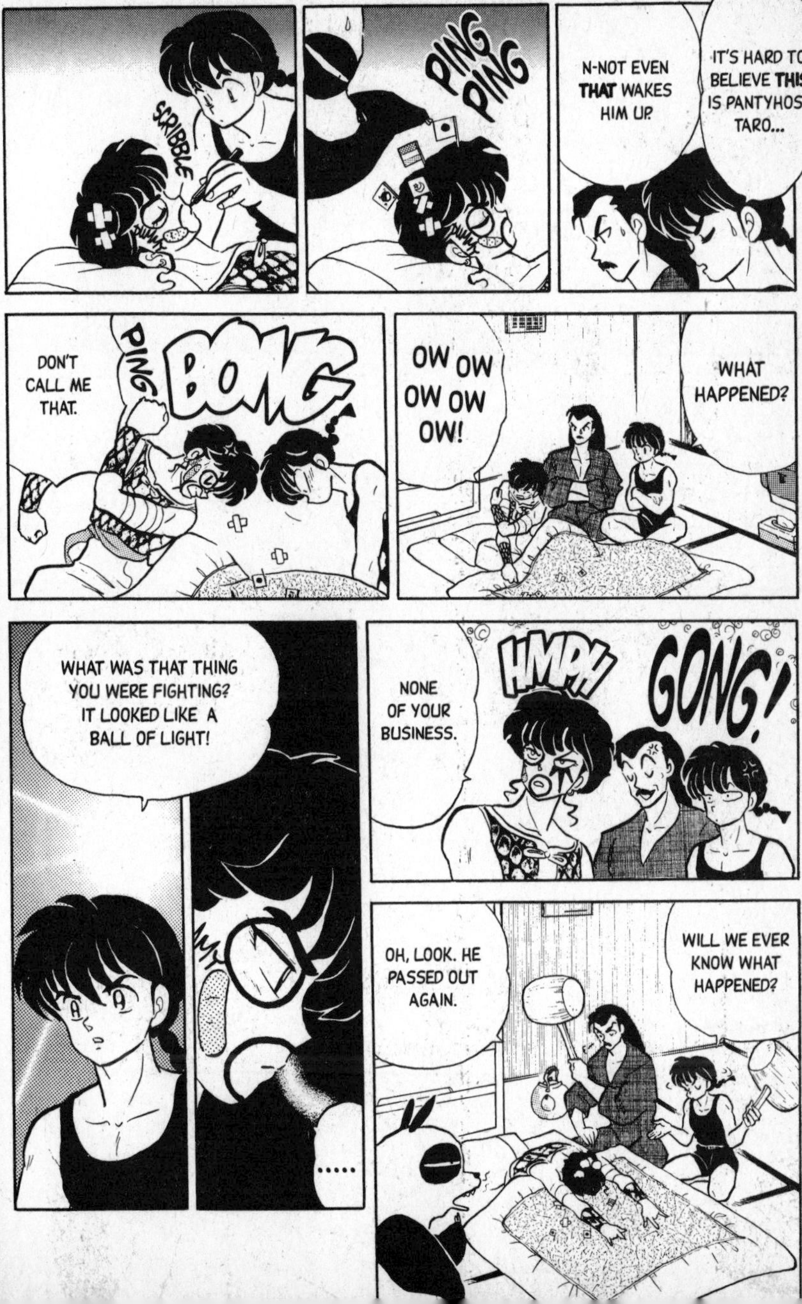
SCRIBBLE
PING PING
N-NOT EVEN THAT WAKES HIM UP.
IT'S HARD TO BELIEVE THIS IS PANTYHOSE TARO...
DON'T CALL ME THAT.
PING
BONG
OW OW OW OW OW!
WHAT HAPPENED?
WHAT WAS THAT THING YOU WERE FIGHTING? IT LOOKED LIKE A BALL OF LIGHT!
.....
NONE OF YOUR BUSINESS.
HMPH
GONG!
OH, LOOK. HE PASSED OUT AGAIN.
WILL WE EVER KNOW WHAT HAPPENED?

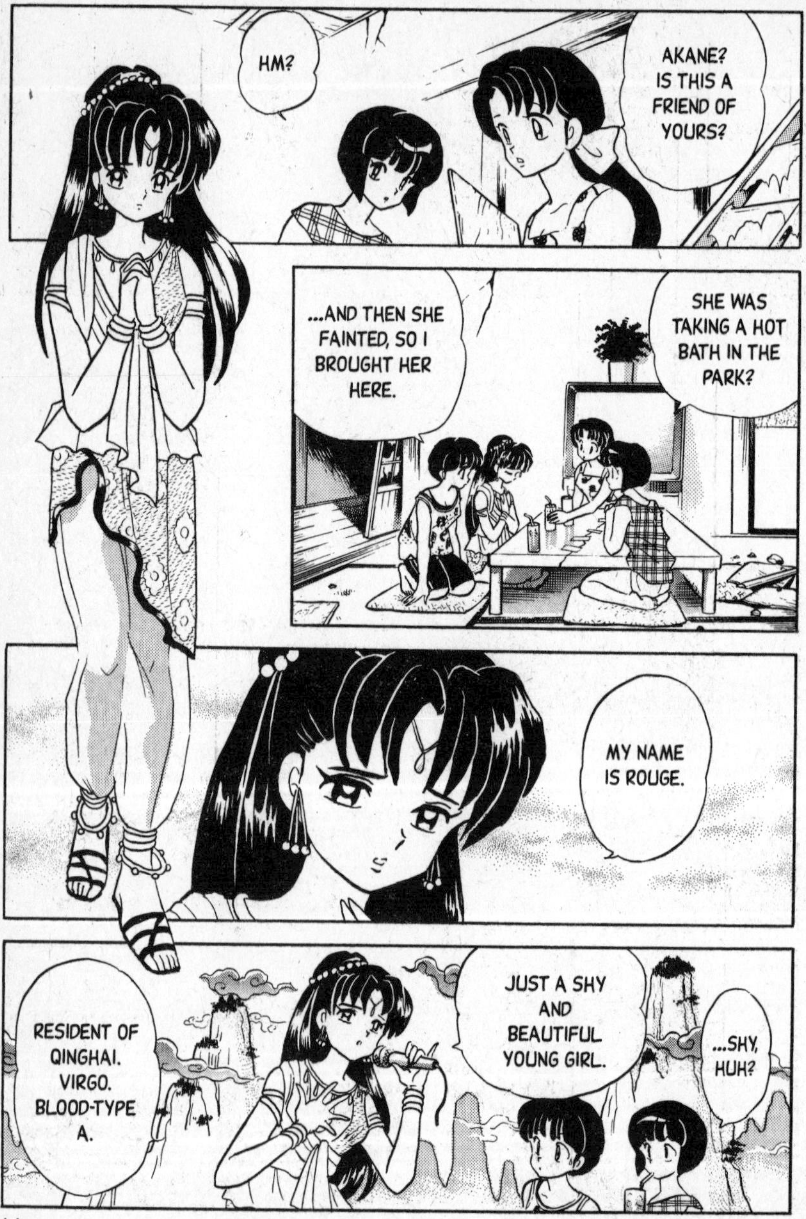
HM?
AKANE? IS THIS A FRIEND OF YOURS?
...AND THEN SHE FAINTED, SO I BROUGHT HER HERE.
SHE WAS TAKING A HOT BATH IN THE PARK?
MY NAME IS ROUGE.
RESIDENT OF QINGHAI. VIRGO. BLOOD-TYPE A.
JUST A SHY AND BEAUTIFUL YOUNG GIRL.
...SHY, HUH?

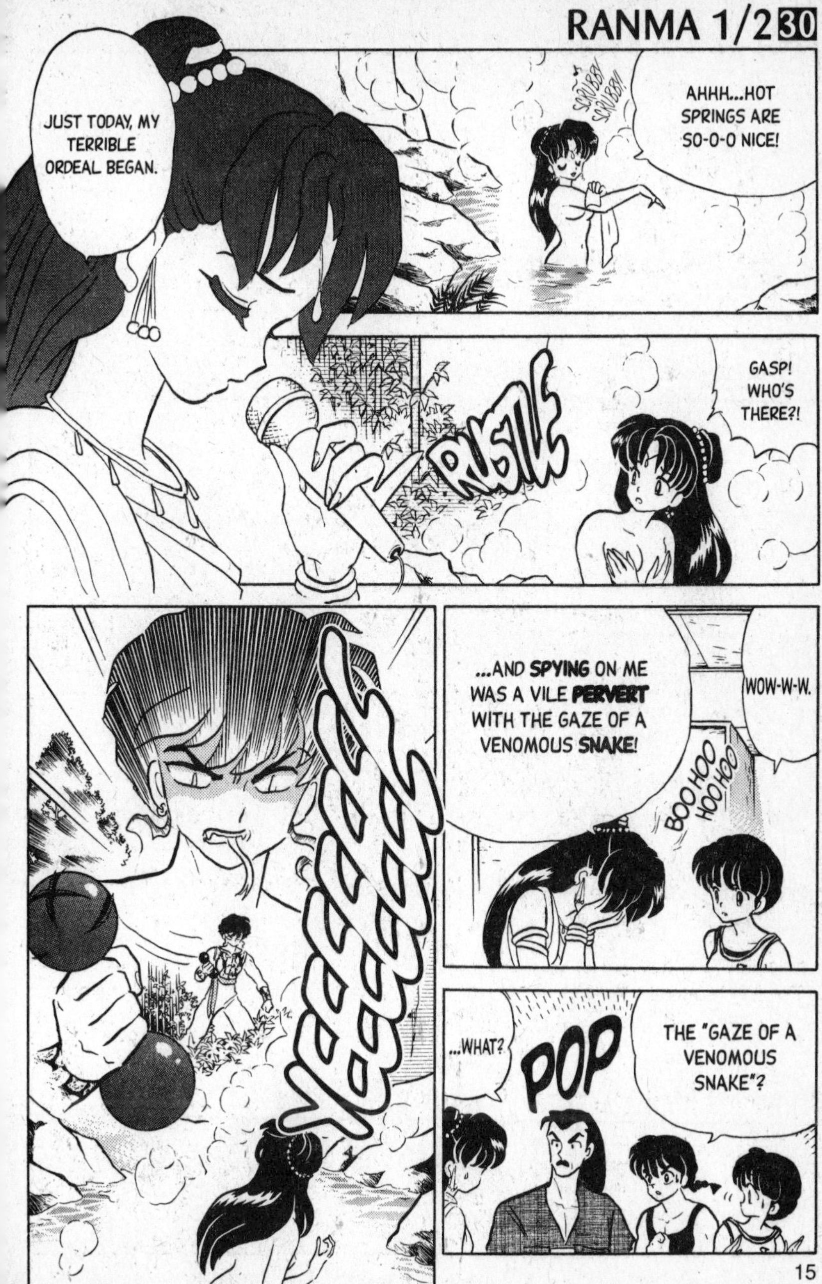
JUST TODAY, MY TERRIBLE ORDEAL BEGAN.
SCRUBBY SCRUBBY
AHHH...HOT SPRINGS ARE SO-O-O NICE!
RUSTLE
GASP! WHO'S THERE?!
...AND **SPYING** ON ME WAS A VILE **PERVERT** WITH THE GAZE OF A VENOMOUS **SNAKE**!
WOW-W-W.
BOO HOO HOO HOO
...WHAT?
POP
THE "GAZE OF A VENOMOUS SNAKE"?

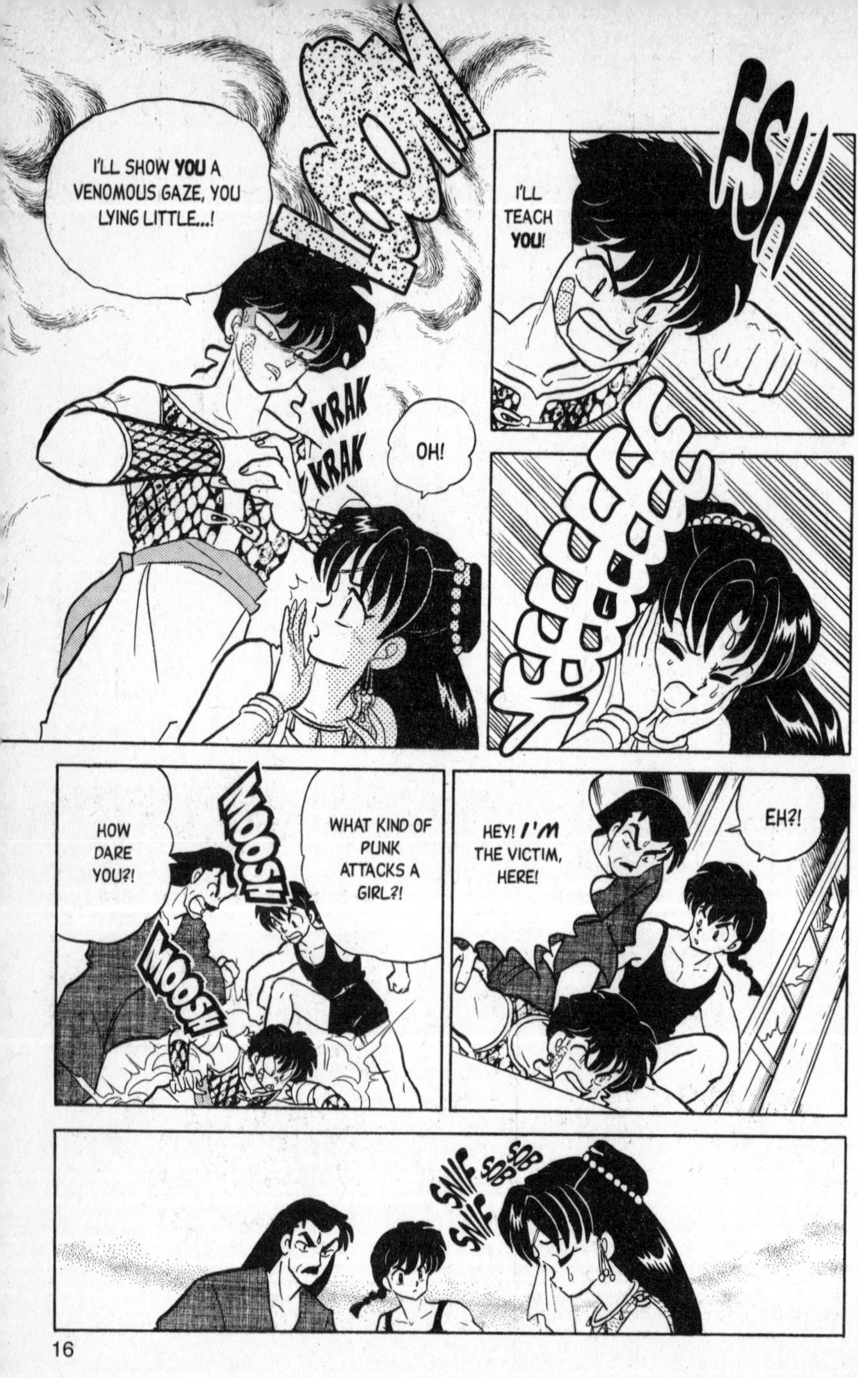
I'LL SHOW YOU A VENOMOUS GAZE, YOU LYING LITTLE...!
KRAK KRAK
OH!
FSH
I'LL TEACH YOU!
HOW DARE YOU?!
MOOSH
MOOSH
WHAT KIND OF PUNK ATTACKS A GIRL?!
HEY! I'M THE VICTIM, HERE!
EH?!
SNIF SNIF
SOB SOB

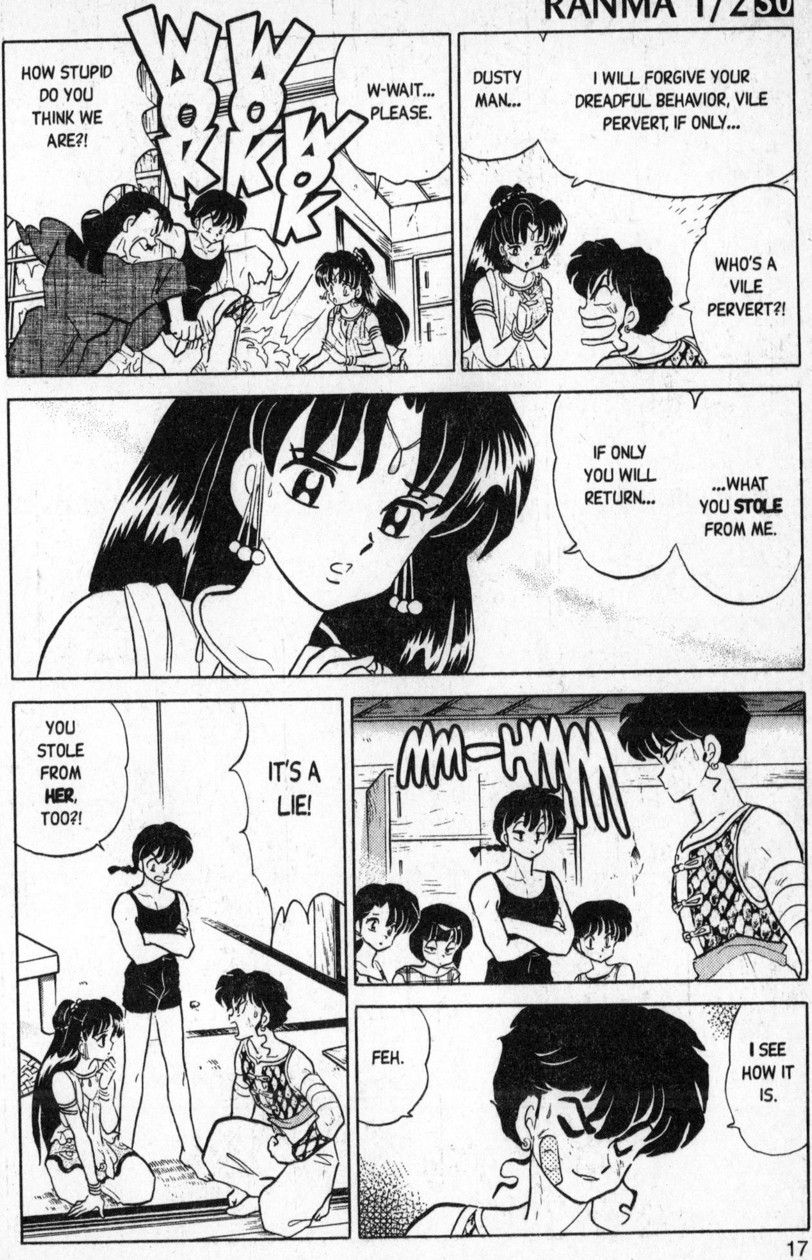
HOW STUPID DO YOU THINK WE ARE?!
WOK WOK WOK
W-WAIT... PLEASE.
DUSTY MAN...
I WILL FORGIVE YOUR DREADFUL BEHAVIOR, VILE PERVERT, IF ONLY...
WHO'S A VILE PERVERT?!
IF ONLY YOU WILL RETURN...
...WHAT YOU **STOLE** FROM ME.
YOU STOLE FROM **HER**, TOO?!
IT'S A LIE!
MM-HMM
FEH.
I SEE HOW IT IS.

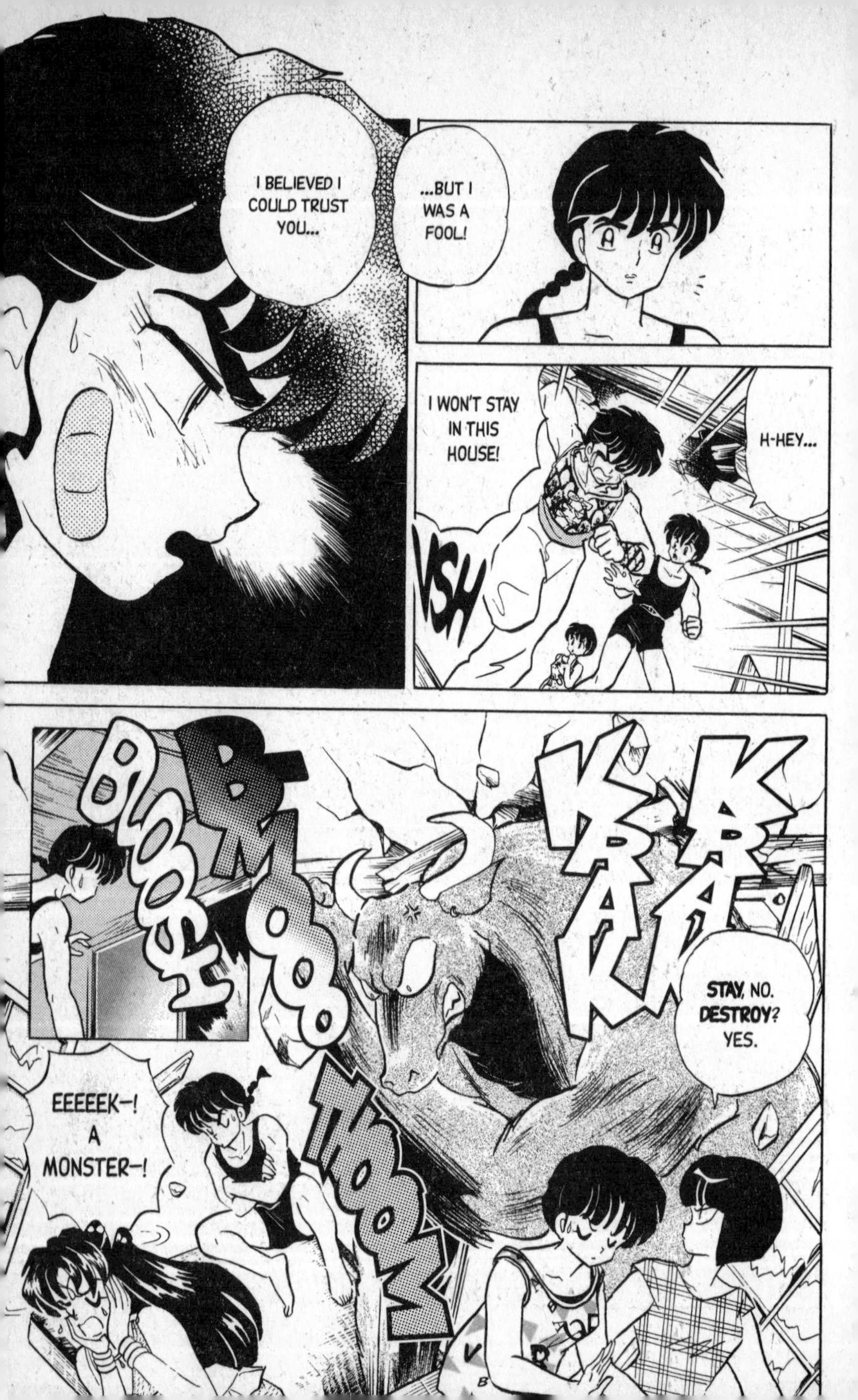
I BELIEVED I COULD TRUST YOU...
...BUT I WAS A FOOL!
I WON'T STAY IN THIS HOUSE!
VSH
H-HEY...
BLOOOSH
BMOOOO
THOOM
KRAK
KRAAK
STAY, NO. DESTROY? YES.
EEEEEK–! A MONSTER–!

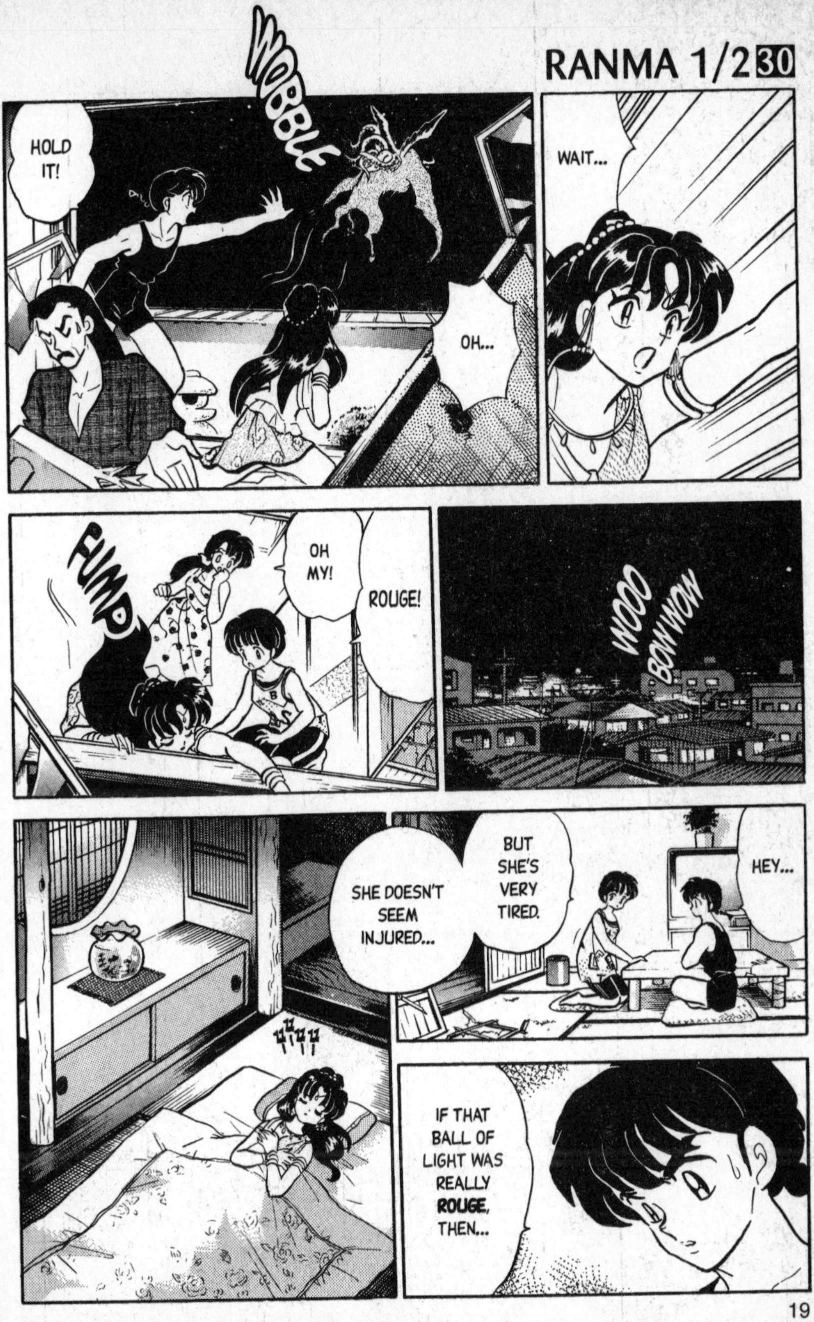
WOBBLE
HOLD IT!
OH...
WAIT...
FUMP
OH MY!
ROUGE!
WOOO
BOW WOW
SHE DOESN'T SEEM INJURED...
BUT SHE'S VERY TIRED.
HEY...
IF THAT BALL OF LIGHT WAS REALLY **ROUGE**, THEN...

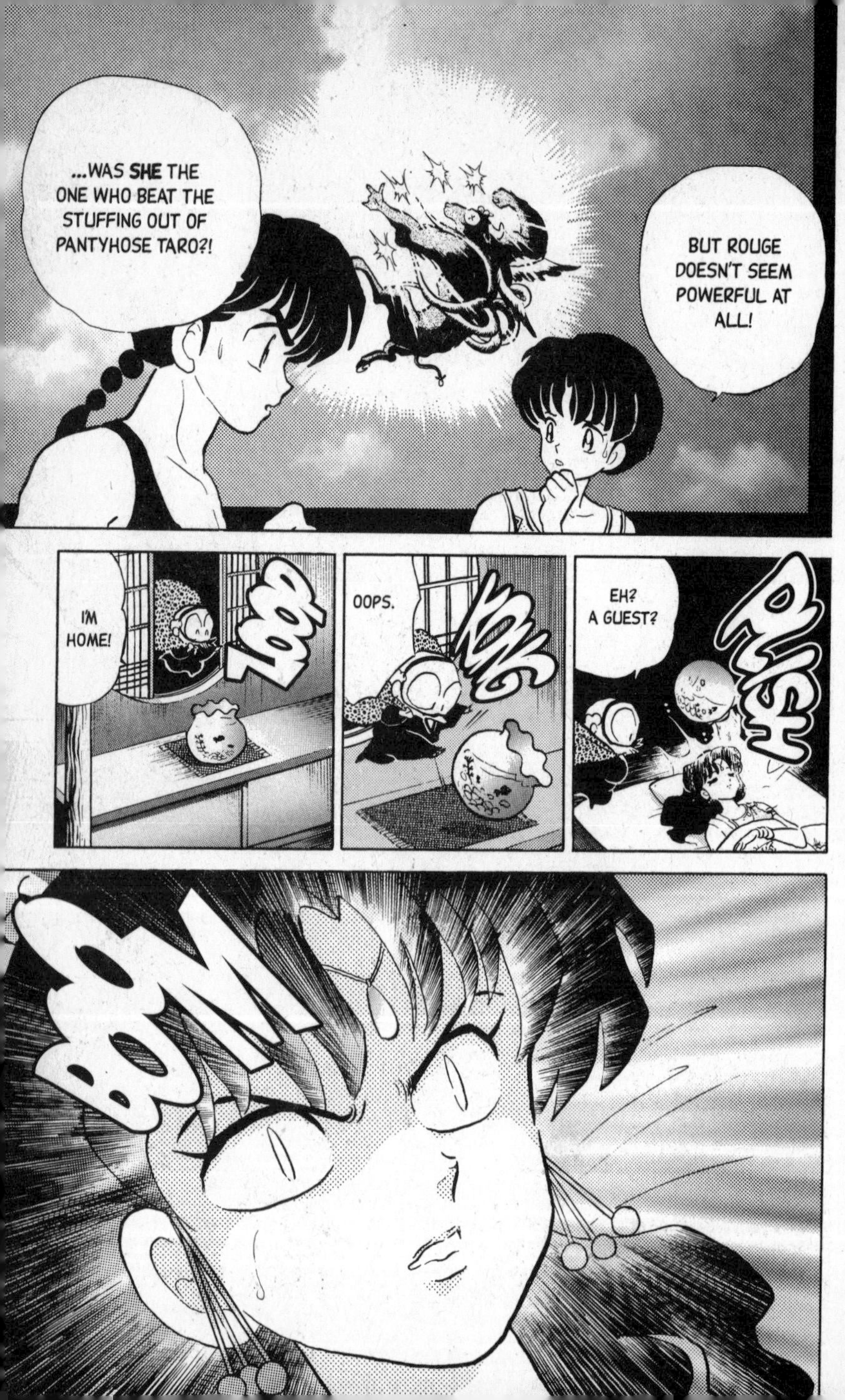
...WAS SHE THE ONE WHO BEAT THE STUFFING OUT OF PANTYHOSE TARO?!
BUT ROUGE DOESN'T SEEM POWERFUL AT ALL!
I'M HOME!
OOPS.
EH? A GUEST?
PLISH
BOOM

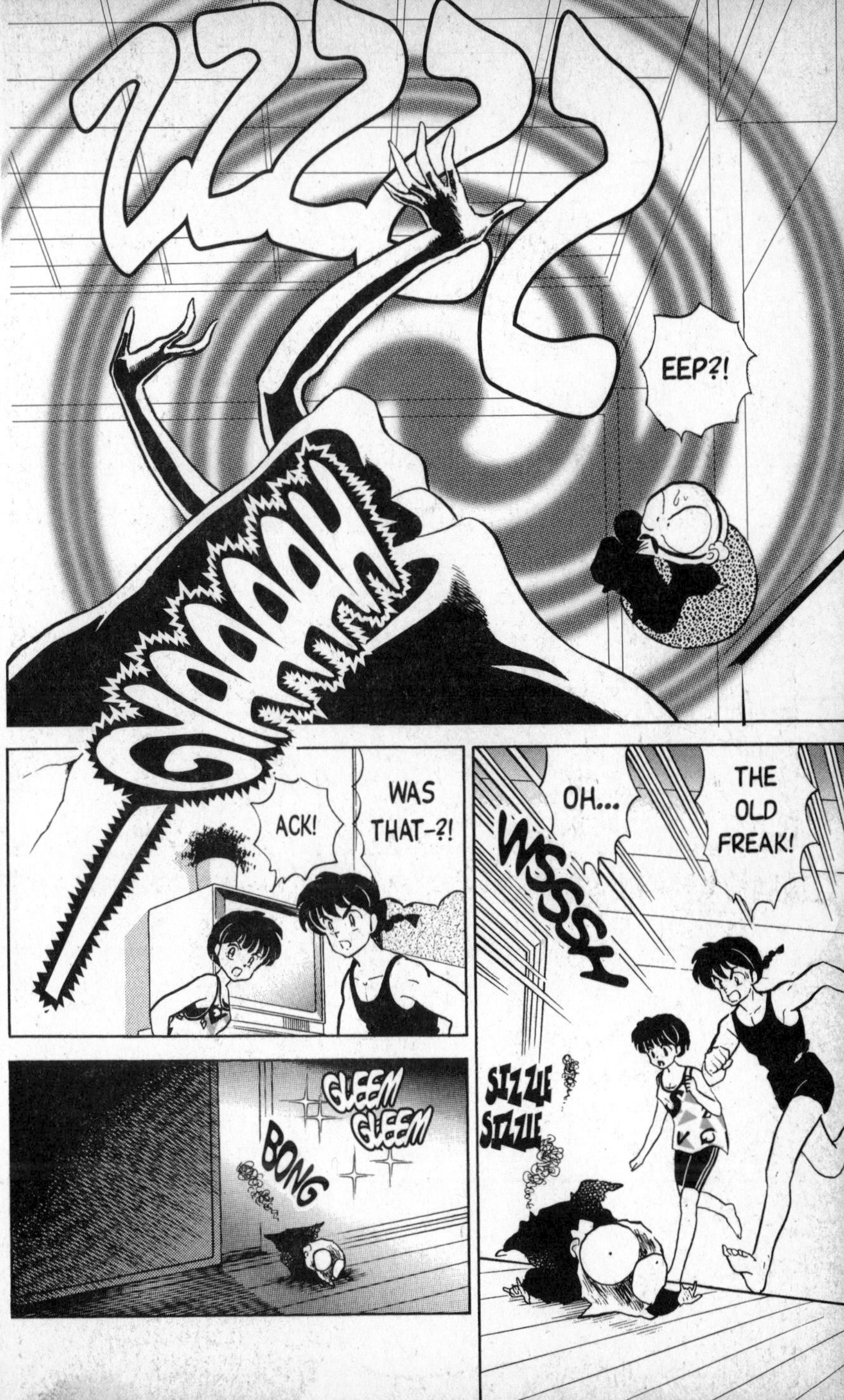
ZZZZ
EEP?!
GNAAAH
ACK!
WAS THAT-?!
GLEEM GLEEM
BONG
OH...
THE OLD FREAK!
WSSSH
SIZZLE SIZZLE

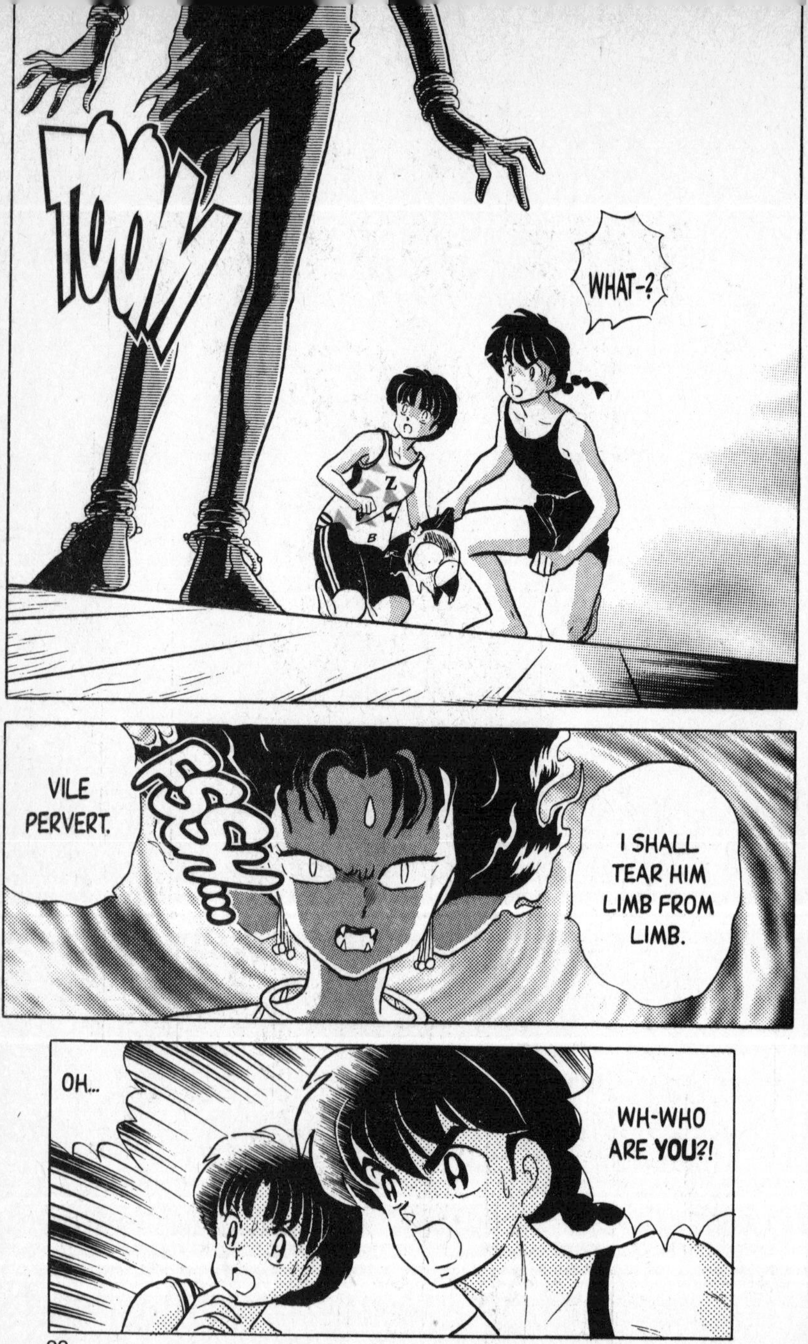
TOOM
WHAT-?
VILE PERVERT.
FSSH...
I SHALL TEAR HIM LIMB FROM LIMB.
OH...
WH-WHO ARE YOU?!

PART 2

THE OTHER ROUGE!!

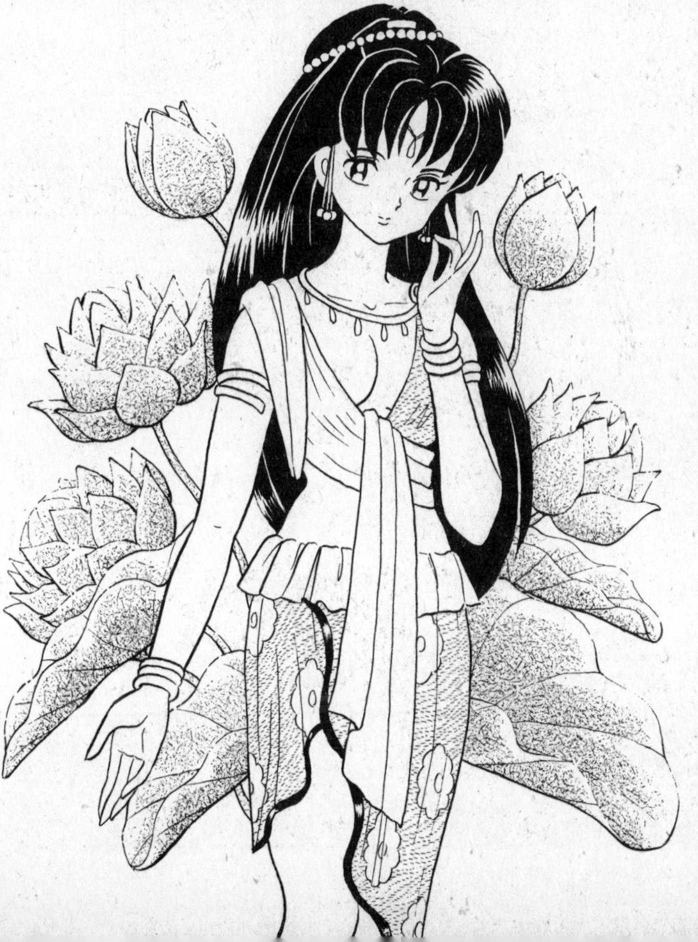

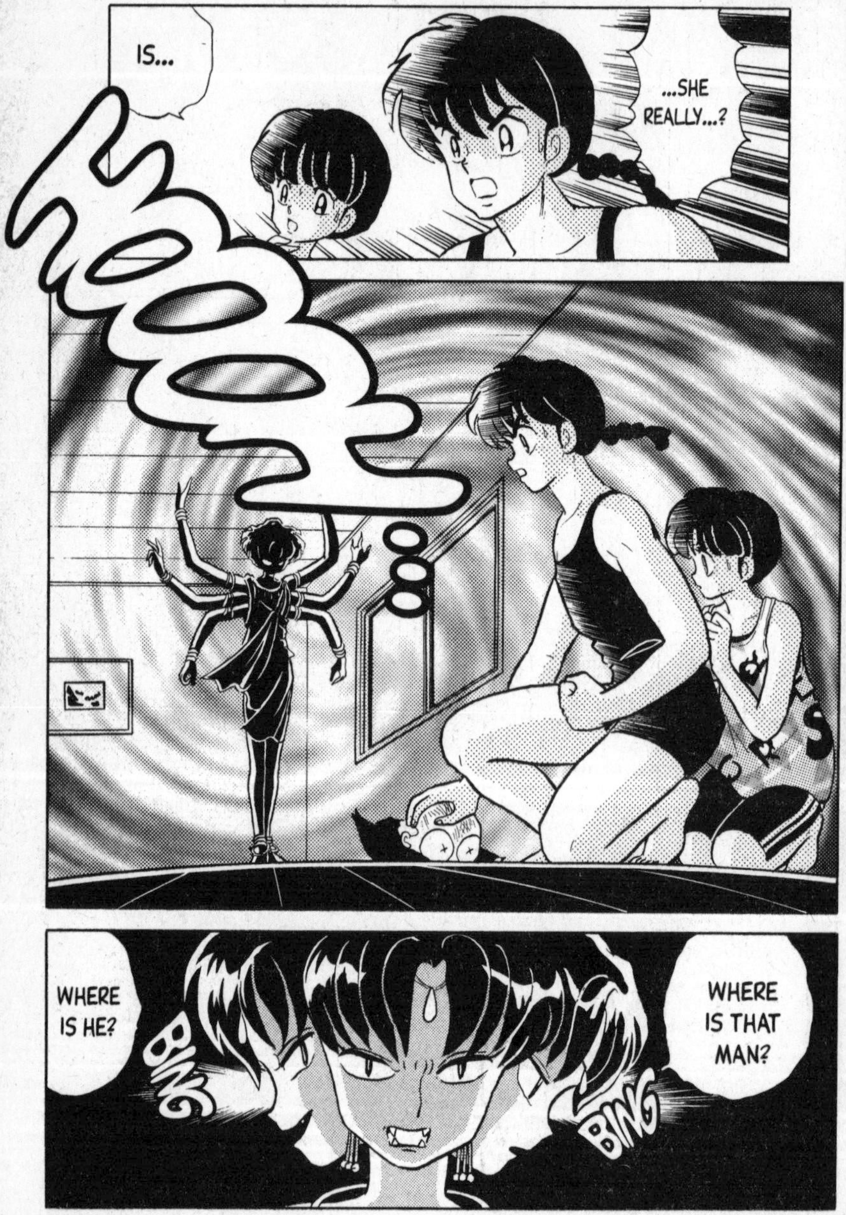
IS...
...SHE REALLY...?
WHERE IS HE?
BING
WHERE IS THAT MAN?
BING

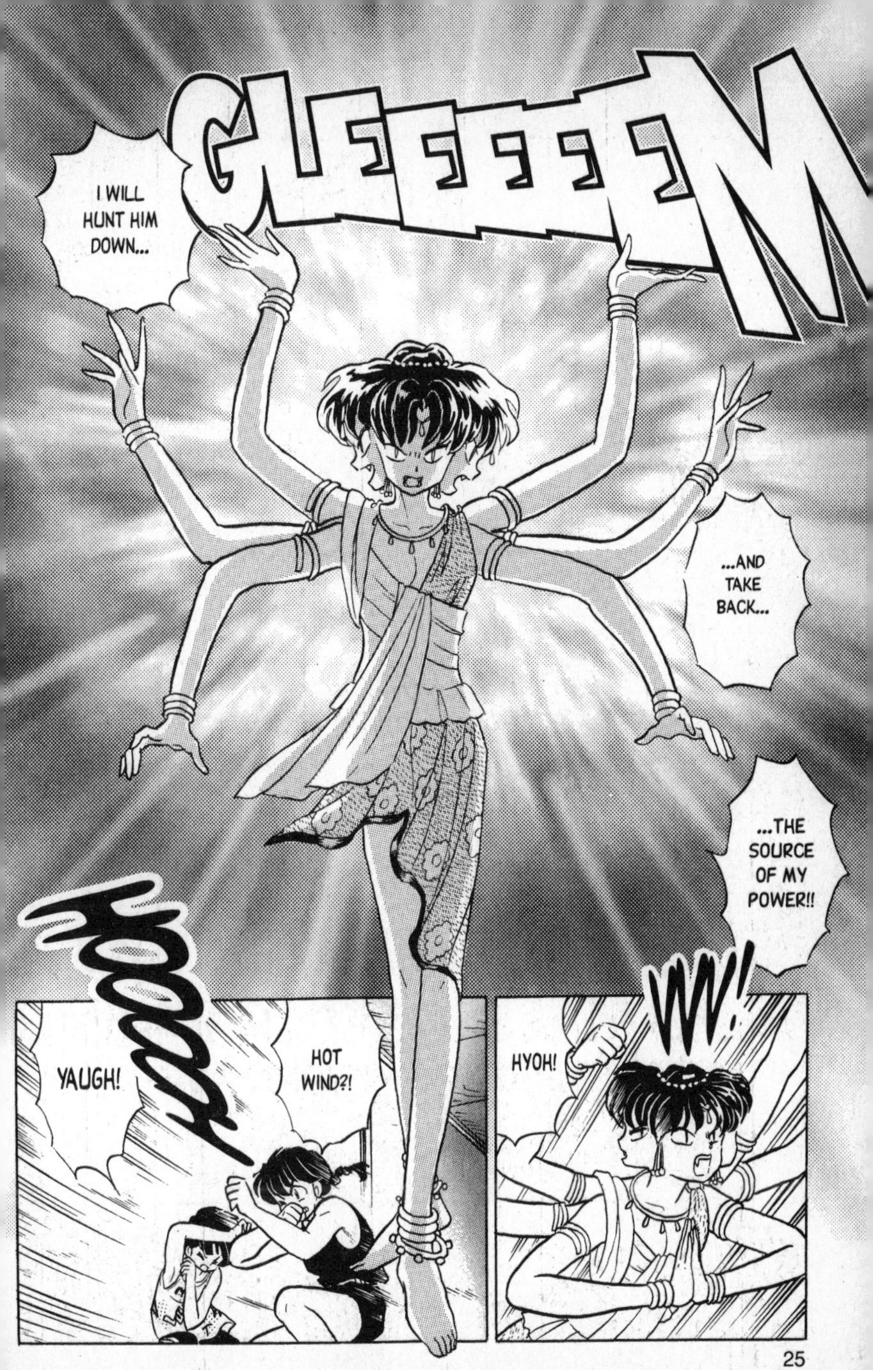
GLEEEEEM
I WILL HUNT HIM DOWN...
...AND TAKE BACK...
...THE SOURCE OF MY POWER!!
YAUGH!
HOT WIND?!
HYOH!

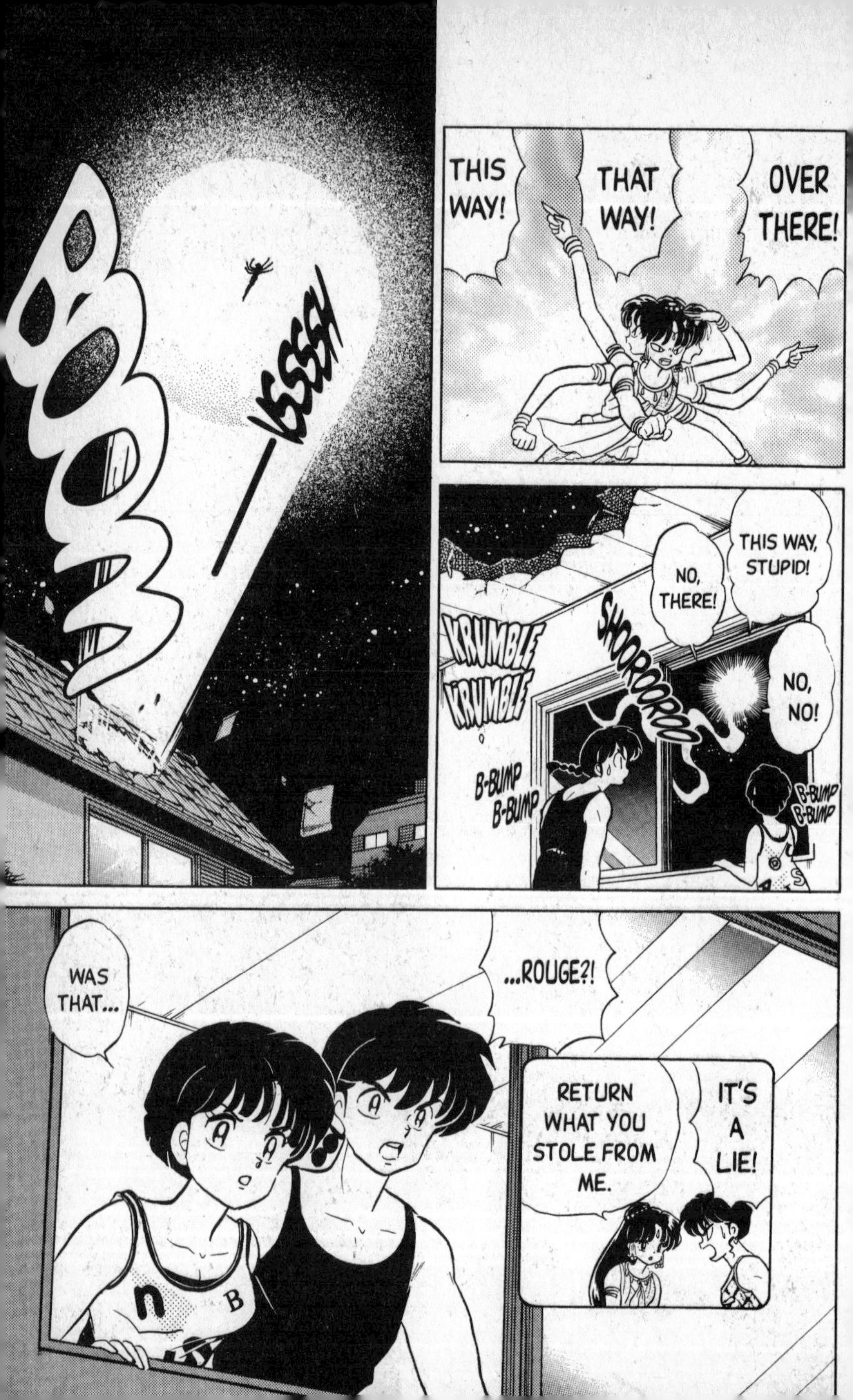
BOOM
—VSSSSH
THIS WAY!
THAT WAY!
OVER THERE!
KRUMBLE KRUMBLE
SHOOROOROO
NO, THERE!
THIS WAY, STUPID!
NO, NO!
B-BUMP B-BUMP
B-BUMP B-BUMP
WAS THAT...
...ROUGE?!
RETURN WHAT YOU STOLE FROM ME.
IT'S A LIE!

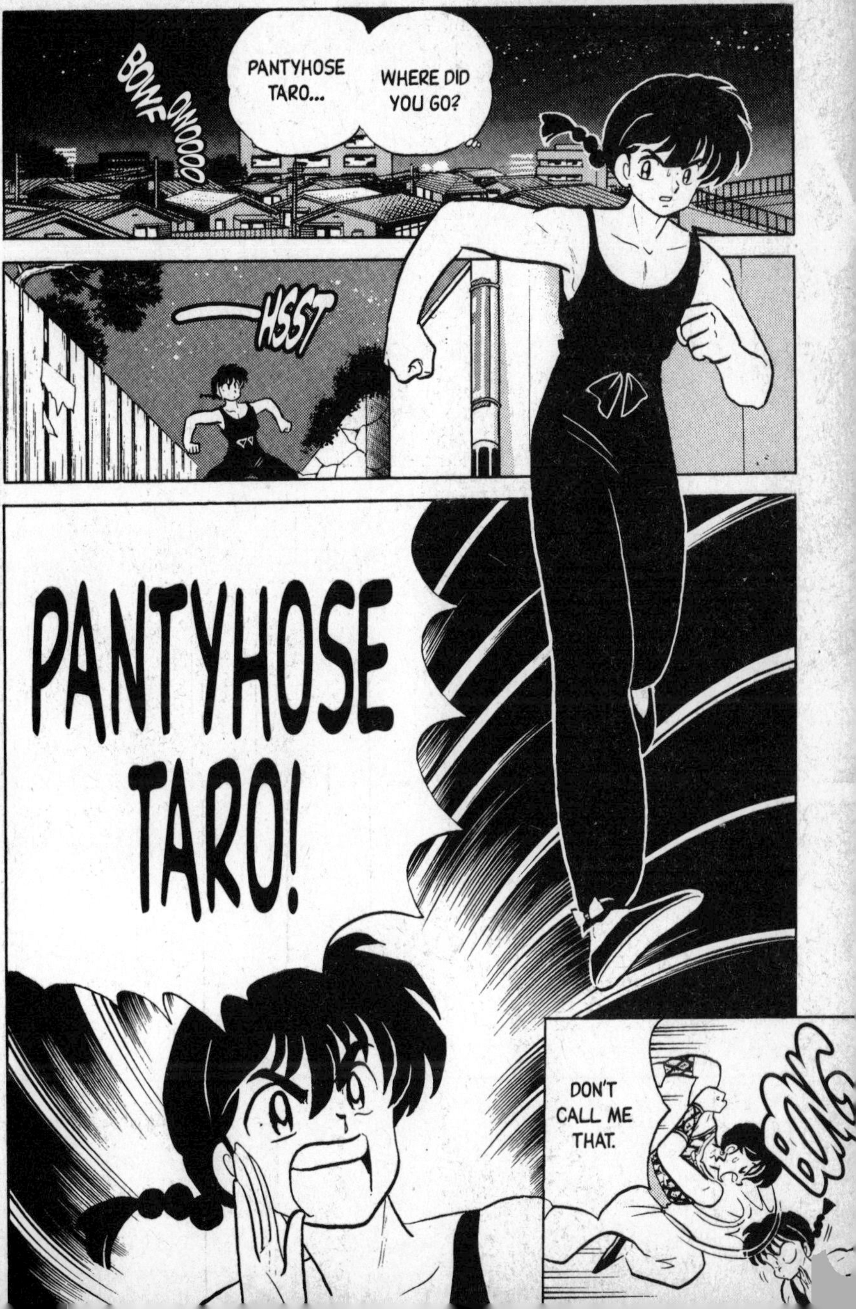
BOWF
OWOOOOO...
PANTYHOSE TARO...
WHERE DID YOU GO?
HSST
PANTYHOSE TARO!
DON'T CALL ME THAT.
BONG

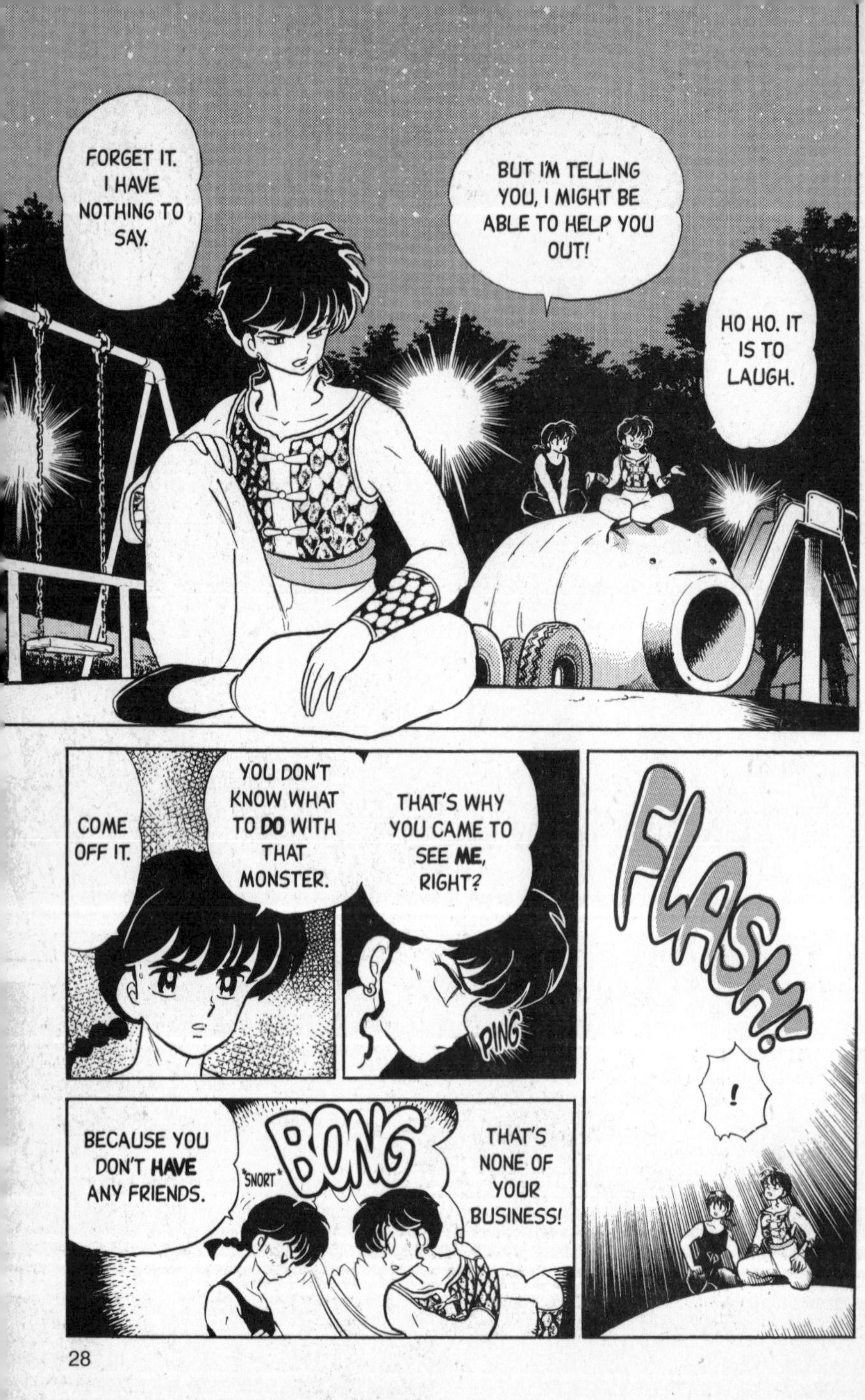
FORGET IT. I HAVE NOTHING TO SAY.
BUT I'M TELLING YOU, I MIGHT BE ABLE TO HELP YOU OUT!
HO HO. IT IS TO LAUGH.
COME OFF IT.
YOU DON'T KNOW WHAT TO DO WITH THAT MONSTER.
THAT'S WHY YOU CAME TO SEE ME, RIGHT?
PING
FLASH!
!
BECAUSE YOU DON'T HAVE ANY FRIENDS.
SNORT
BONG
THAT'S NONE OF YOUR BUSINESS!

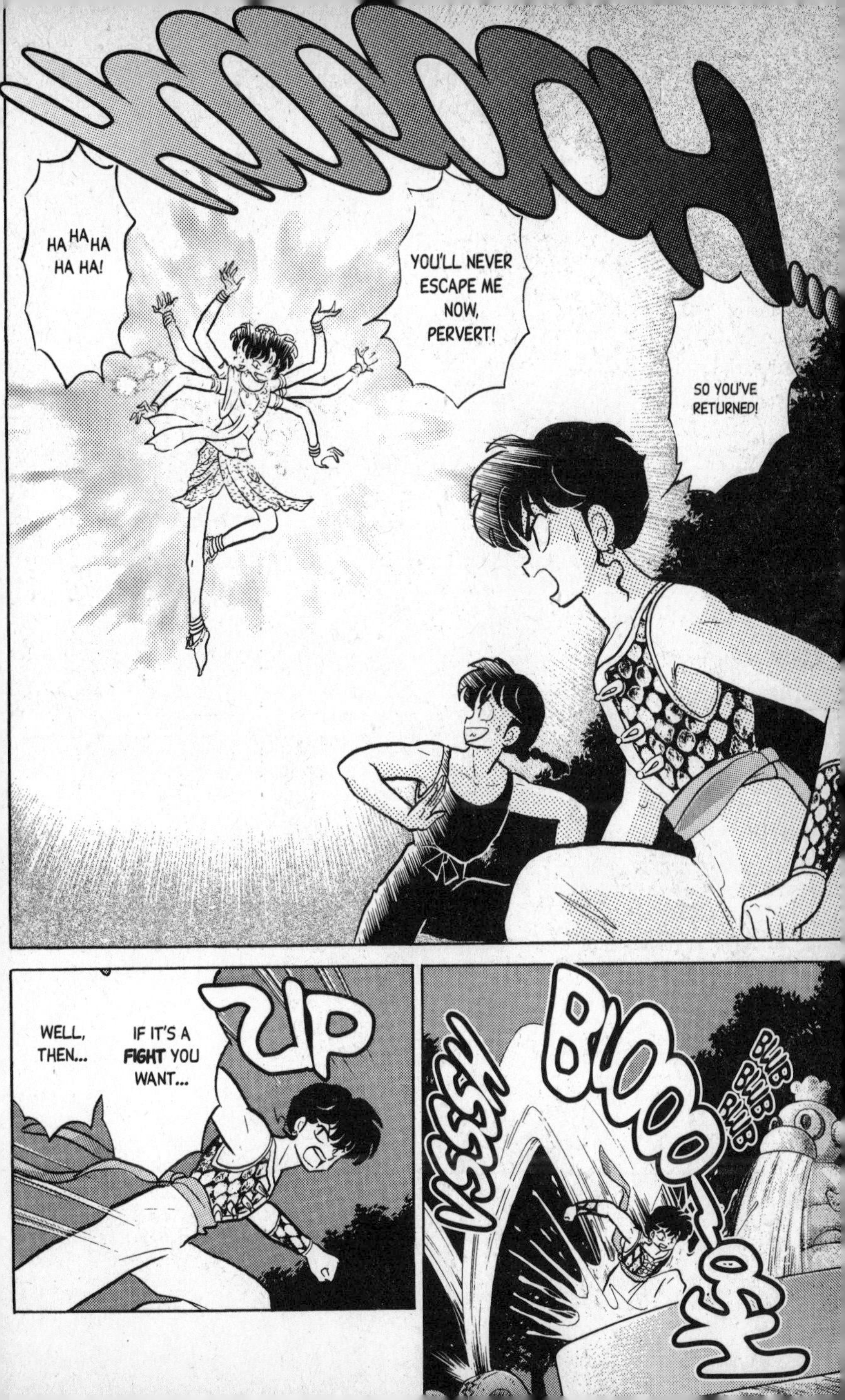
HA HA HA HA HA!
YOU'LL NEVER ESCAPE ME NOW, PERVERT!
SO YOU'VE RETURNED!
WELL, THEN...
IF IT'S A **FIGHT** YOU WANT...
ZIP
BWUB BWUB BWUB

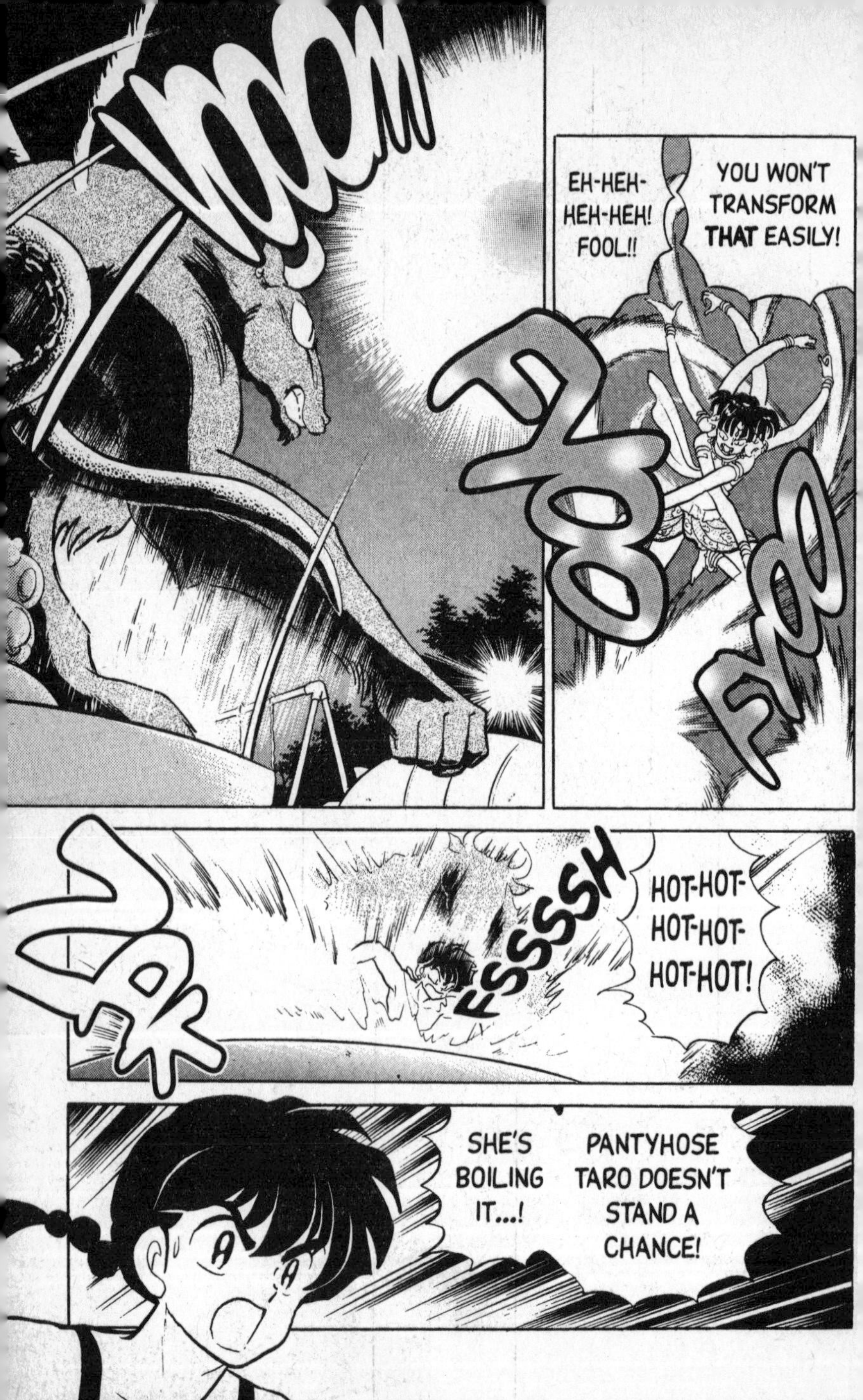
VOOOM
EH-HEH-HEH-HEH! FOOL!!
YOU WON'T TRANSFORM THAT EASILY!
FWOOM
FWOO
VOK
FSSSSH
HOT-HOT-HOT-HOT-HOT-HOT!
SHE'S BOILING IT...!
PANTYHOSE TARO DOESN'T STAND A CHANCE!

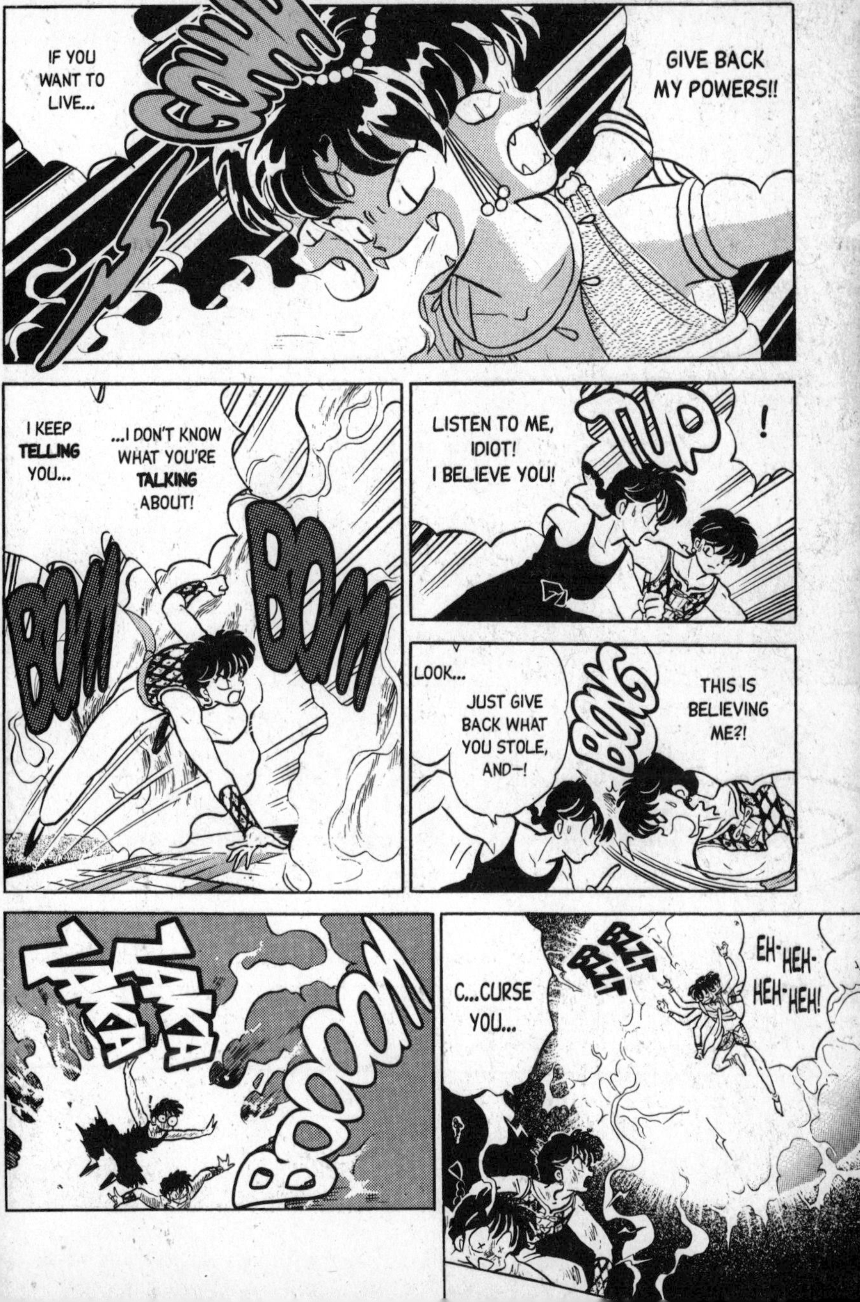
IF YOU WANT TO LIVE...
CRUNCH
GIVE BACK MY POWERS!!
I KEEP TELLING YOU...
...I DON'T KNOW WHAT YOU'RE TALKING ABOUT!
BOM
BOM
LISTEN TO ME, IDIOT! I BELIEVE YOU!
TUP
!
LOOK...
JUST GIVE BACK WHAT YOU STOLE, AND—!
BONG
THIS IS BELIEVING ME?!
ZAKA ZAKA
BOOOOM
C...CURSE YOU...
BZZT BZZT
EH-HEH-HEH-HEH!

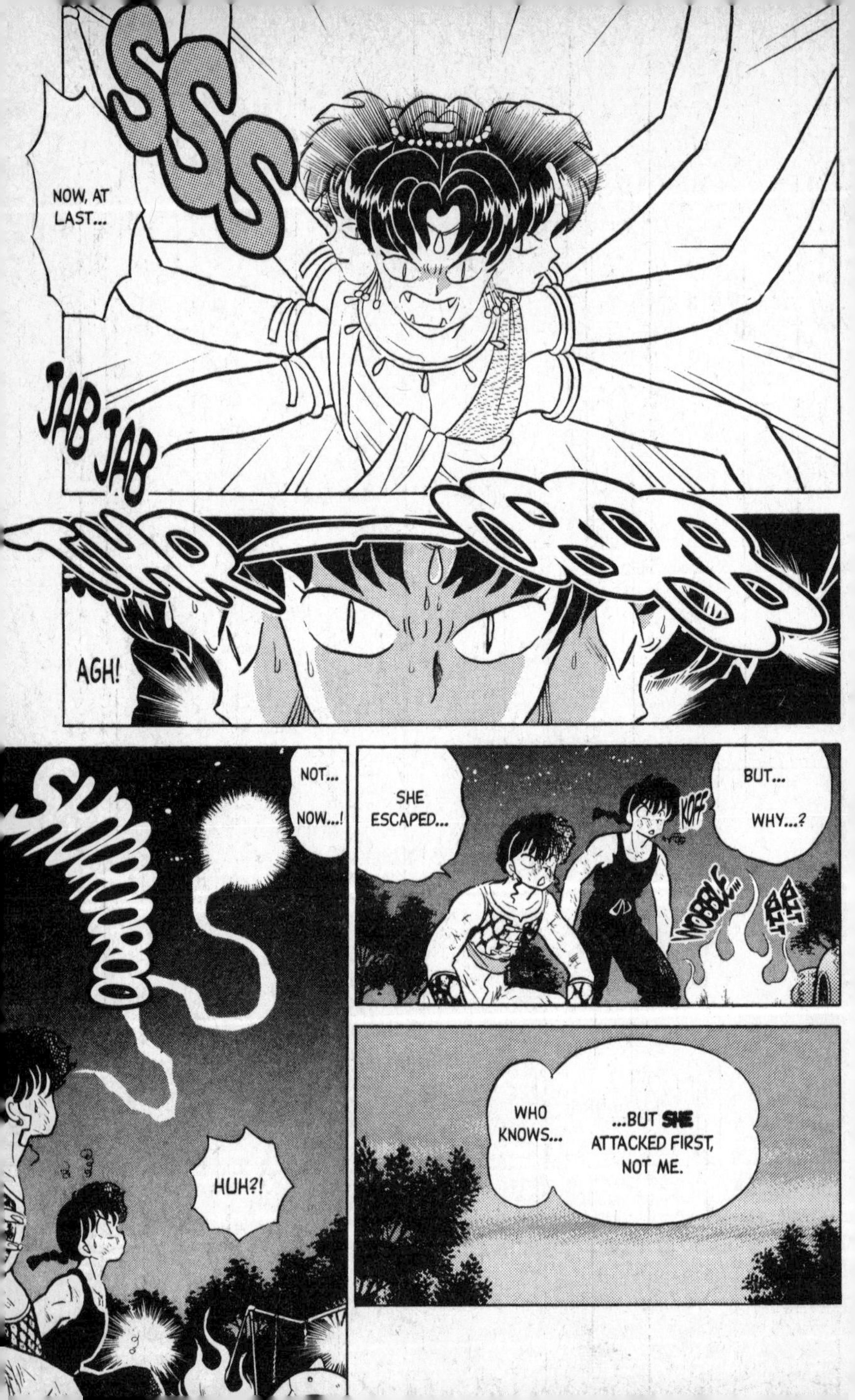
SSS
NOW, AT LAST...
JAB JAB
AGH!
NOT... NOW...!
HUH?!
SHE ESCAPED...
BUT... WHY...?
KOFF
WOBBLE...
WHO KNOWS...
...BUT **SHE** ATTACKED FIRST, NOT ME.

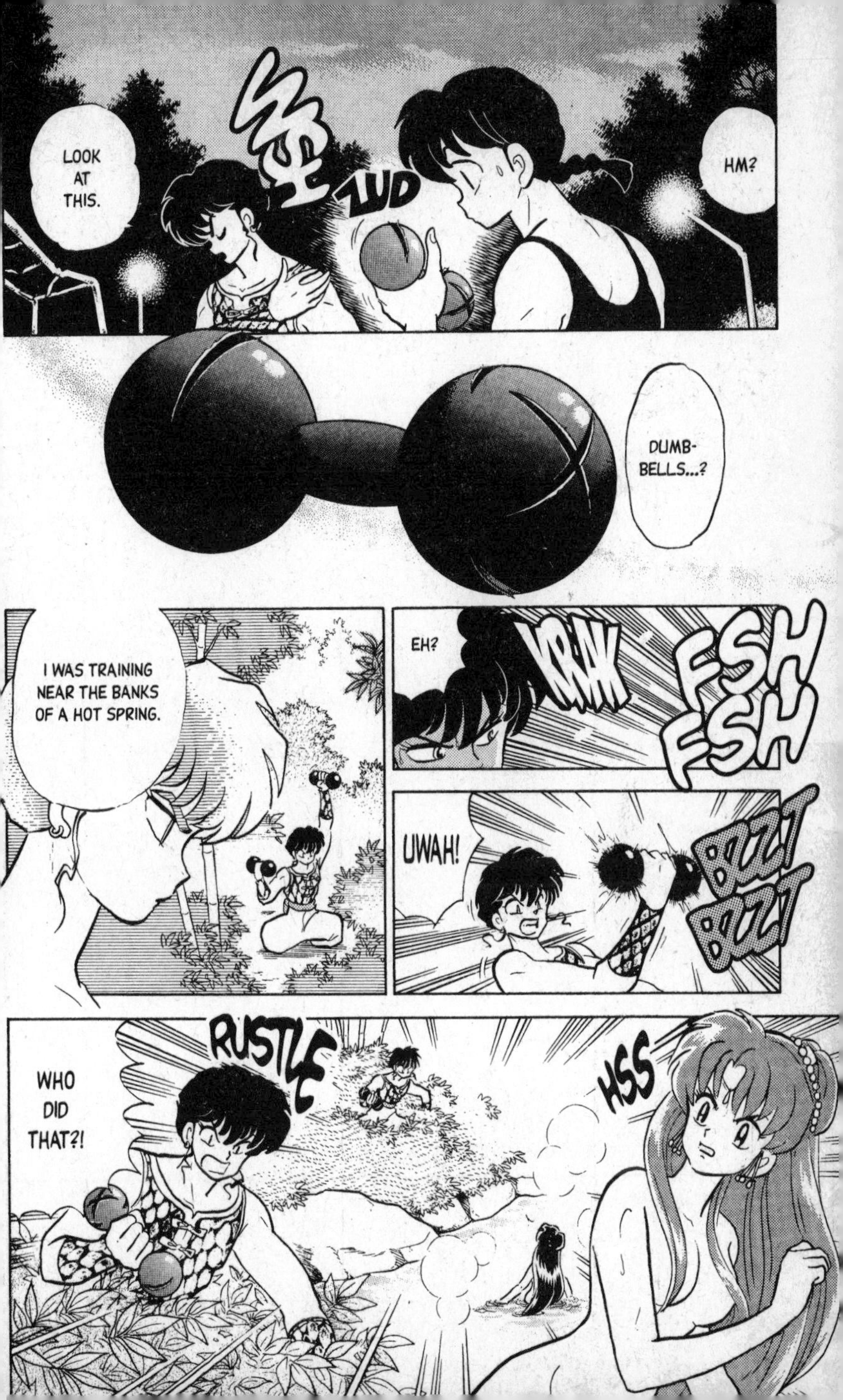
LOOK AT THIS.
WSH
ZUD
HM?
DUMB-BELLS...?
I WAS TRAINING NEAR THE BANKS OF A HOT SPRING.
EH?
KRAK
FSH FSH
UWAH!
BZZT BZZT
RUSTLE
WHO DID THAT?!
HSS

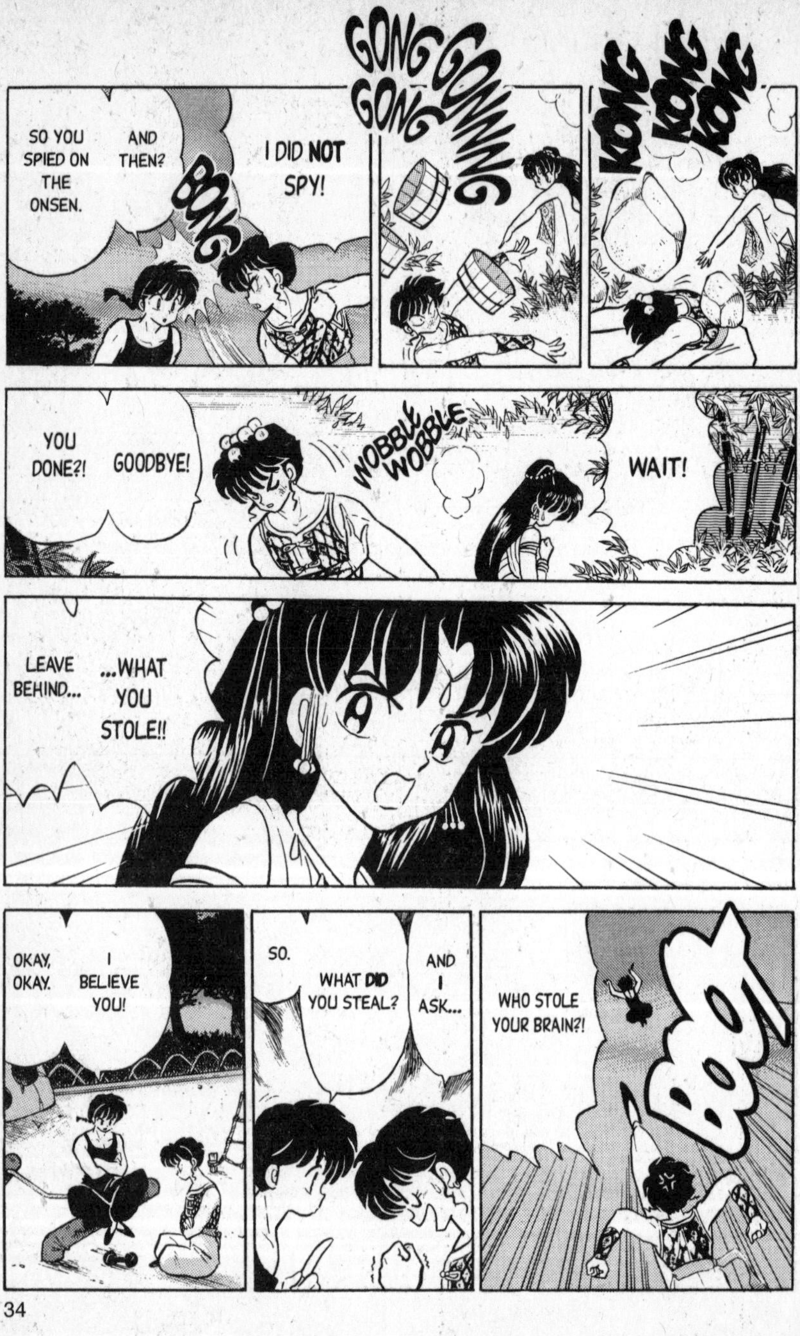

SO YOU SPIED ON THE ONSEN.
AND THEN?
BONG
I DID **NOT** SPY!
GONG GONG GONNNG
KONG KONG KONG
YOU DONE?!
GOODBYE!
WOBBLE WOBBLE
WAIT!
LEAVE BEHIND...
...WHAT YOU STOLE!!
OKAY, OKAY.
I BELIEVE YOU!
SO.
WHAT **DID** YOU STEAL?
AND I ASK...
WHO STOLE YOUR BRAIN?!
BOOM

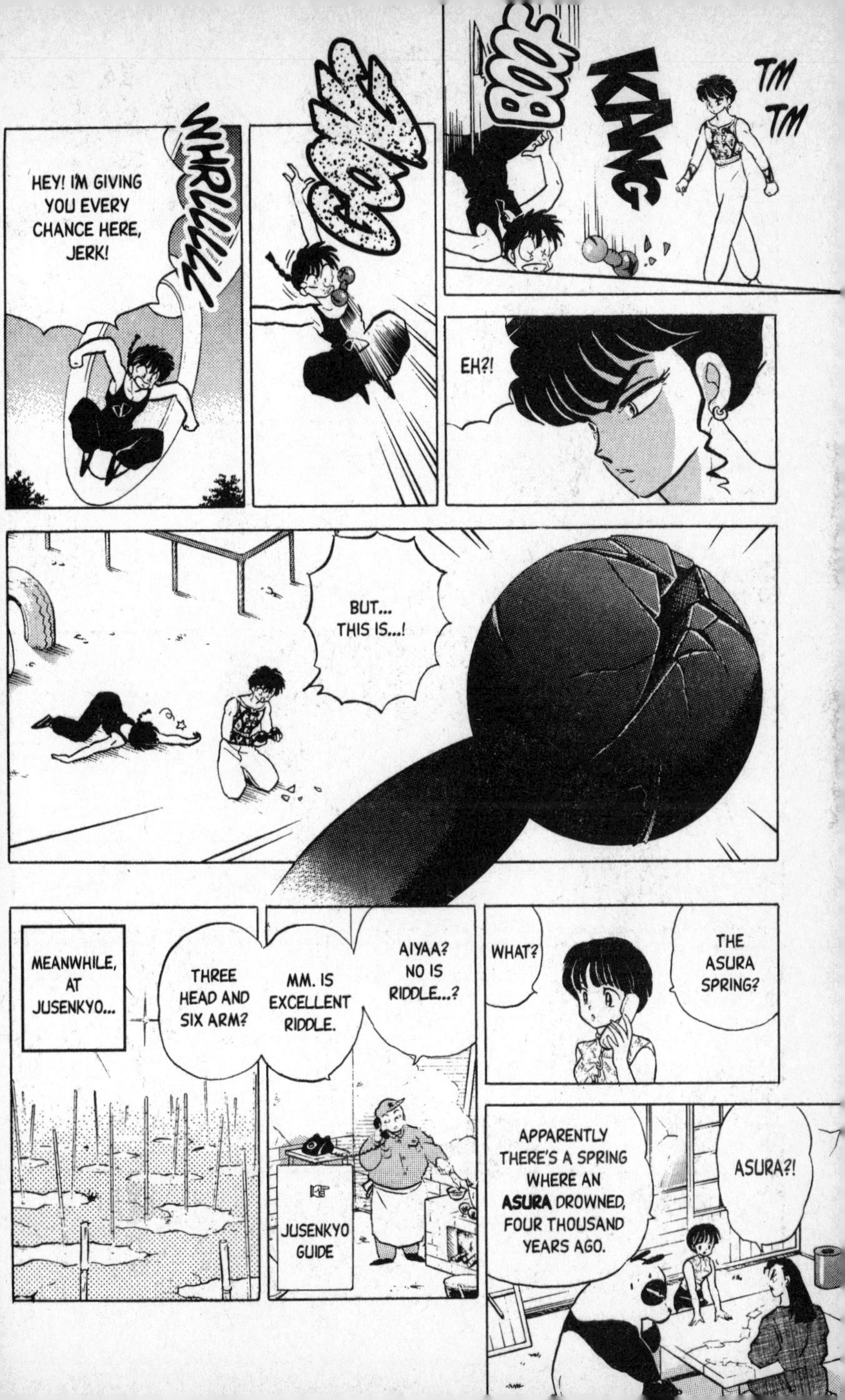
WHRLLLLL
HEY! I'M GIVING YOU EVERY CHANCE HERE, JERK!
BOOT
KANG
TM
TM
EH?!
BUT... THIS IS...!
MEANWHILE, AT JUSENKYO...
THREE HEAD AND SIX ARM?
MM. IS EXCELLENT RIDDLE.
AIYAA? NO IS RIDDLE...?
JUSENKYO GUIDE
WHAT?
THE ASURA SPRING?
APPARENTLY THERE'S A SPRING WHERE AN ASURA DROWNED, FOUR THOUSAND YEARS AGO.
ASURA?!

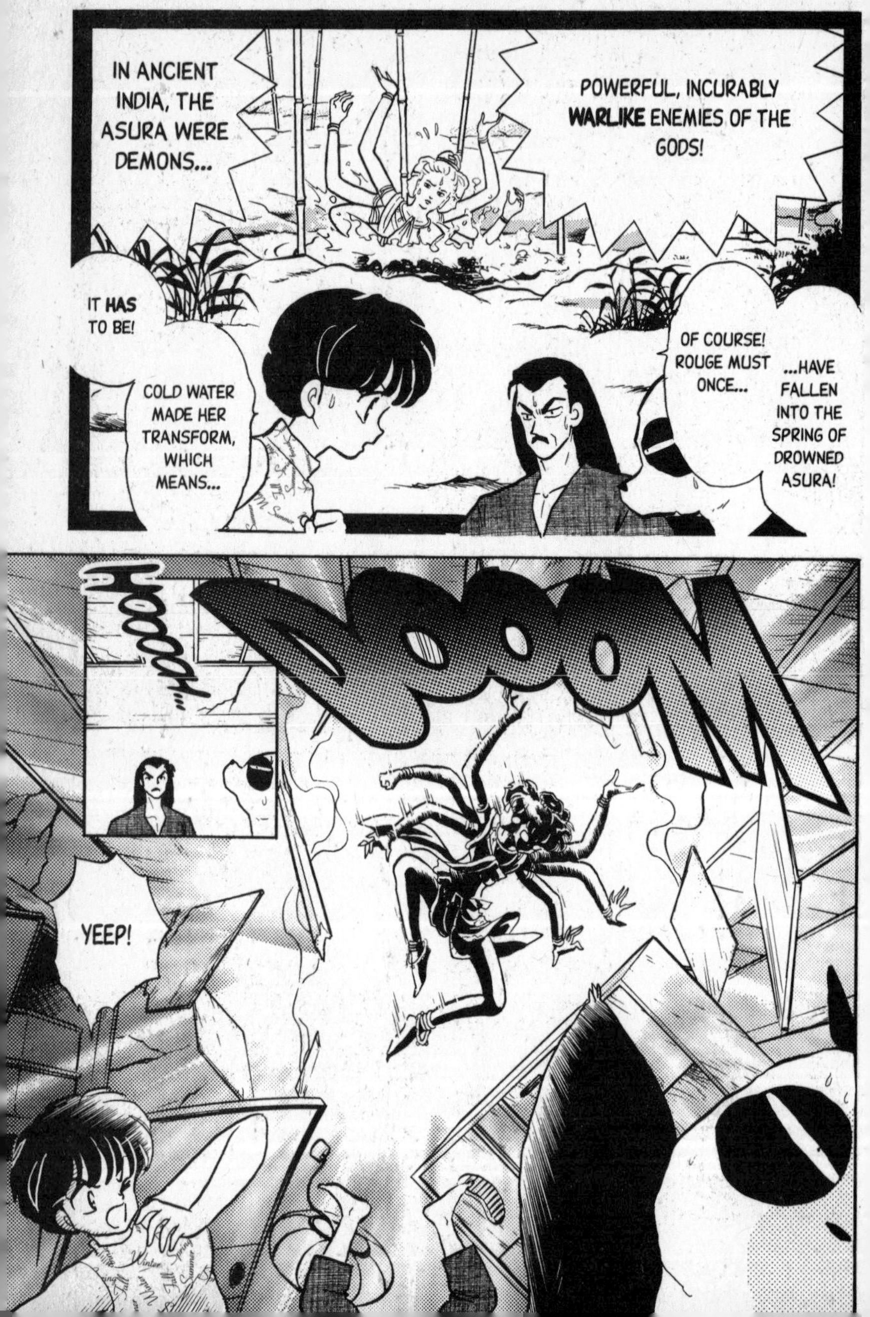
IN ANCIENT INDIA, THE ASURA WERE DEMONS...
POWERFUL, INCURABLY WARLIKE ENEMIES OF THE GODS!
IT HAS TO BE!
COLD WATER MADE HER TRANSFORM, WHICH MEANS...
OF COURSE! ROUGE MUST ONCE...
...HAVE FALLEN INTO THE SPRING OF DROWNED ASURA!
HOOOOO...
VOOOOM
YEEP!

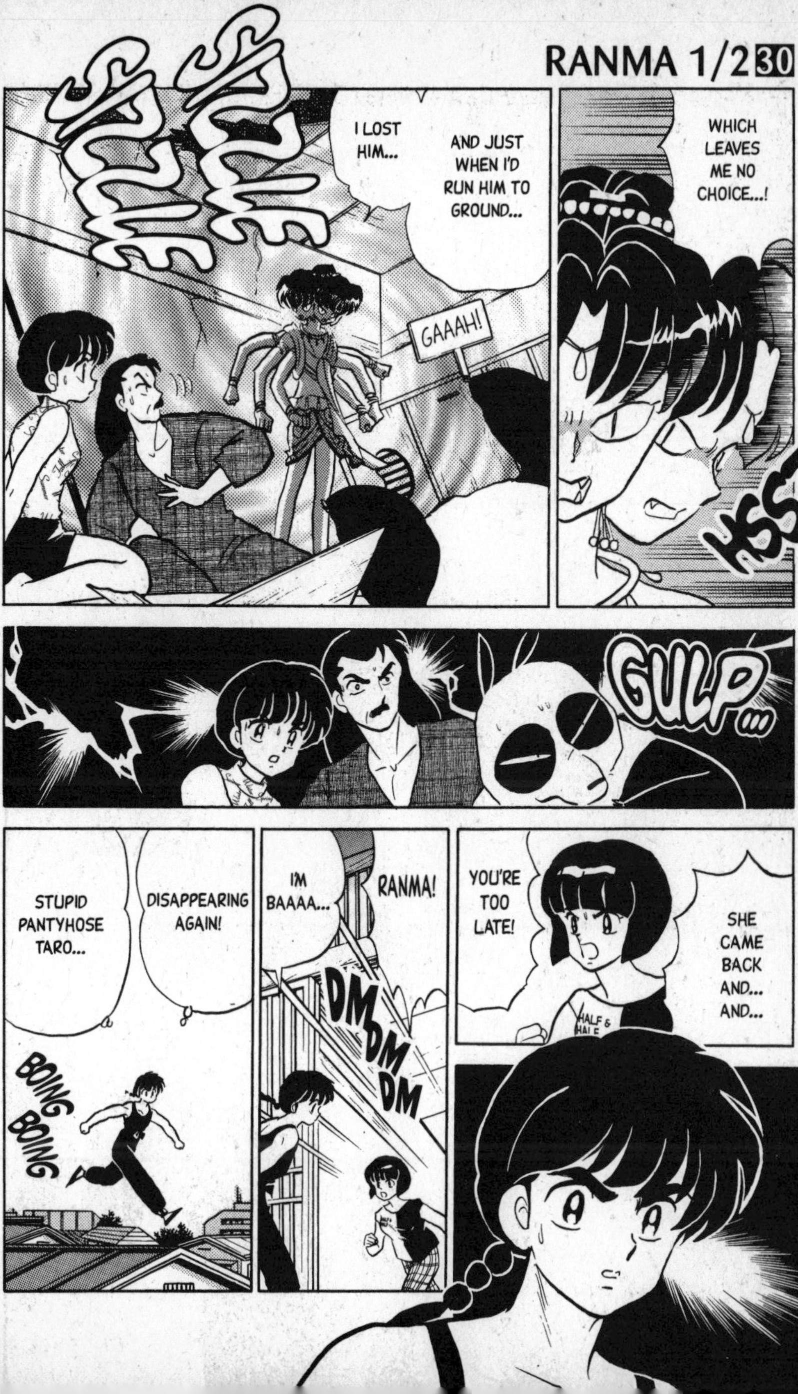
I LOST HIM...
AND JUST WHEN I'D RUN HIM TO GROUND...
GAAAH!
WHICH LEAVES ME NO CHOICE...!
HSST
GULP...
STUPID PANTYHOSE TARO...
DISAPPEARING AGAIN!
BOING BOING
I'M BAAAA...
RANMA!
DM DM DM DM
YOU'RE TOO LATE!
SHE CAME BACK AND... AND...
HALF & HALF

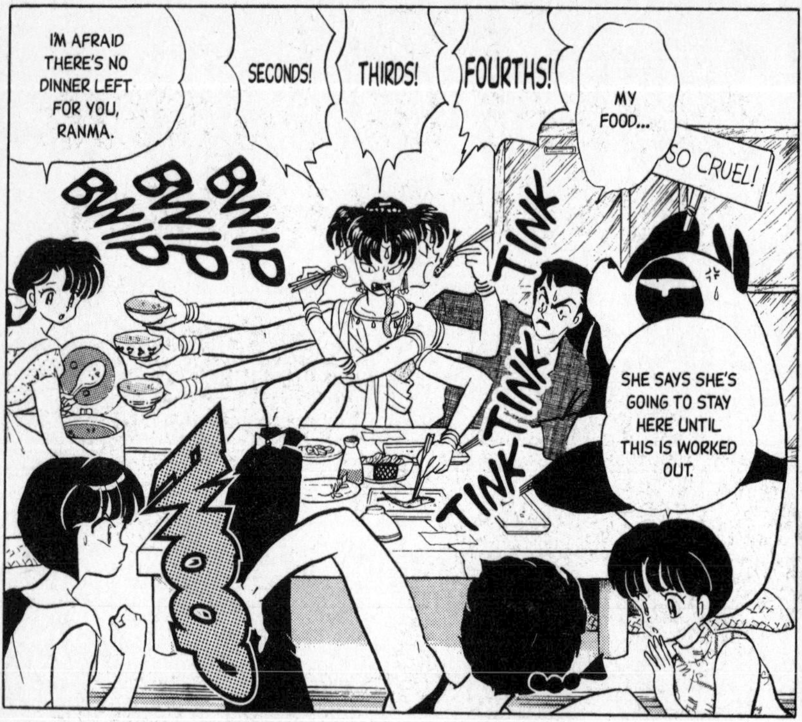
I'M AFRAID THERE'S NO DINNER LEFT FOR YOU, RANMA.
BWIP BWIP BWIP
SECONDS!
THIRDS!
FOURTHS!
MY FOOD...
SO CRUEL!
TINK TINK TINK TINK
SHE SAYS SHE'S GOING TO STAY HERE UNTIL THIS IS WORKED OUT.

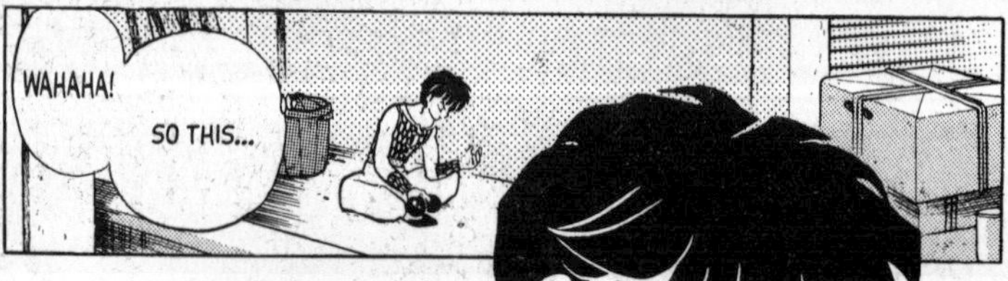
WAHAHA!
SO THIS...

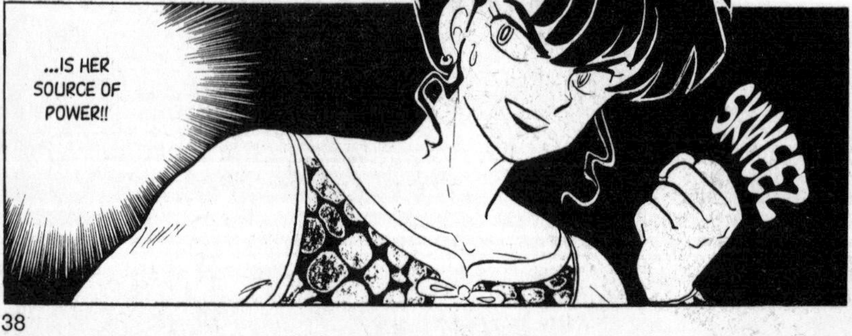
...IS HER SOURCE OF POWER!!
SKWEEZ

PART 3

SOURCE OF POWER: OWNER'S MANUAL

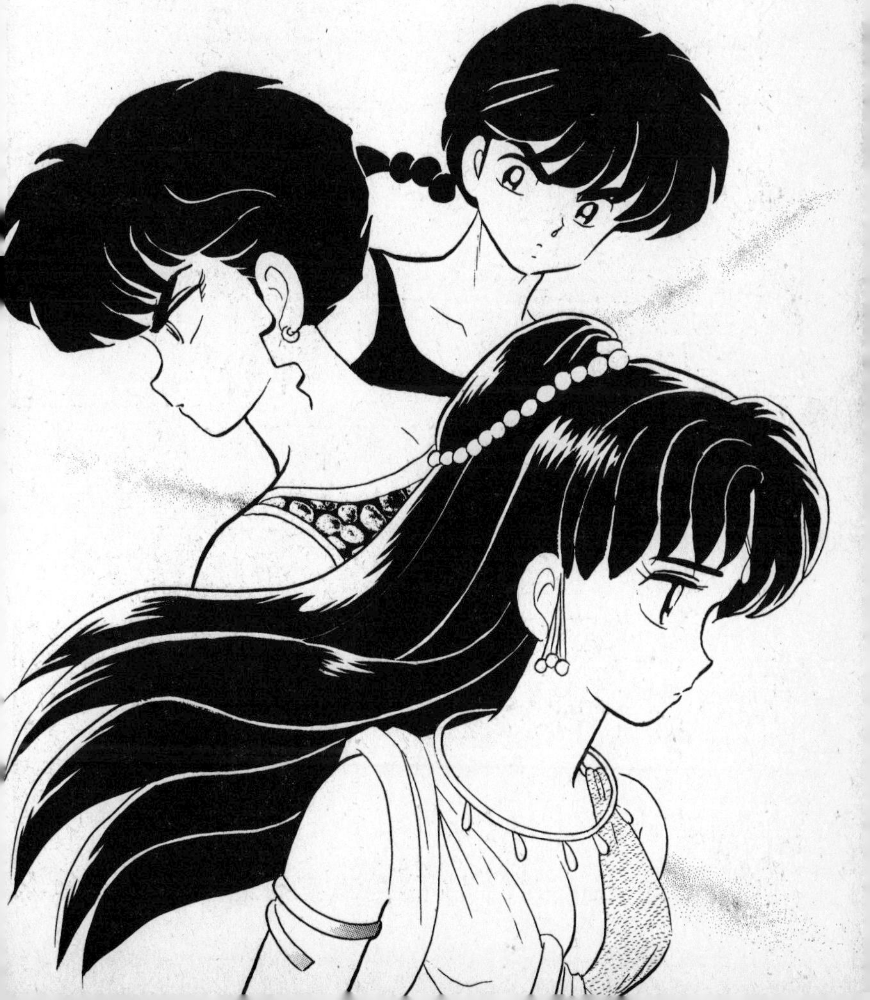

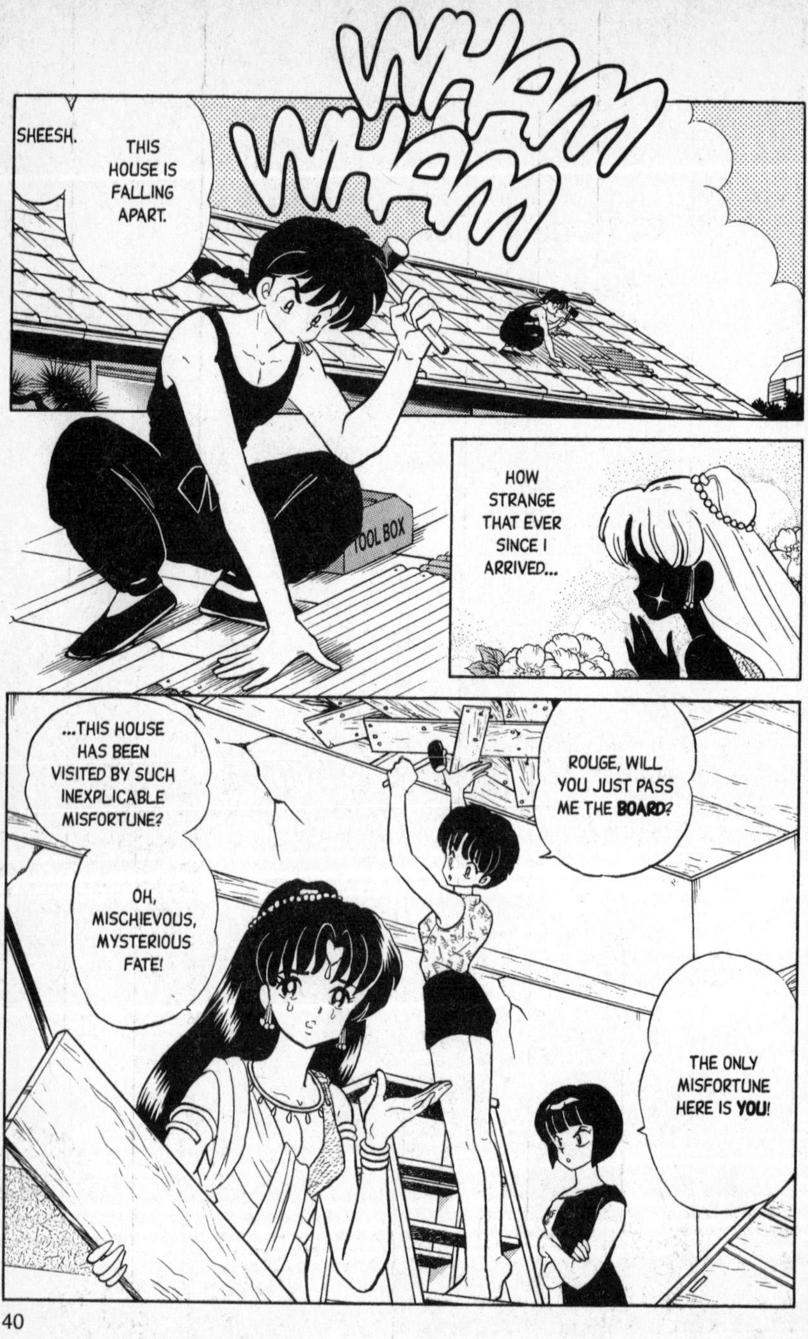
WHAM WHAM
SHEESH.
THIS HOUSE IS FALLING APART.
HOW STRANGE THAT EVER SINCE I ARRIVED...
...THIS HOUSE HAS BEEN VISITED BY SUCH INEXPLICABLE MISFORTUNE?
OH, MISCHIEVOUS, MYSTERIOUS FATE!
ROUGE, WILL YOU JUST PASS ME THE **BOARD**?
THE ONLY MISFORTUNE HERE IS **YOU**!
TOOL BOX

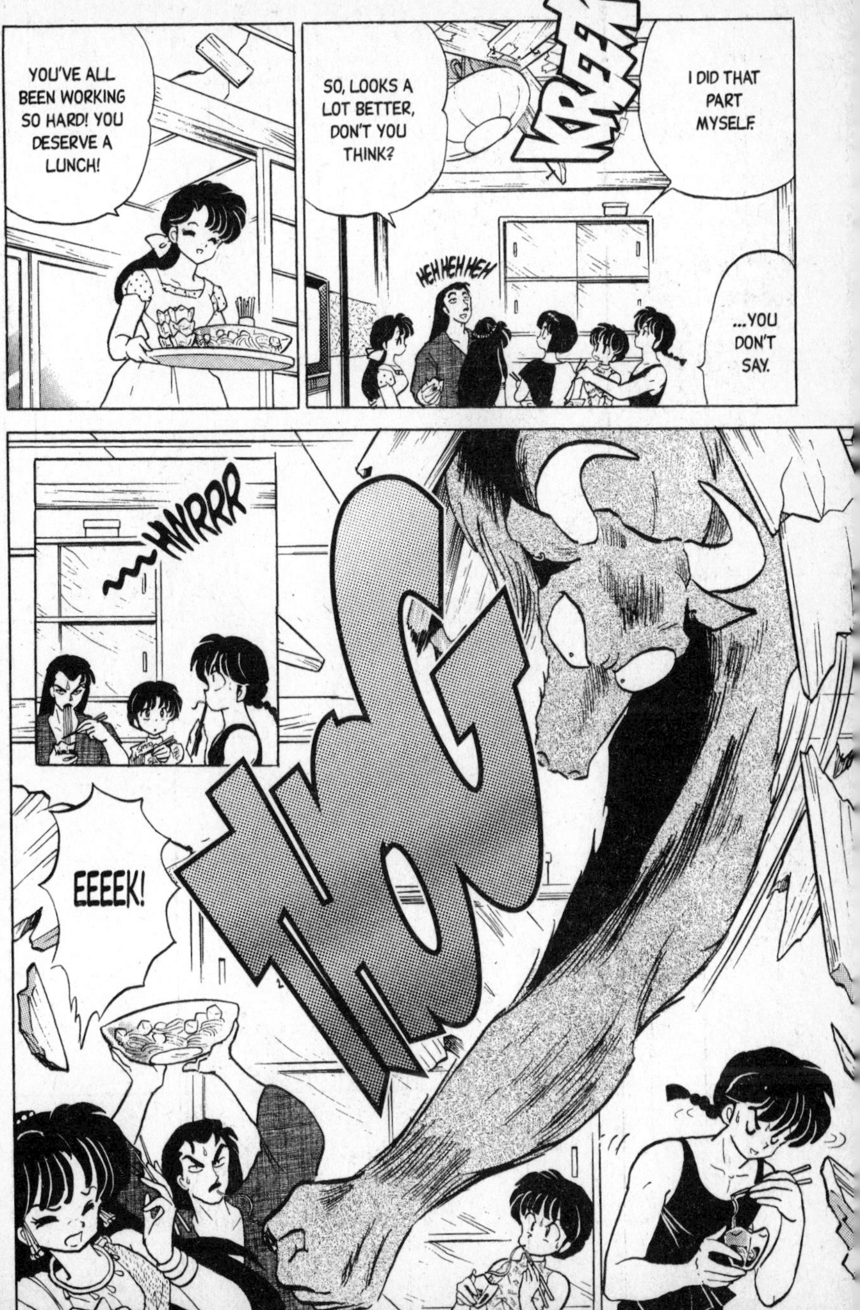
YOU'VE ALL BEEN WORKING SO HARD! YOU DESERVE A LUNCH!
SO, LOOKS A LOT BETTER, DON'T YOU THINK?
KREEK
I DID THAT PART MYSELF.
HEH HEH HEH
...YOU DON'T SAY.
~~HNRRR
THOC
EEEEK!

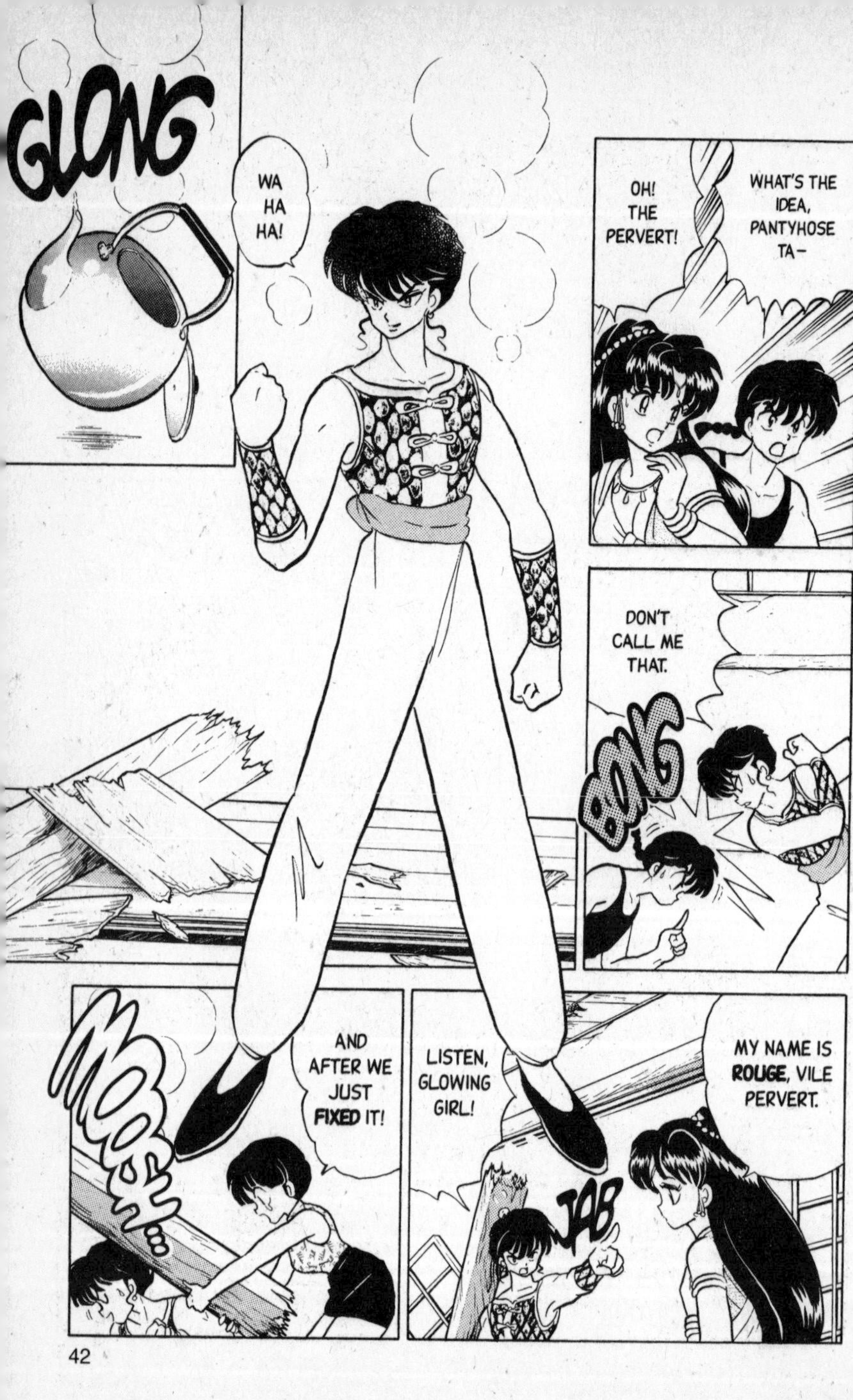
GLONG
WA HA HA!
OH! THE PERVERT!
WHAT'S THE IDEA, PANTYHOSE TA—
DON'T CALL ME THAT.
BONG
MOOSH
AND AFTER WE JUST **FIXED** IT!
LISTEN, GLOWING GIRL!
JAB
MY NAME IS **ROUGE**, VILE PERVERT.

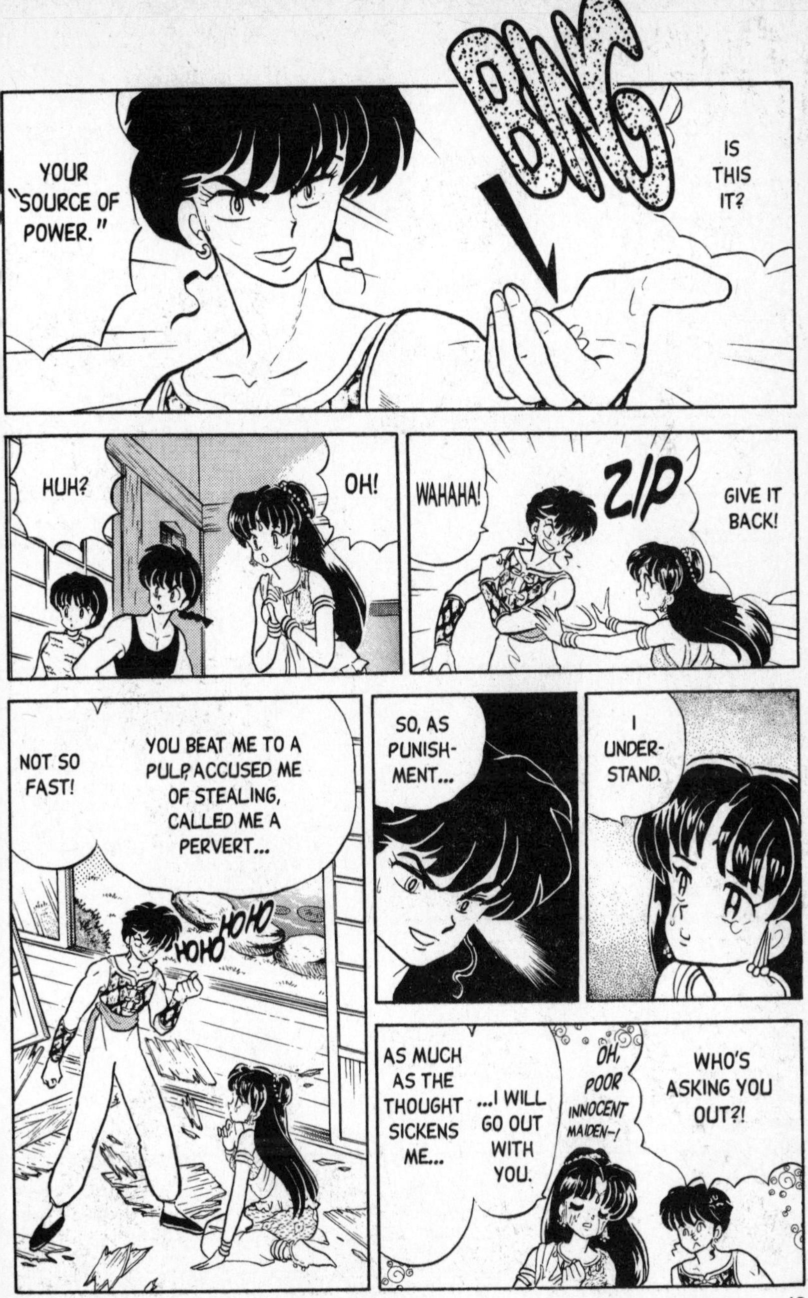
YOUR "SOURCE OF POWER."
BING
IS THIS IT?
HUH?
OH!
WAHAHA!
ZIP
GIVE IT BACK!
NOT SO FAST!
YOU BEAT ME TO A PULP, ACCUSED ME OF STEALING, CALLED ME A PERVERT...
HOHO HOHO
SO, AS PUNISH-MENT...
I UNDER-STAND.
AS MUCH AS THE THOUGHT SICKENS ME...
...I WILL GO OUT WITH YOU.
OH, POOR INNOCENT MAIDEN—!
WHO'S ASKING YOU OUT?!

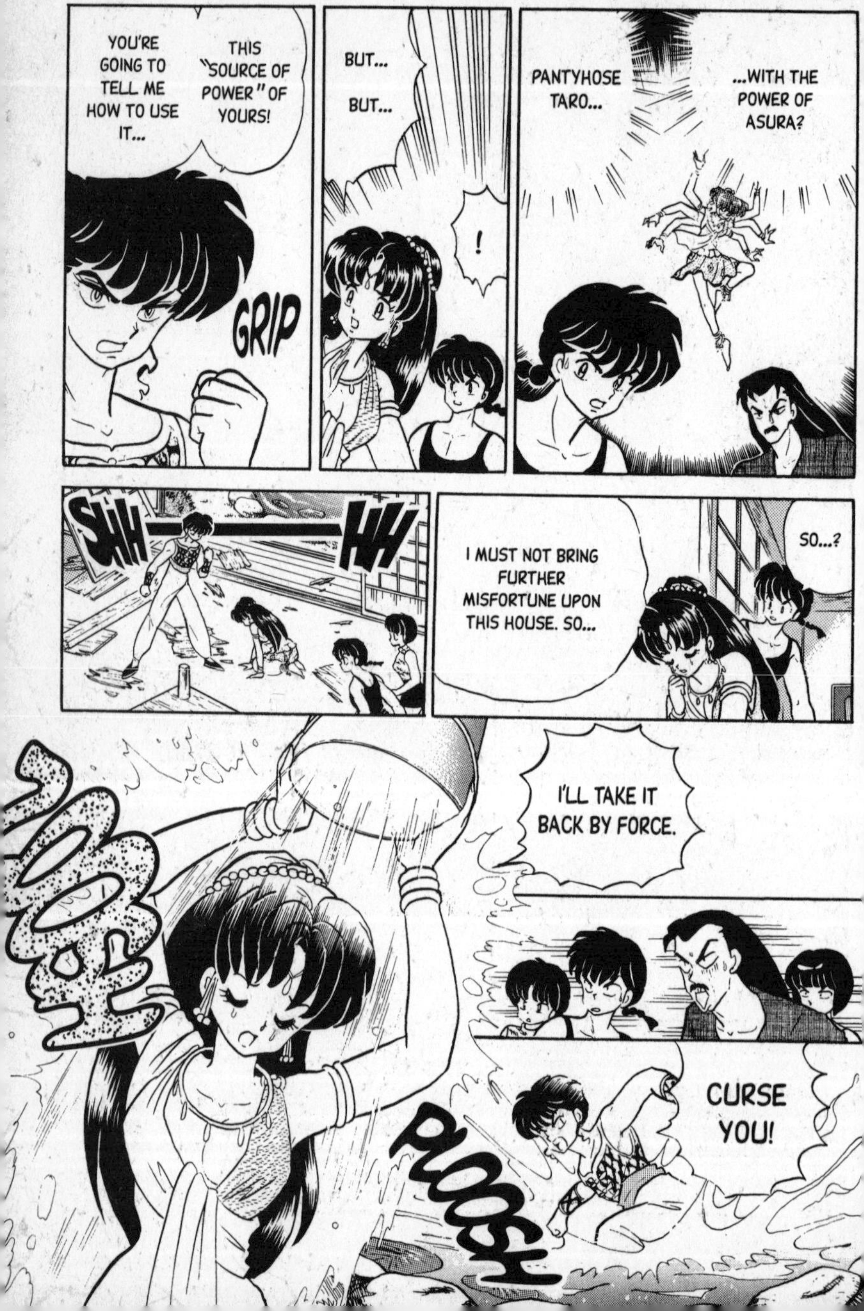
YOU'RE GOING TO TELL ME HOW TO USE IT...
THIS "SOURCE OF POWER" OF YOURS!
GRIP
BUT...
BUT...
!
PANTYHOSE TARO...
...WITH THE POWER OF ASURA?
SHH
HH
I MUST NOT BRING FURTHER MISFORTUNE UPON THIS HOUSE. SO...
SO...?
I'LL TAKE IT BACK BY FORCE.
PLOOSH
CURSE YOU!

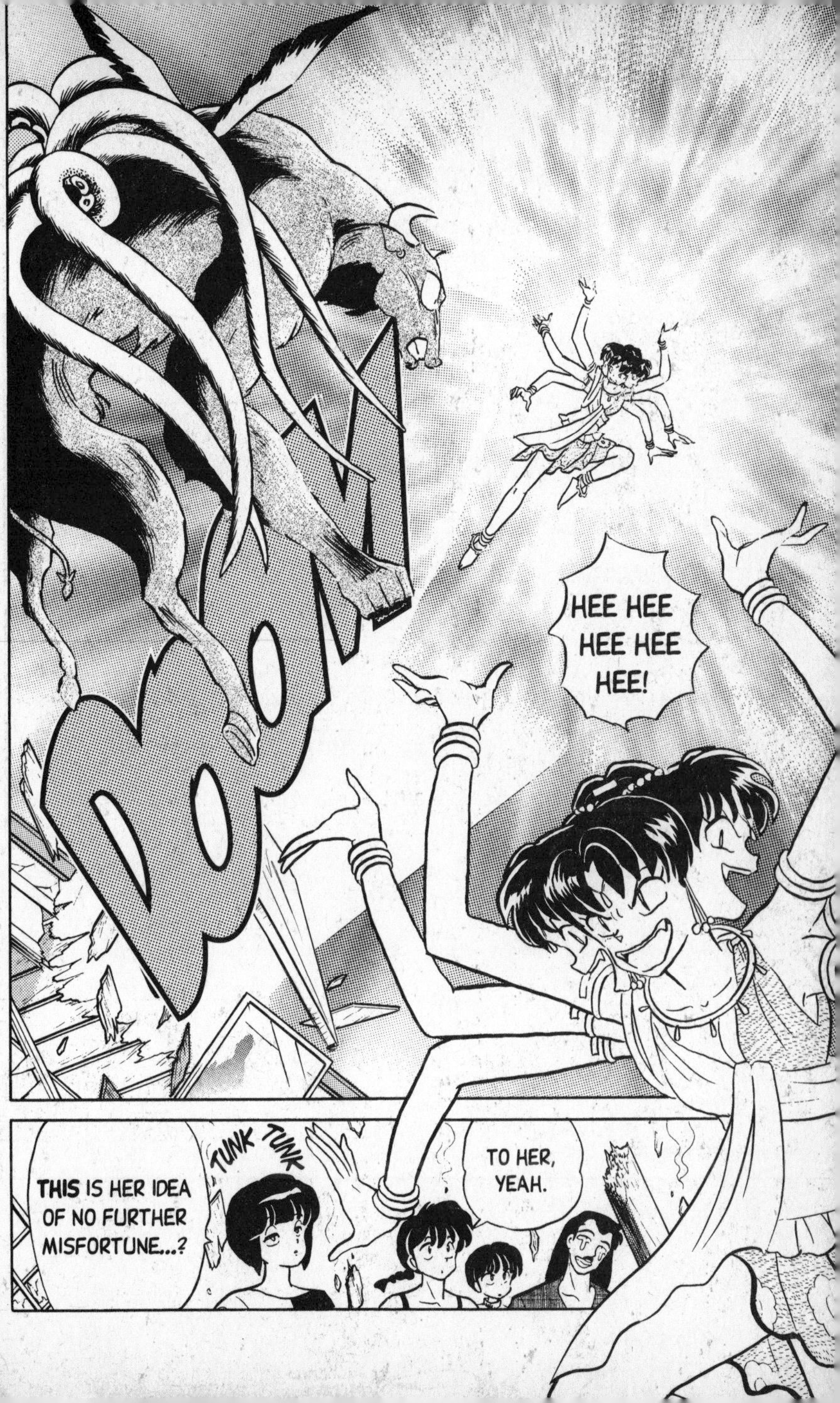
BOOM
HEE HEE HEE HEE HEE!
THIS IS HER IDEA OF NO FURTHER MISFORTUNE...?
TUNK TUNK
TO HER, YEAH.

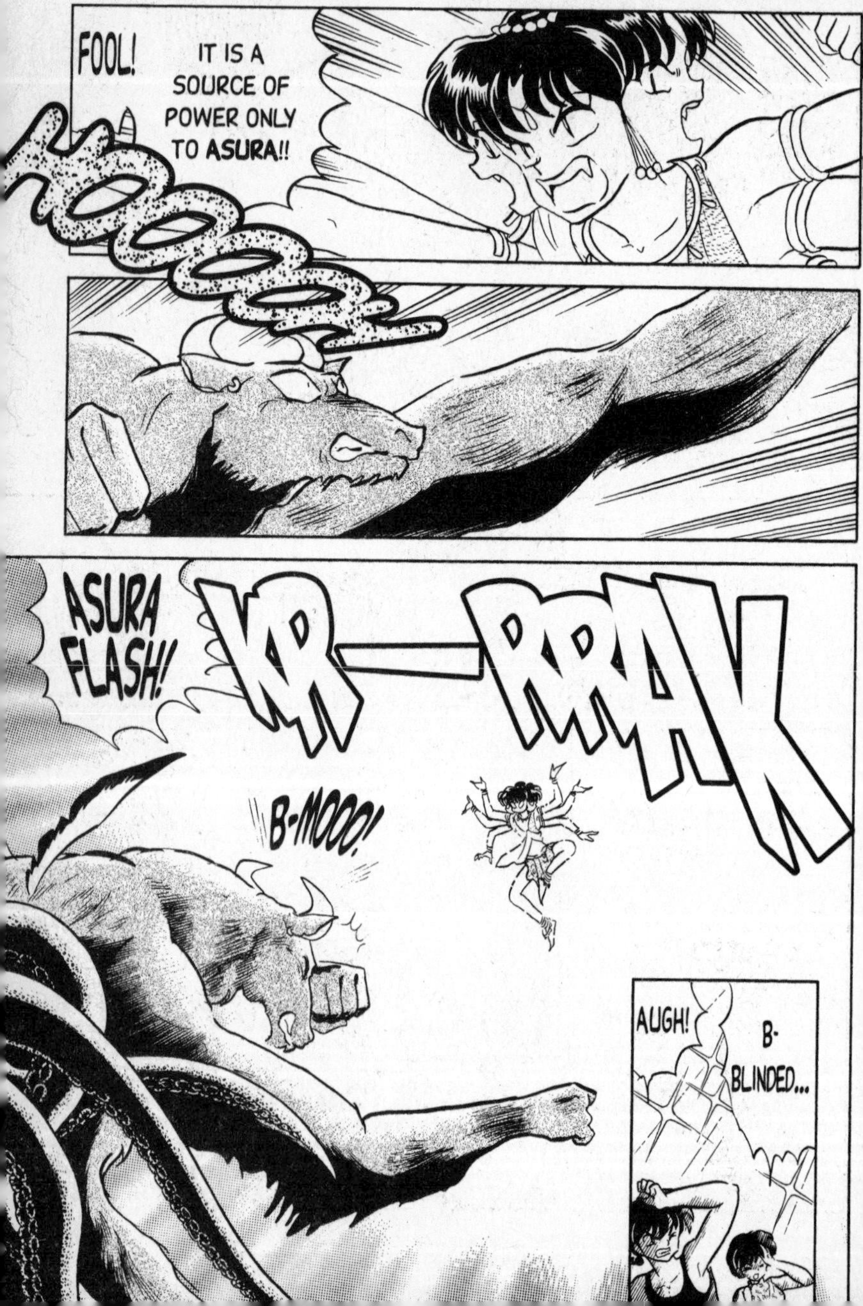
FOOL!
IT IS A SOURCE OF POWER ONLY TO ASURA!!
ASURA FLASH!
KR—RRRAK
B-MOOO!
AUGH!
B-BLINDED...

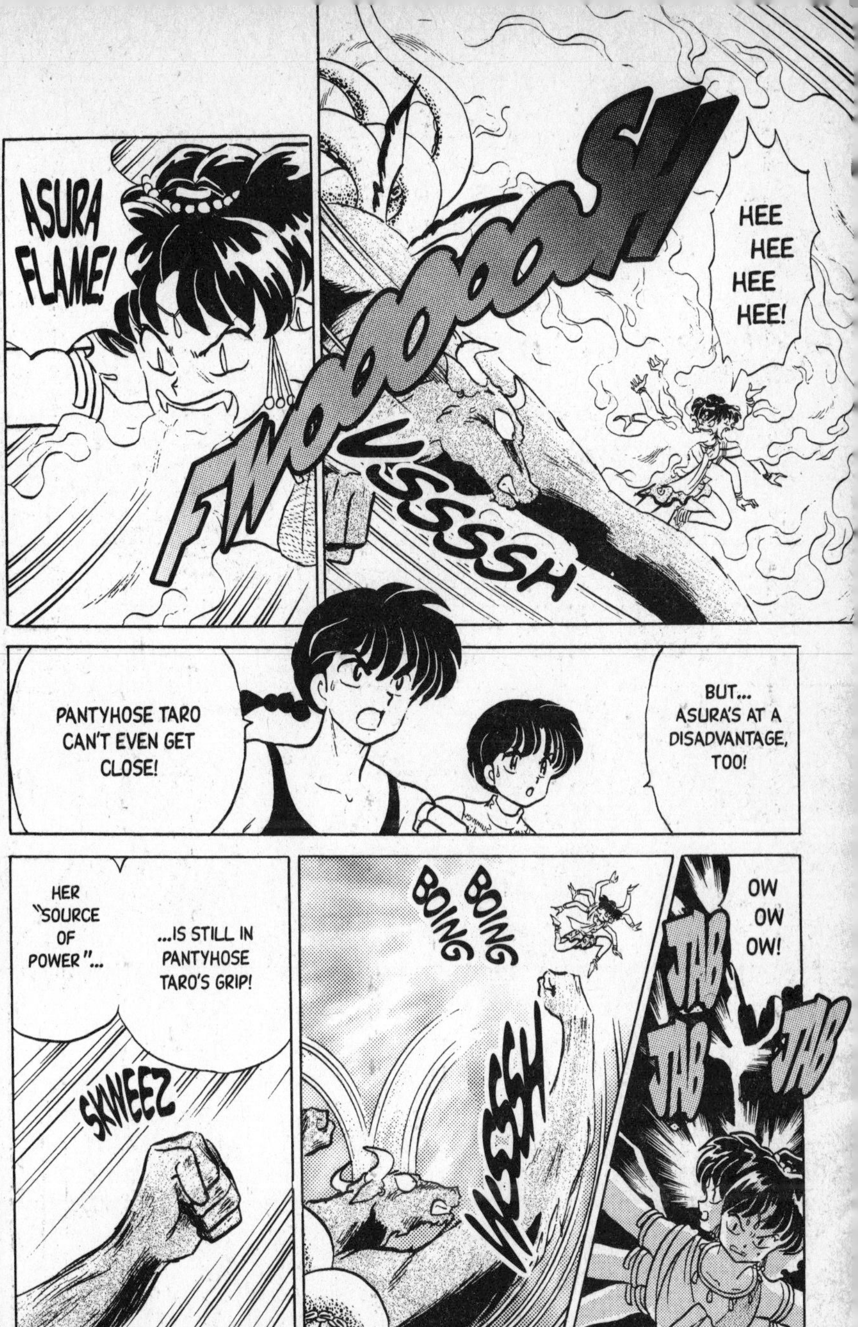
ASURA FLAME!
FWOOOOOOSH
VSSSSSH
HEE HEE HEE HEE!
PANTYHOSE TARO CAN'T EVEN GET CLOSE!
BUT... ASURA'S AT A DISADVANTAGE, TOO!
HER "SOURCE OF POWER"...
...IS STILL IN PANTYHOSE TARO'S GRIP!
SKWEEZ
BOING BOING
WSSSH
OW OW OW!
JAB JAB JAB

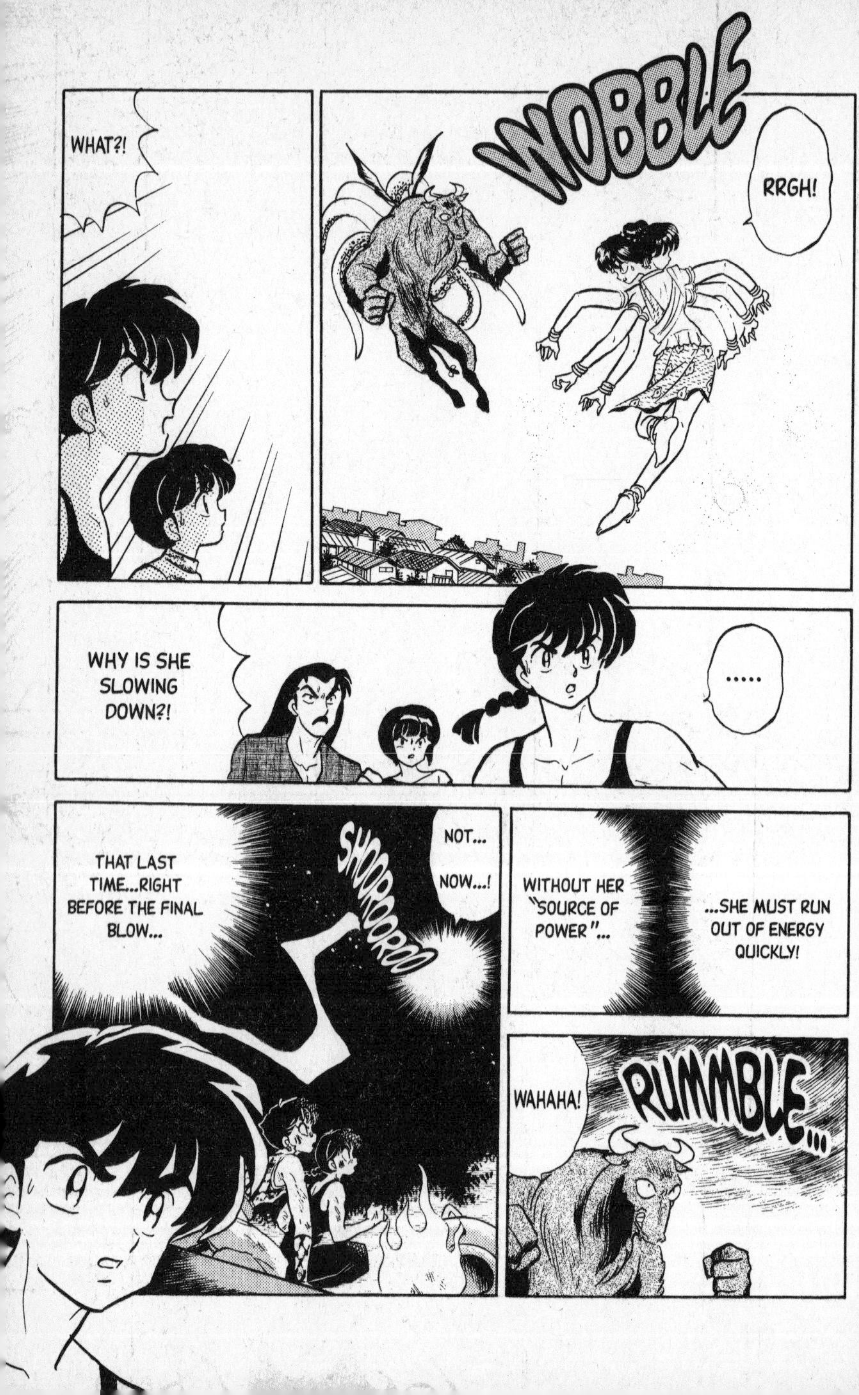
WHAT?!
WOBBLE
RRGH!
WHY IS SHE SLOWING DOWN?!
.....
THAT LAST TIME...RIGHT BEFORE THE FINAL BLOW...
SHOROOROO
NOT... NOW...!
WITHOUT HER "SOURCE OF POWER"...
...SHE MUST RUN OUT OF ENERGY QUICKLY!
WAHAHA!
RUMMBLE...

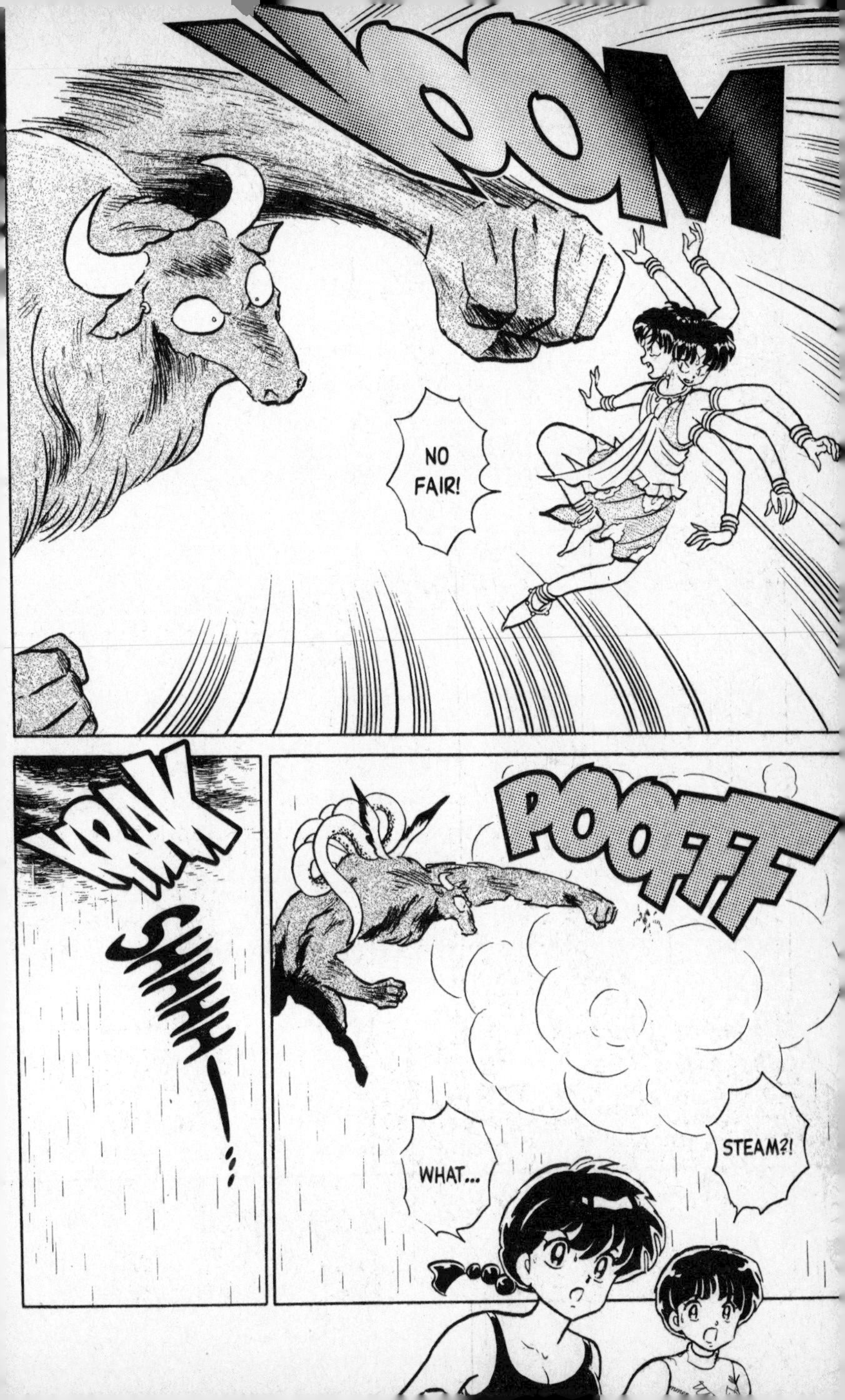
VOOOM
NO FAIR!
KRAK
SHHHH—!!
POOFFF
WHAT...
STEAM?!

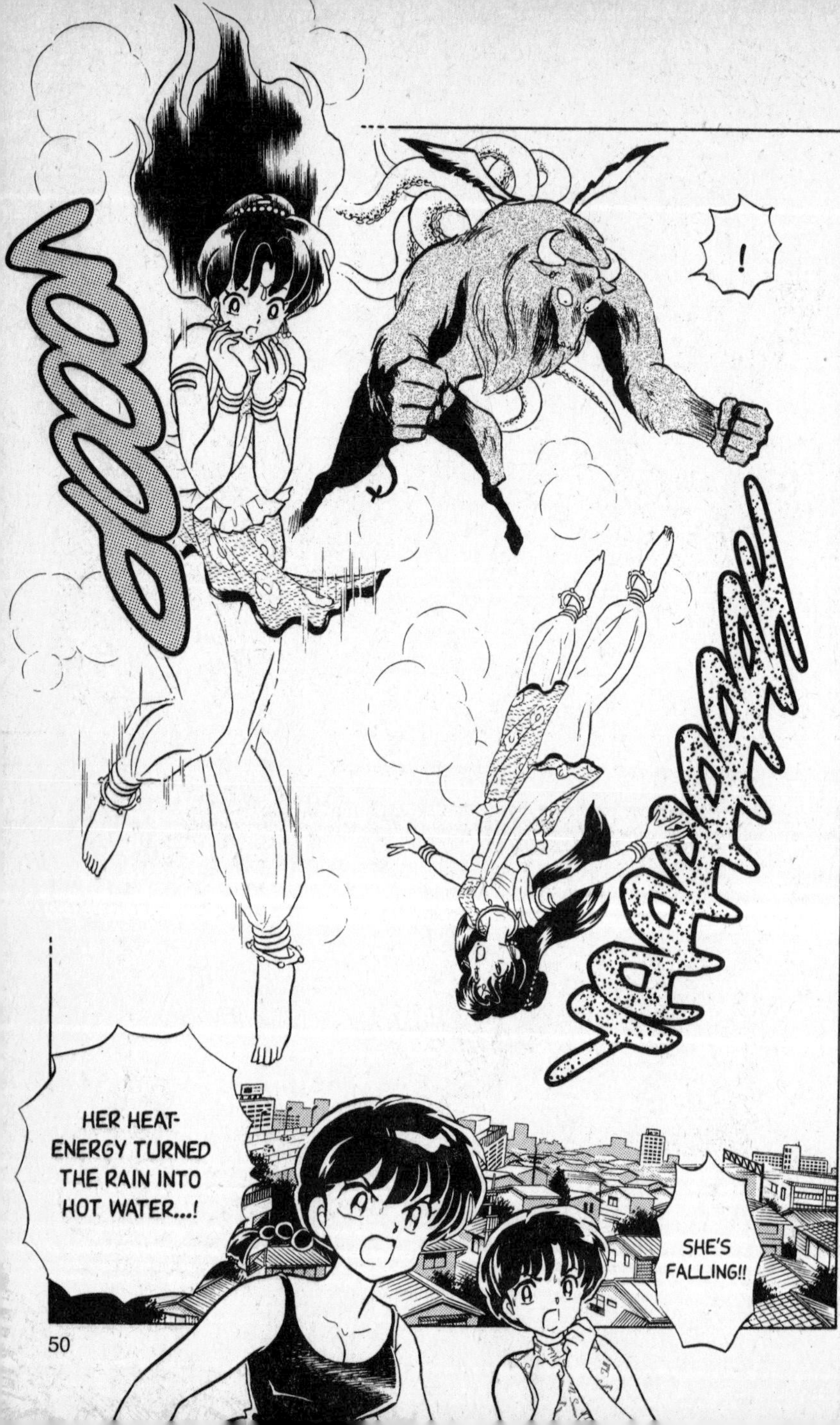
!
HER HEAT-ENERGY TURNED THE RAIN INTO HOT WATER...!
SHE'S FALLING!!

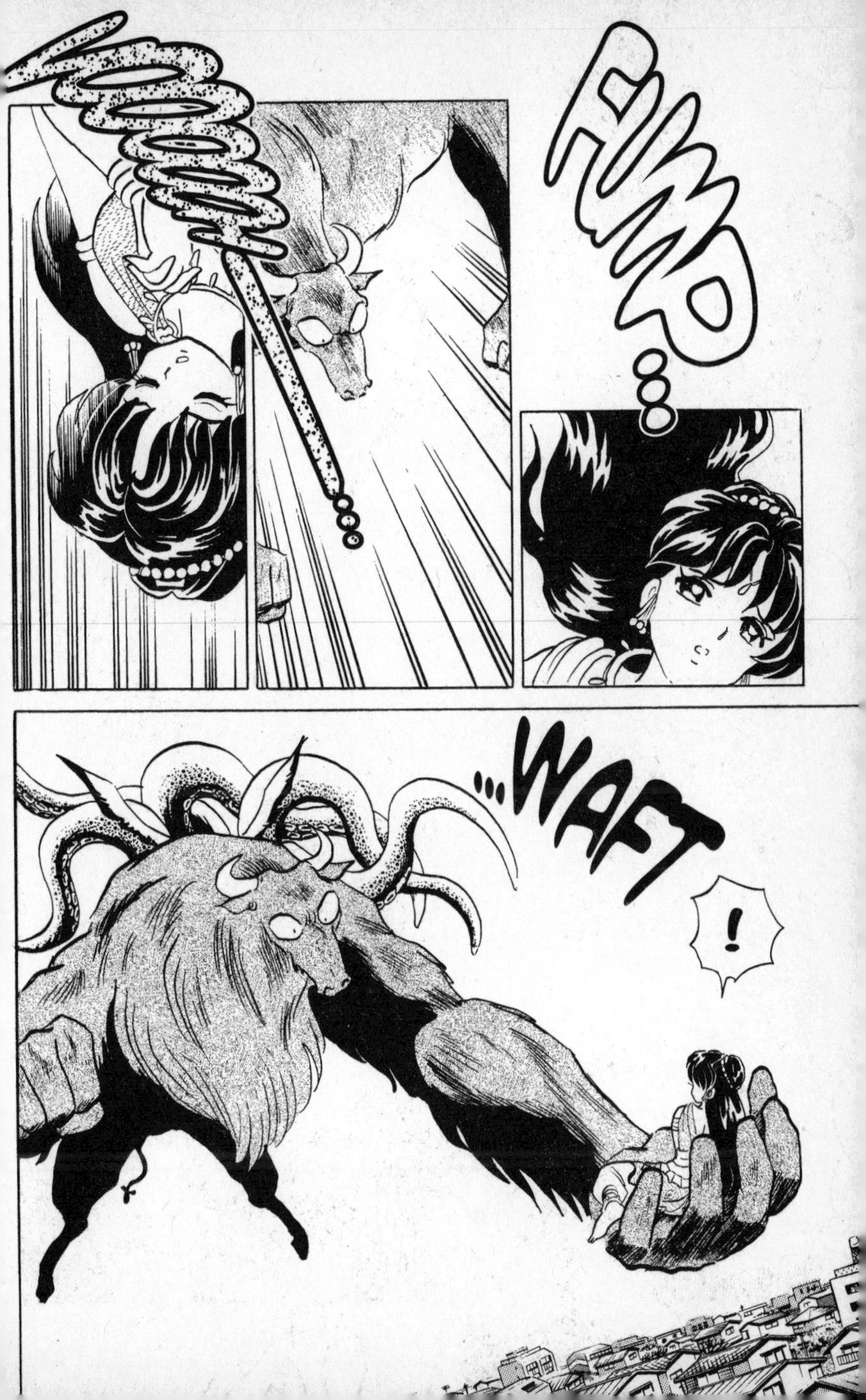
WOOOOOM...
FWMP...
...WAFT
!

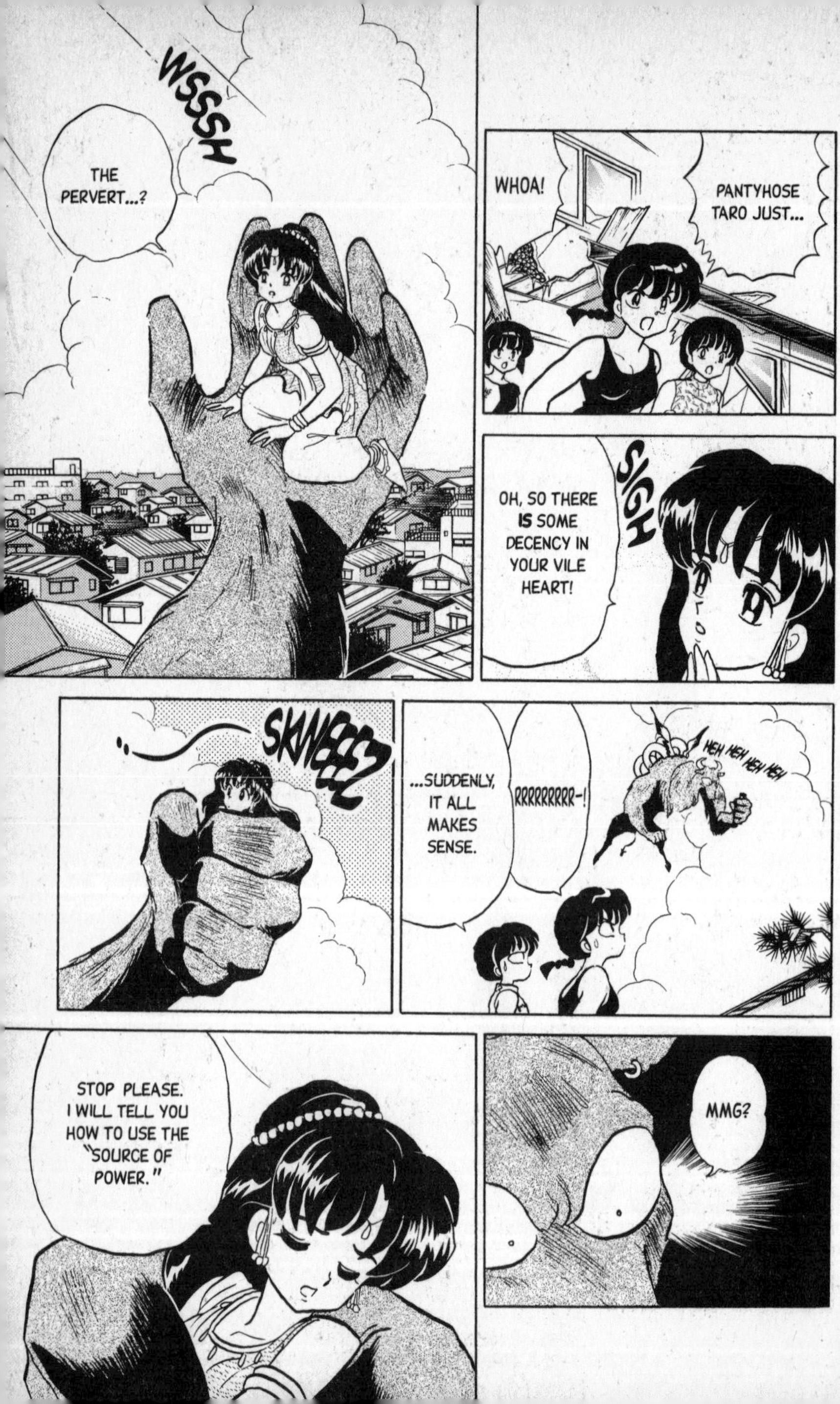
WSSSH
THE PERVERT...?
WHOA!
PANTYHOSE TARO JUST...
OH, SO THERE **IS** SOME DECENCY IN YOUR VILE HEART!
SIGH
SKWEEEZ
...SUDDENLY, IT ALL MAKES SENSE.
RRRRRRRRR-!
HEH HEH HEH HEH
STOP PLEASE. I WILL TELL YOU HOW TO USE THE "SOURCE OF POWER."
MMG?

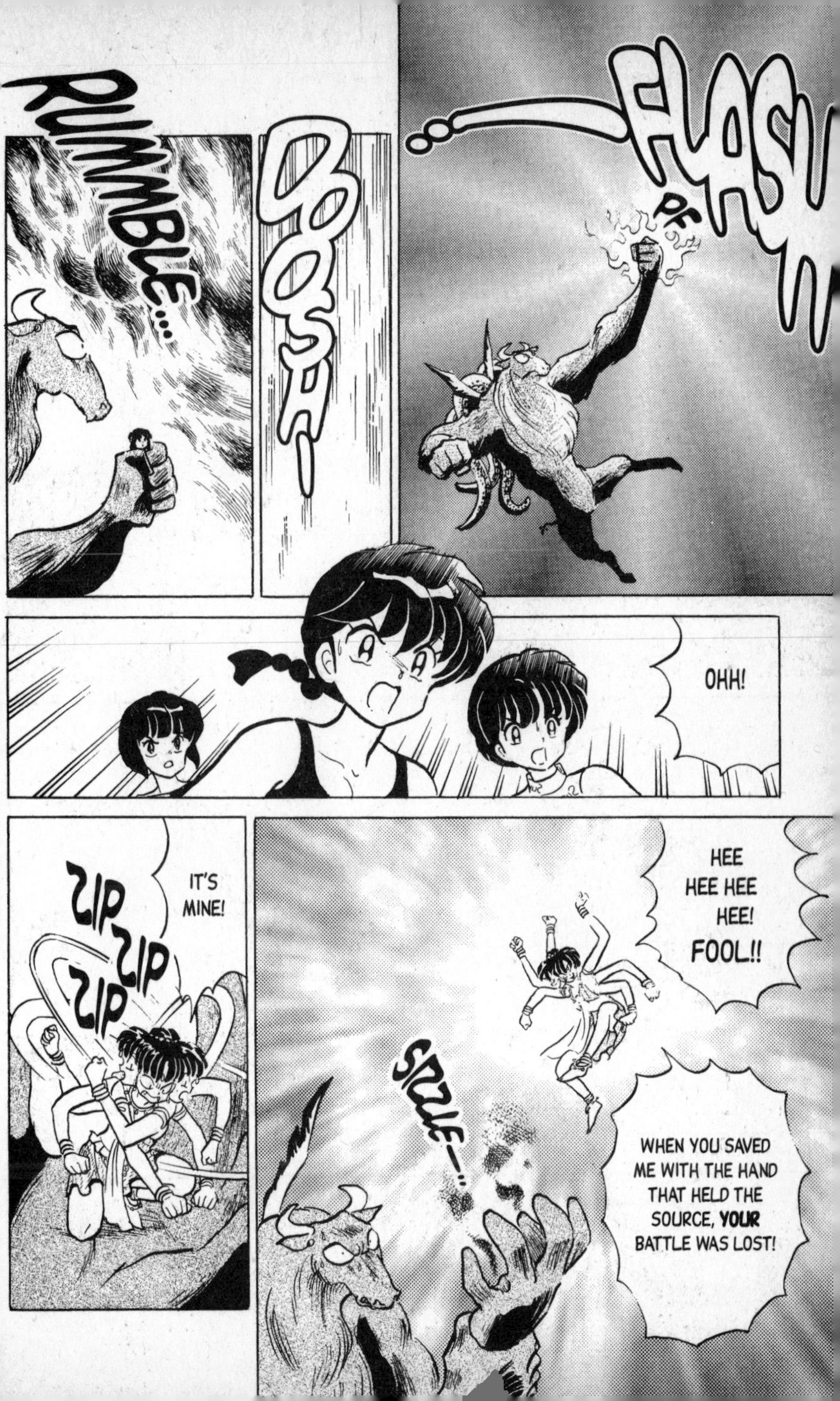
RUMMBLE...
DOOSH
...FLASH
PF
OHH!
IT'S MINE!
ZIP ZIP ZIP
HEE HEE HEE HEE! FOOL!!
SIZZLE...!!
WHEN YOU SAVED ME WITH THE HAND THAT HELD THE SOURCE, YOUR BATTLE WAS LOST!

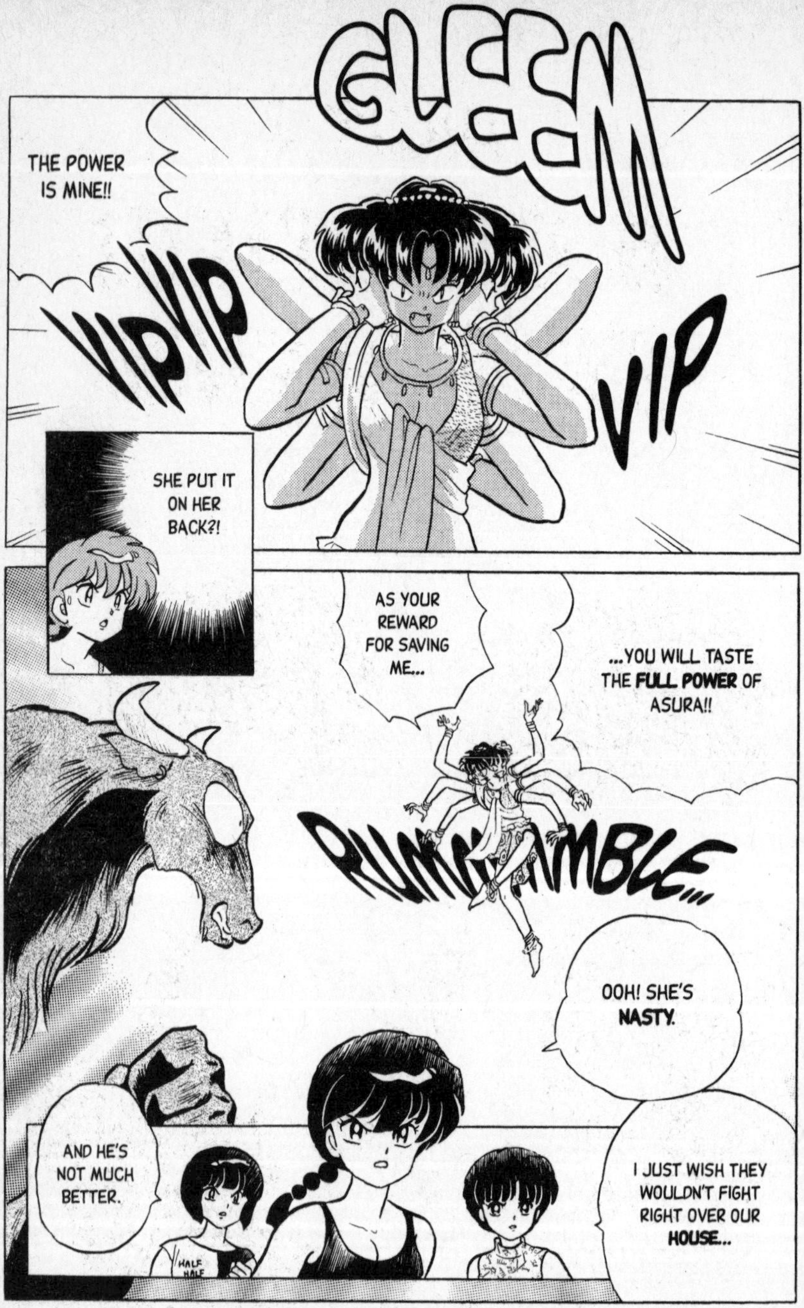
GLEEM
THE POWER IS MINE!!
VIPVIP
VIP
SHE PUT IT ON HER BACK?!
AS YOUR REWARD FOR SAVING ME...
...YOU WILL TASTE THE **FULL POWER** OF ASURA!!
OOH! SHE'S **NASTY**.
AND HE'S NOT MUCH BETTER.
HALF HALF
I JUST WISH THEY WOULDN'T FIGHT RIGHT OVER OUR **HOUSE**...

PART 4

A BEAUTIFUL FRIENDSHIP

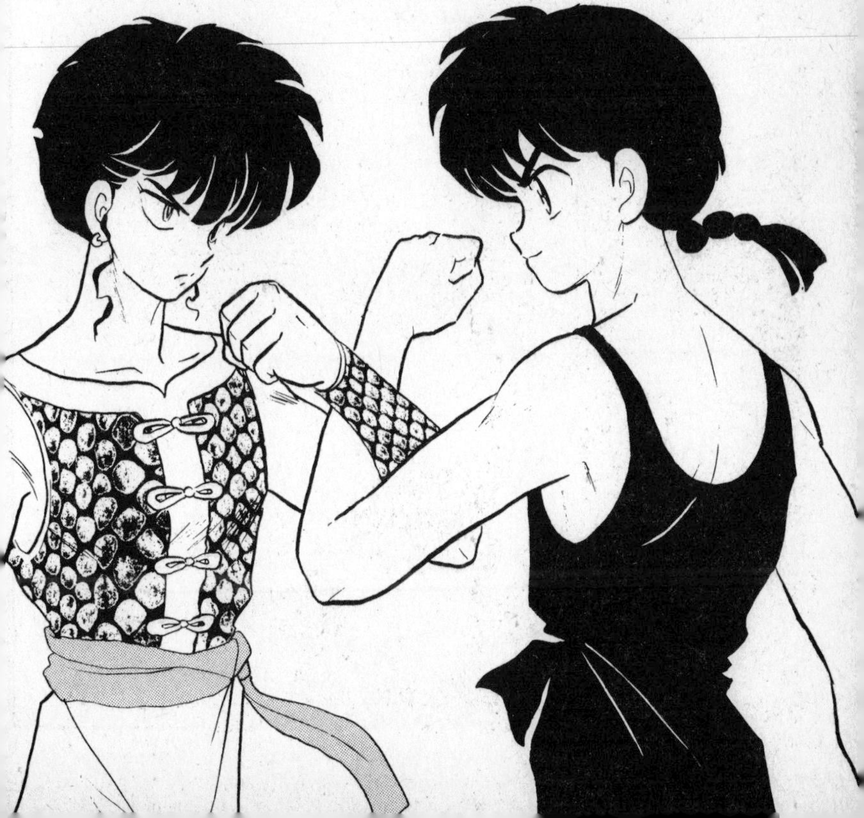

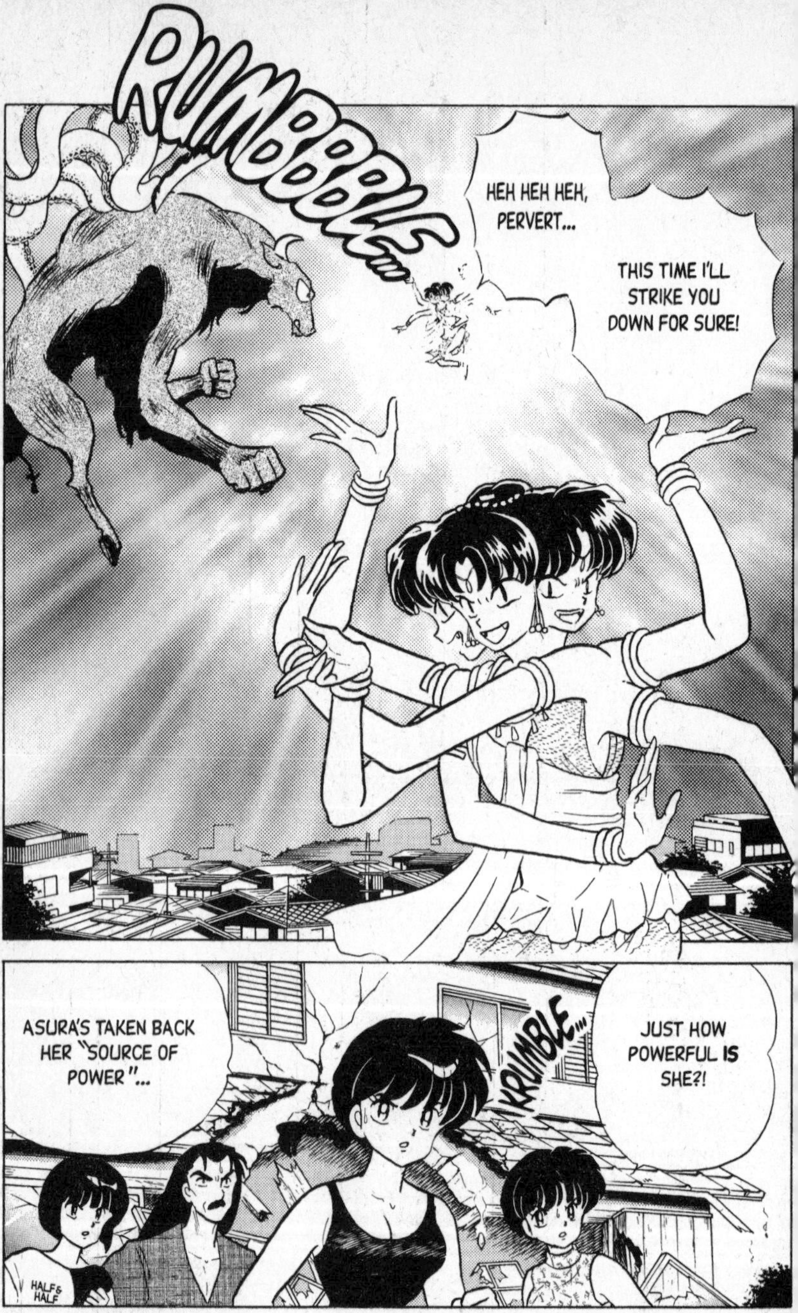
RUMBBBLE...
HEH HEH HEH, PERVERT...
THIS TIME I'LL STRIKE YOU DOWN FOR SURE!
ASURA'S TAKEN BACK HER "SOURCE OF POWER"...
KRUMBLE...
JUST HOW POWERFUL **IS** SHE?!
HALF & HALF

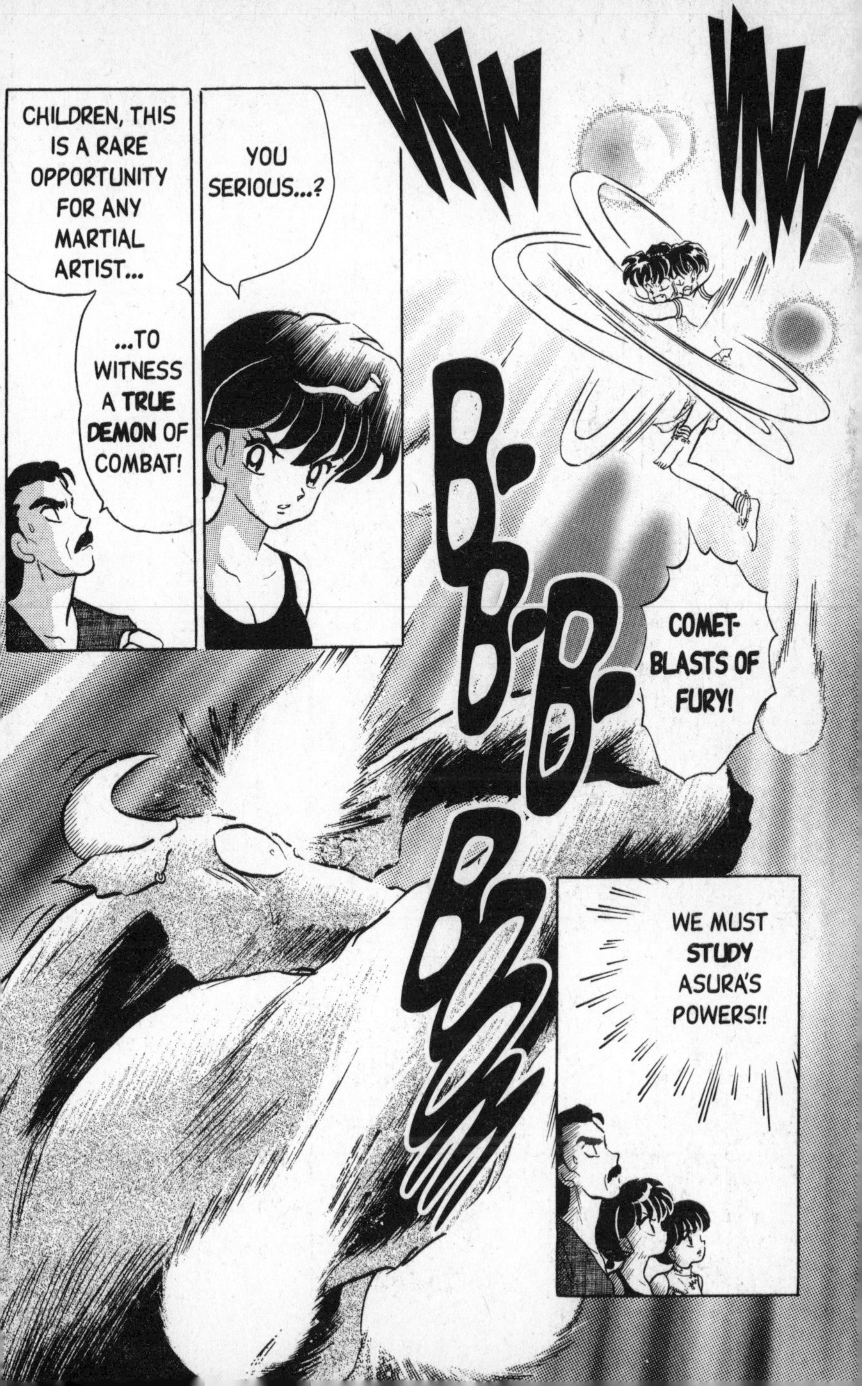
CHILDREN, THIS IS A RARE OPPORTUNITY FOR ANY MARTIAL ARTIST...
...TO WITNESS A TRUE DEMON OF COMBAT!
YOU SERIOUS...?
VNNN
VNNN
B-B-B-B-BOOM
COMET-BLASTS OF FURY!
WE MUST STUDY ASURA'S POWERS!!

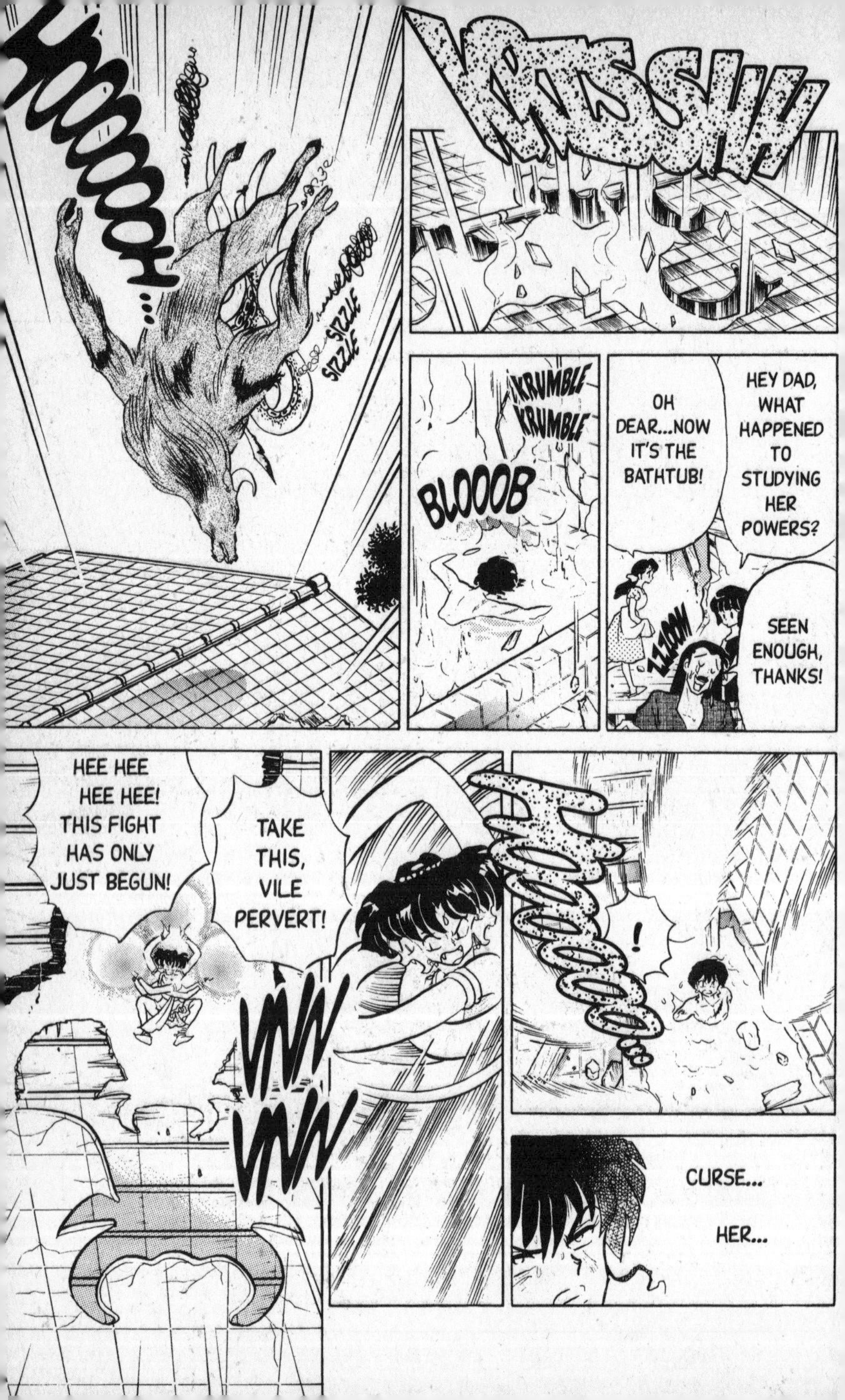
HOOOOOOH...
SIZZLE SIZZLE
KRUMBLE KRUMBLE
BLOOOB
OH DEAR...NOW IT'S THE BATHTUB!
HEY DAD, WHAT HAPPENED TO STUDYING HER POWERS?
SEEN ENOUGH, THANKS!
HEE HEE HEE HEE! THIS FIGHT HAS ONLY JUST BEGUN!
TAKE THIS, VILE PERVERT!
VWW VWW
!
CURSE...
HER...

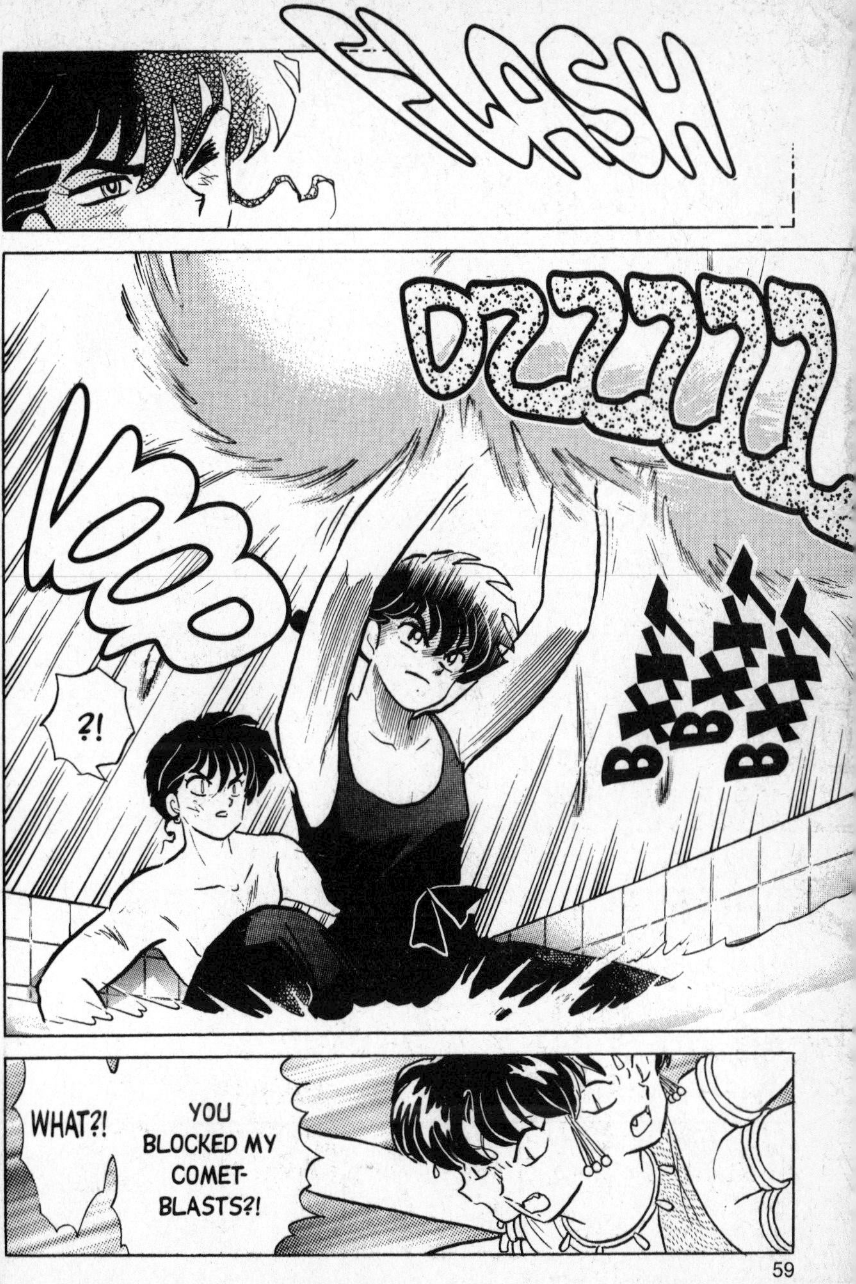
FLASH
DZZZZZ
VOOO
BZZT BZZT BZZT
?!
WHAT?!
YOU BLOCKED MY COMET-BLASTS?!

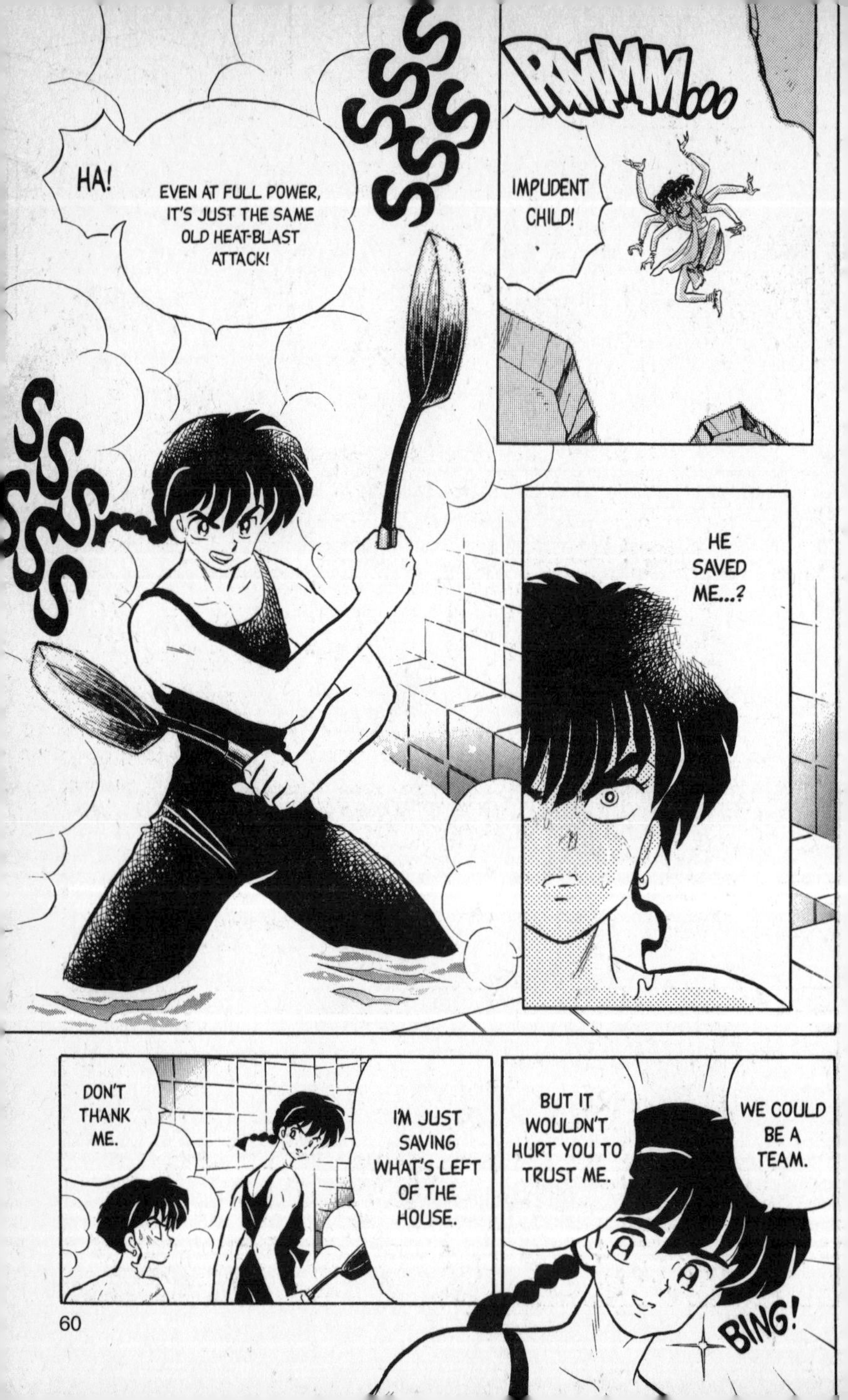
HA!
EVEN AT FULL POWER, IT'S JUST THE SAME OLD HEAT-BLAST ATTACK!
RMMMM...
IMPUDENT CHILD!
HE SAVED ME...?
DON'T THANK ME.
I'M JUST SAVING WHAT'S LEFT OF THE HOUSE.
BUT IT WOULDN'T HURT YOU TO TRUST ME.
WE COULD BE A TEAM.
BING!

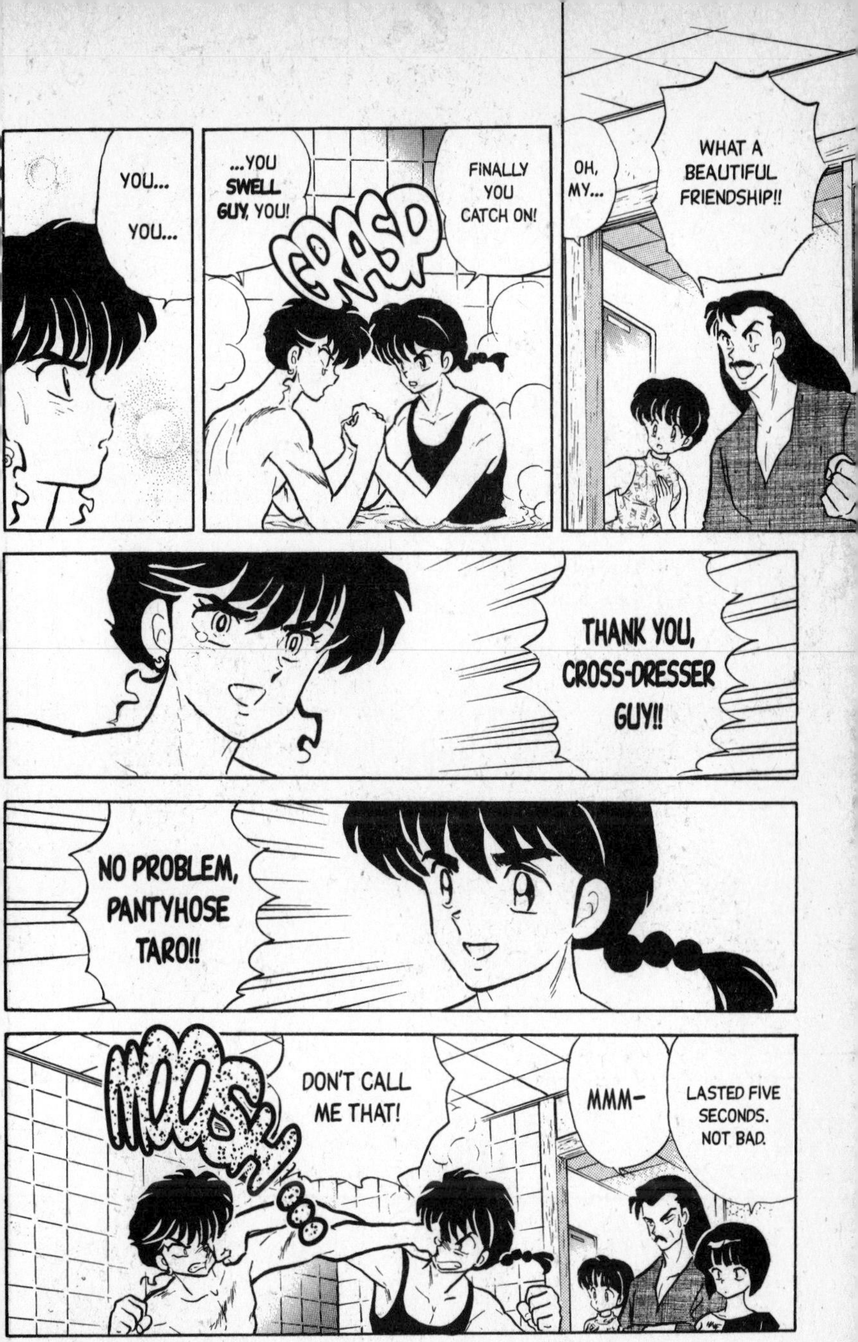
YOU... YOU...
...YOU **SWELL GUY**, YOU!
GRASP
FINALLY YOU CATCH ON!
OH, MY...
WHAT A BEAUTIFUL FRIENDSHIP!!
THANK YOU, CROSS-DRESSER GUY!!
NO PROBLEM, PANTYHOSE TARO!!
DON'T CALL ME THAT!
MMM-
LASTED FIVE SECONDS. NOT BAD.

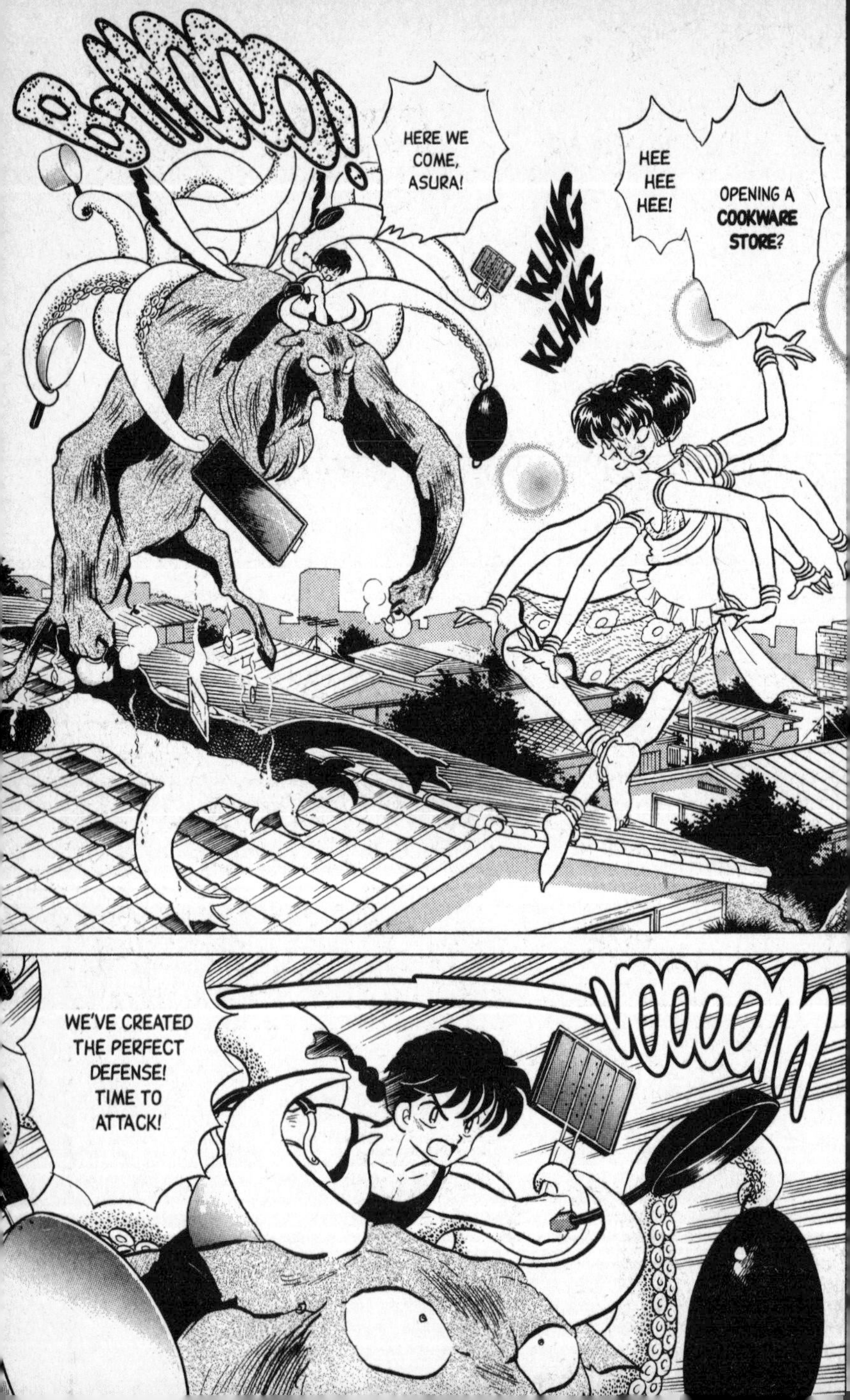
HERE WE COME, ASURA!
KLANG KLANG
HEE HEE HEE!
OPENING A **COOKWARE** STORE?
WE'VE CREATED THE PERFECT DEFENSE! TIME TO ATTACK!
VOOOOM

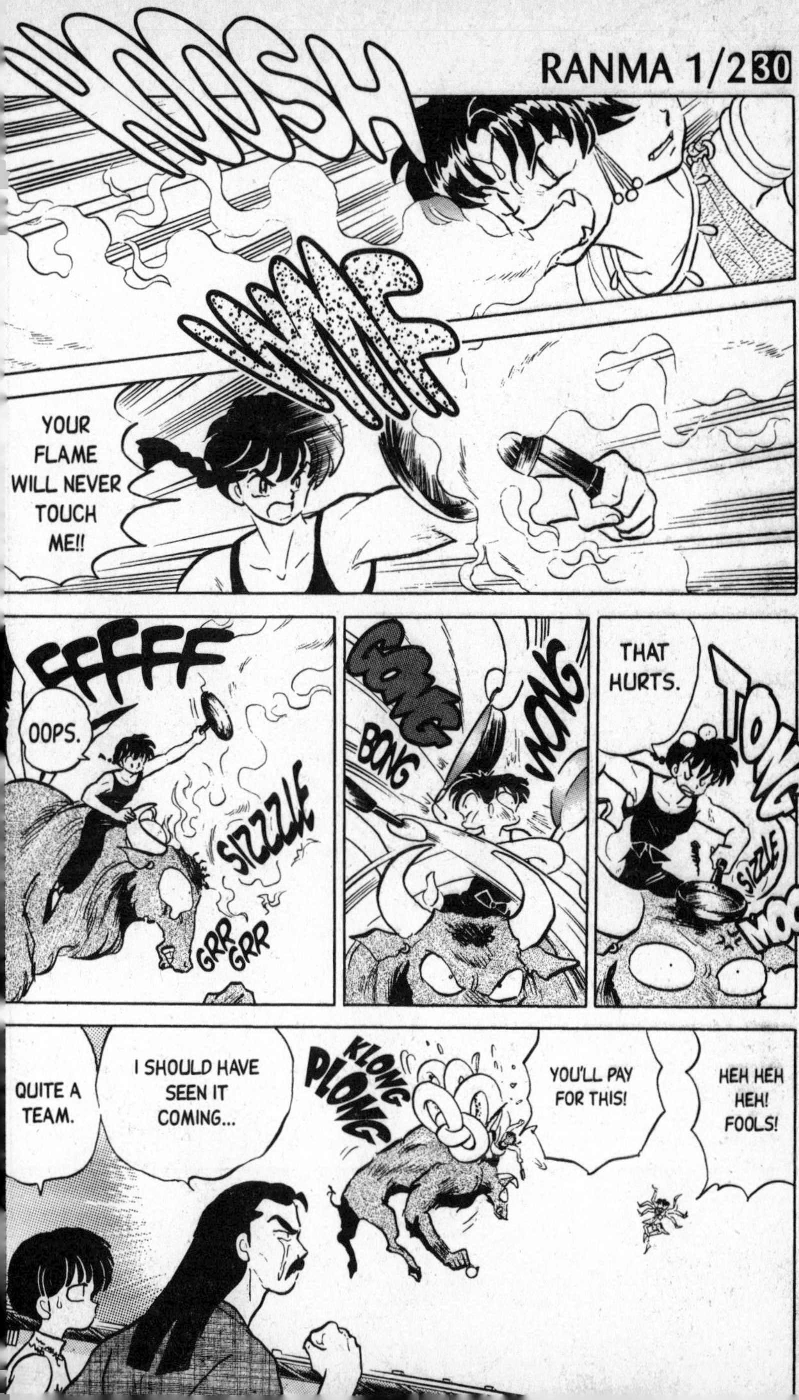
WHOOSH
WHIP
YOUR FLAME WILL NEVER TOUCH ME!!
FFFFF
OOPS.
SIZZZLE
GRR GRR
GONG
BONG
WONG
THAT HURTS.
TONG
SIZZLE
MOO!
QUITE A TEAM.
I SHOULD HAVE SEEN IT COMING...
KLONG
PLONG
YOU'LL PAY FOR THIS!
HEH HEH HEH! FOOLS!

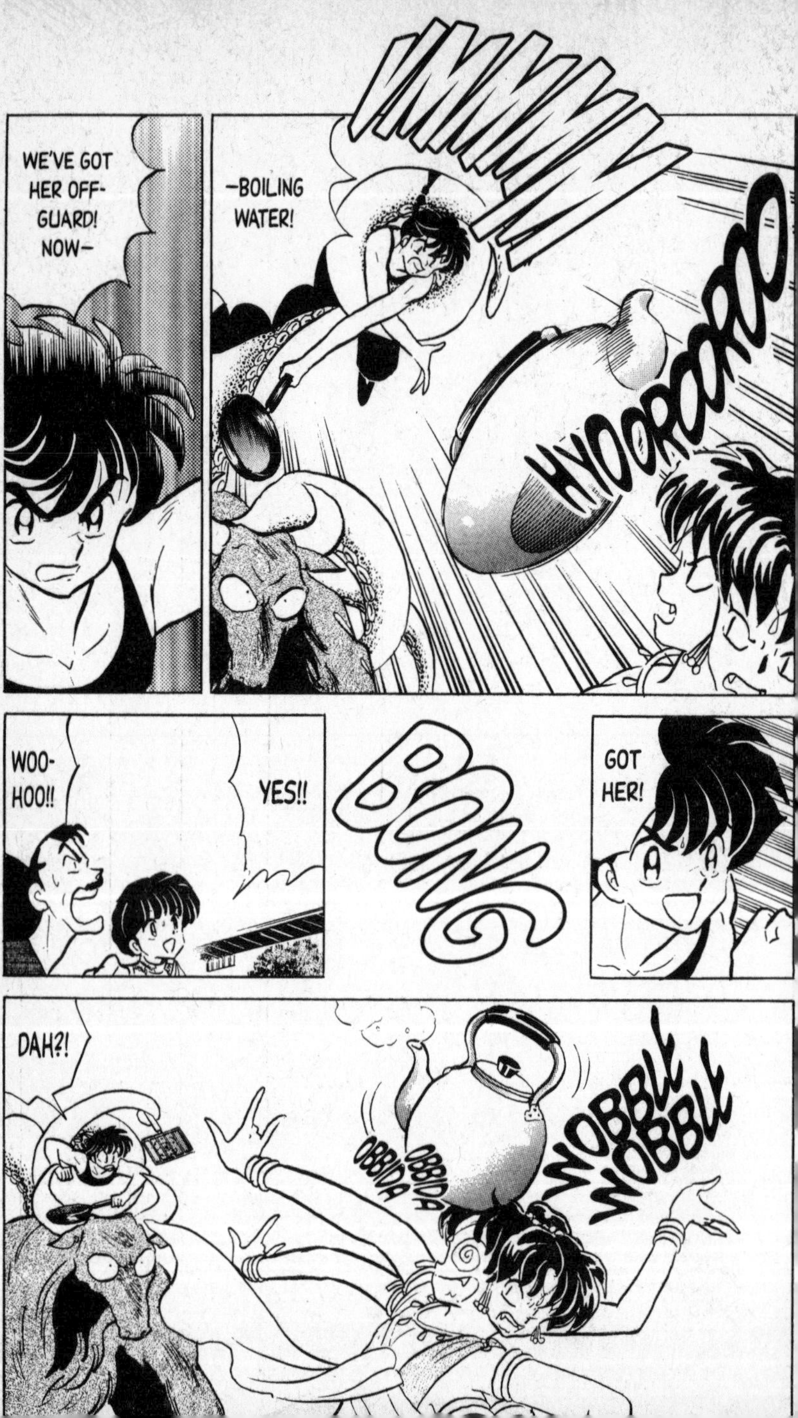
WE'VE GOT HER OFF-GUARD! NOW—
VMMMMMM
—BOILING WATER!
HYOOROOROO
WOO-HOO!!
YES!!
BONG
GOT HER!
DAH?!
OBBIDA OBBIDA
WOBBLE WOBBLE

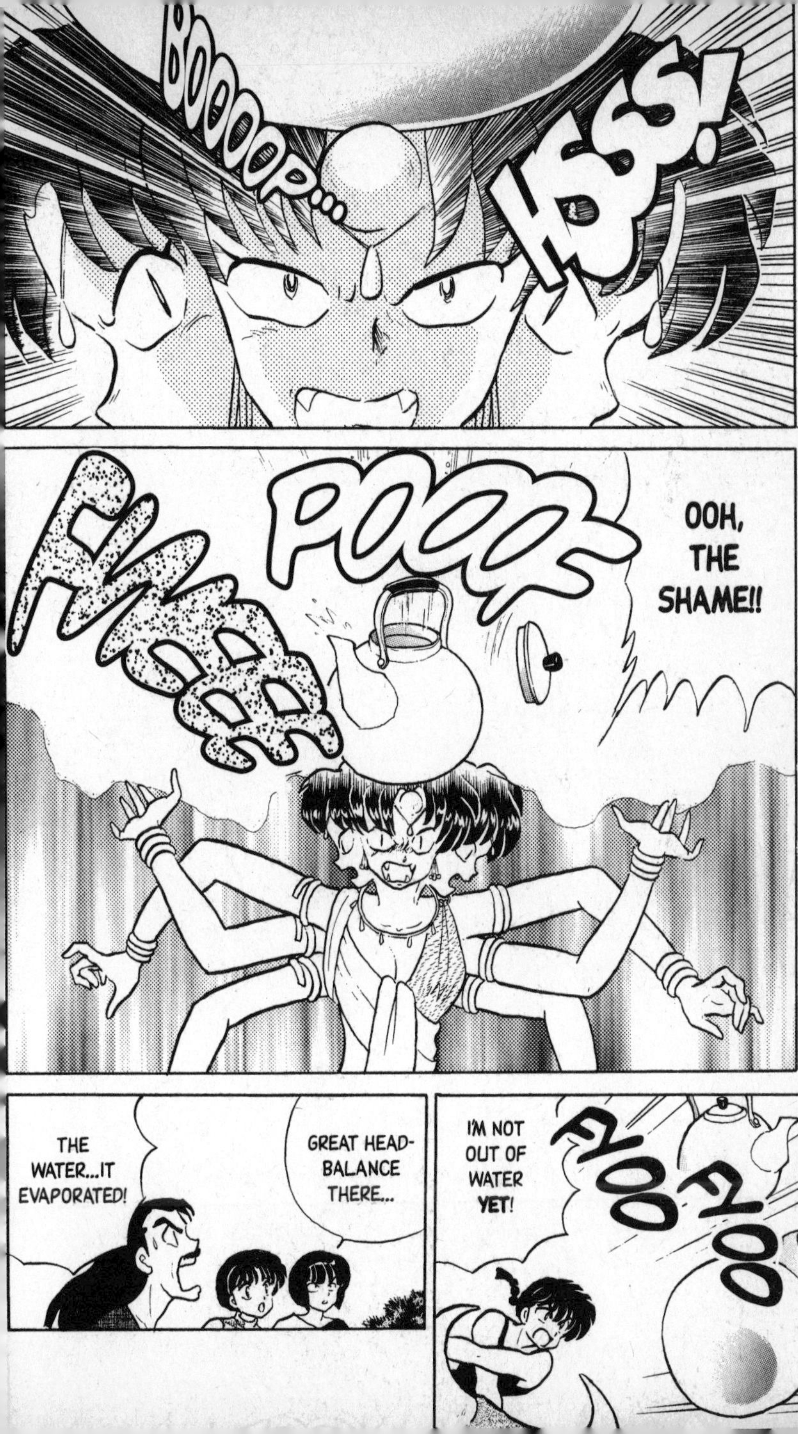
BOOOOOP...
HISS!
FWEEE
POOF
OOH, THE SHAME!!
THE WATER...IT EVAPORATED!
GREAT HEAD-BALANCE THERE...
I'M NOT OUT OF WATER YET!
FYOO FYOO

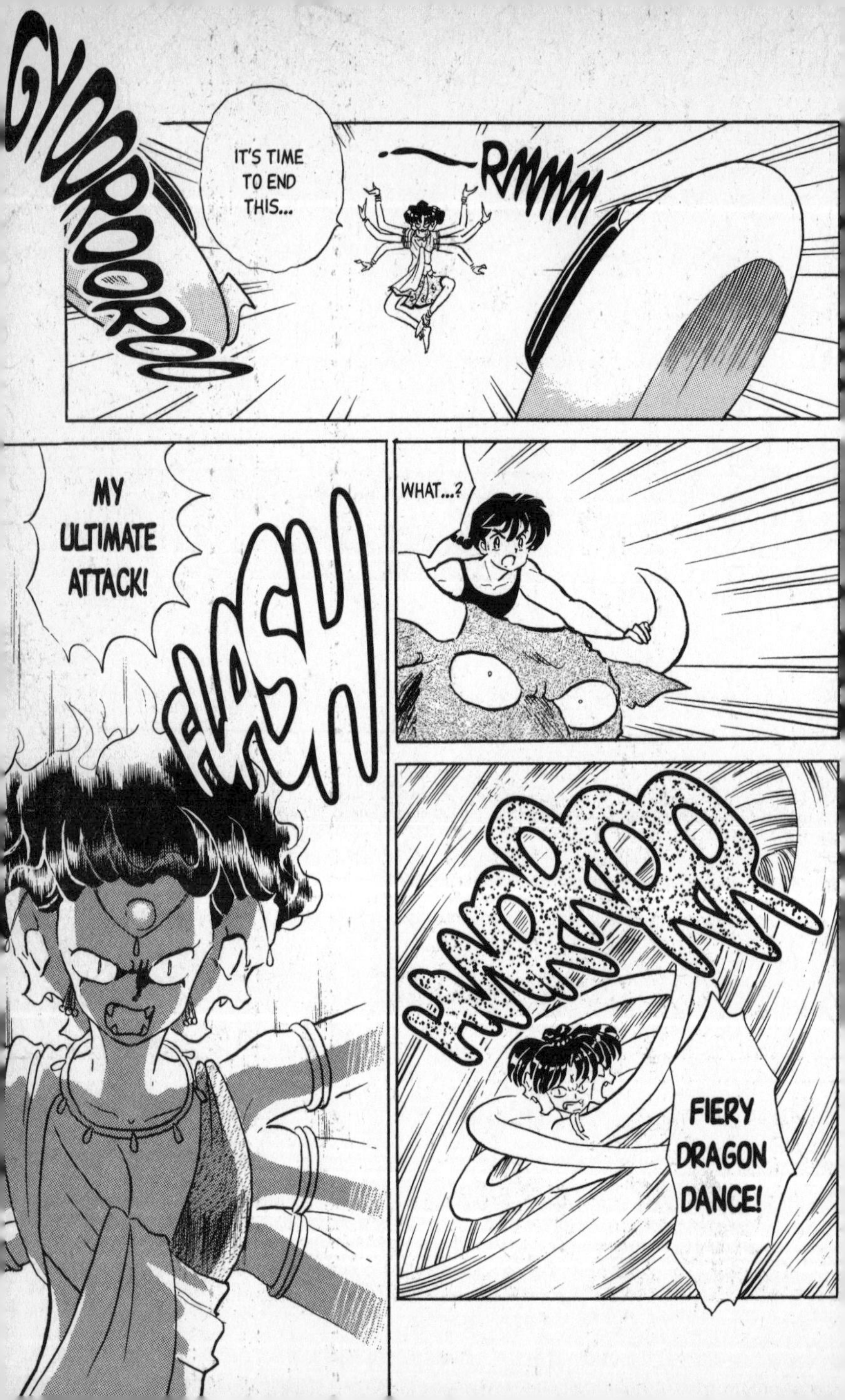
IT'S TIME TO END THIS...
MY ULTIMATE ATTACK!
FLASH
WHAT...?
FIERY DRAGON DANCE!

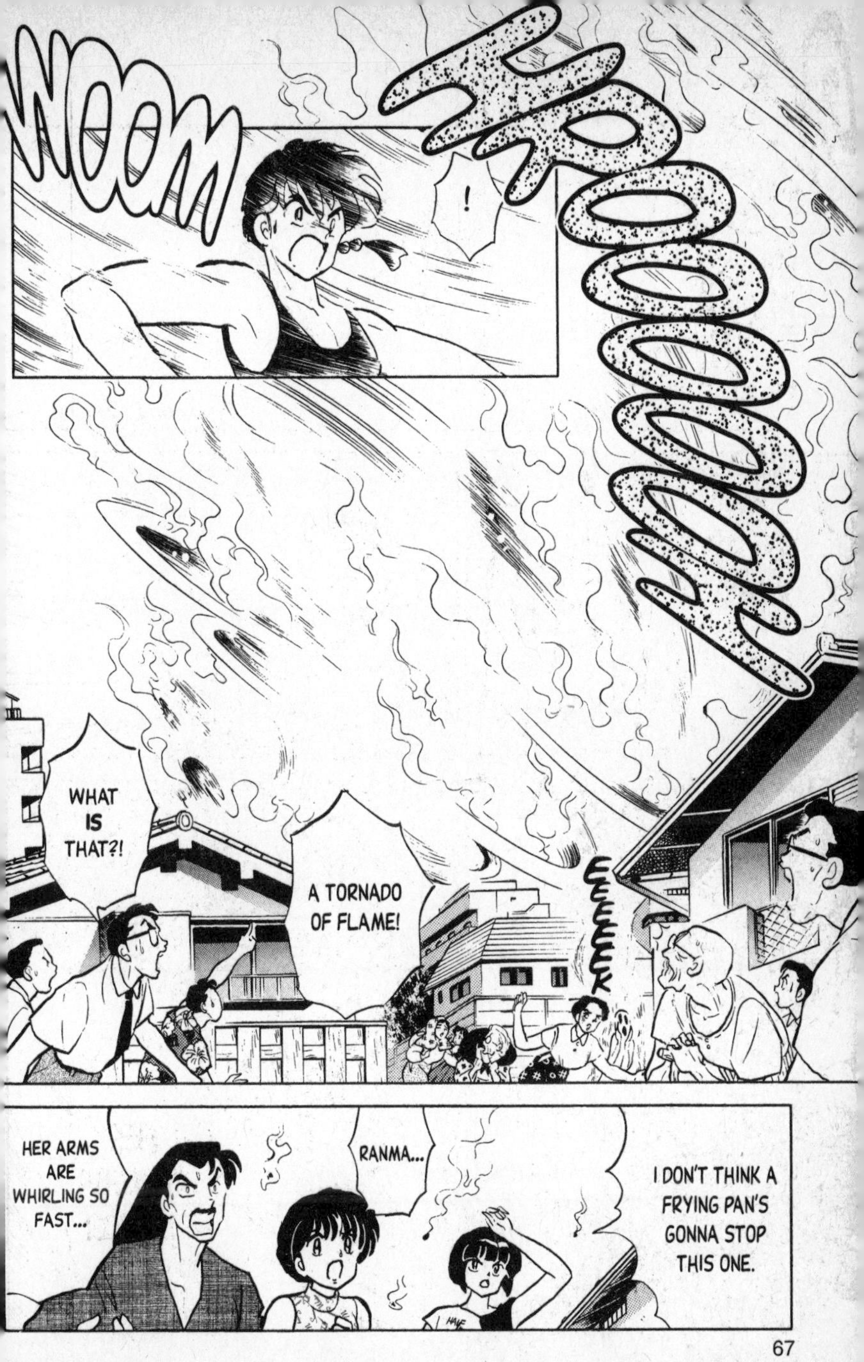
WOOM
!
HROOOOMH
WHAT IS THAT?!
A TORNADO OF FLAME!
EEEEEEK
HER ARMS ARE WHIRLING SO FAST...
RANMA...
I DON'T THINK A FRYING PAN'S GONNA STOP THIS ONE.

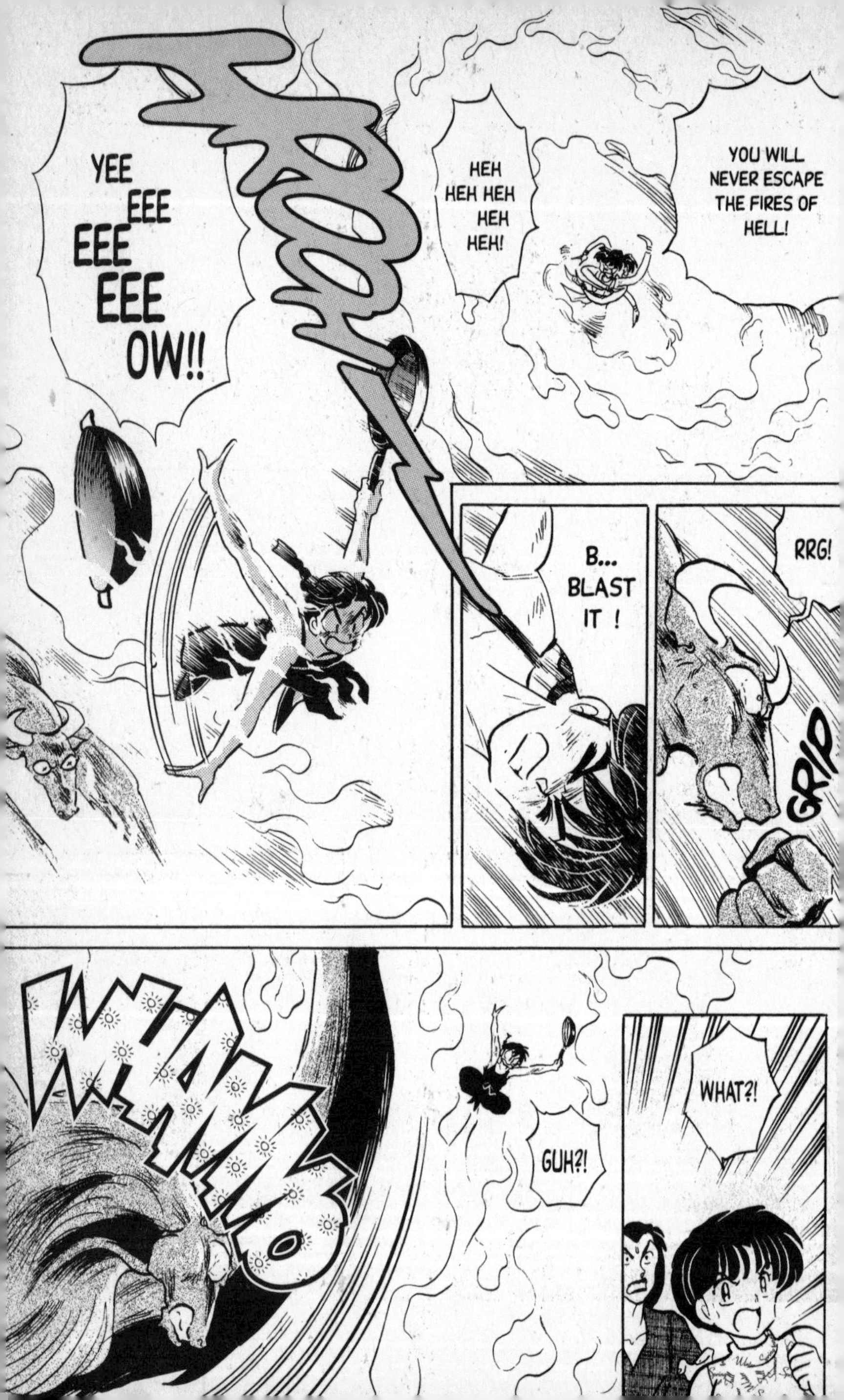
YEE EEE EEE EEE OW!!
HEH HEH HEH HEH HEH!
YOU WILL NEVER ESCAPE THE FIRES OF HELL!
B... BLAST IT !
RRG!
GRIP
GUH?!
WHAT?!

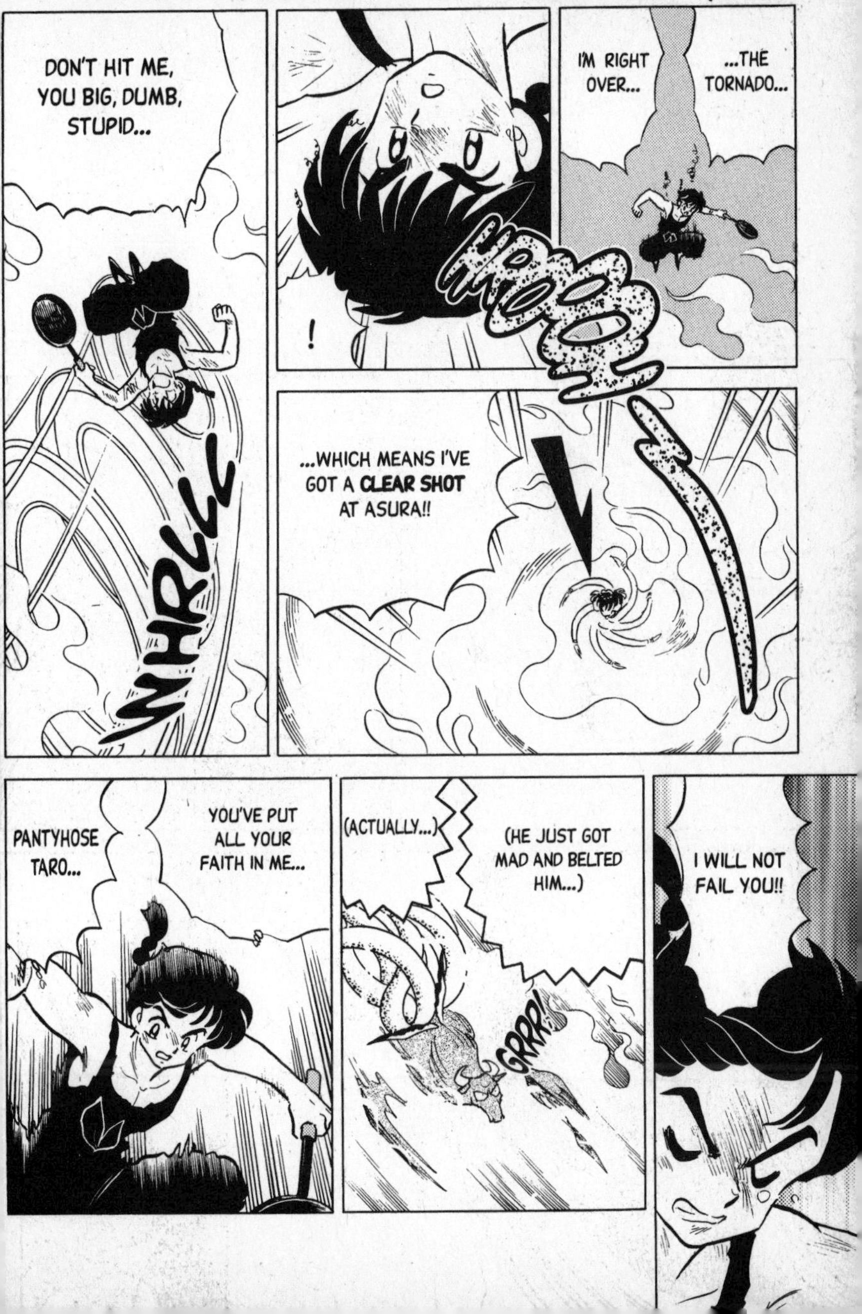
DON'T HIT ME, YOU BIG, DUMB, STUPID...
WHRLLL
!
I'M RIGHT OVER...
...THE TORNADO...
...WHICH MEANS I'VE GOT A **CLEAR SHOT** AT ASURA!!
PANTYHOSE TARO...
YOU'VE PUT ALL YOUR FAITH IN ME...
(ACTUALLY...)
(HE JUST GOT MAD AND BELTED HIM...)
GRRR!
I WILL NOT FAIL YOU!!

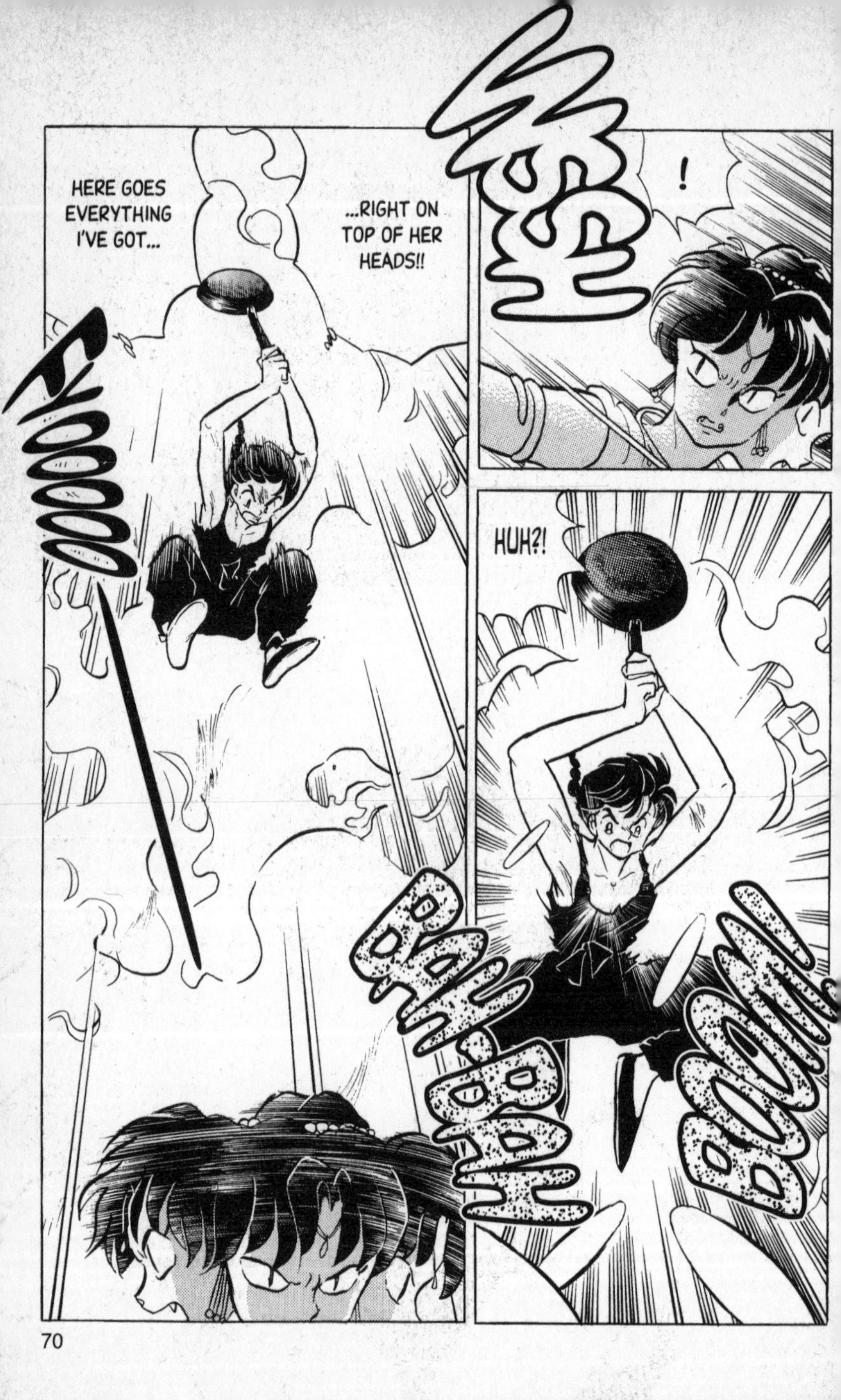
HERE GOES EVERYTHING I'VE GOT...
...RIGHT ON TOP OF HER HEADS!!
FYOOOOO
!
HUH?!
BAH-BAH
BOOM!

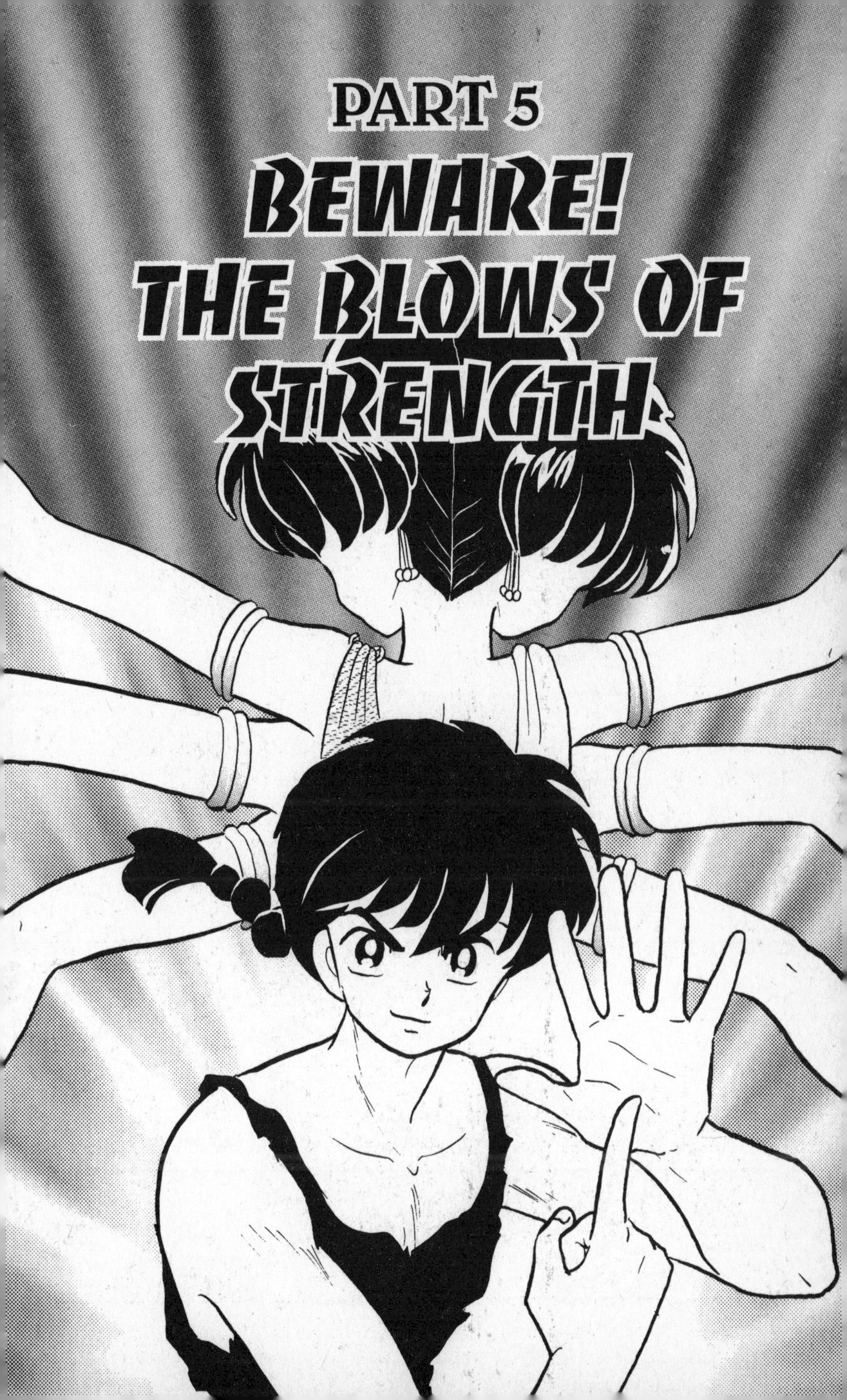
PART 5
BEWARE! THE BLOWS OF STRENGTH

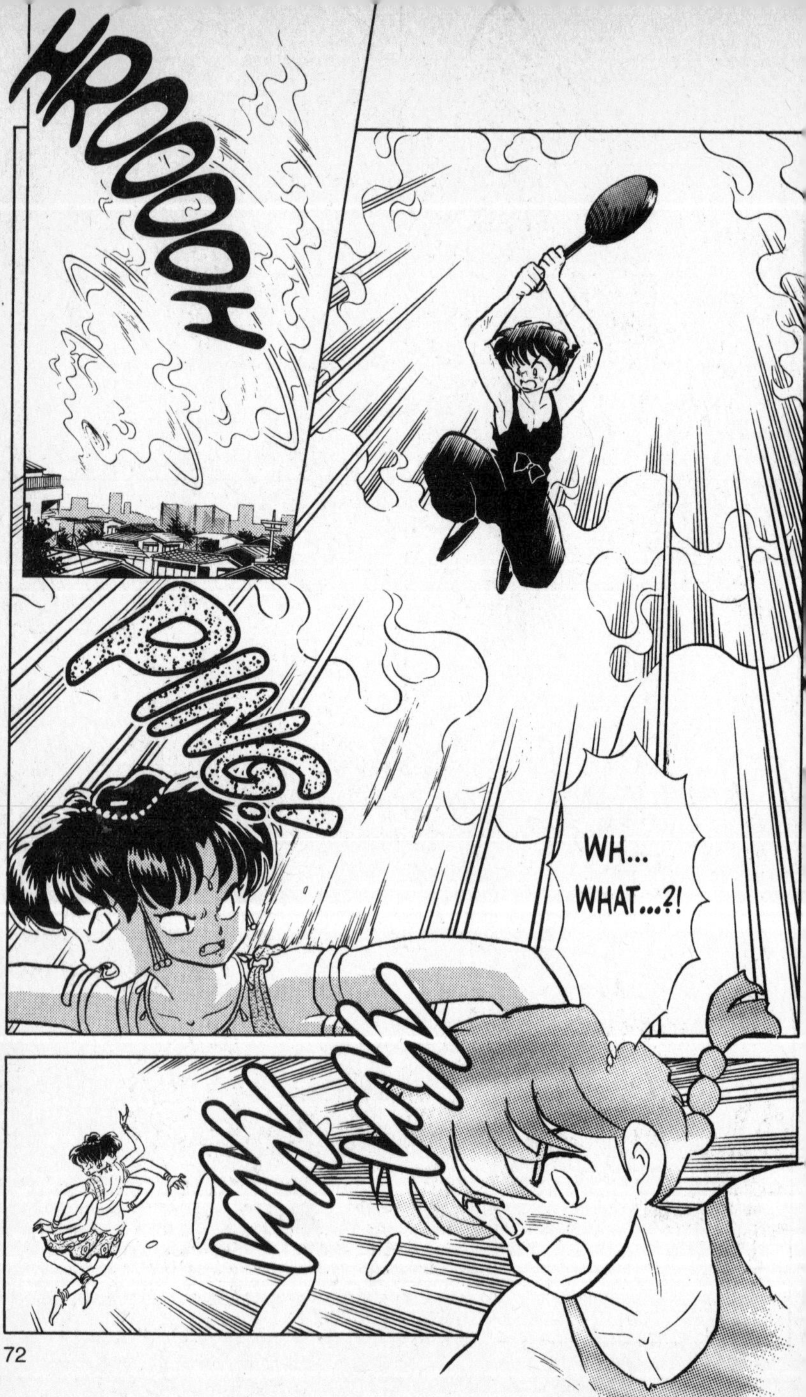
HROOOOH
PING!
WH...
WHAT...?!

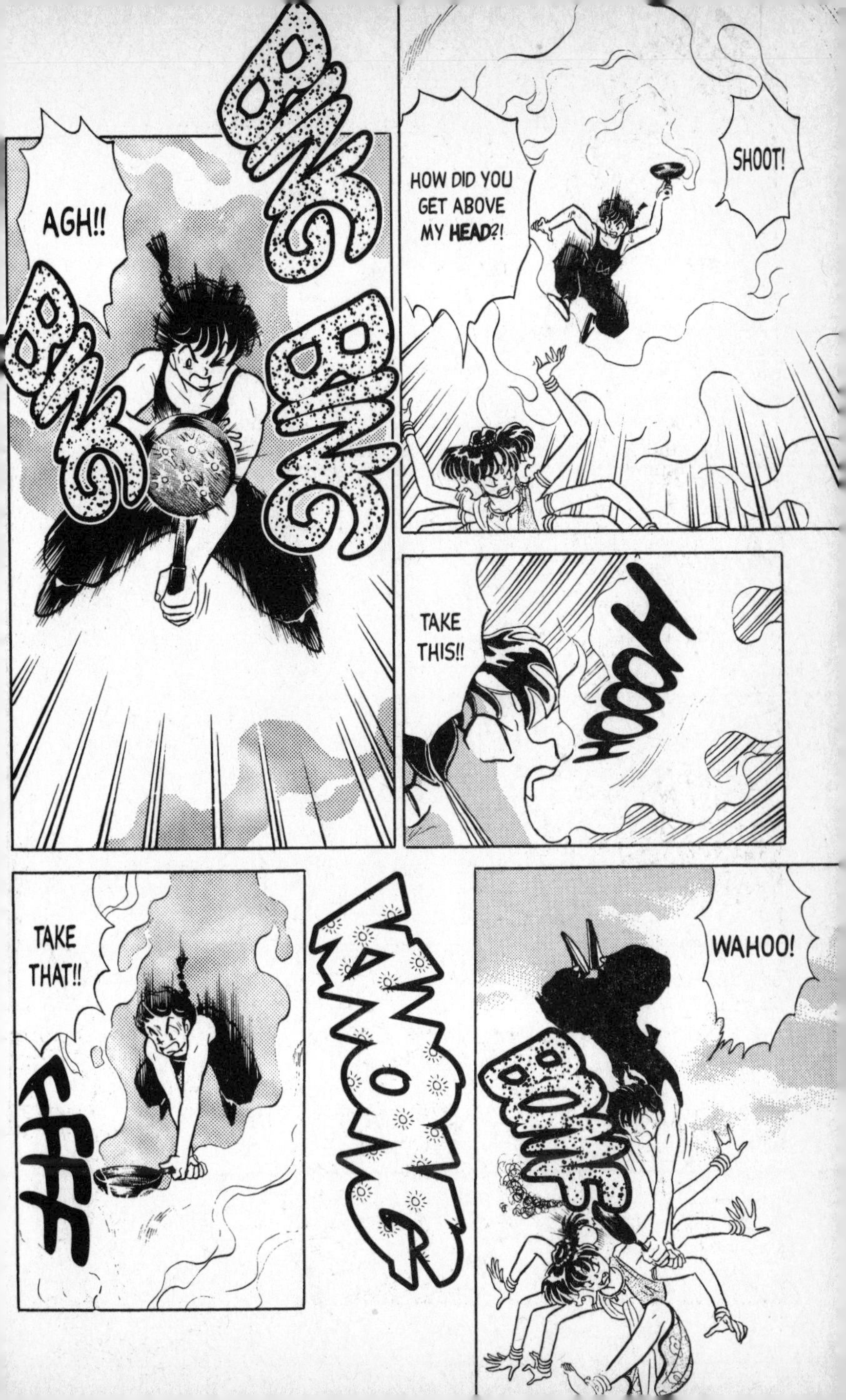
AGH!!
BING BING
BING
HOW DID YOU GET ABOVE MY HEAD?!
SHOOT!
TAKE THIS!!
TAKE THAT!!
KWONG
WAHOO!
BOING

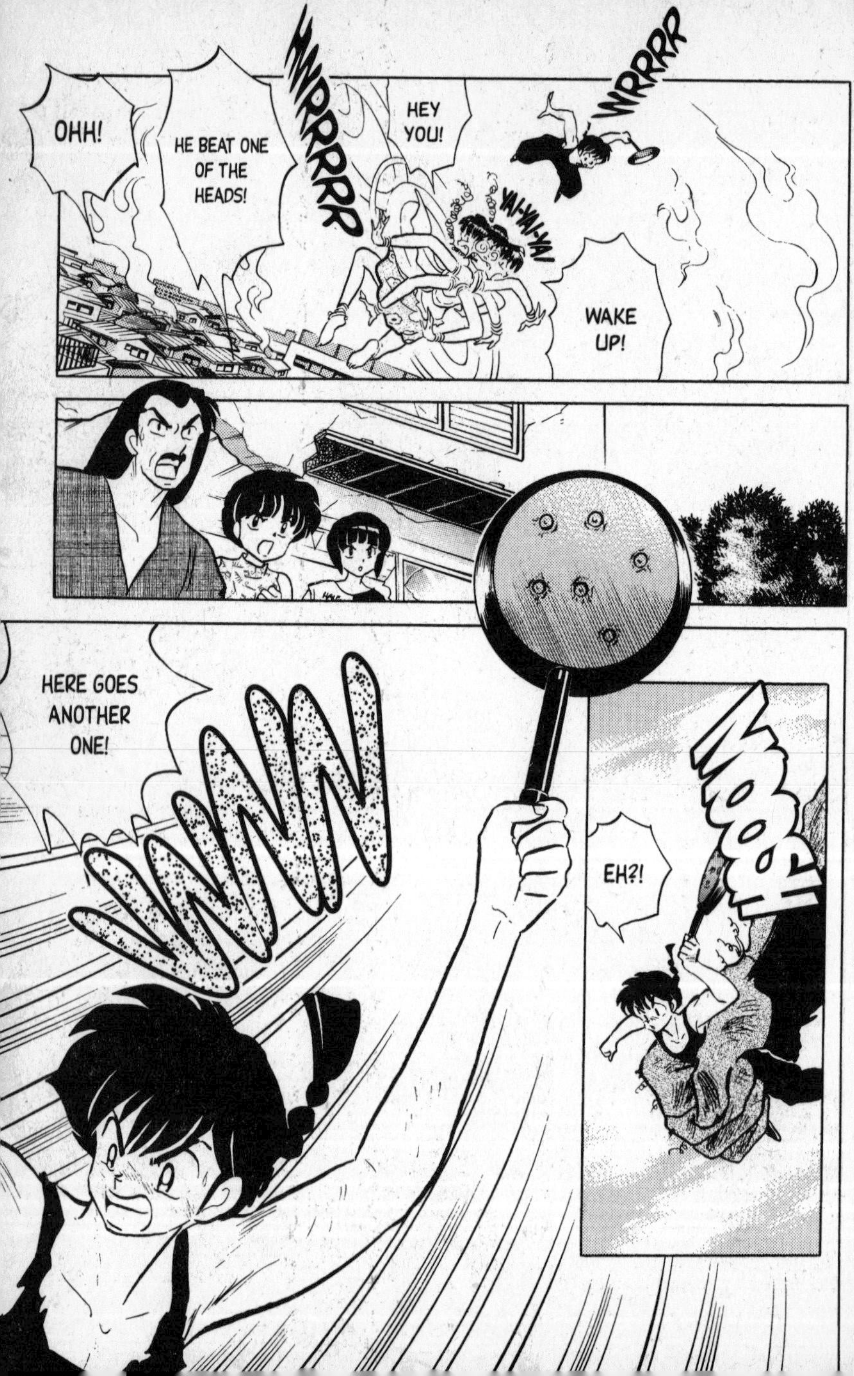
OHH!
HE BEAT ONE OF THE HEADS!
WRRRRRR
HEY YOU!
YAI-YAI-YAI!
WRRRRR
WAKE UP!
HERE GOES ANOTHER ONE!
WWWW
EH?!
WHOOSH

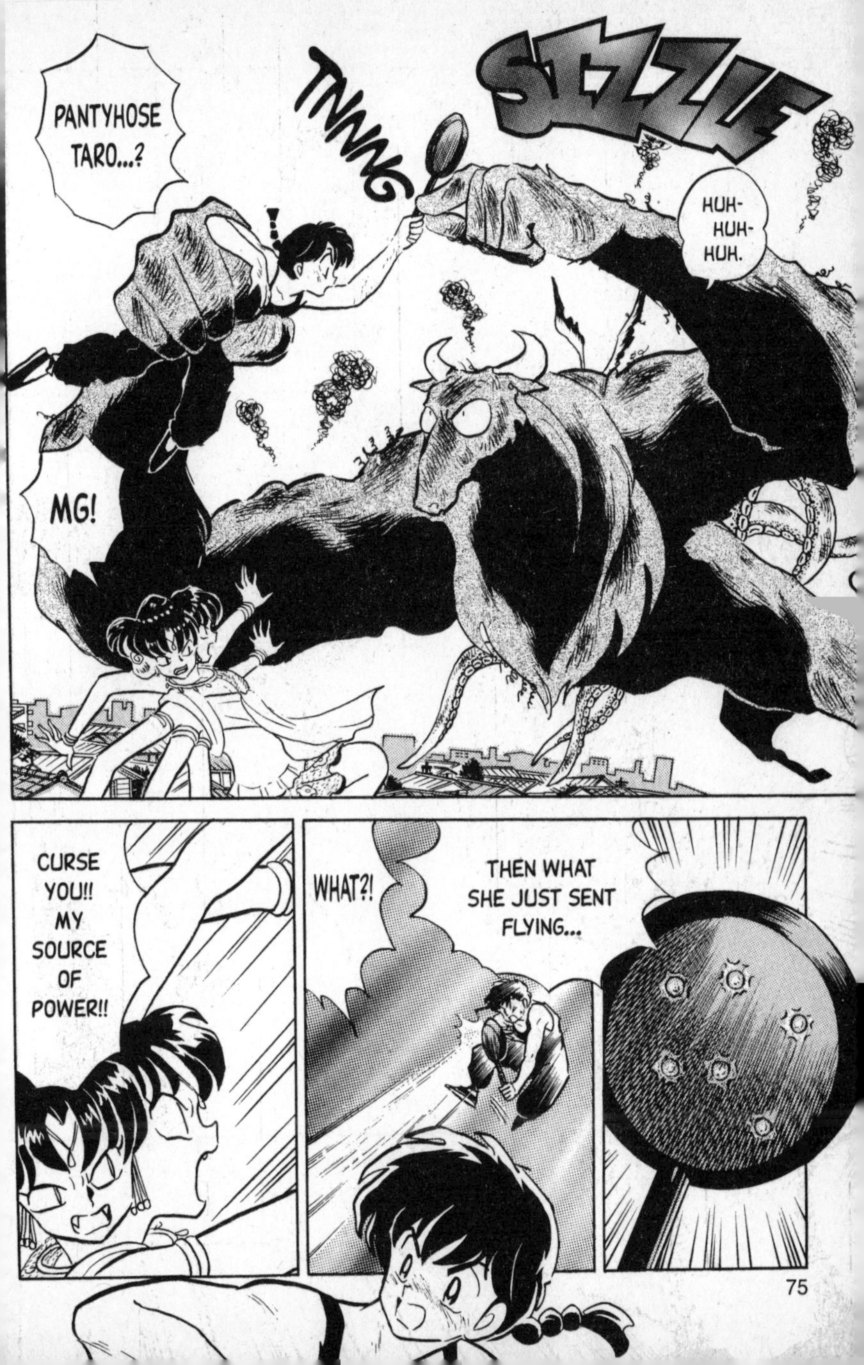
PANTYHOSE TARO...?
TWANG
SIZZLE
HUH-HUH-HUH.
MG!
CURSE YOU!! MY SOURCE OF POWER!!
WHAT?!
THEN WHAT SHE JUST SENT FLYING...

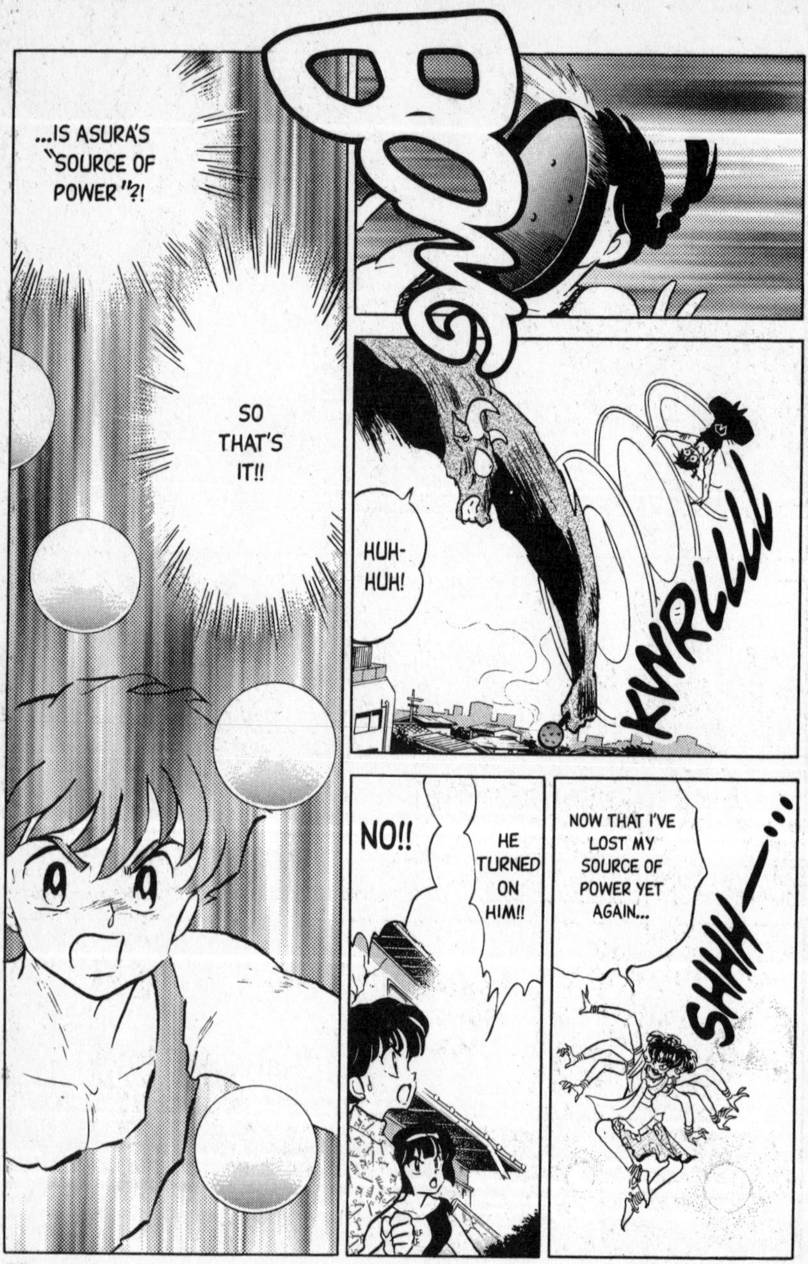
...IS ASURA'S "SOURCE OF POWER"?!
SO THAT'S IT!!
BONG
HUH-HUH!
KWRLLLL
NO!!
HE TURNED ON HIM!!
NOW THAT I'VE LOST MY SOURCE OF POWER YET AGAIN...
SHHH—...

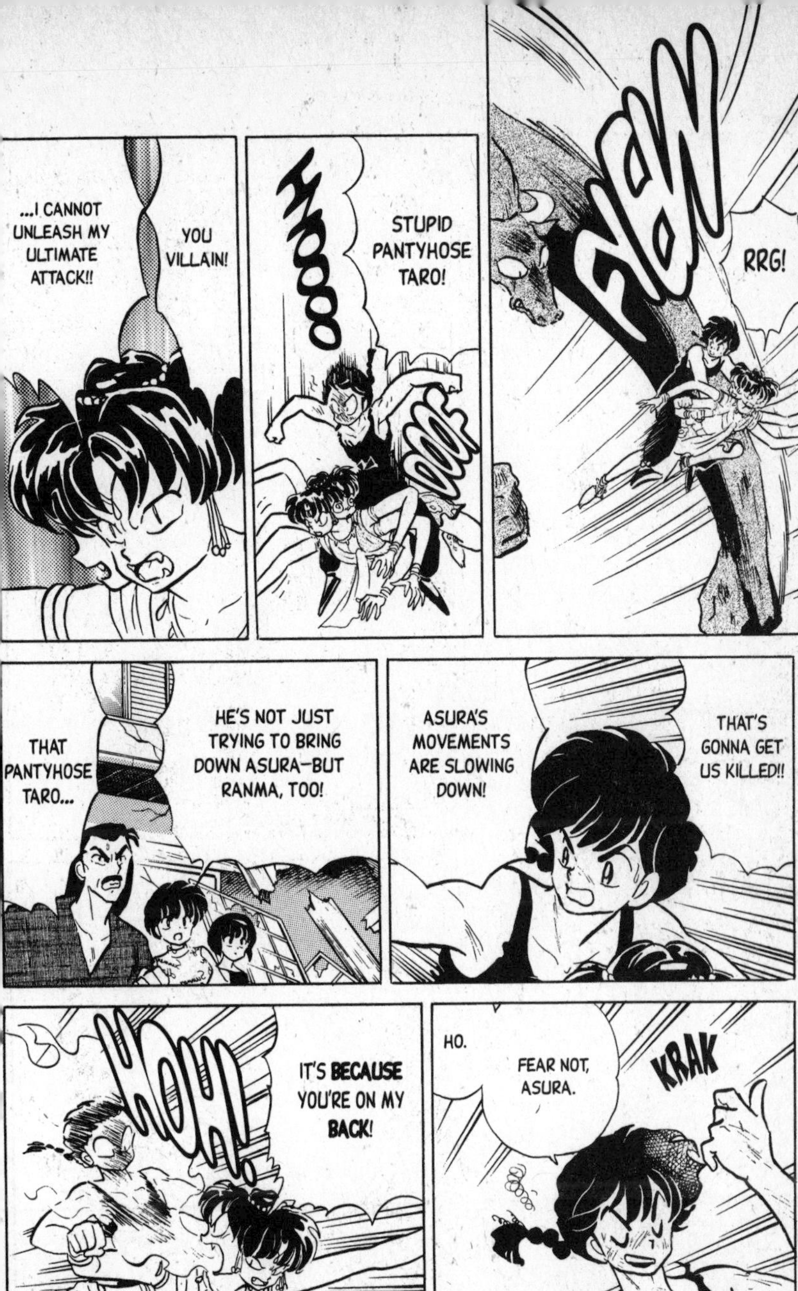
...I CANNOT UNLEASH MY ULTIMATE ATTACK!!
YOU VILLAIN!
STUPID PANTYHOSE TARO!
RRG!
THAT PANTYHOSE TARO...
HE'S NOT JUST TRYING TO BRING DOWN ASURA—BUT RANMA, TOO!
ASURA'S MOVEMENTS ARE SLOWING DOWN!
THAT'S GONNA GET US KILLED!!
IT'S **BECAUSE** YOU'RE ON MY **BACK!**
HO.
FEAR NOT, ASURA.
KRAK

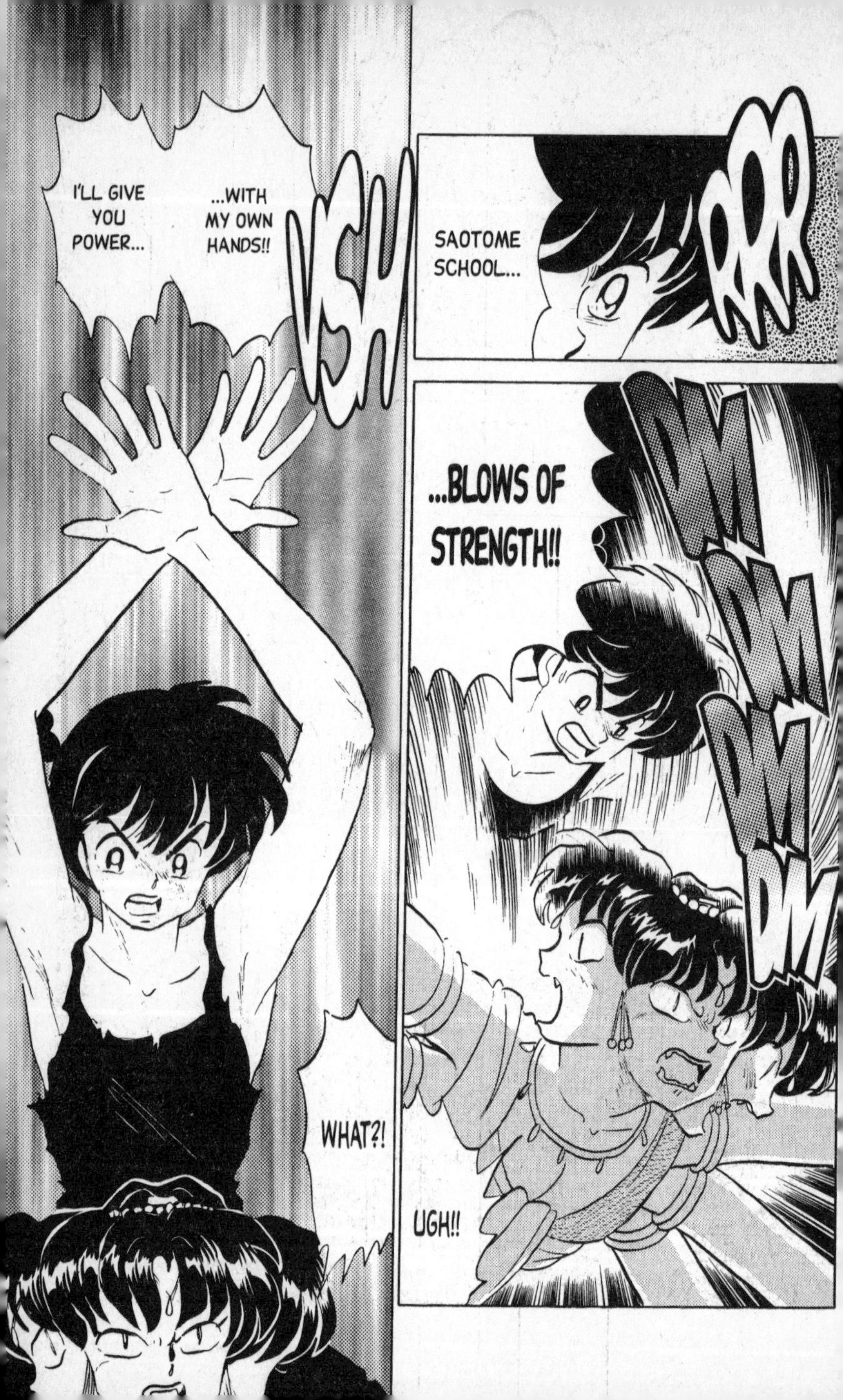
I'LL GIVE YOU POWER...
...WITH MY OWN HANDS!!
WHAT?!
SAOTOME SCHOOL...
...BLOWS OF STRENGTH!!
UGH!!

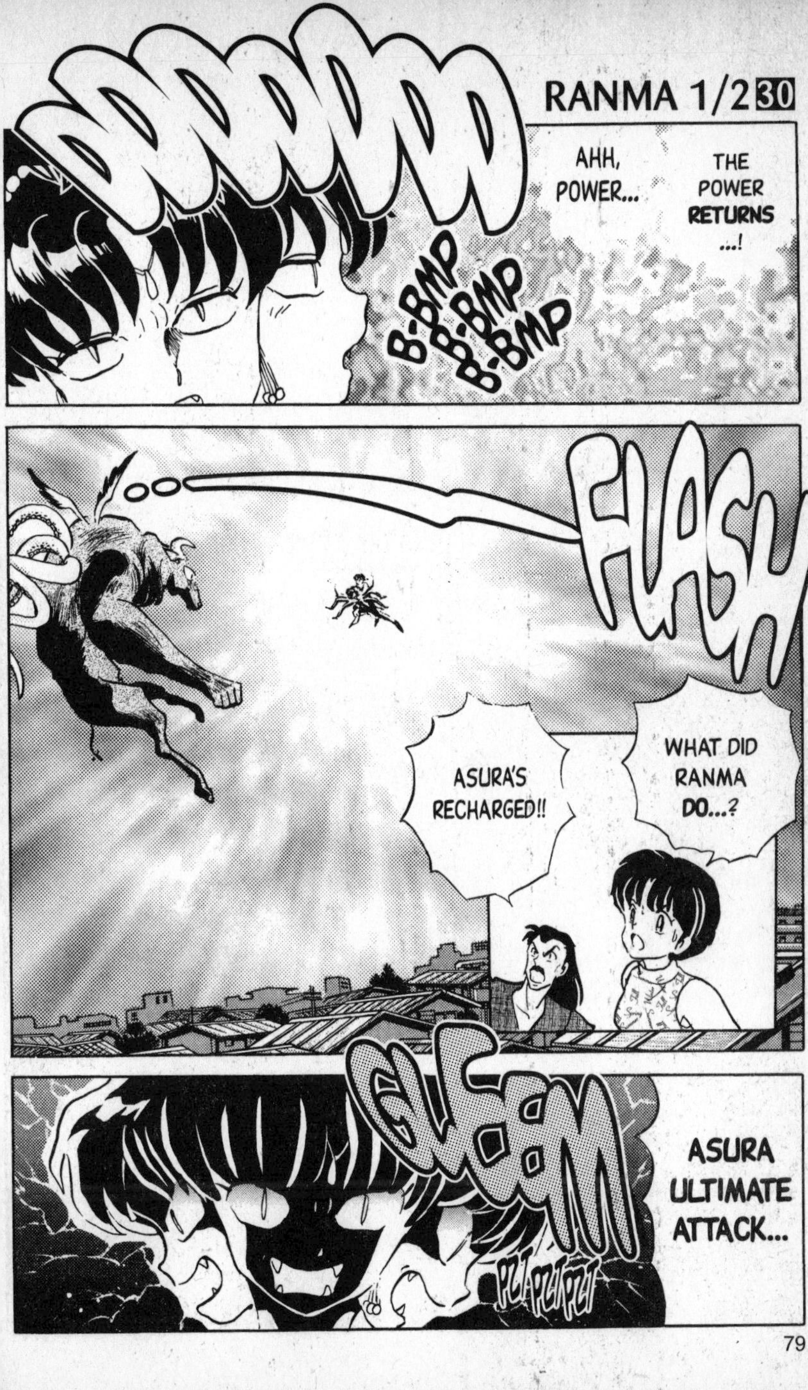
AHH, POWER...
THE POWER RETURNS ...!
B-BMP B-BMP B-BMP
FLASH
ASURA'S RECHARGED!!
WHAT DID RANMA DO...?
ASURA ULTIMATE ATTACK...

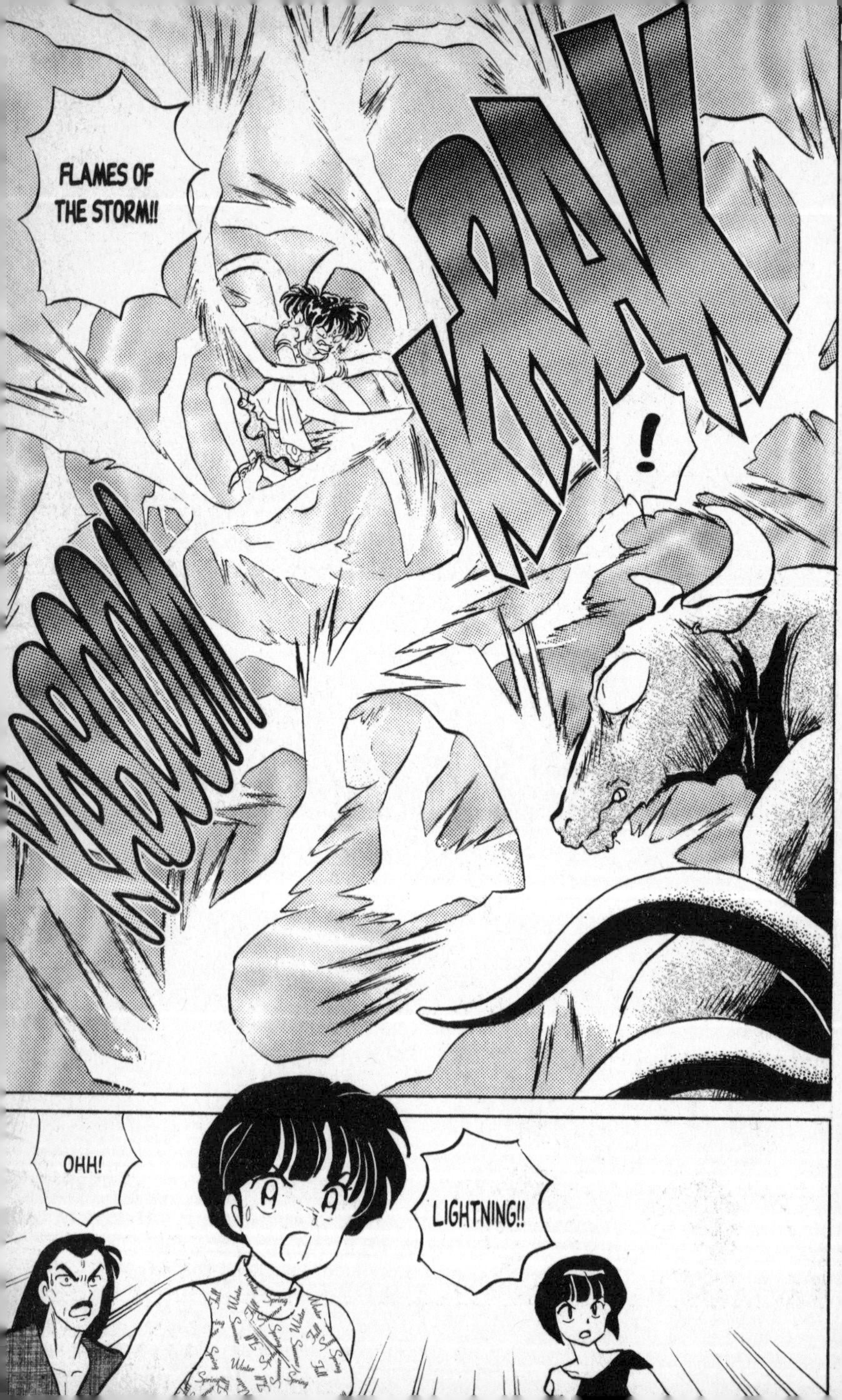
FLAMES OF THE STORM!!
!
OHH!
LIGHTNING!!

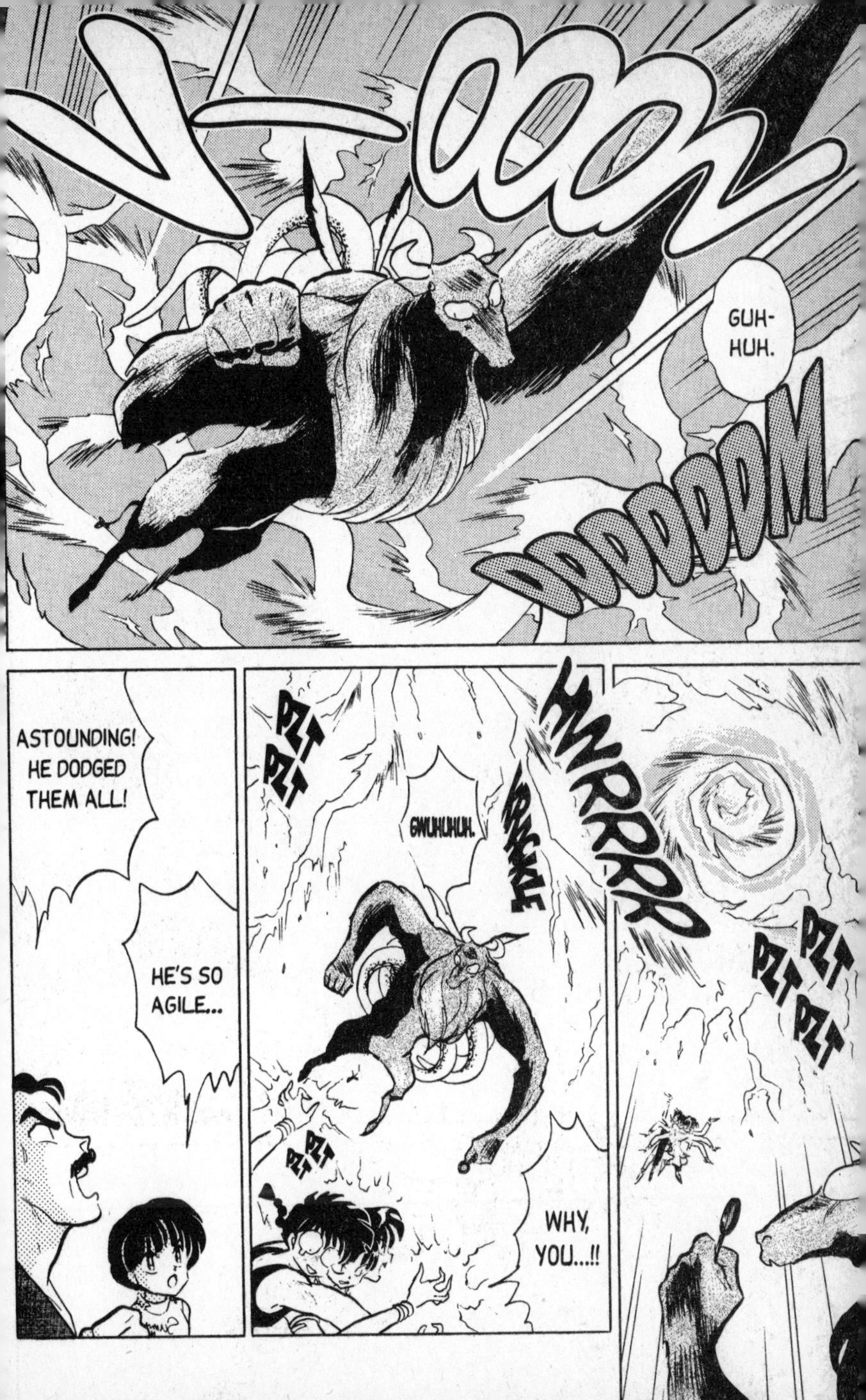
VOOON
GUH-HUH.
DDDDDDDM
ASTOUNDING! HE DODGED THEM ALL!
HE'S SO AGILE...
PZT PZT
GWUHUHUH.
HWRRRR
PZT PZT PZT
WHY, YOU...!!
PZT PZT PZT PZT

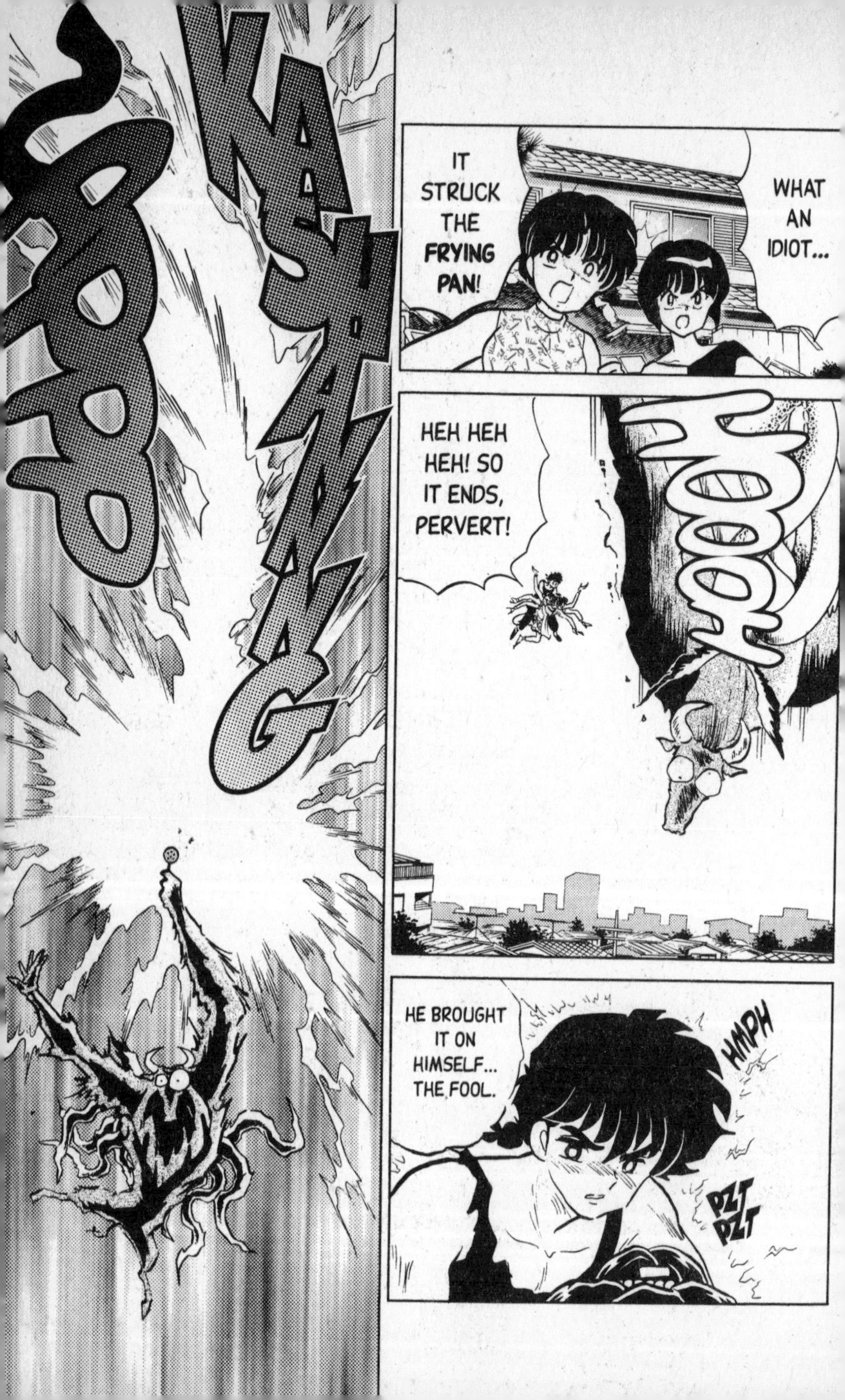
IT STRUCK THE FRYING PAN!
WHAT AN IDIOT...
HEH HEH HEH! SO IT ENDS, PERVERT!
HE BROUGHT IT ON HIMSELF... THE FOOL.
HMPH
PZT PZT

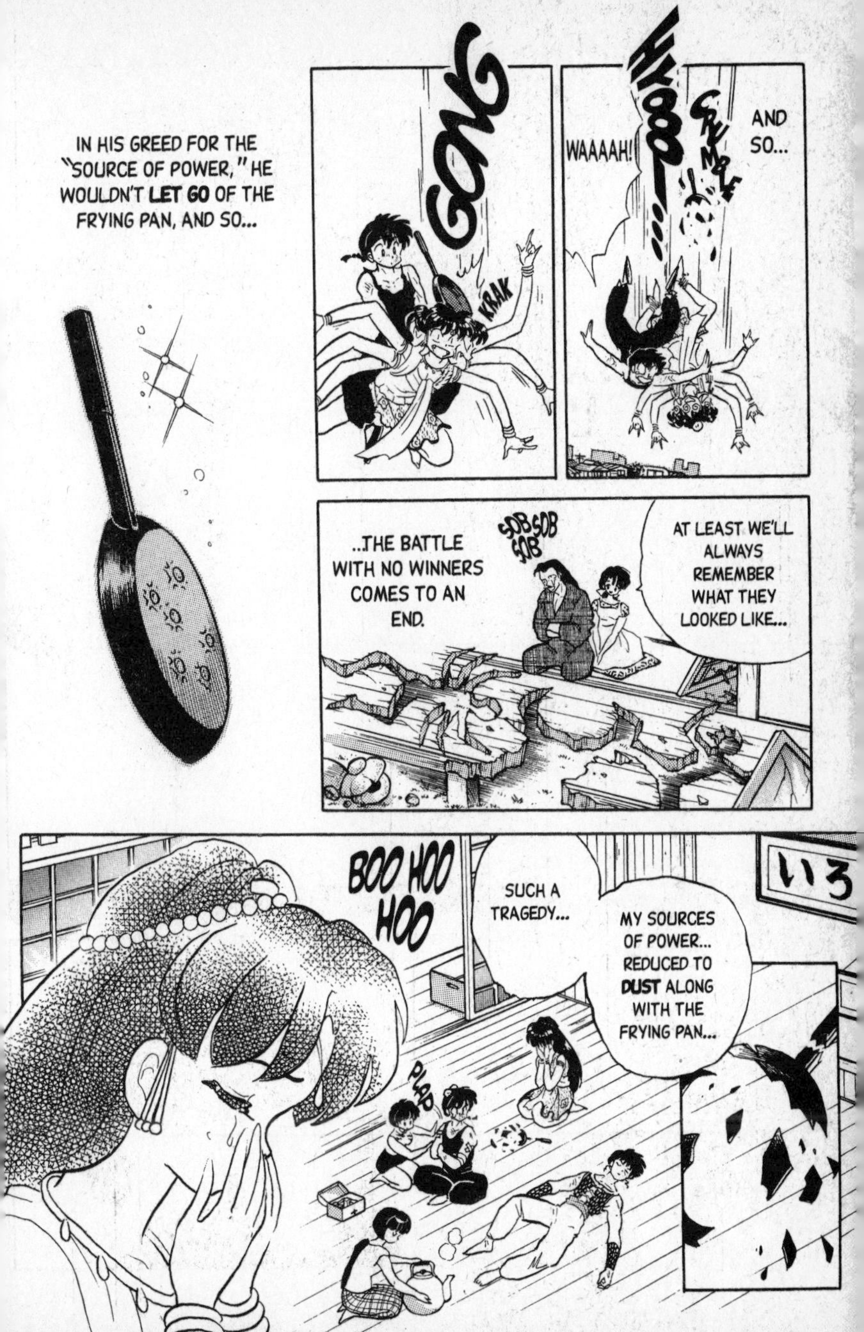
IN HIS GREED FOR THE "SOURCE OF POWER," HE WOULDN'T **LET GO** OF THE FRYING PAN, AND SO...
GONG
KRAK
HYOOO...!!
WAAAAH!
CRUMBLE
AND SO...
...THE BATTLE WITH NO WINNERS COMES TO AN END.
SOB SOB SOB
AT LEAST WE'LL ALWAYS REMEMBER WHAT THEY LOOKED LIKE...
BOO HOO HOO
SUCH A TRAGEDY...
MY SOURCES OF POWER... REDUCED TO **DUST** ALONG WITH THE FRYING PAN...
PLAP
いろ

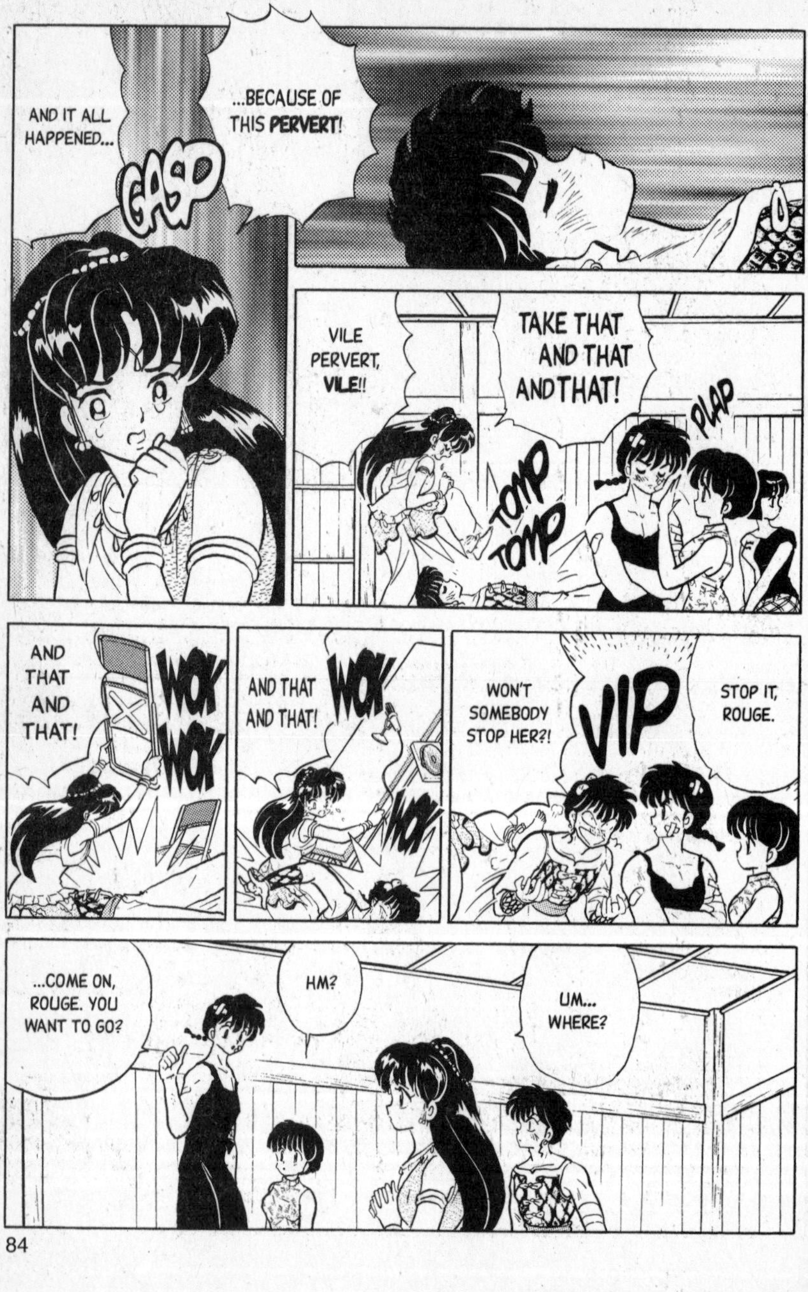
AND IT ALL HAPPENED...
...BECAUSE OF THIS PERVERT!
GASP
VILE PERVERT, VILE!!
TAKE THAT AND THAT AND THAT!
PLAP
TOMP
TOMP
AND THAT AND THAT!
WOK
WOK
AND THAT AND THAT!
WOK
WOK
WON'T SOMEBODY STOP HER?!
VIP
STOP IT, ROUGE.
...COME ON, ROUGE. YOU WANT TO GO?
HM?
UM... WHERE?

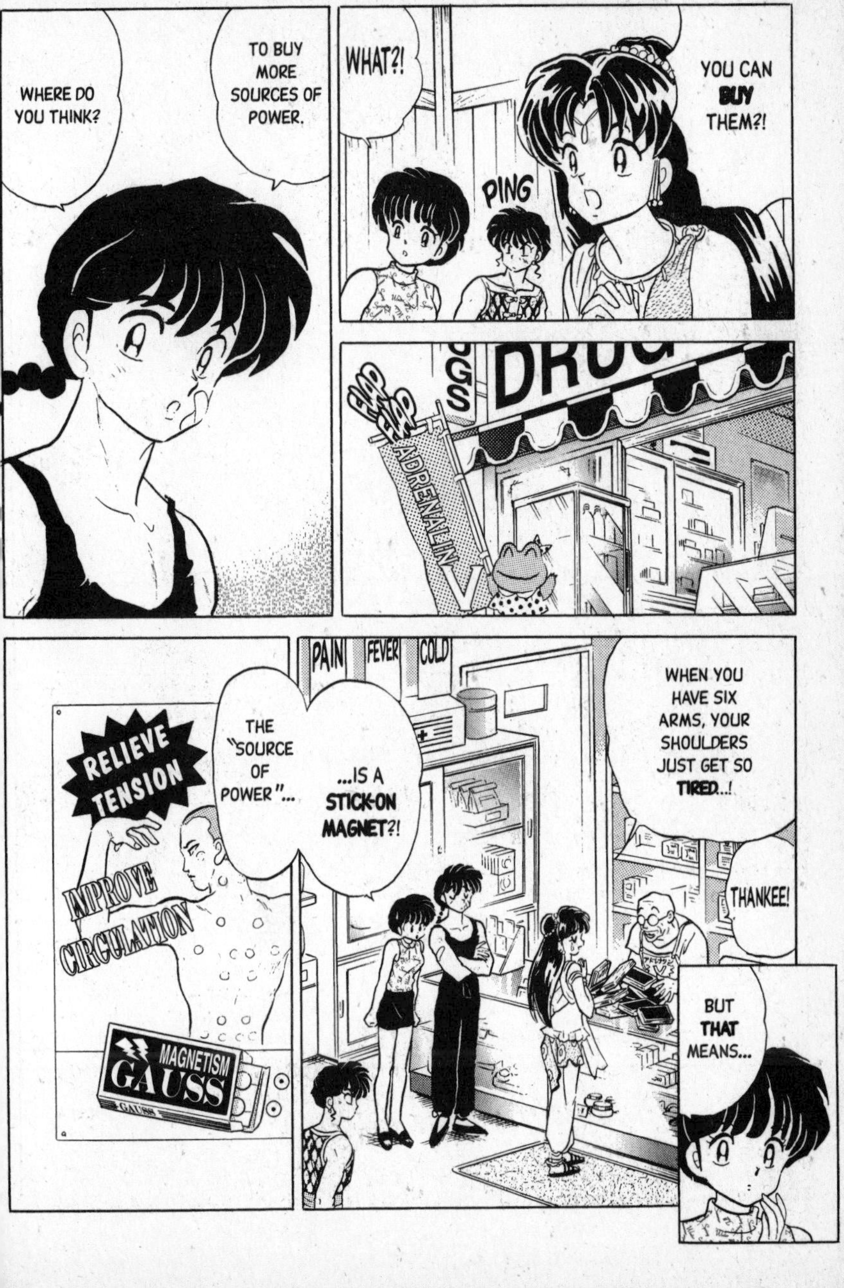
WHERE DO YOU THINK?
TO BUY MORE SOURCES OF POWER.
WHAT?!
PING
YOU CAN **BUY** THEM?!
GS
DRUG
ADRENALIN V
RELIEVE TENSION
IMPROVE CIRCULATION
MAGNETISM
GAUSS
THE "SOURCE OF POWER"...
...IS A **STICK-ON MAGNET**?!
PAIN
FEVER
COLD
WHEN YOU HAVE SIX ARMS, YOUR SHOULDERS JUST GET SO **TIRED**...!
THANKEE!
BUT **THAT** MEANS...

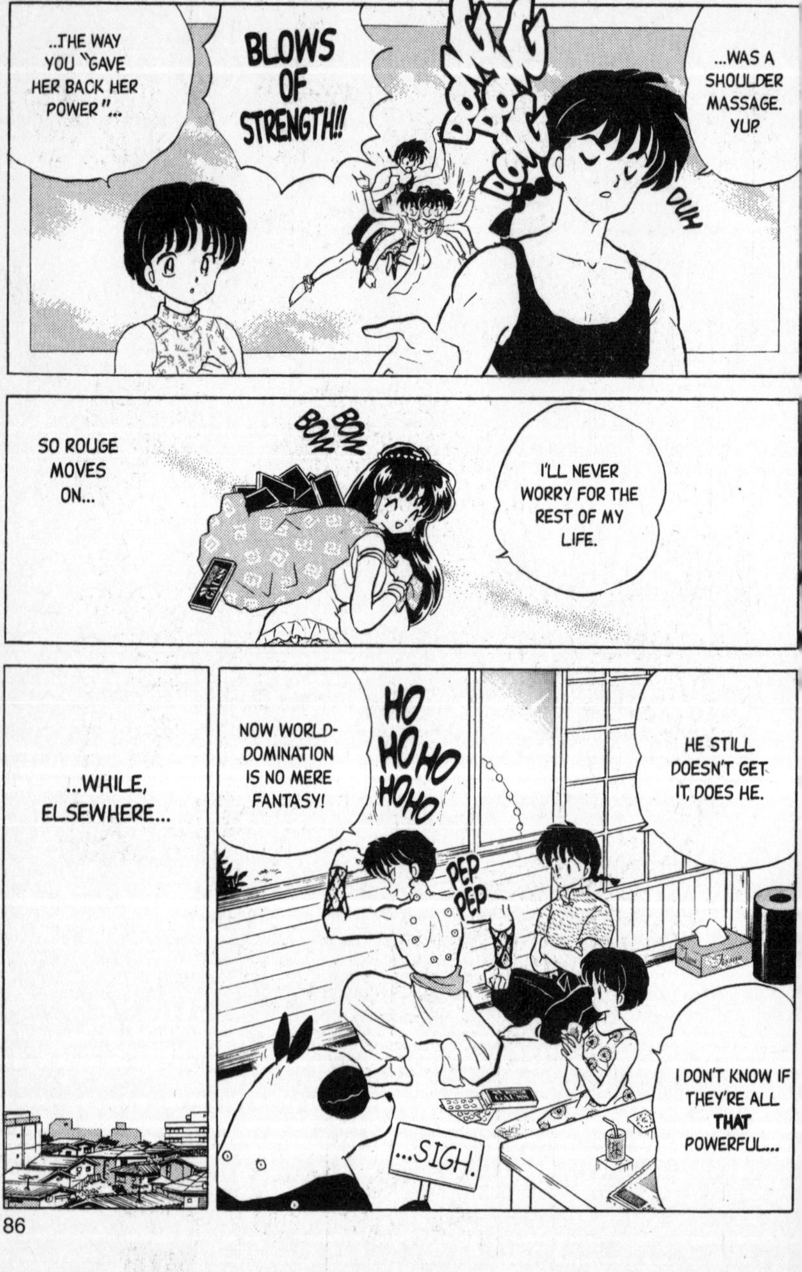

...THE WAY YOU "GAVE HER BACK HER POWER"...
BLOWS OF STRENGTH!!
...WAS A SHOULDER MASSAGE. YUP.
DUH
SO ROUGE MOVES ON...
BOW BOW
I'LL NEVER WORRY FOR THE REST OF MY LIFE.
...WHILE, ELSEWHERE...
NOW WORLD-DOMINATION IS NO MERE FANTASY!
HO HO HO HO HO HO HO
PEP PEP
HE STILL DOESN'T GET IT, DOES HE.
...SIGH.
I DON'T KNOW IF THEY'RE ALL **THAT** POWERFUL...

PART 6

THE WHITE LILY

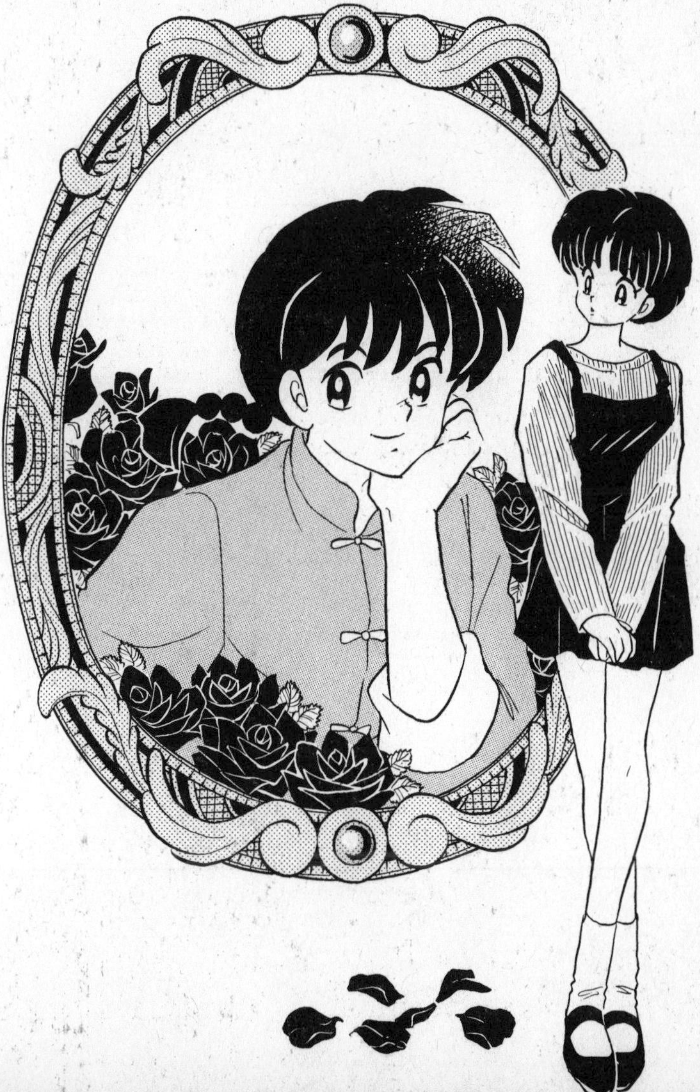

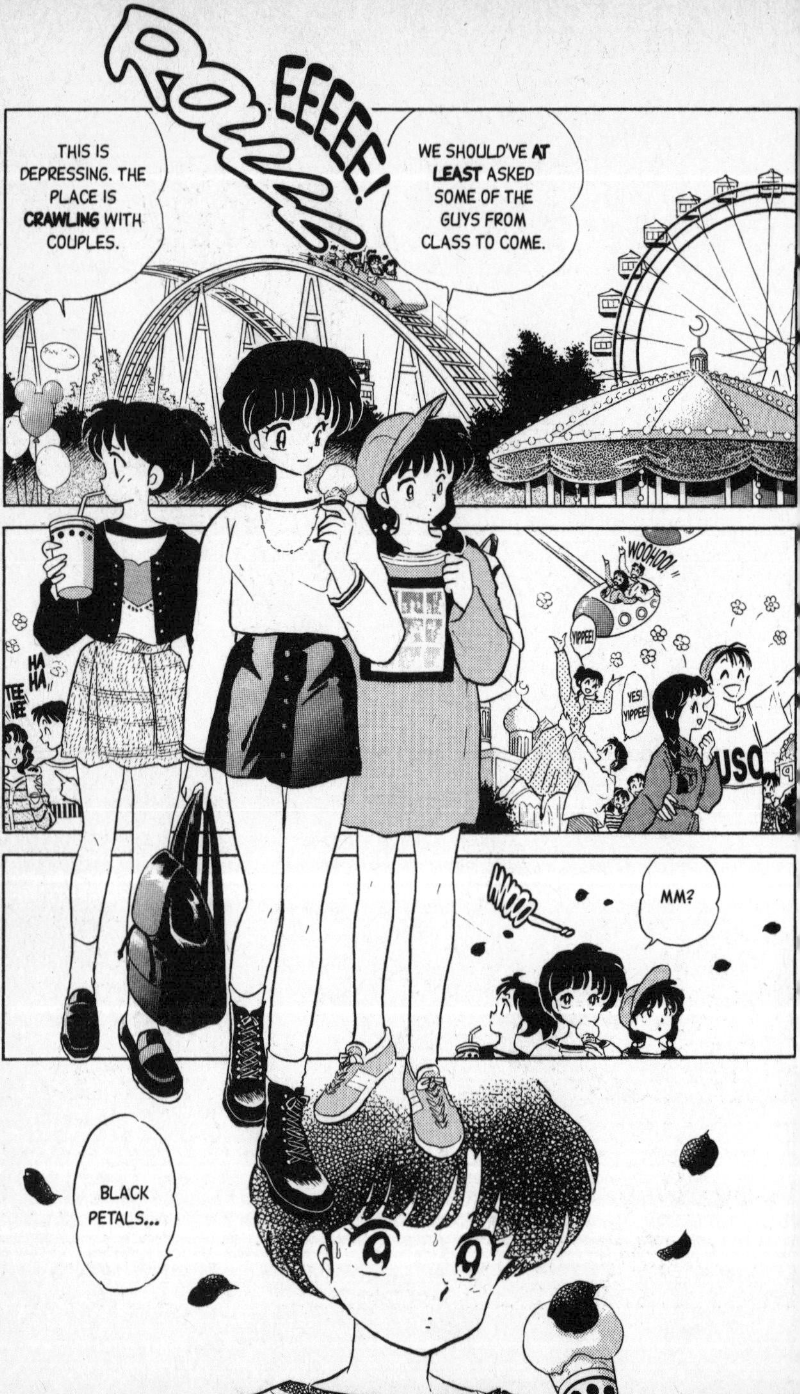
EEEEEE!
THIS IS DEPRESSING. THE PLACE IS **CRAWLING** WITH COUPLES.
WE SHOULD'VE **AT LEAST** ASKED SOME OF THE GUYS FROM CLASS TO COME.
TEE HEE
HA HA
WOOHOO!
YIPPEE!
YES! YIPPEE!
USO
MM?
BLACK PETALS...

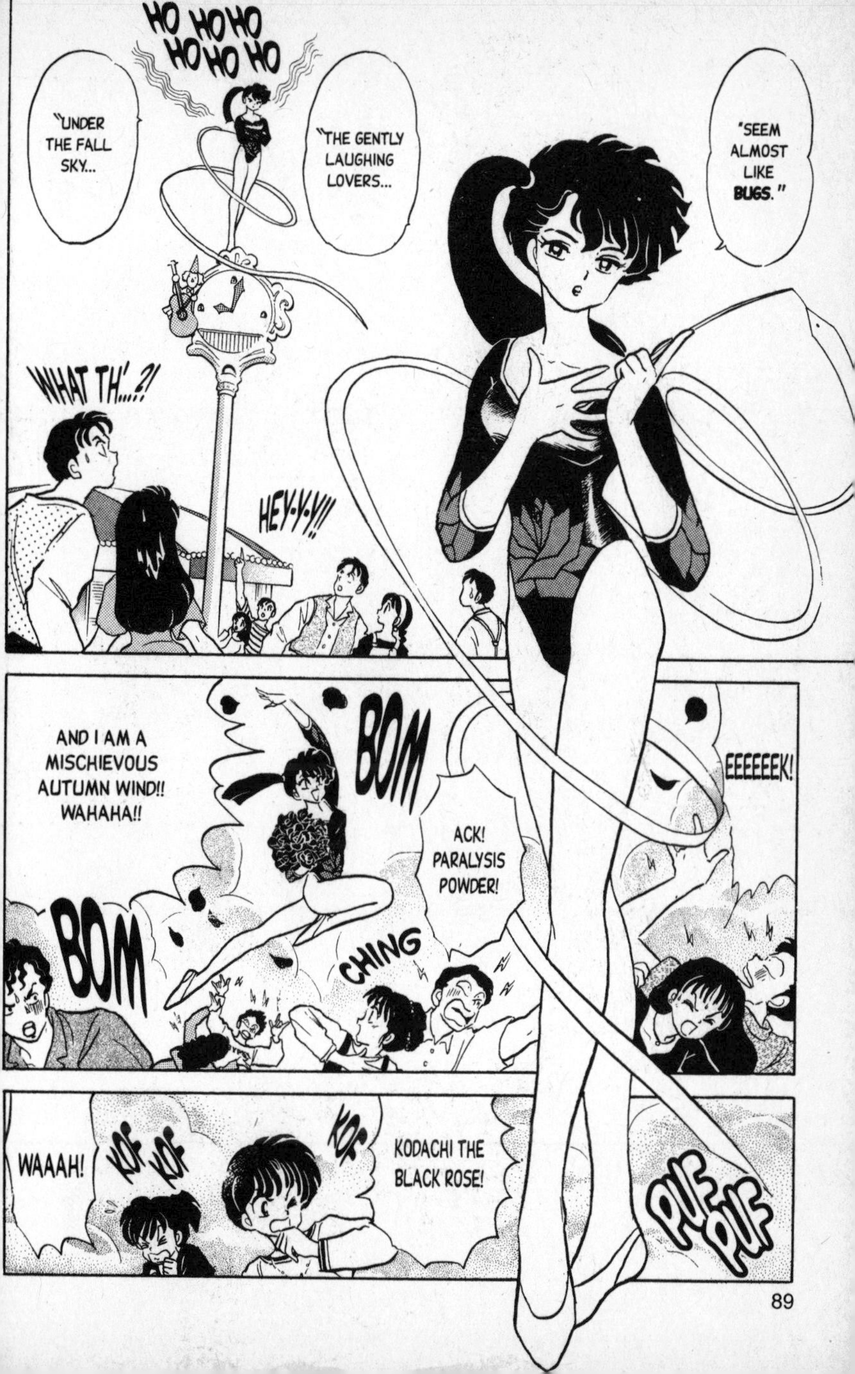

HO HO HO HO HO HO
"UNDER THE FALL SKY...
"THE GENTLY LAUGHING LOVERS...
"SEEM ALMOST LIKE BUGS."
WHAT TH'...?!
HEY-Y-Y!!
AND I AM A MISCHIEVOUS AUTUMN WIND!! WAHAHA!!
BOM
ACK! PARALYSIS POWDER!
EEEEEEK!
BOM
CHING
WAAAH!
KOF KOF
KOF
KODACHI THE BLACK ROSE!
PUF PUF

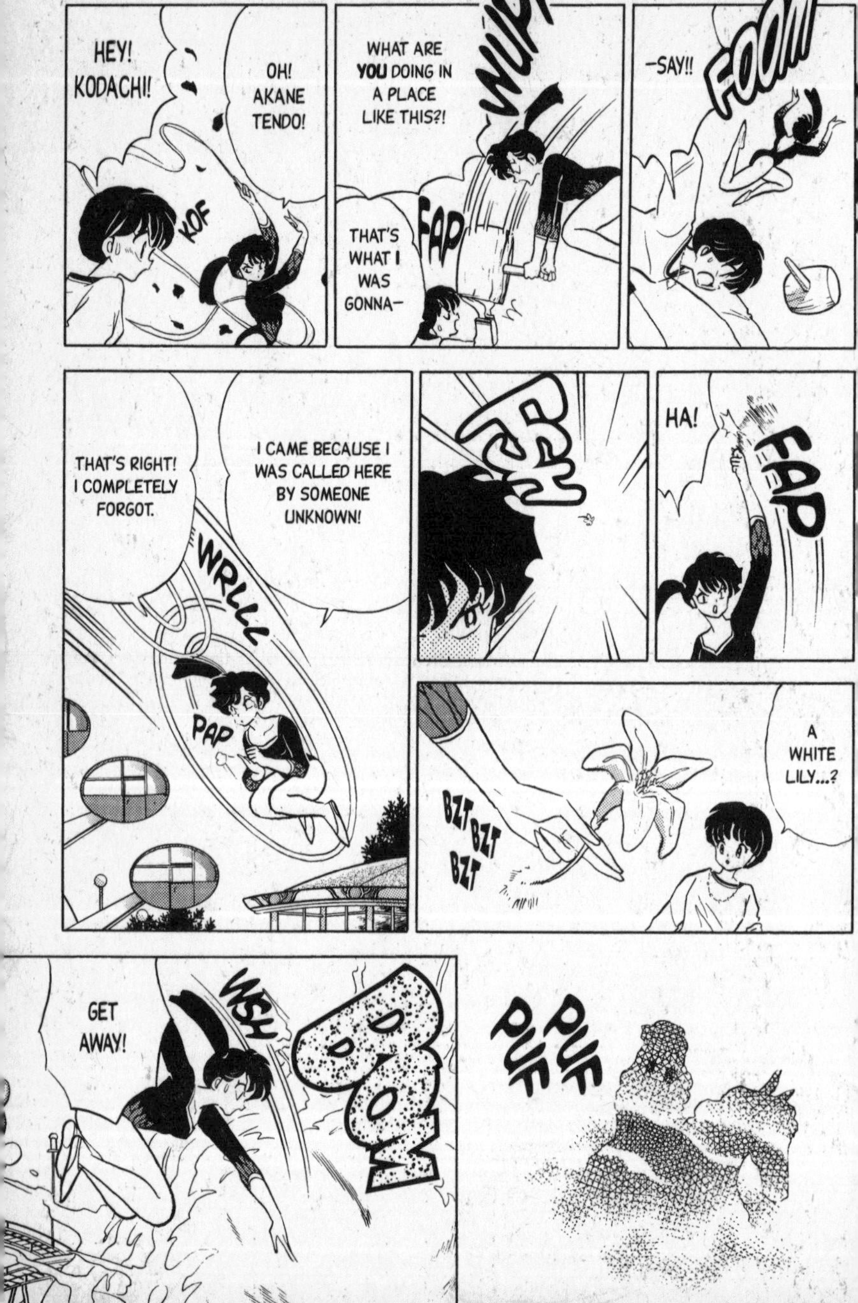

HEY! KODACHI!
KOF
OH! AKANE TENDO!
WHAT ARE YOU DOING IN A PLACE LIKE THIS?!
WUPP
FAP
THAT'S WHAT I WAS GONNA—
—SAY!!
FOOM
THAT'S RIGHT! I COMPLETELY FORGOT.
I CAME BECAUSE I WAS CALLED HERE BY SOMEONE UNKNOWN!
WRLLL
PAP
HA!
FAP
A WHITE LILY...?
BZT BZT BZT
GET AWAY!
WSH
BOOM
PUF PUF PUF PUF

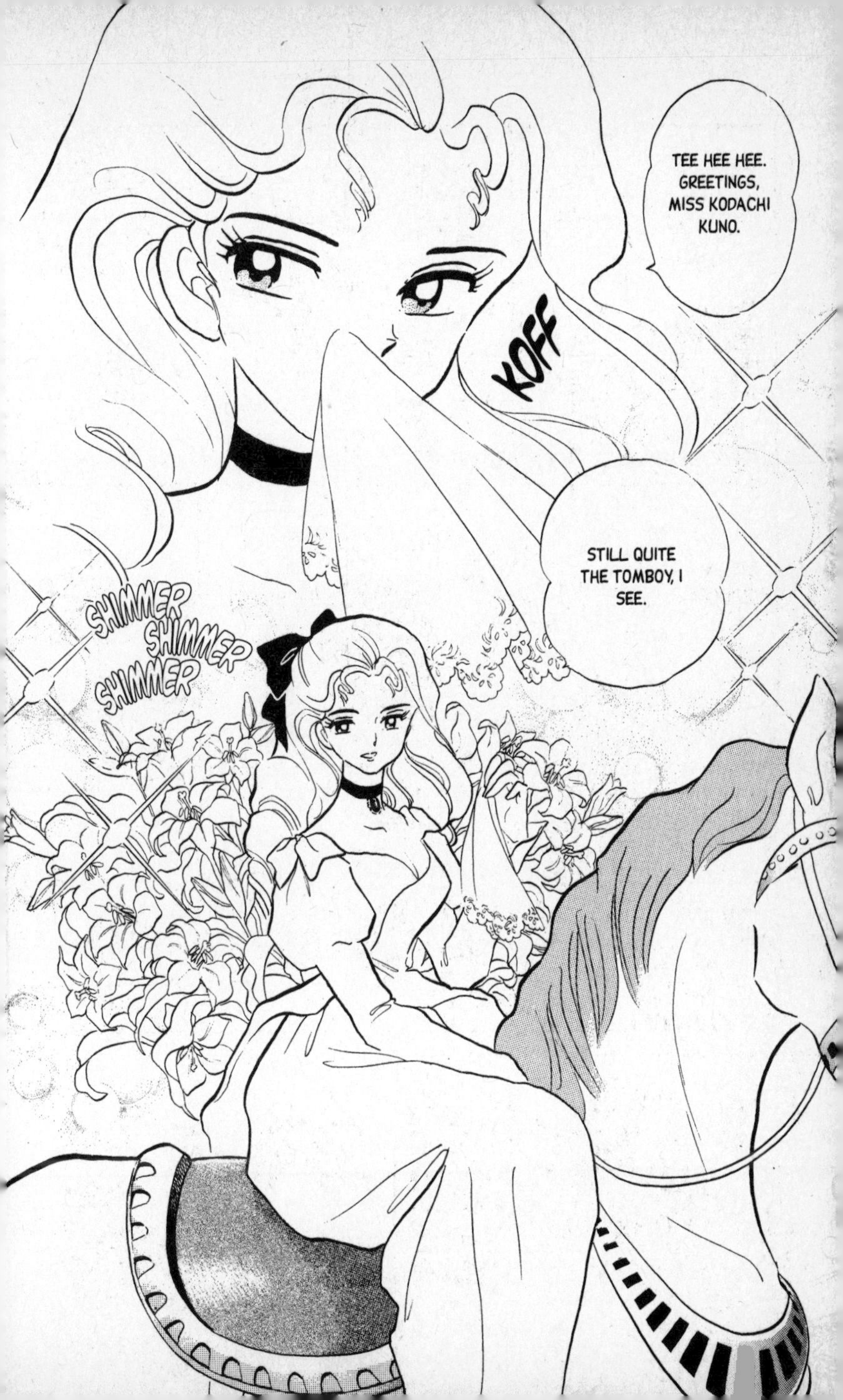
TEE HEE HEE. GREETINGS, MISS KODACHI KUNO.
KOFF
STILL QUITE THE TOMBOY, I SEE.
SHIMMER
SHIMMER
SHIMMER

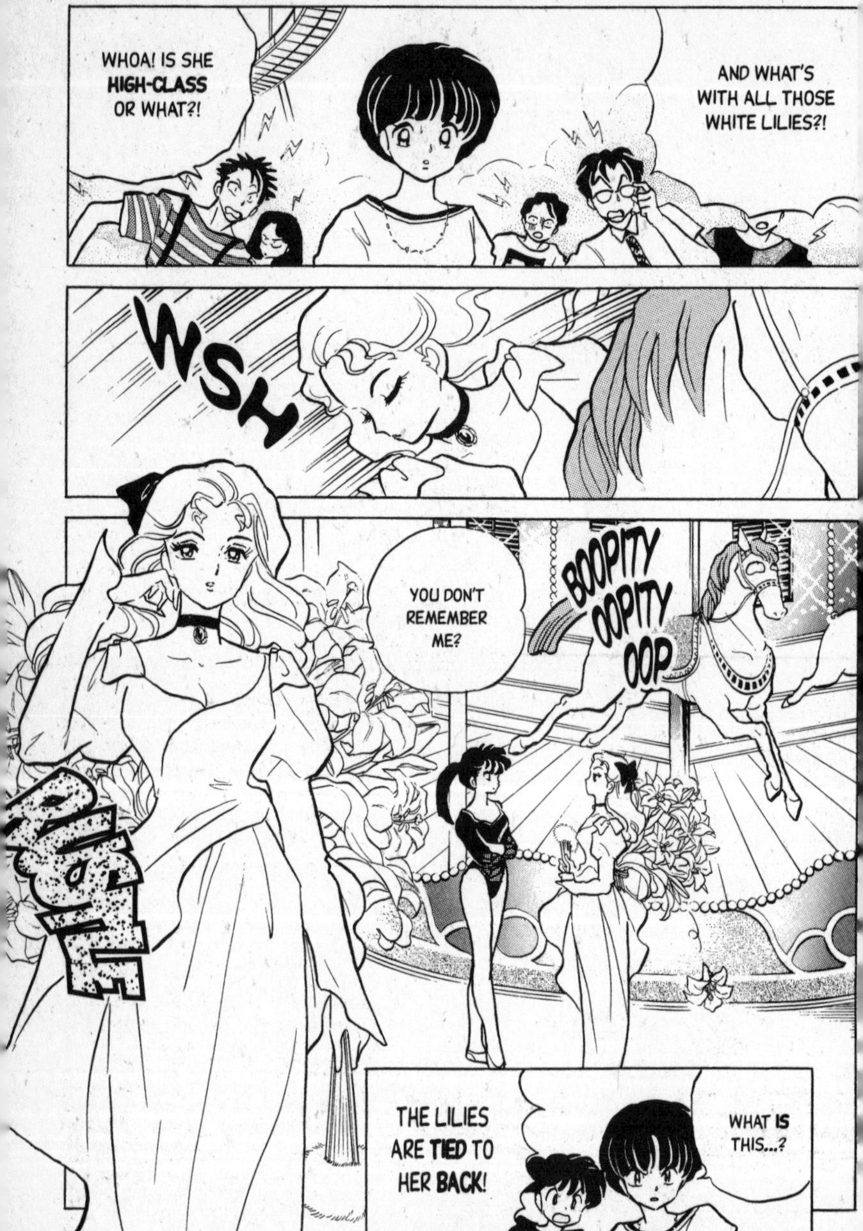
WHOA! IS SHE HIGH-CLASS OR WHAT?!
AND WHAT'S WITH ALL THOSE WHITE LILIES?!
WSH
RUSTLE
YOU DON'T REMEMBER ME?
BOOPITY OOPITY OOP
THE LILIES ARE TIED TO HER BACK!
WHAT IS THIS...?

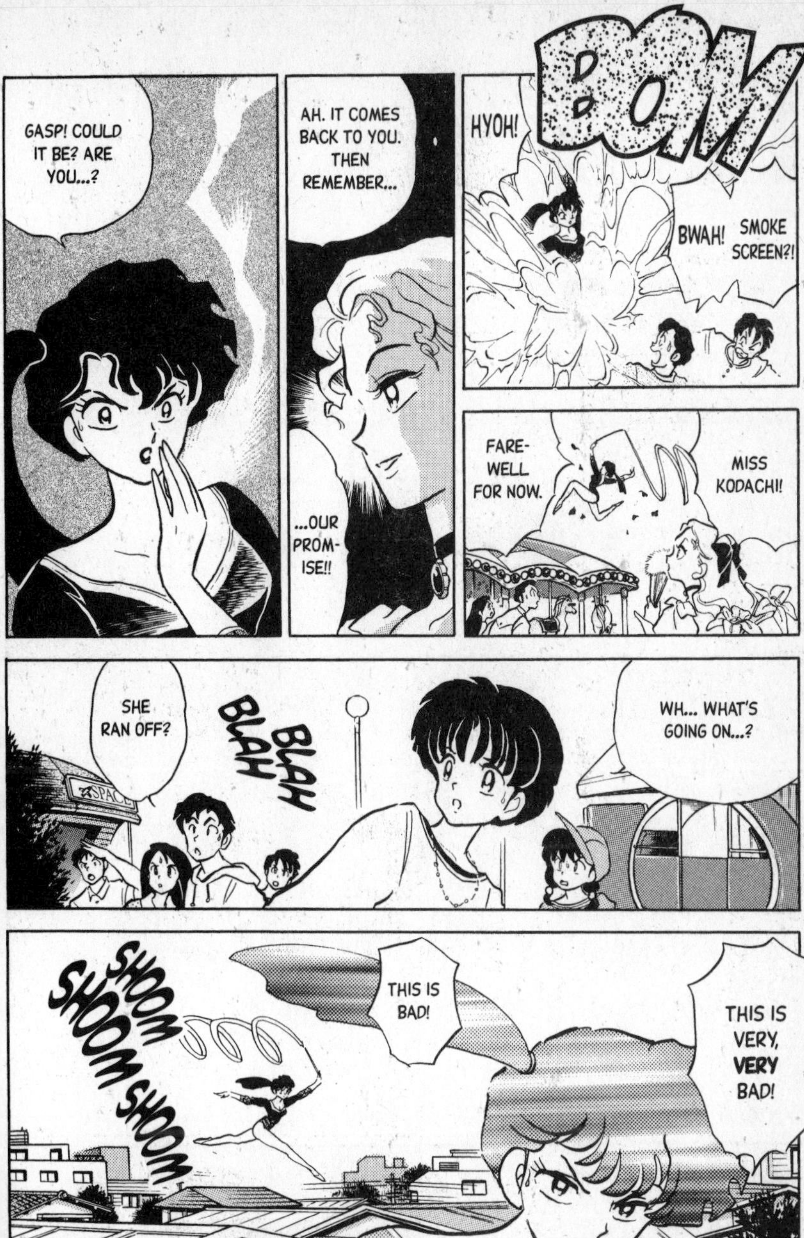
GASP! COULD IT BE? ARE YOU...?
AH. IT COMES BACK TO YOU. THEN REMEMBER...
...OUR PROMISE!!
BOOM
HYOH!
BWAH!
SMOKE SCREEN?!
FAREWELL FOR NOW.
MISS KODACHI!
SHE RAN OFF?
BLAH BLAH
WH... WHAT'S GOING ON...?
SPACE
SHOOM SHOOM SHOOM SHOOM
THIS IS BAD!
THIS IS VERY, **VERY** BAD!

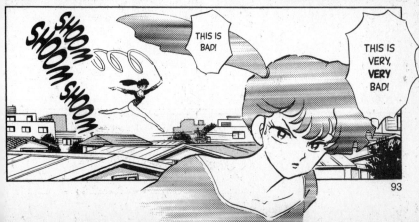

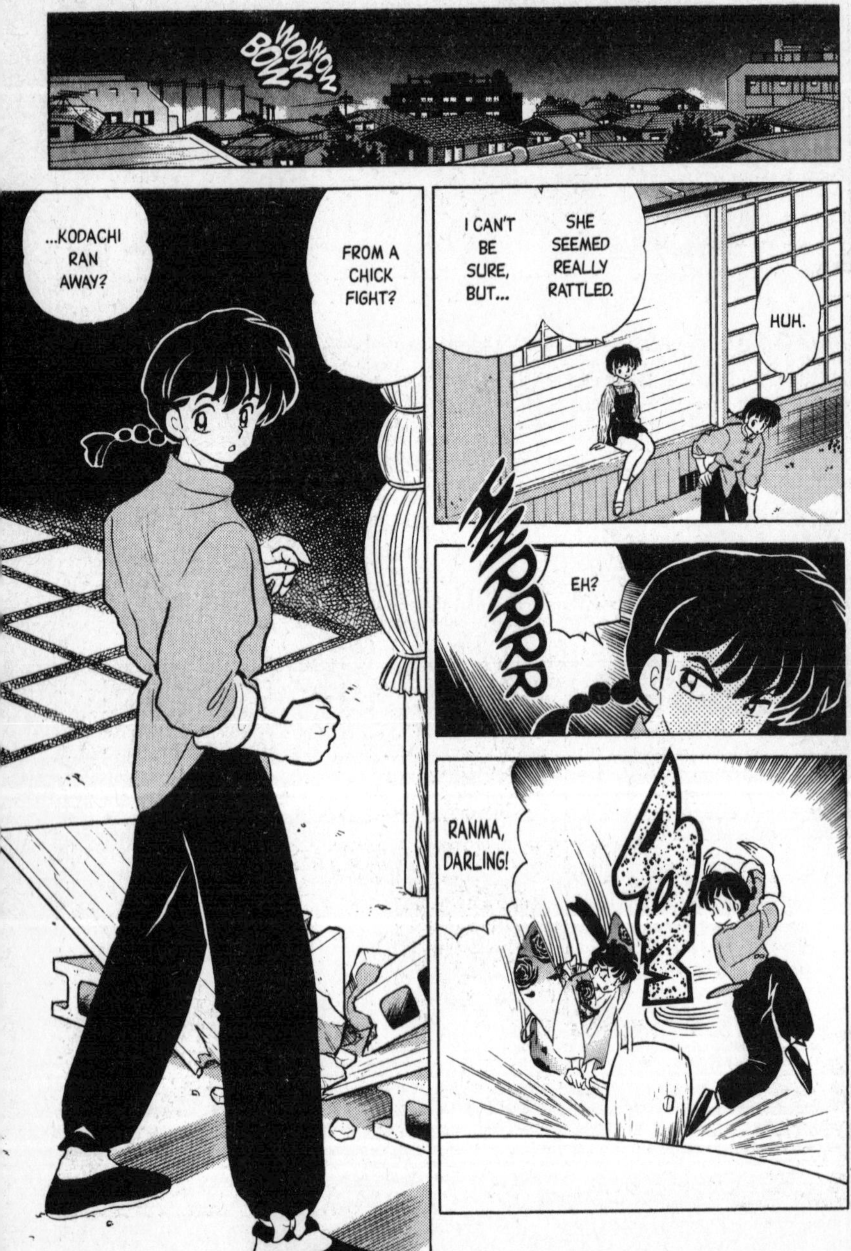
WOWWOW BOW
...KODACHI RAN AWAY?
FROM A CHICK FIGHT?
I CAN'T BE SURE, BUT...
SHE SEEMED REALLY RATTLED.
HUH.
HWRRRRR
EH?
RANMA, DARLING!

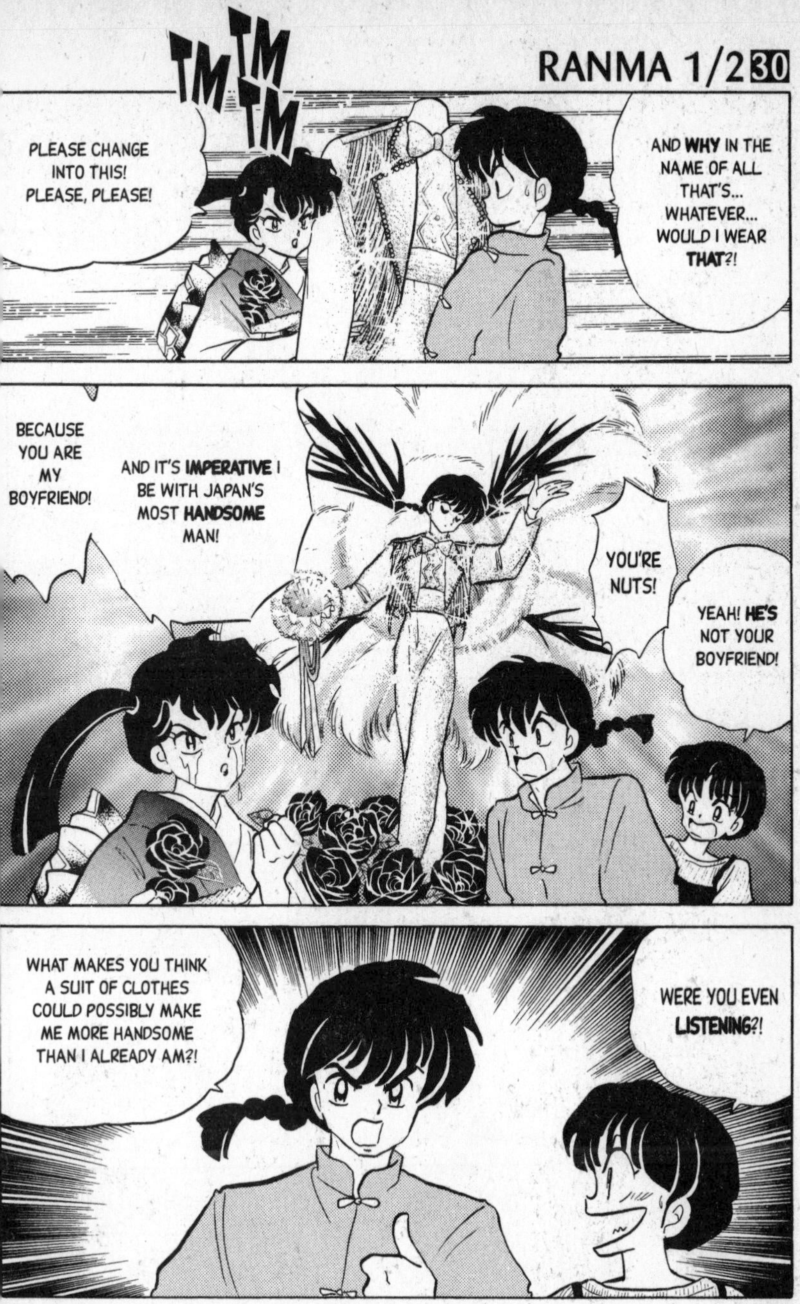
TM TM TM TM
PLEASE CHANGE INTO THIS! PLEASE, PLEASE!
AND WHY IN THE NAME OF ALL THAT'S... WHATEVER... WOULD I WEAR THAT?!
BECAUSE YOU ARE MY BOYFRIEND!
AND IT'S IMPERATIVE I BE WITH JAPAN'S MOST HANDSOME MAN!
YOU'RE NUTS!
YEAH! HE'S NOT YOUR BOYFRIEND!
WHAT MAKES YOU THINK A SUIT OF CLOTHES COULD POSSIBLY MAKE ME MORE HANDSOME THAN I ALREADY AM?!
WERE YOU EVEN LISTENING?!

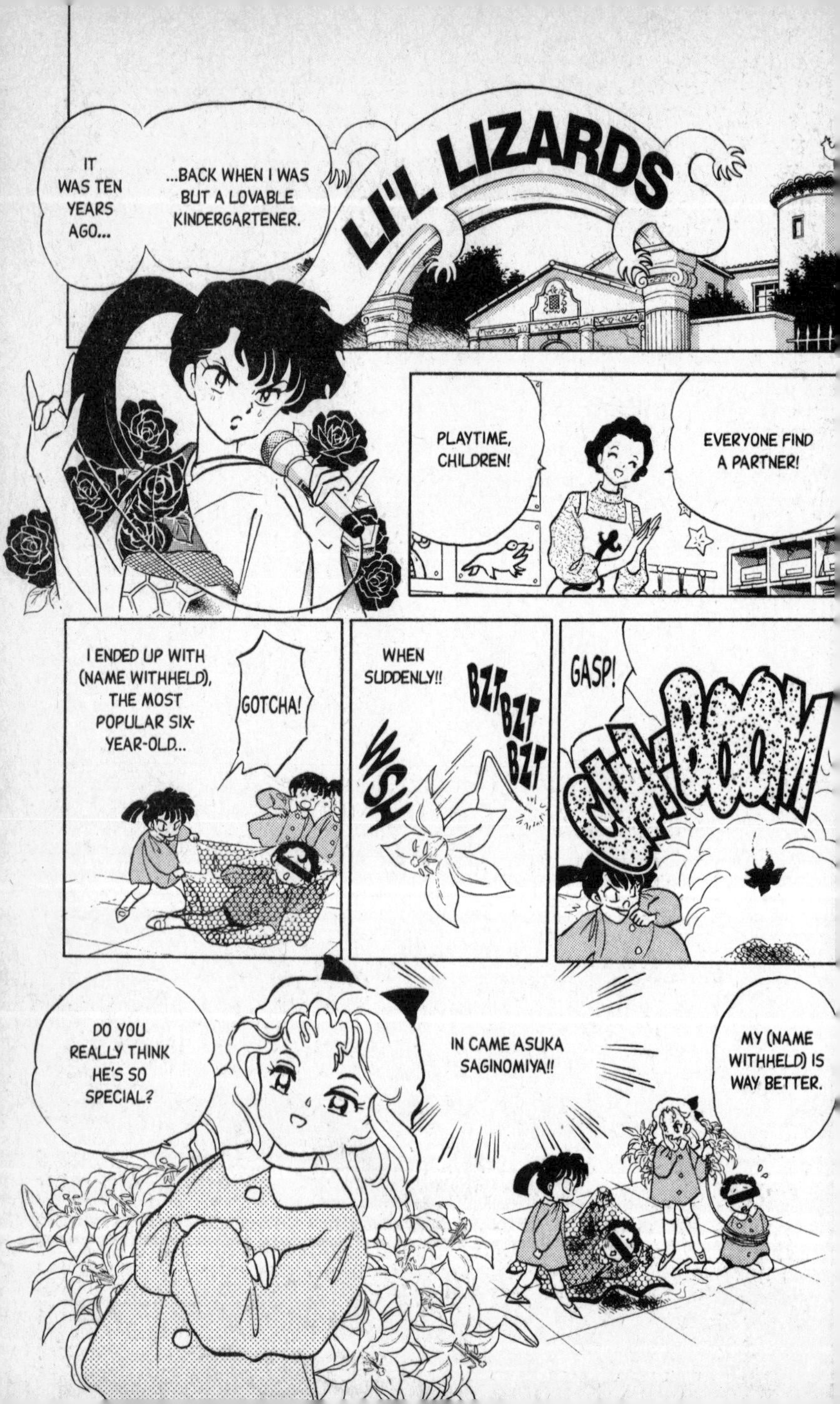
IT WAS TEN YEARS AGO...
...BACK WHEN I WAS BUT A LOVABLE KINDERGARTENER.
LI'L LIZARDS
PLAYTIME, CHILDREN!
EVERYONE FIND A PARTNER!
I ENDED UP WITH (NAME WITHHELD), THE MOST POPULAR SIX-YEAR-OLD...
GOTCHA!
WHEN SUDDENLY!!
BZT BZT BZT
WSH
GASP!
CHA-BOOM
DO YOU REALLY THINK HE'S SO SPECIAL?
IN CAME ASUKA SAGINOMIYA!!
MY (NAME WITHHELD) IS WAY BETTER.

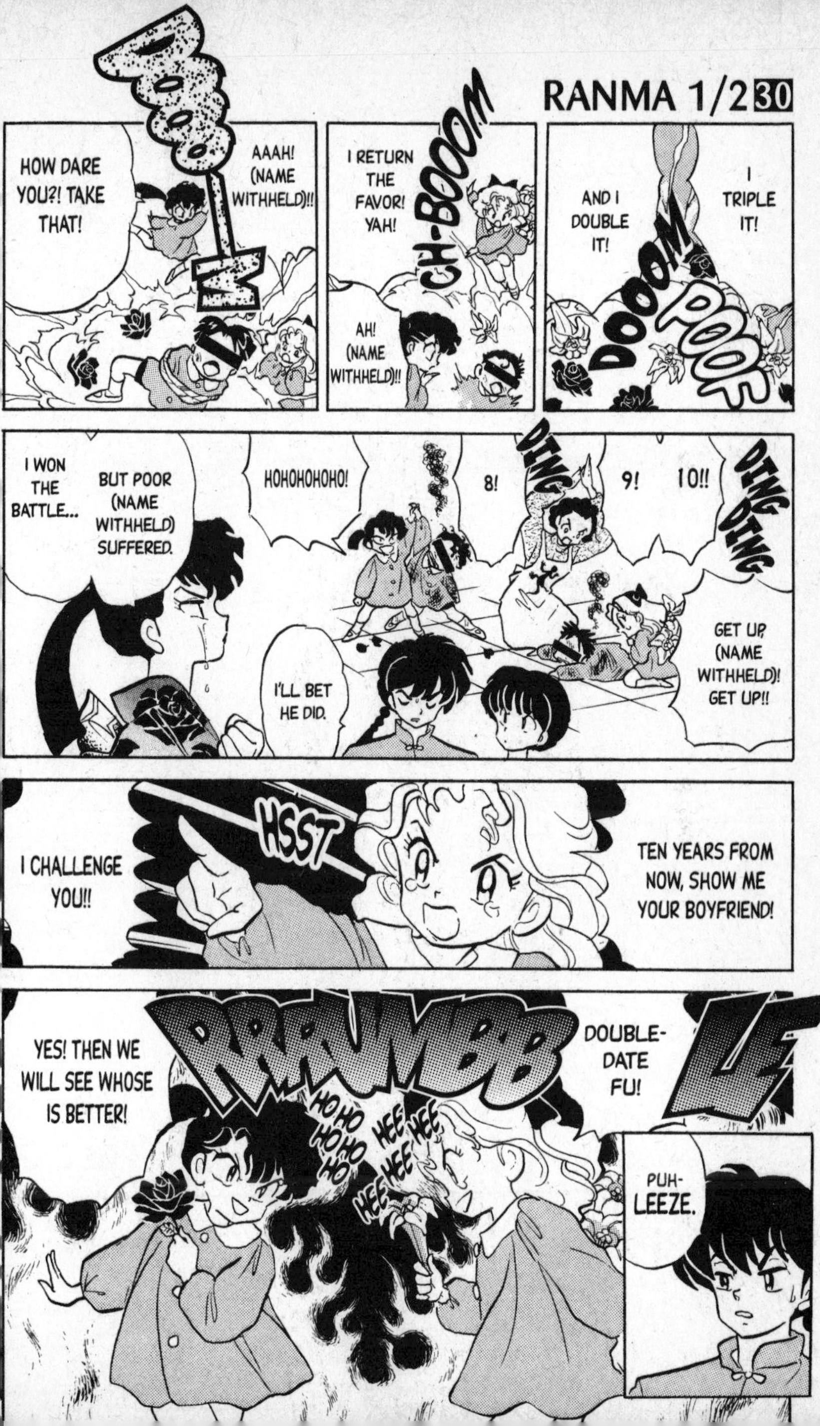
DOOOOM
HOW DARE YOU?! TAKE THAT!
AAAH! (NAME WITHHELD)!!
I RETURN THE FAVOR! YAH!
CH-BOOOM
AH! (NAME WITHHELD)!!
AND I DOUBLE IT!
I TRIPLE IT!
DOOOM
POOF
I WON THE BATTLE...
BUT POOR (NAME WITHHELD) SUFFERED.
HOHOHOHOHO!
8!
DING
9!
10!!
DING DING DING
I'LL BET HE DID.
GET UP, (NAME WITHHELD)! GET UP!!
I CHALLENGE YOU!!
HSST
TEN YEARS FROM NOW, SHOW ME YOUR BOYFRIEND!
YES! THEN WE WILL SEE WHOSE IS BETTER!
RRRUMBBLE
DOUBLE-DATE FU!
HO HO HO HO HO
HEE HEE HEE HEE HEE
PUH-LEEZE.

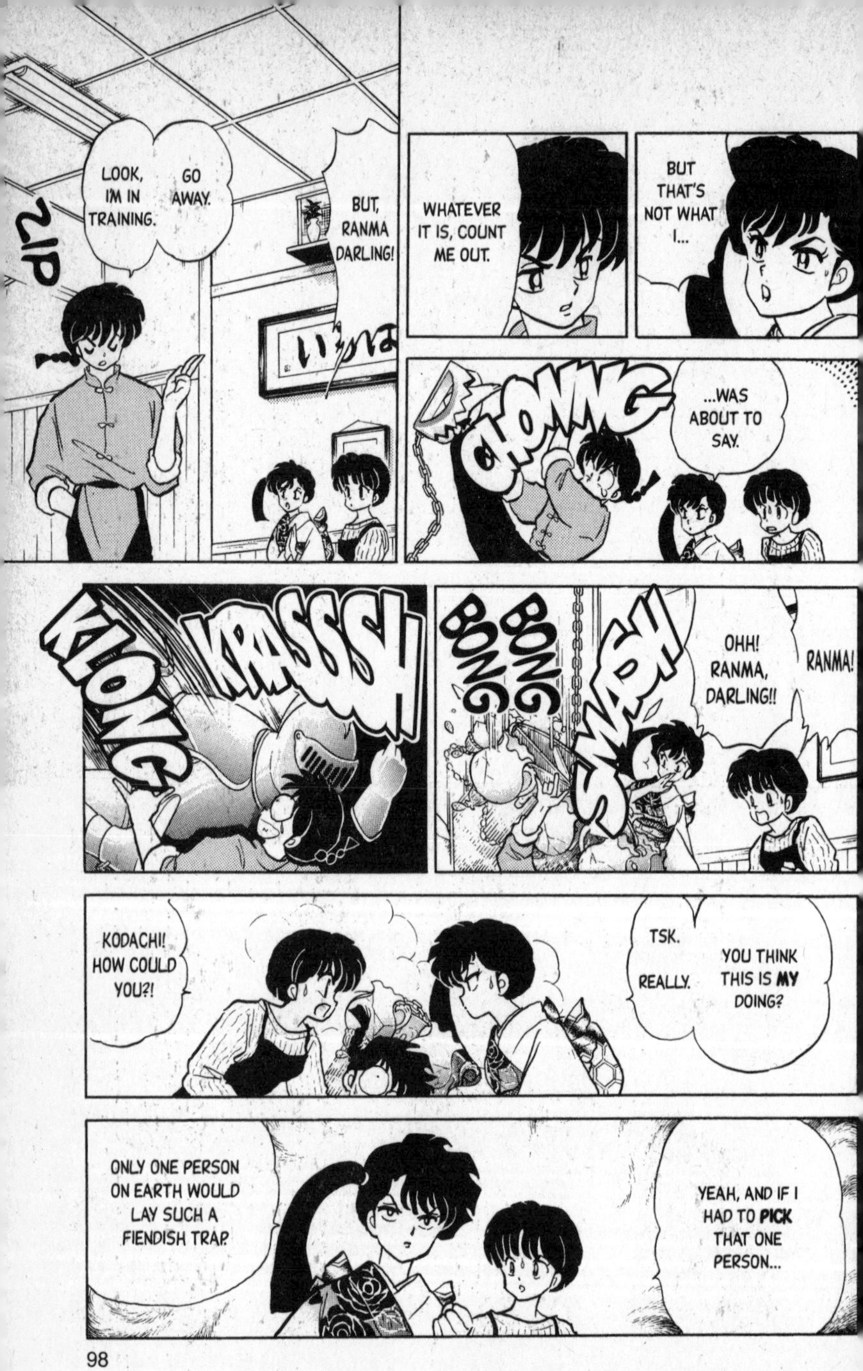

ZIP
LOOK, I'M IN TRAINING.
GO AWAY.
BUT, RANMA DARLING!
WHATEVER IT IS, COUNT ME OUT.
BUT THAT'S NOT WHAT I...
CLONNG
...WAS ABOUT TO SAY.
KLONG
KRASSSH
BONG BONG
SMASH
OHH! RANMA, DARLING!!
RANMA!
KODACHI! HOW COULD YOU?!
TSK. REALLY.
YOU THINK THIS IS MY DOING?
ONLY ONE PERSON ON EARTH WOULD LAY SUCH A FIENDISH TRAP.
YEAH, AND IF I HAD TO PICK THAT ONE PERSON...

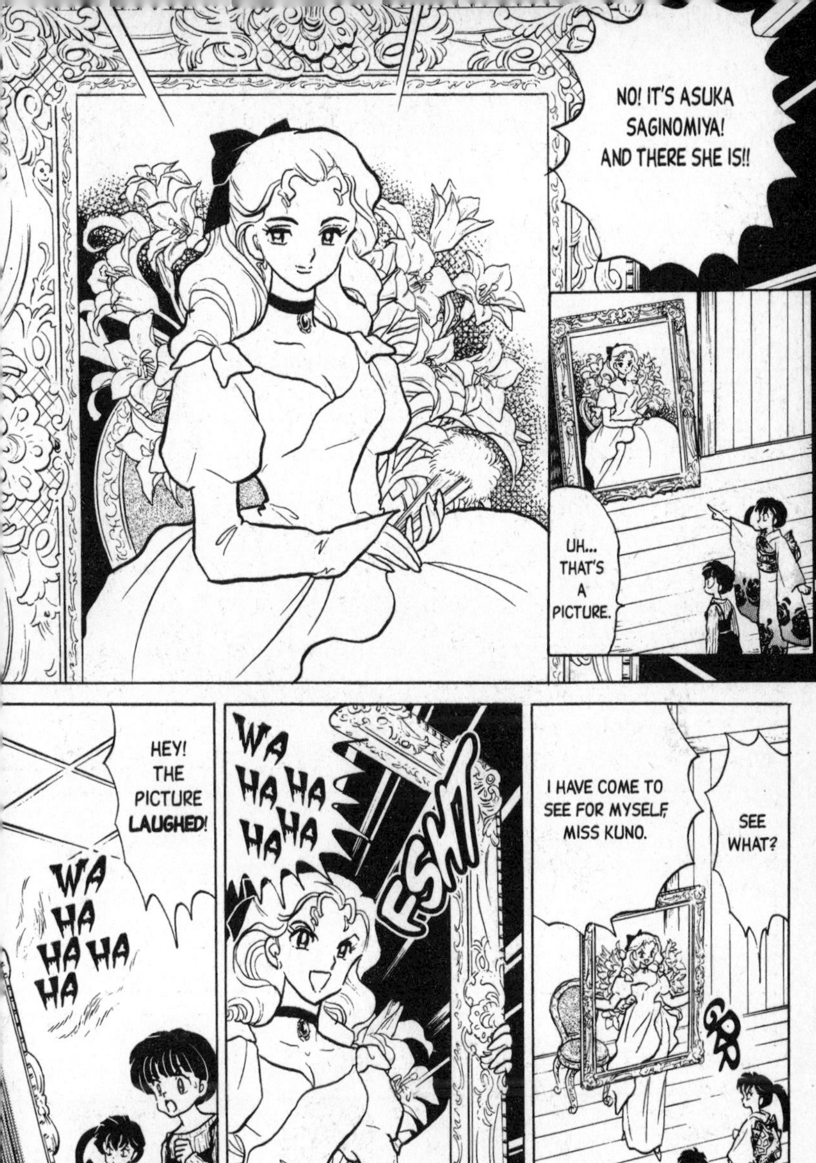

NO! IT'S ASUKA SAGINOMIYA! AND THERE SHE IS!!
UH... THAT'S A PICTURE.
HEY! THE PICTURE LAUGHED!
WA HA HA HA HA HA
WA HA HA HA HA HA
FSHT
I HAVE COME TO SEE FOR MYSELF, MISS KUNO.
SEE WHAT?
GRR

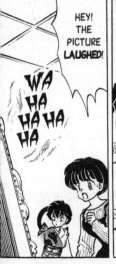

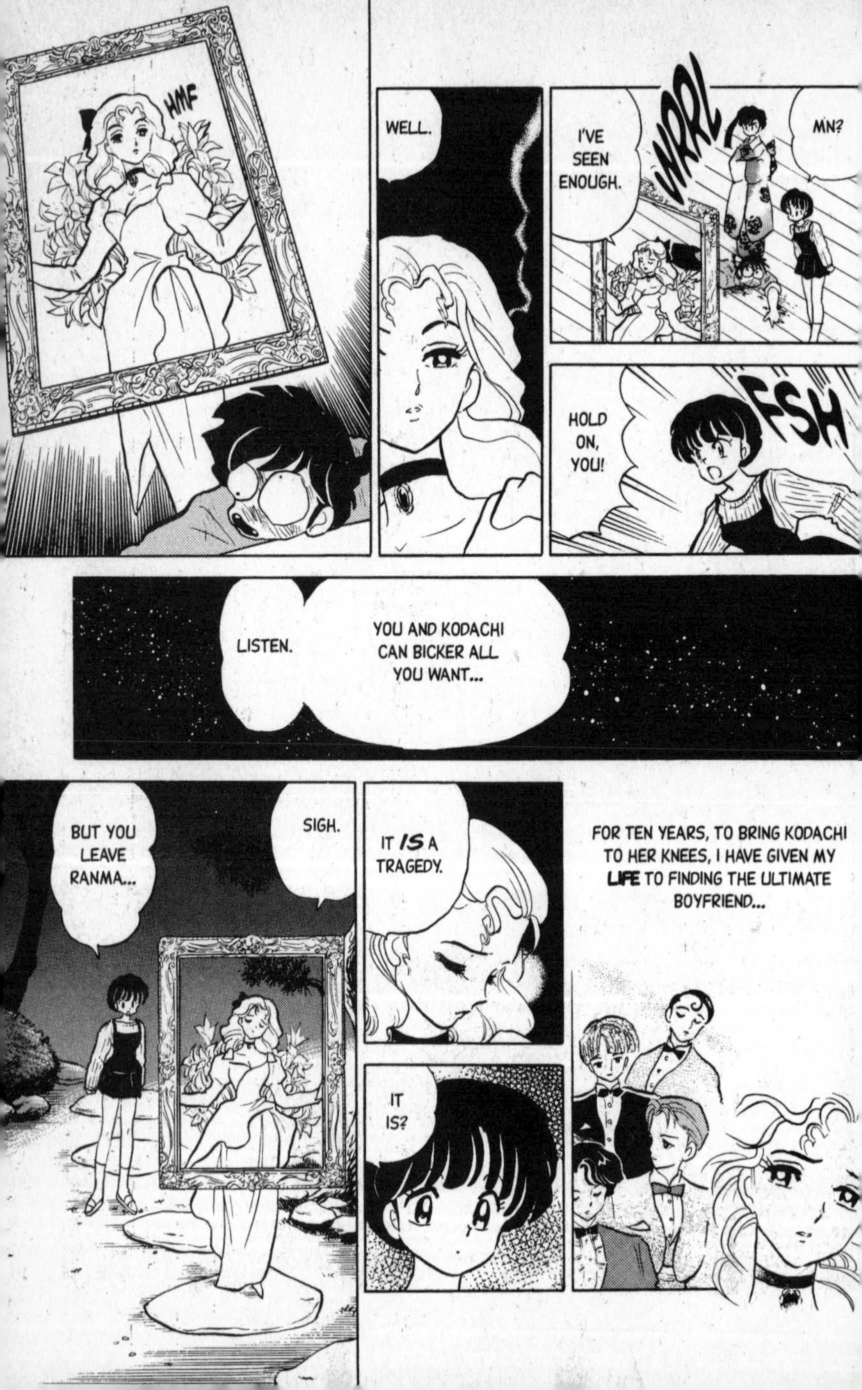
HMF
WELL.
I'VE SEEN ENOUGH.
WRRL
MN?
HOLD ON, YOU!
FSH
LISTEN.
YOU AND KODACHI CAN BICKER ALL YOU WANT...
BUT YOU LEAVE RANMA...
SIGH.
IT IS A TRAGEDY.
IT IS?
FOR TEN YEARS, TO BRING KODACHI TO HER KNEES, I HAVE GIVEN MY LIFE TO FINDING THE ULTIMATE BOYFRIEND...

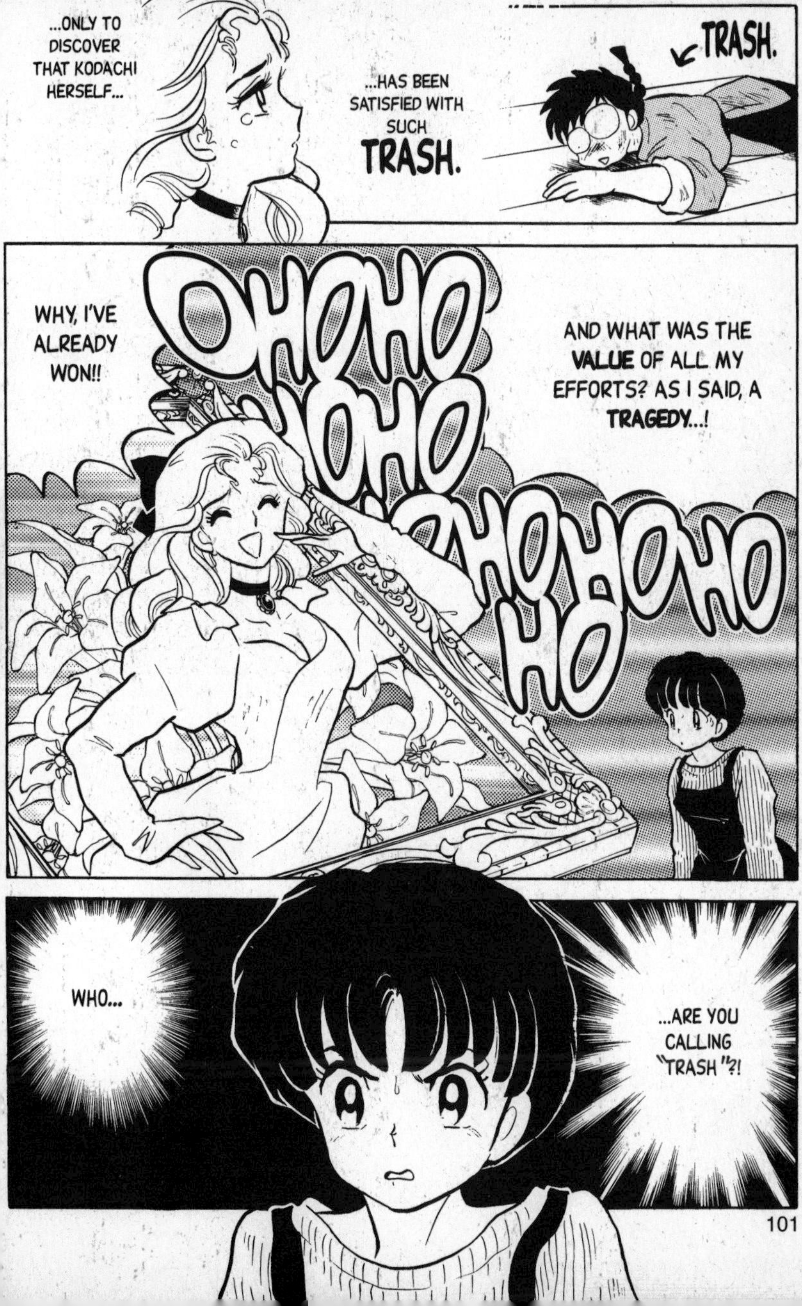
...ONLY TO DISCOVER THAT KODACHI HERSELF...
...HAS BEEN SATISFIED WITH SUCH TRASH.
TRASH.
WHY, I'VE ALREADY WON!!
OHOHO HOHO HOHOHOHOHOHO HO
AND WHAT WAS THE VALUE OF ALL MY EFFORTS? AS I SAID, A TRAGEDY...!
WHO...
...ARE YOU CALLING "TRASH"?!

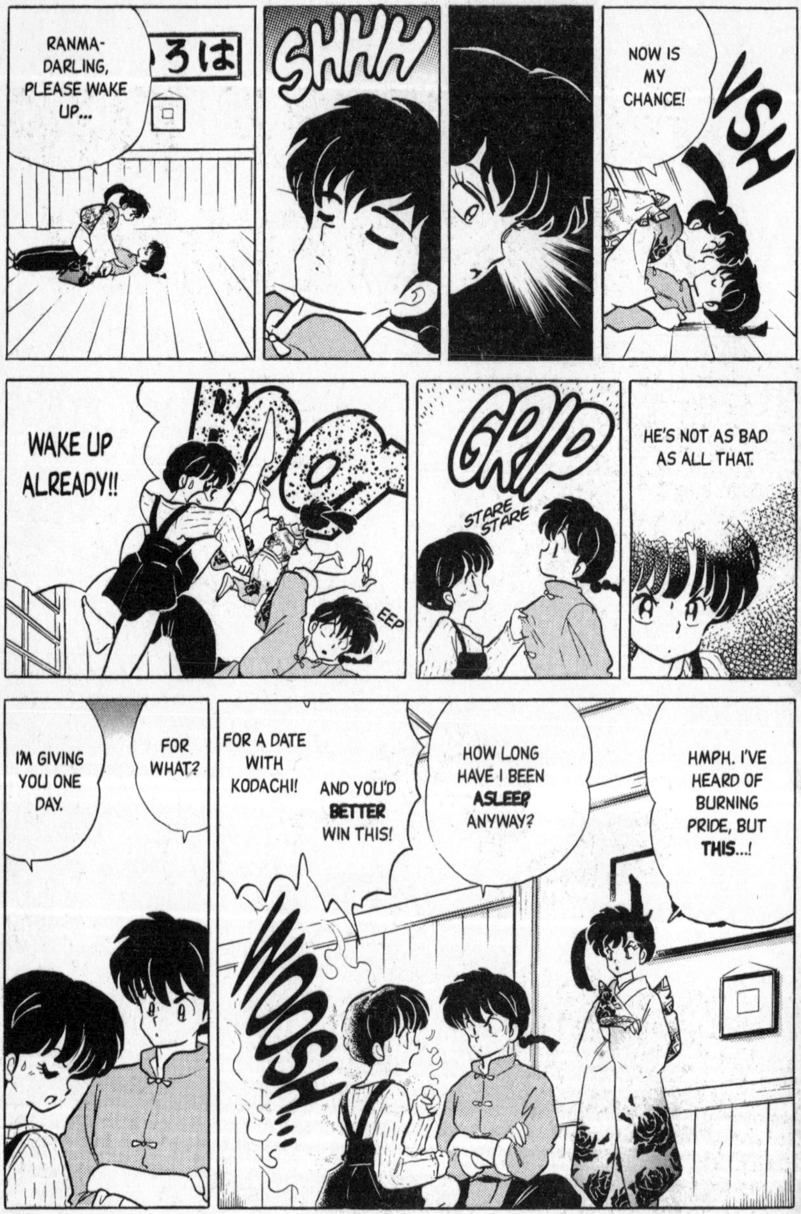
RANMA-DARLING, PLEASE WAKE UP...
SHHH
NOW IS MY CHANCE!
VSH
WAKE UP ALREADY!!
EEP
GRIP
STARE STARE
HE'S NOT AS BAD AS ALL THAT.
I'M GIVING YOU ONE DAY.
FOR WHAT?
FOR A DATE WITH KODACHI!
AND YOU'D BETTER WIN THIS!
HOW LONG HAVE I BEEN ASLEEP ANYWAY?
HMPH. I'VE HEARD OF BURNING PRIDE, BUT THIS...!
WOOSH...

PART 7

BATTLE OF THE BOYFRIENDS!

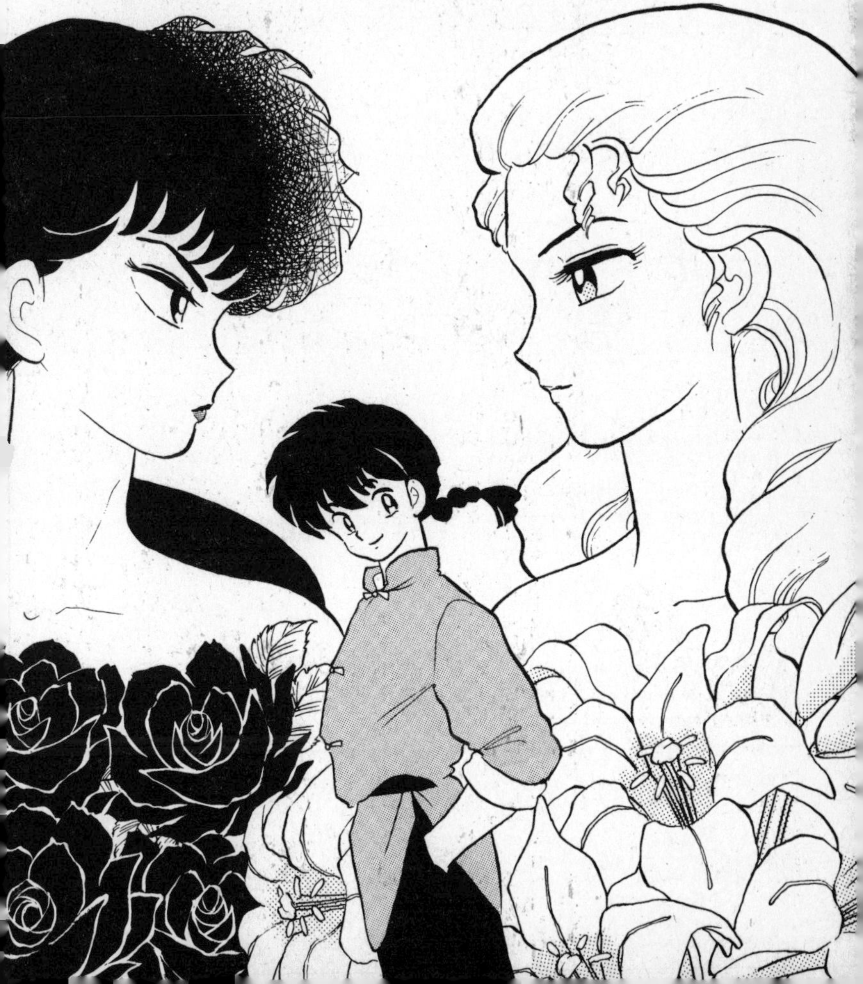

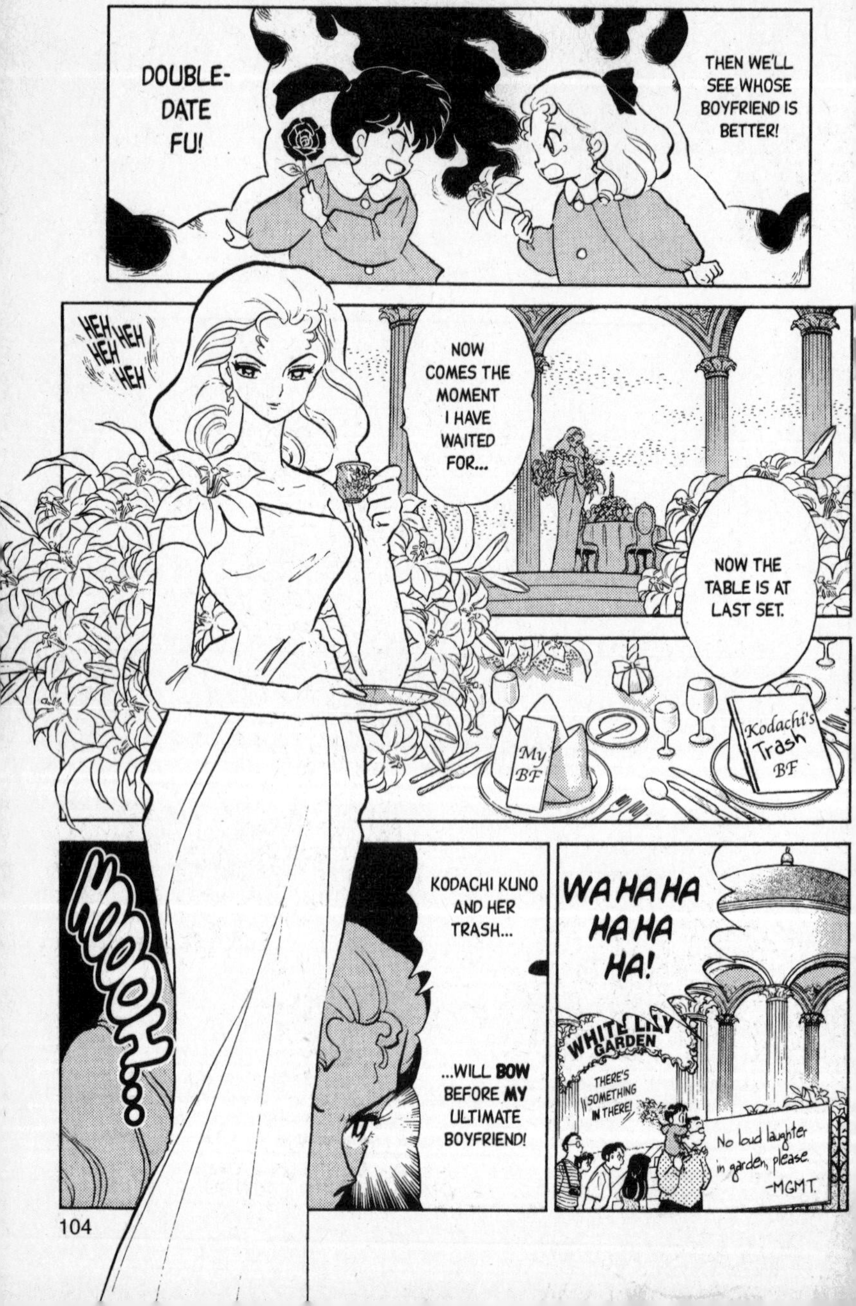
DOUBLE-DATE FU!
THEN WE'LL SEE WHOSE BOYFRIEND IS BETTER!
HEH HEH HEH HEH HEH
NOW COMES THE MOMENT I HAVE WAITED FOR...
NOW THE TABLE IS AT LAST SET.
My BF
Kodachi's Trash BF
HOOOOH...
KODACHI KUNO AND HER TRASH...
...WILL BOW BEFORE MY ULTIMATE BOYFRIEND!
WA HA HA HA HA HA!
WHITE LILY GARDEN
THERE'S SOMETHING IN THERE!
No loud laughter in garden, please. -MGMT.

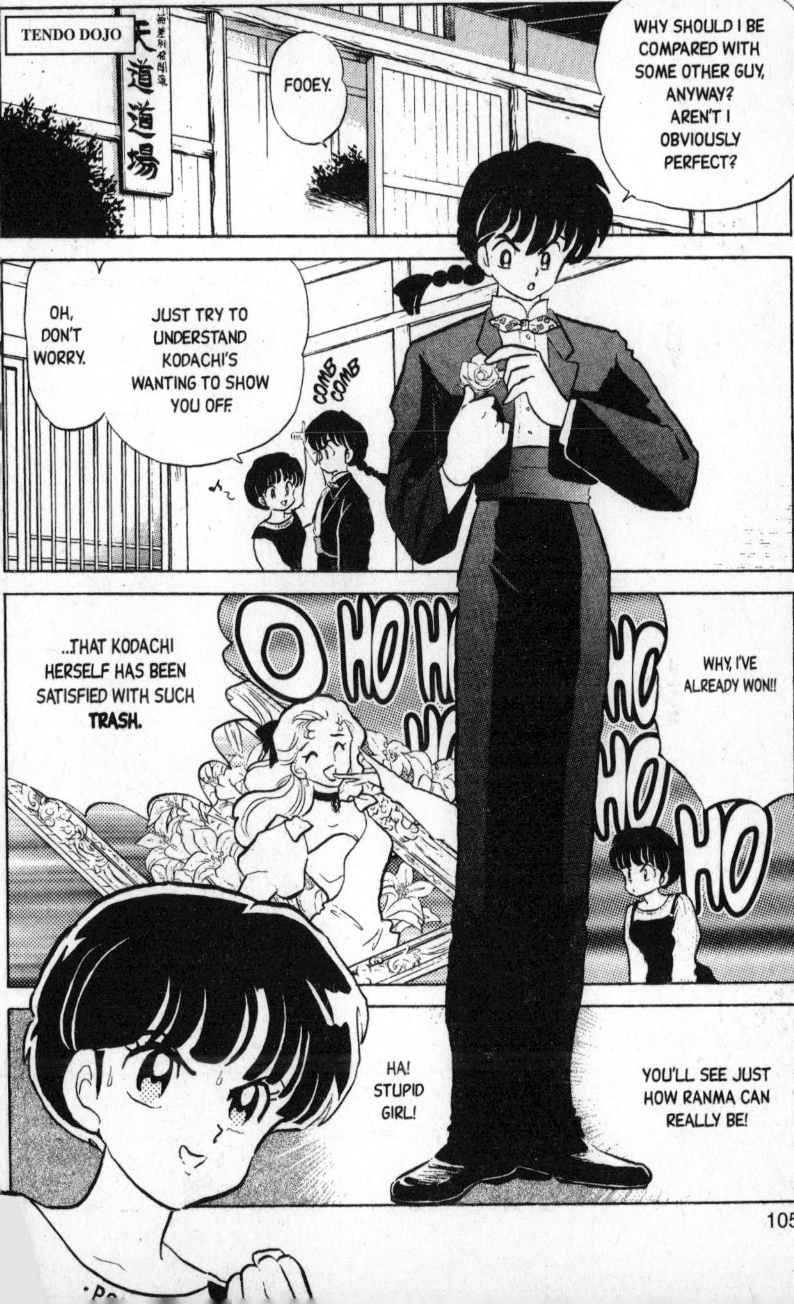
TENDO DOJO
無差別格闘流
天道道場
FOOEY.
WHY SHOULD I BE COMPARED WITH SOME OTHER GUY, ANYWAY? AREN'T I OBVIOUSLY PERFECT?
OH, DON'T WORRY.
JUST TRY TO UNDERSTAND KODACHI'S WANTING TO SHOW YOU OFF.
COMB COMB
...THAT KODACHI HERSELF HAS BEEN SATISFIED WITH SUCH **TRASH.**
O HO HO HO HO HO HO HO
WHY, I'VE ALREADY WON!!
HA! STUPID GIRL!
YOU'LL SEE JUST HOW RANMA CAN REALLY BE!

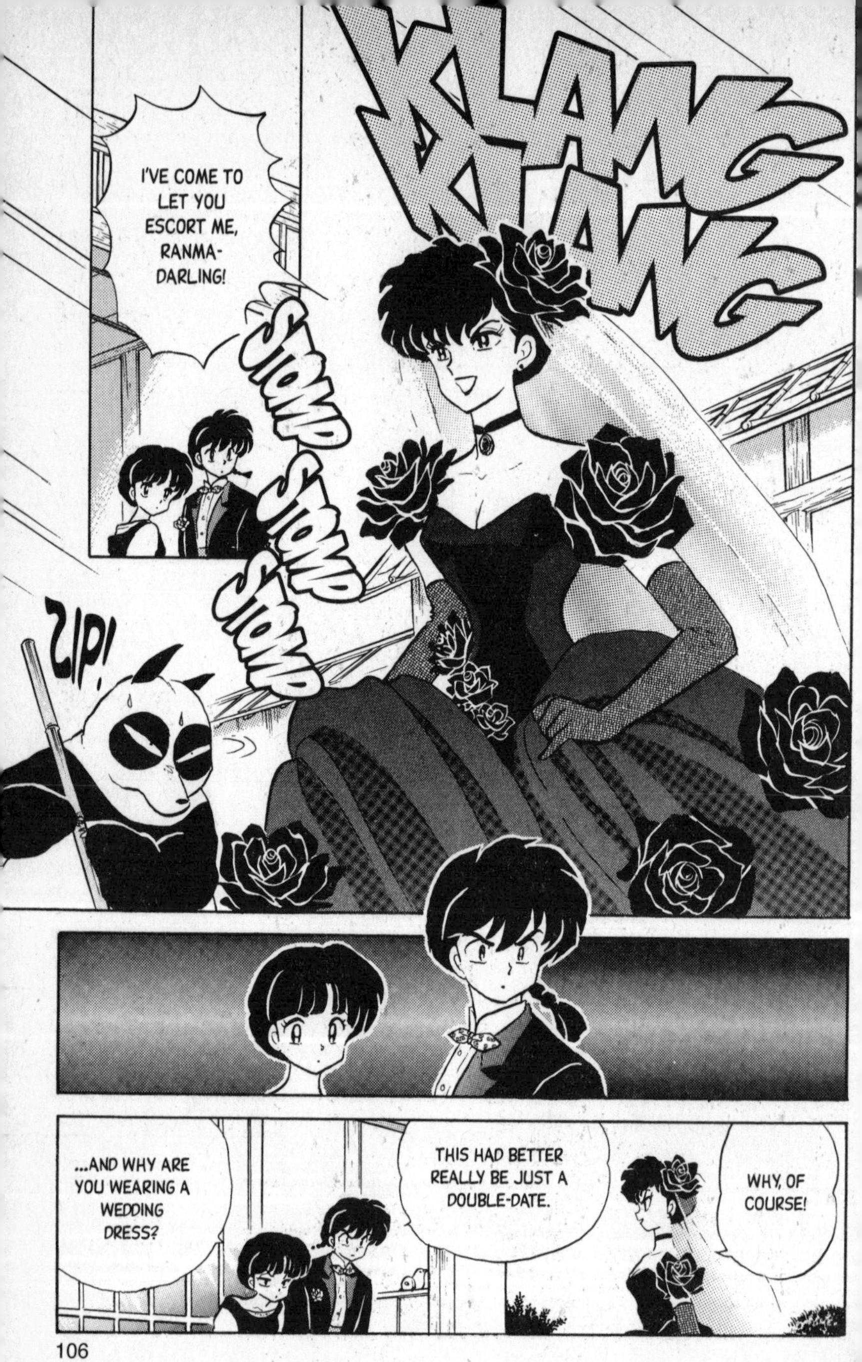
I'VE COME TO LET YOU ESCORT ME, RANMA-DARLING!
KLANG KLANG
STOMP STOMP STOMP
ZIP!
...AND WHY ARE YOU WEARING A WEDDING DRESS?
THIS HAD BETTER REALLY BE JUST A DOUBLE-DATE.
WHY, OF COURSE!

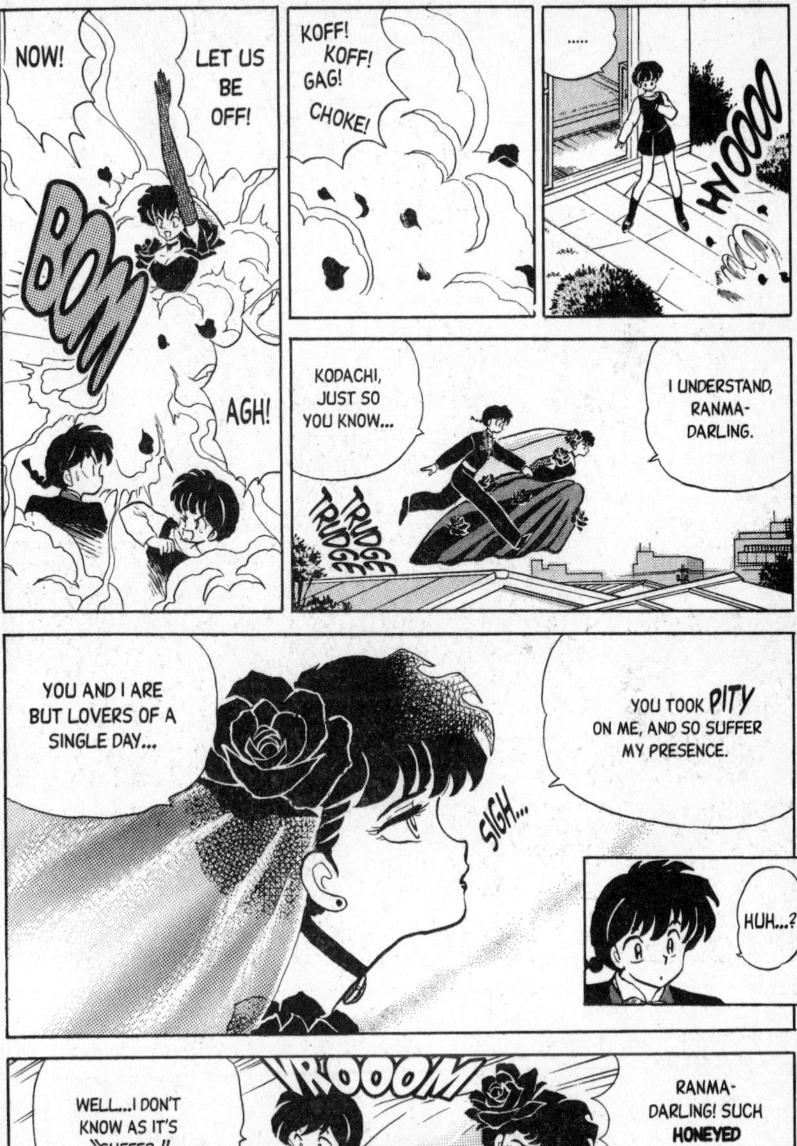
NOW!
LET US BE OFF!
BOM
AGH!
KOFF! KOFF! GAG! CHOKE!
.....
HYOOOO
KODACHI, JUST SO YOU KNOW...
TRUDGE TRUDGE
I UNDERSTAND, RANMA-DARLING.
YOU AND I ARE BUT LOVERS OF A SINGLE DAY...
SIGH...
YOU TOOK PITY ON ME, AND SO SUFFER MY PRESENCE.
HUH...?
WELL...I DON'T KNOW AS IT'S "SUFFER," EXACTLY...
VROOOM
RANMA-DARLING! SUCH HONEYED WORDS!

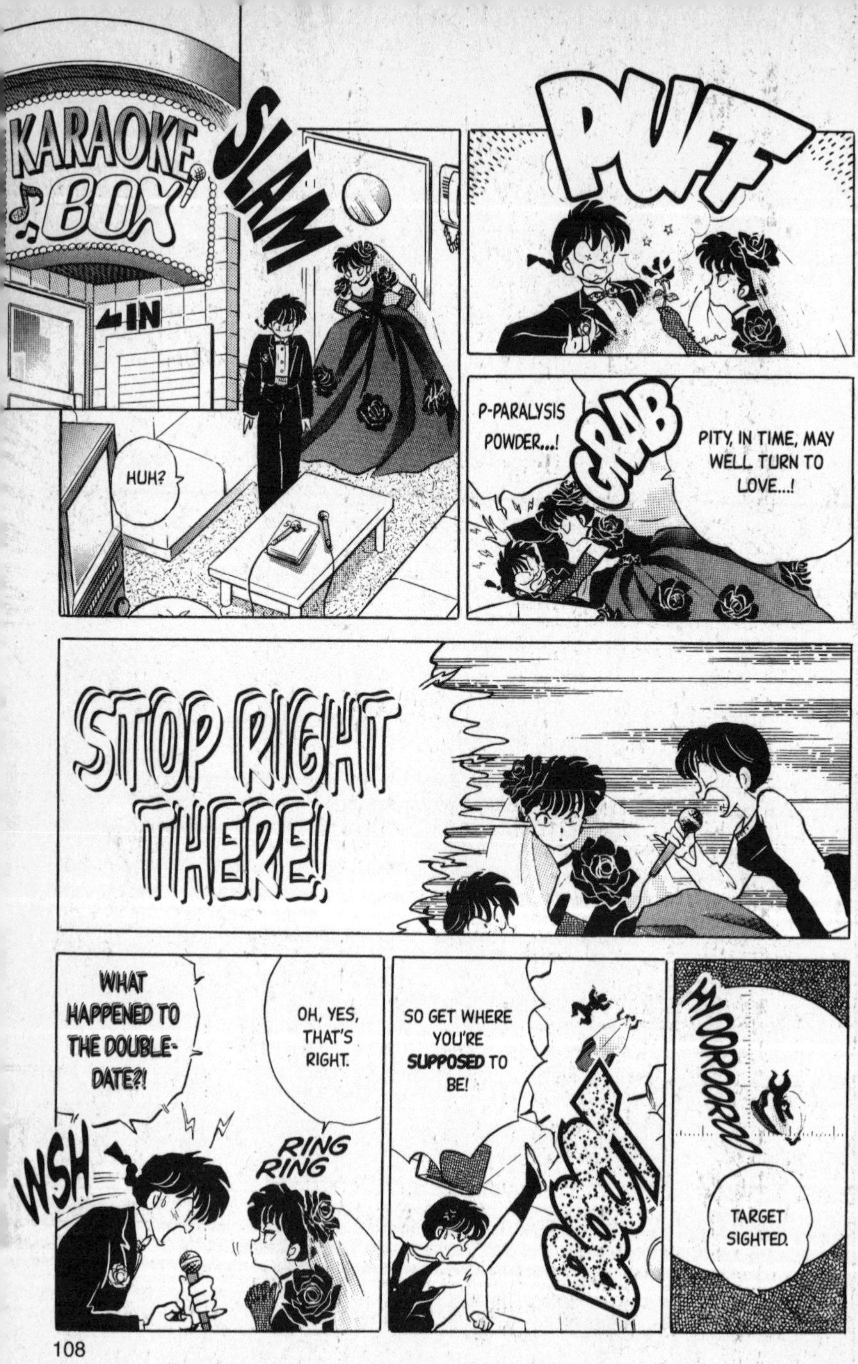
KARAOKE BOX
IN
SLAM
HUH?
PUFF
P-PARALYSIS POWDER...!
CRAB
PITY, IN TIME, MAY WELL TURN TO LOVE...!
STOP RIGHT THERE!
WHAT HAPPENED TO THE DOUBLE-DATE?!
WSH
OH, YES, THAT'S RIGHT.
RING RING
SO GET WHERE YOU'RE **SUPPOSED** TO BE!
BOOT
HYOOROOROO
TARGET SIGHTED.

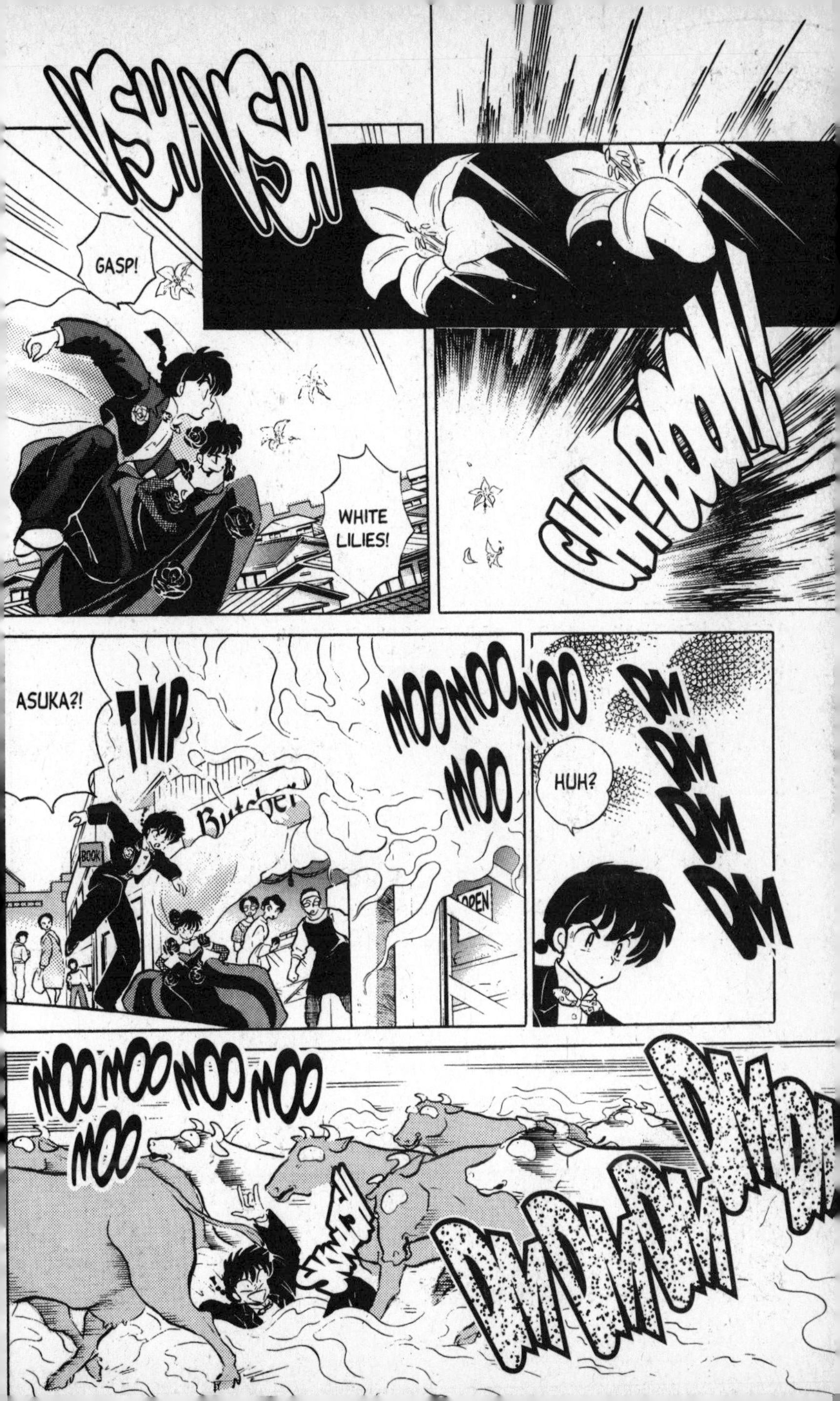
GASP!
WHITE LILIES!
CHA-BOOM!
ASUKA?!
TMP
MOO MOO MOO
MOO
HUH?
DM DM DM DM
MOO MOO MOO MOO
MOO

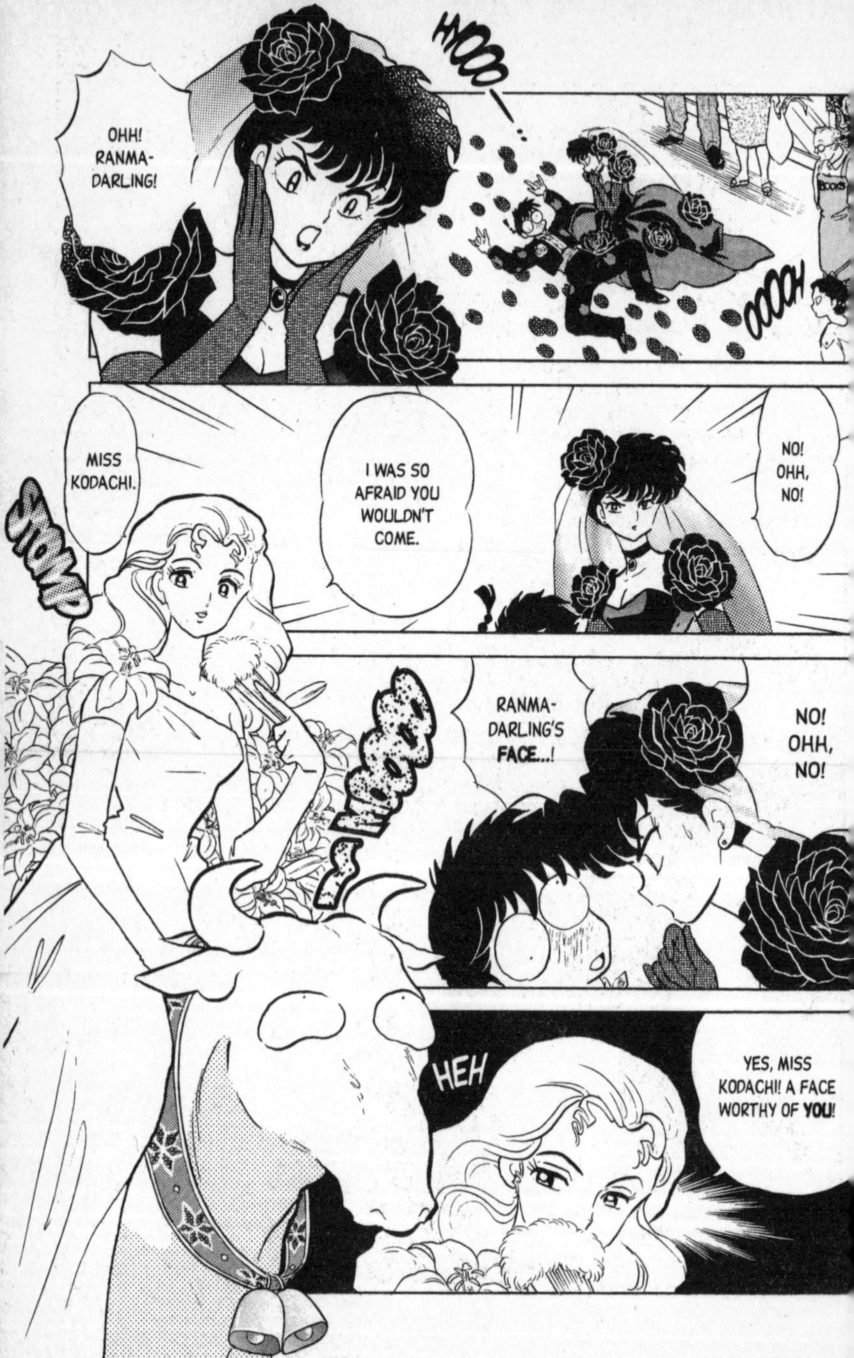
OHH! RANMA-DARLING!
HYOOO—!!
OOOOH
MISS KODACHI.
STOMP
I WAS SO AFRAID YOU WOULDN'T COME.
NO! OHH, NO!
MOOO
RANMA-DARLING'S **FACE**...!
NO! OHH, NO!
HEH
YES, MISS KODACHI! A FACE WORTHY OF **YOU**!

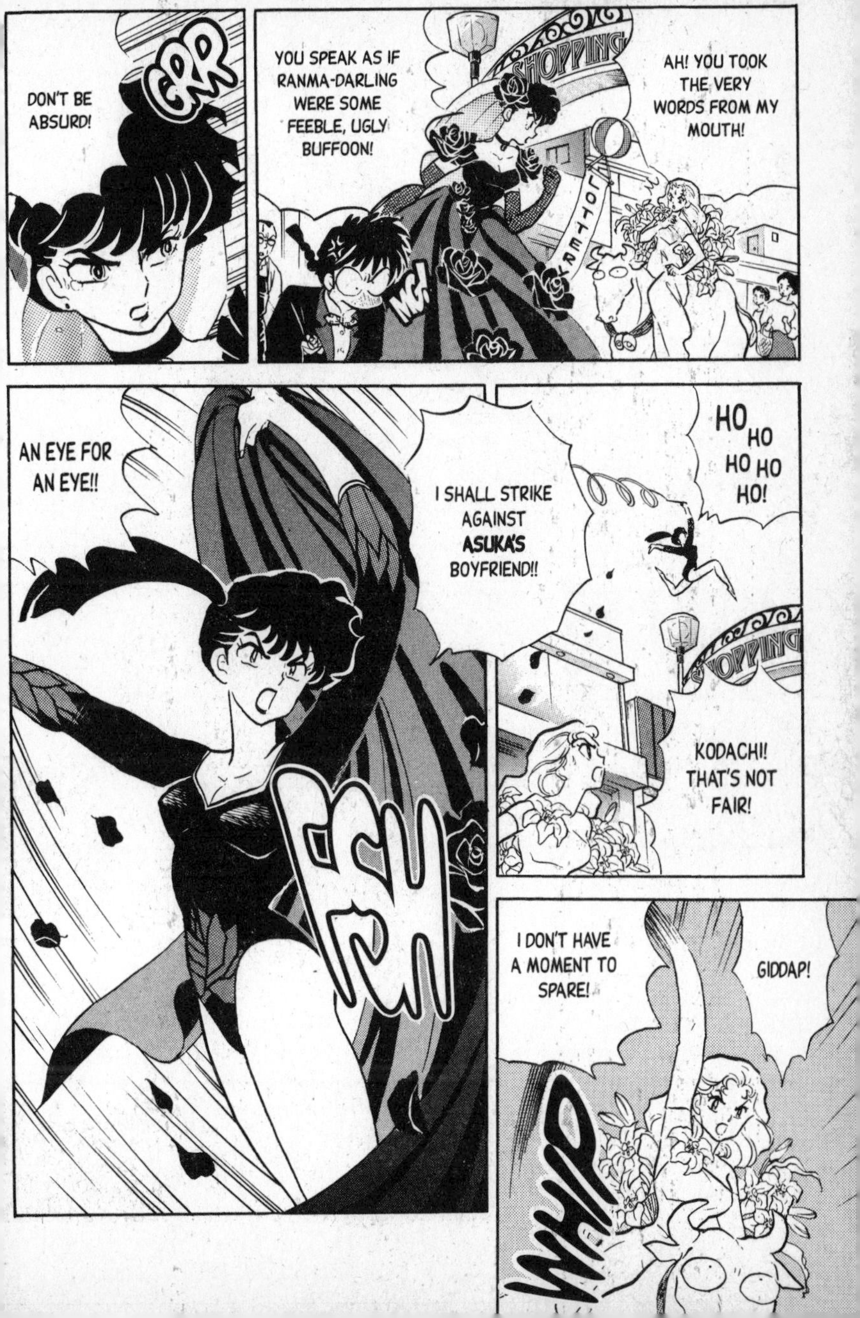
GRR
DON'T BE ABSURD!
YOU SPEAK AS IF RANMA-DARLING WERE SOME FEEBLE, UGLY BUFFOON!
SHOPPING
LOTTERY
MG!
AH! YOU TOOK THE VERY WORDS FROM MY MOUTH!
AN EYE FOR AN EYE!!
I SHALL STRIKE AGAINST ASUKA'S BOYFRIEND!!
FSH
HO HO HO HO HO!
SHOPPING
KODACHI!! THAT'S NOT FAIR!
I DON'T HAVE A MOMENT TO SPARE!
GIDDAP!
WHIP

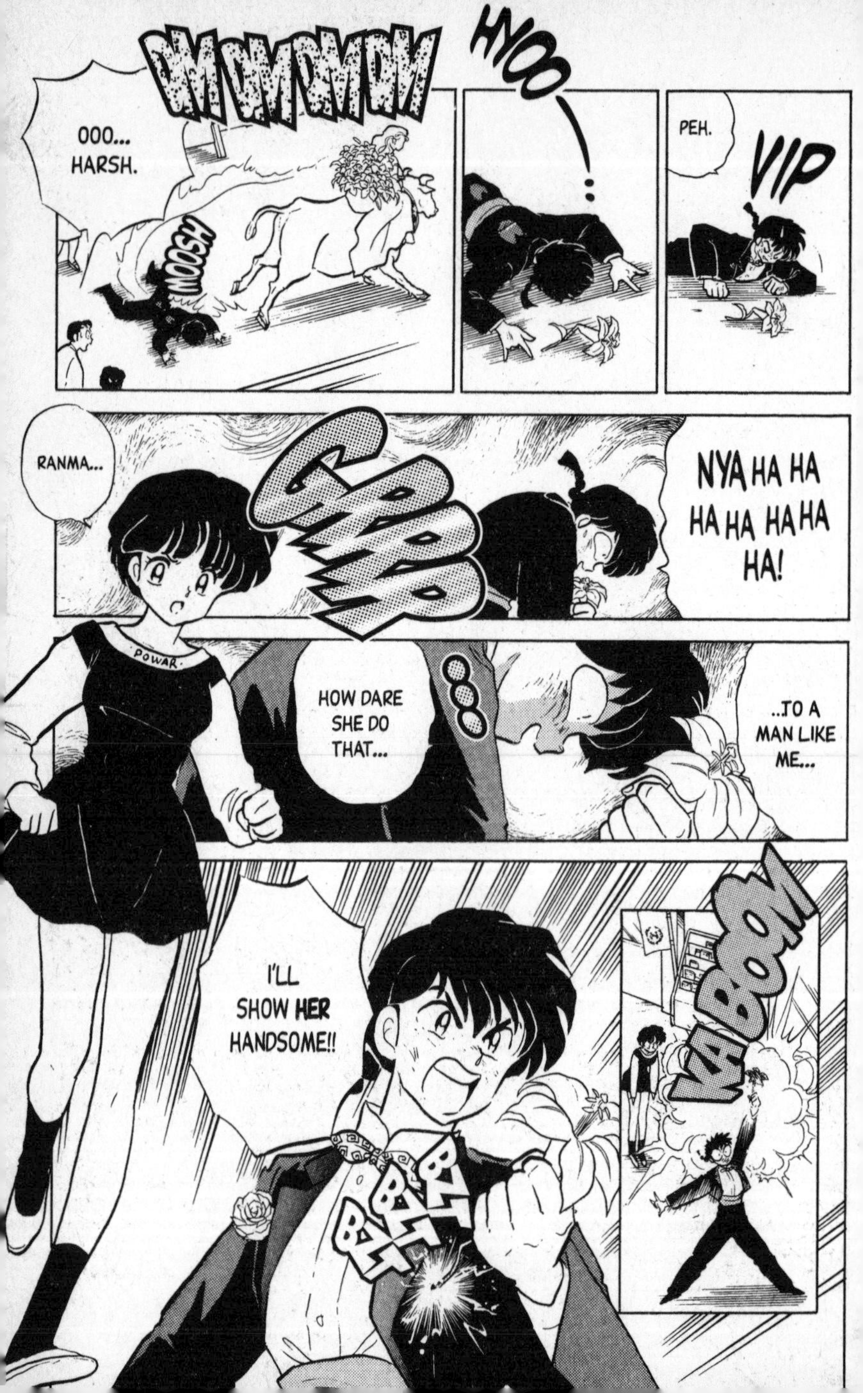
OOO... HARSH.
DMOMOMOM
MOOSH
HYOO
PEH.
VIP
RANMA...
CHOMP
NYA HA HA HA HA HA HA HA!
HOW DARE SHE DO THAT...
...TO A MAN LIKE ME...
I'LL SHOW HER HANDSOME!!
BZZT BZZT BZZT
KA-BOOM

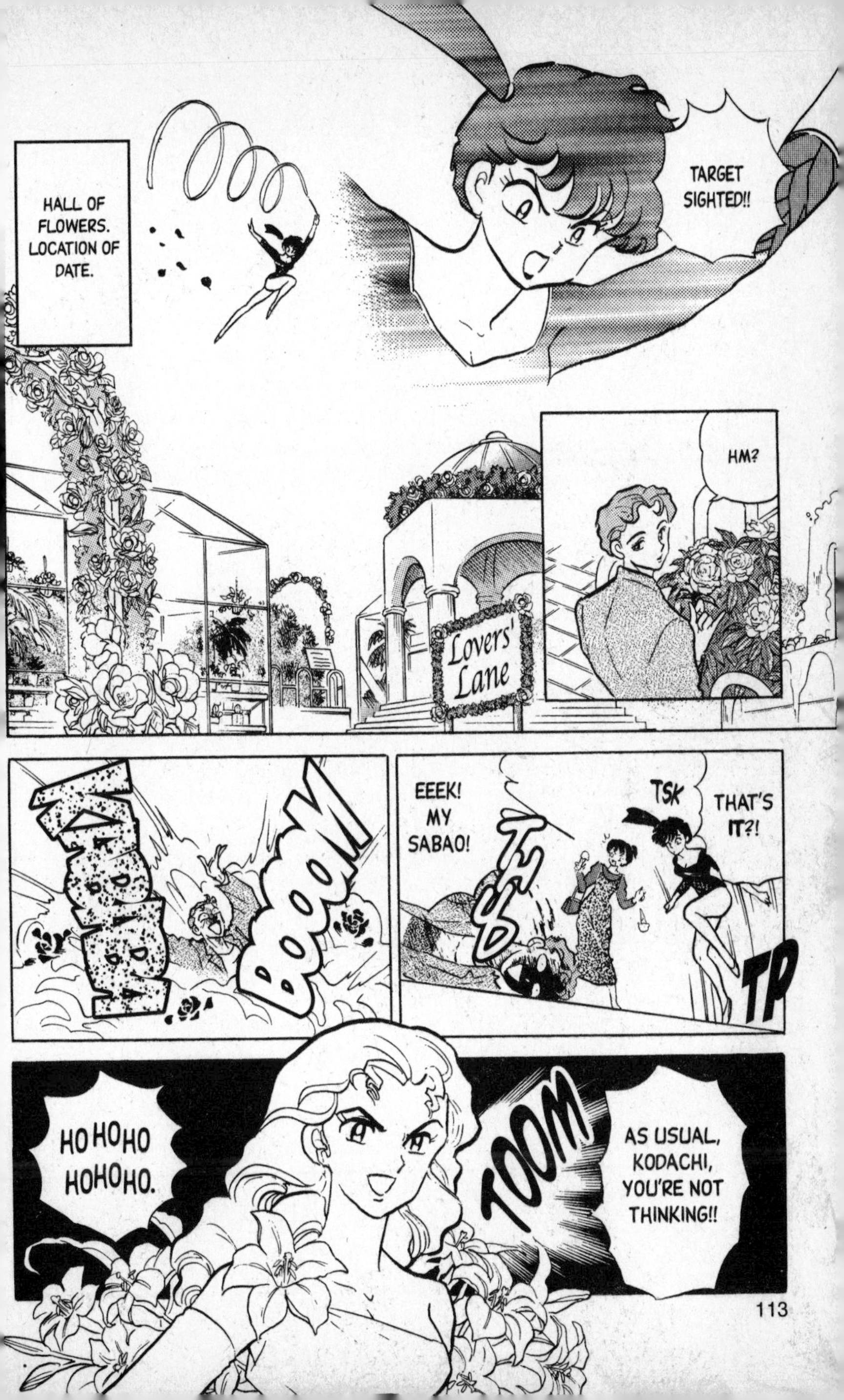
HALL OF FLOWERS. LOCATION OF DATE.
TARGET SIGHTED!!
Lovers' Lane
HM?
KA-BLAM
BOOOM
EEEK! MY SABAO!
THUD
TSK
THAT'S IT?!
TP
HO HO HO HO HO HO.
TOOM
AS USUAL, KODACHI, YOU'RE NOT THINKING!!

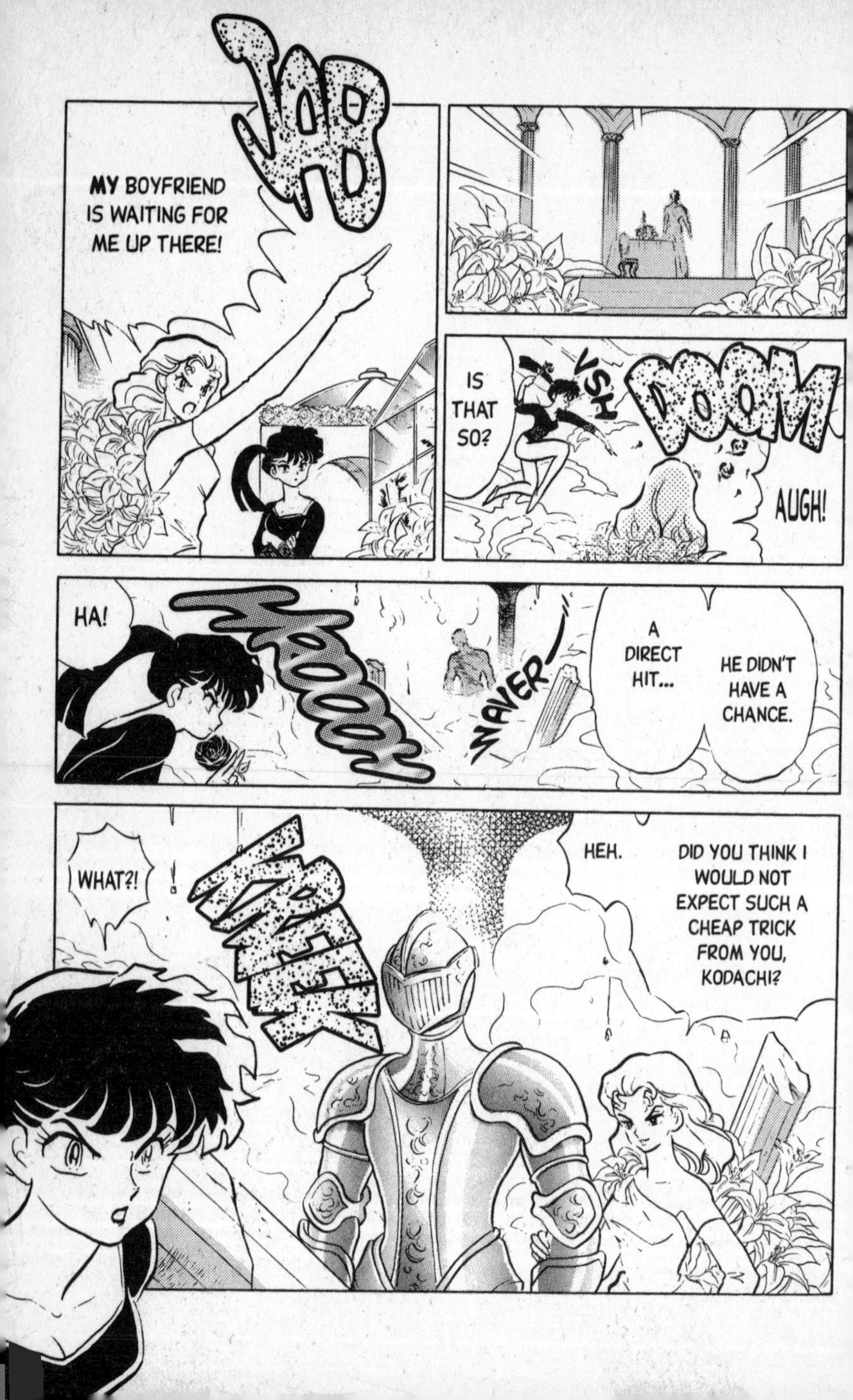
JAB
MY BOYFRIEND IS WAITING FOR ME UP THERE!
IS THAT SO?
VSH
DOOM
AUGH!
HA!
HOOOOH
WAVER
A DIRECT HIT...
HE DIDN'T HAVE A CHANCE.
WHAT?!
KREEK
HEH.
DID YOU THINK I WOULD NOT EXPECT SUCH A CHEAP TRICK FROM YOU, KODACHI?

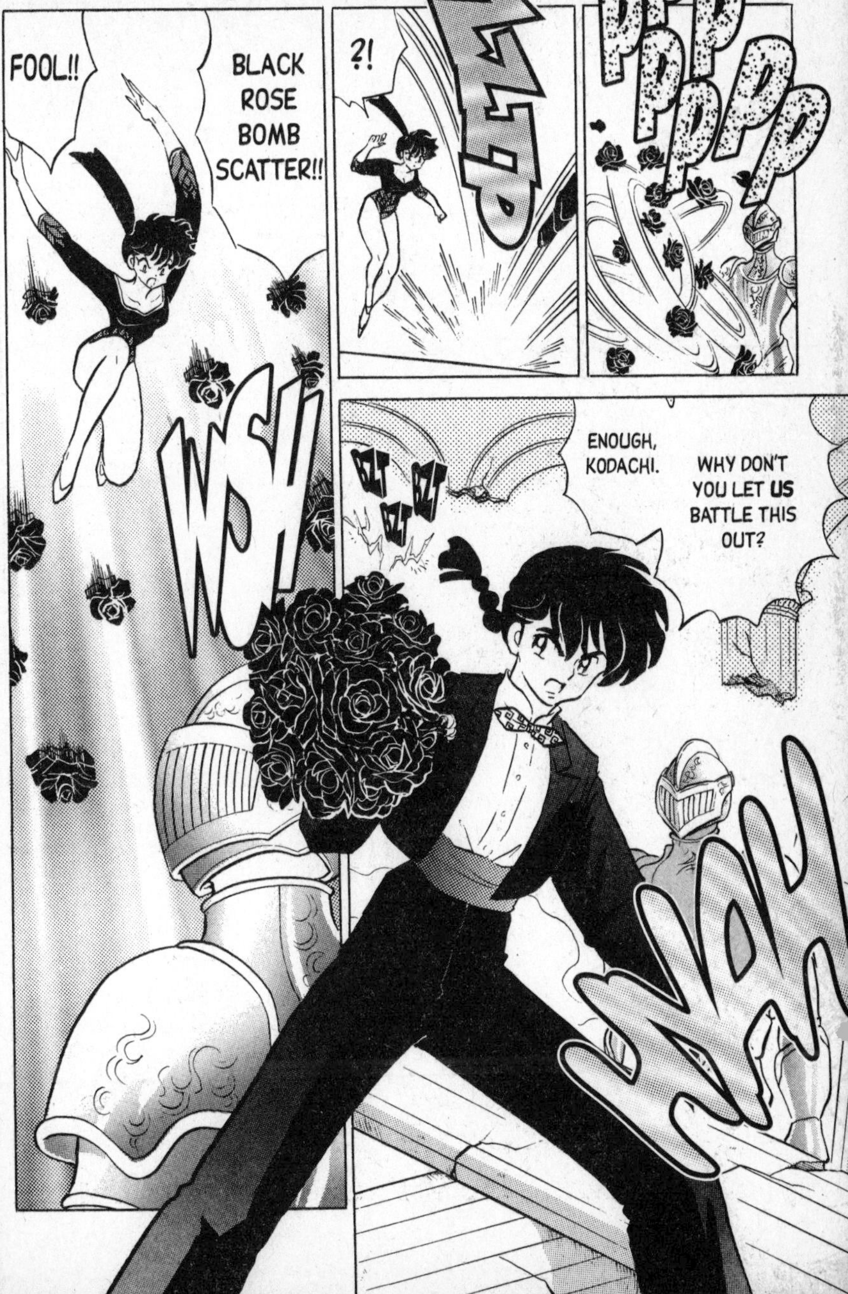
FOOL!!
BLACK ROSE BOMB SCATTER!!
WSH
?!
ZIP
PPPPPPPPP
BZT BZT BZT BZT
ENOUGH, KODACHI.
WHY DON'T YOU LET US BATTLE THIS OUT?
WHOA

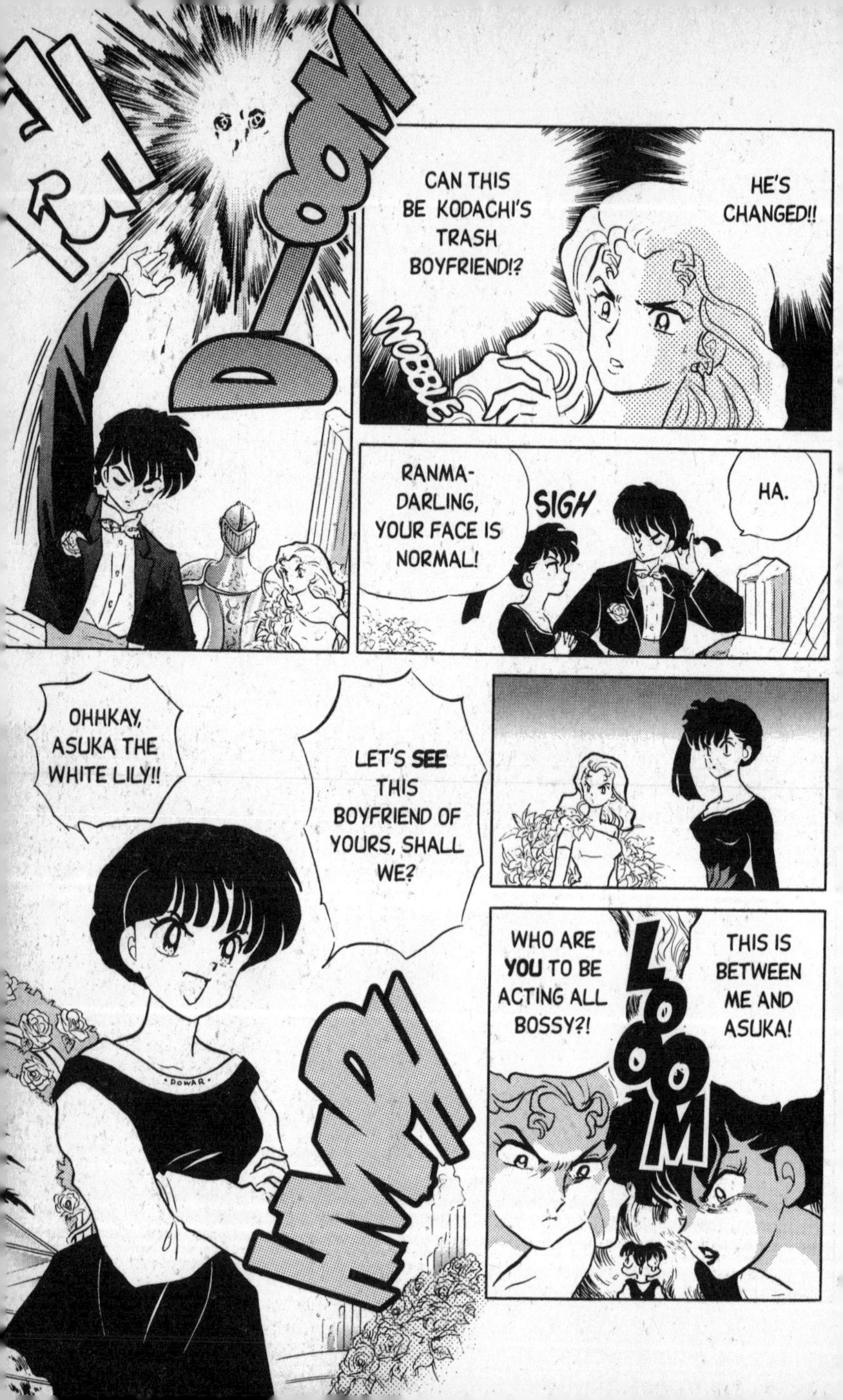
DOOM
CAN THIS BE KODACHI'S TRASH BOYFRIEND!?
HE'S CHANGED!!
WOBBLE
RANMA-DARLING, YOUR FACE IS NORMAL!
SIGH
HA.
OHHKAY, ASUKA THE WHITE LILY!!
LET'S SEE THIS BOYFRIEND OF YOURS, SHALL WE?
HMPH
WHO ARE YOU TO BE ACTING ALL BOSSY?!
LOOOM
THIS IS BETWEEN ME AND ASUKA!

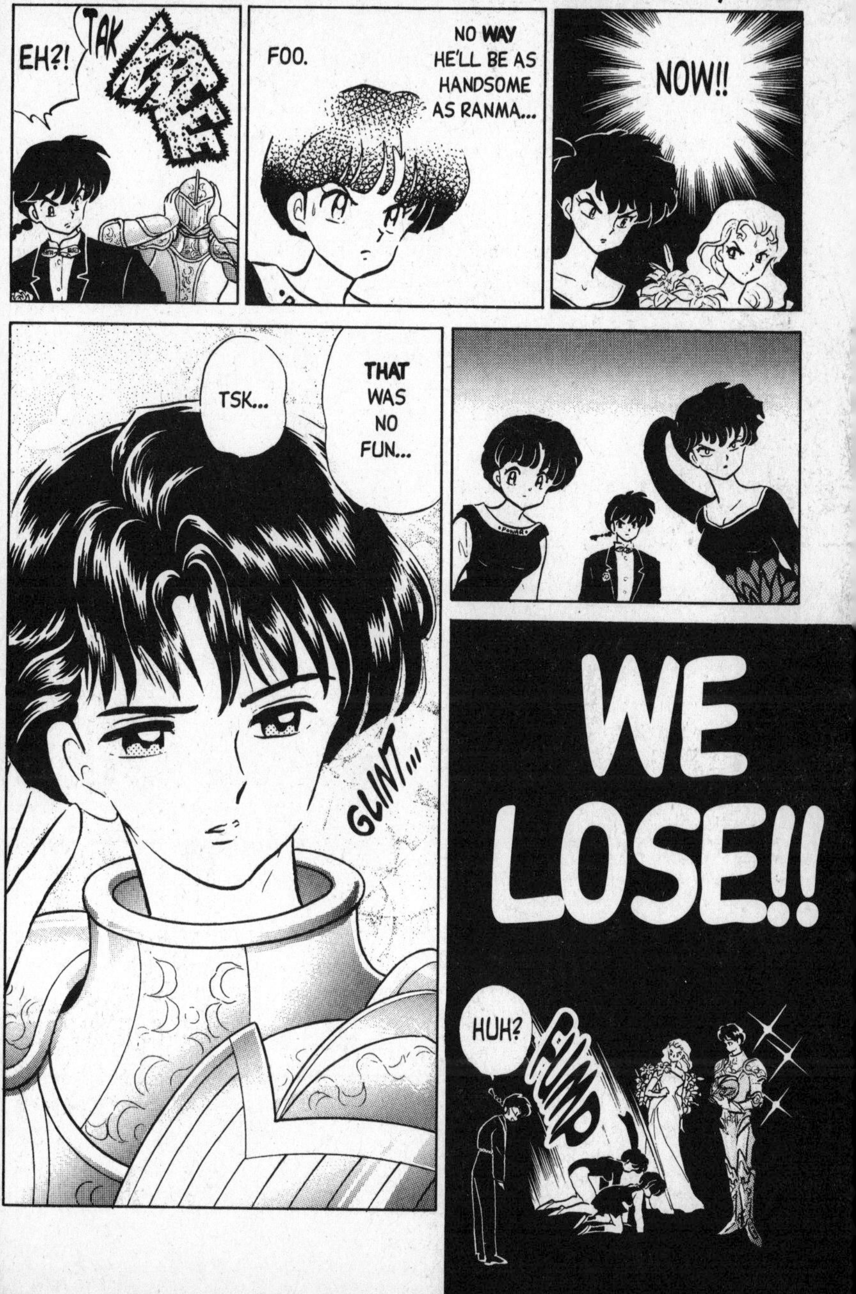
EH?!
TAK
FOO.
NO WAY HE'LL BE AS HANDSOME AS RANMA...
NOW!!
TSK...
THAT WAS NO FUN...
GLINT...
WE LOSE!!
HUH?
CLUMP

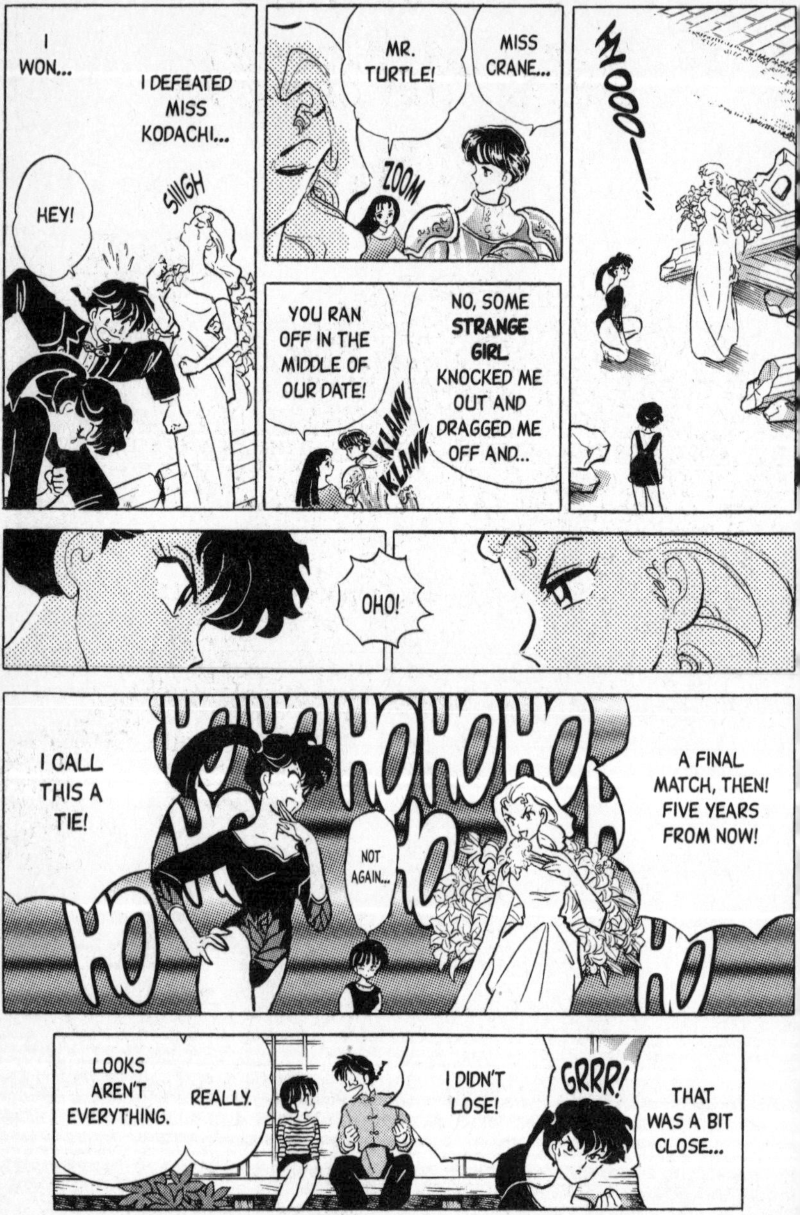

I WON...
I DEFEATED MISS KODACHI...
HEY!
SIIIGH
MR. TURTLE!
MISS CRANE...
ZOOM
YOU RAN OFF IN THE MIDDLE OF OUR DATE!
NO, SOME **STRANGE GIRL** KNOCKED ME OUT AND DRAGGED ME OFF AND...
KLANK
KLANK
WOOO—!!
OHO!
I CALL THIS A TIE!
HOHOHO
NOT AGAIN...
A FINAL MATCH, THEN! FIVE YEARS FROM NOW!
HO
HO
LOOKS AREN'T EVERYTHING.
REALLY.
I DIDN'T LOSE!
GRRR!
THAT WAS A BIT CLOSE...

PART 8

THE CHOSEN ONE

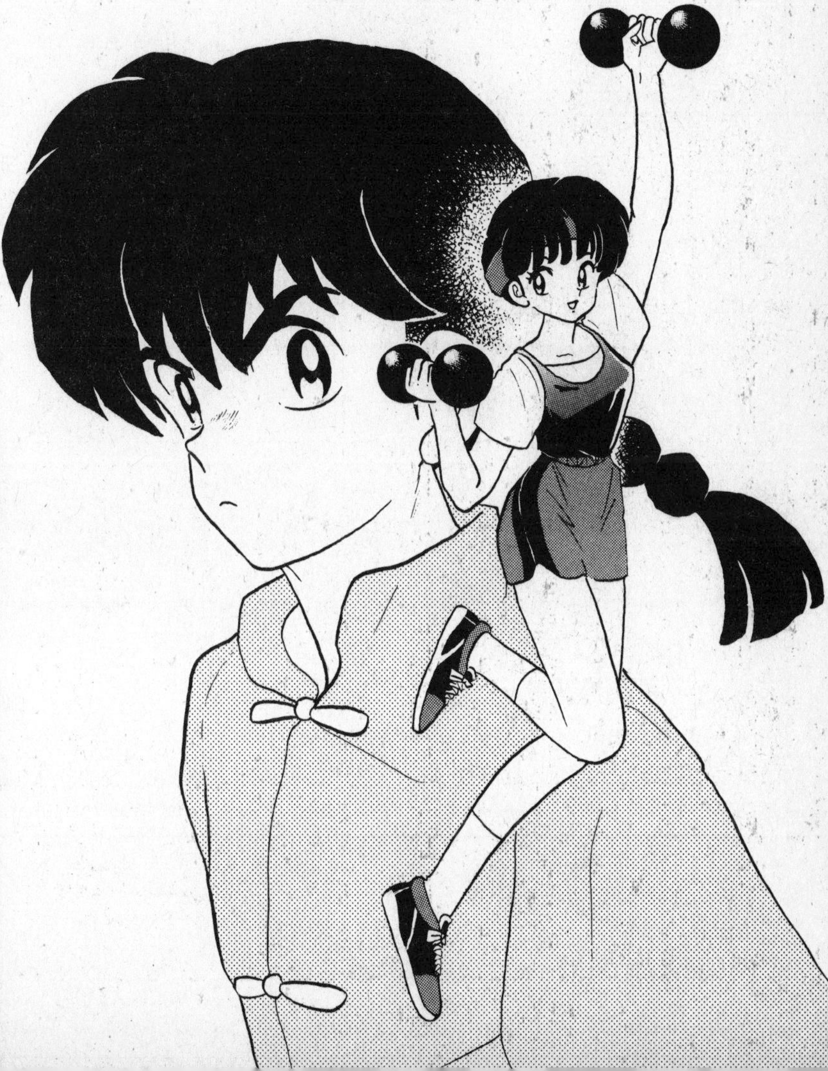

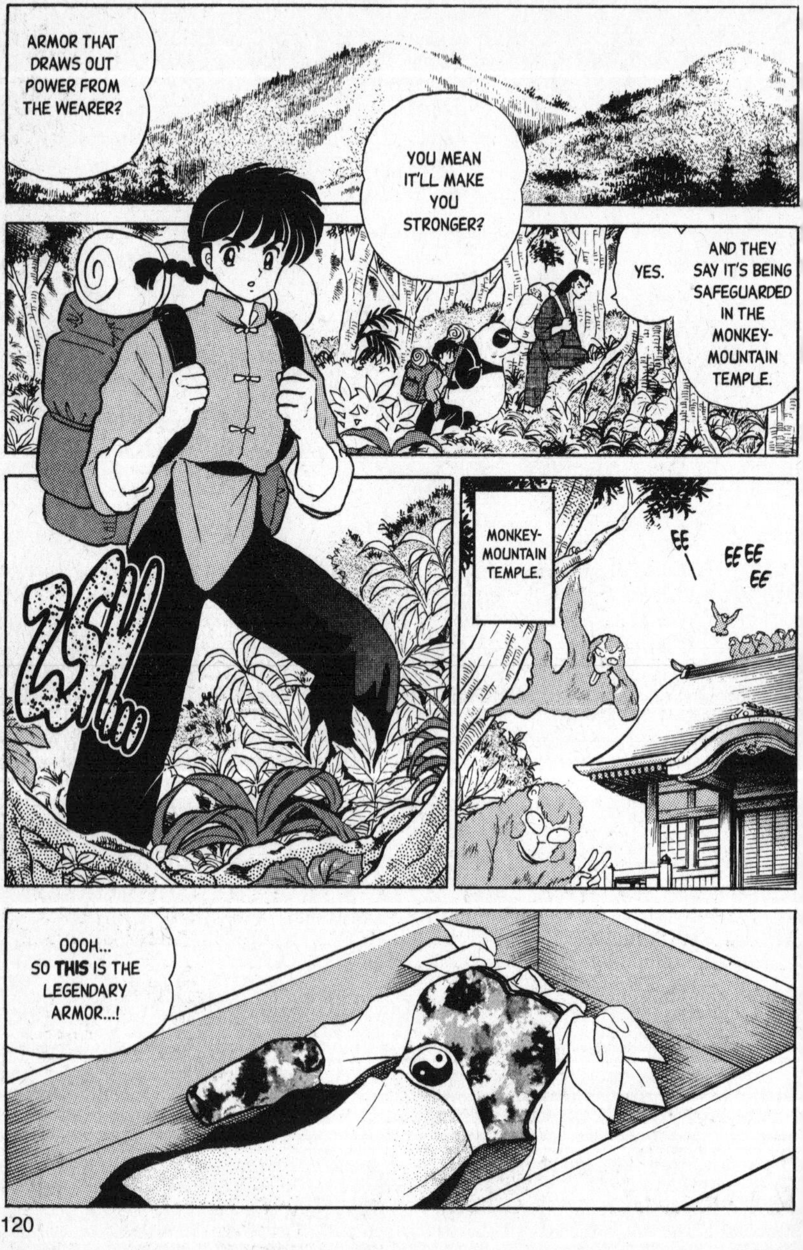
ARMOR THAT DRAWS OUT POWER FROM THE WEARER?
YOU MEAN IT'LL MAKE YOU STRONGER?
YES.
AND THEY SAY IT'S BEING SAFEGUARDED IN THE MONKEY-MOUNTAIN TEMPLE.
MONKEY-MOUNTAIN TEMPLE.
EE
EE EE EE
OOOH... SO **THIS** IS THE LEGENDARY ARMOR...!

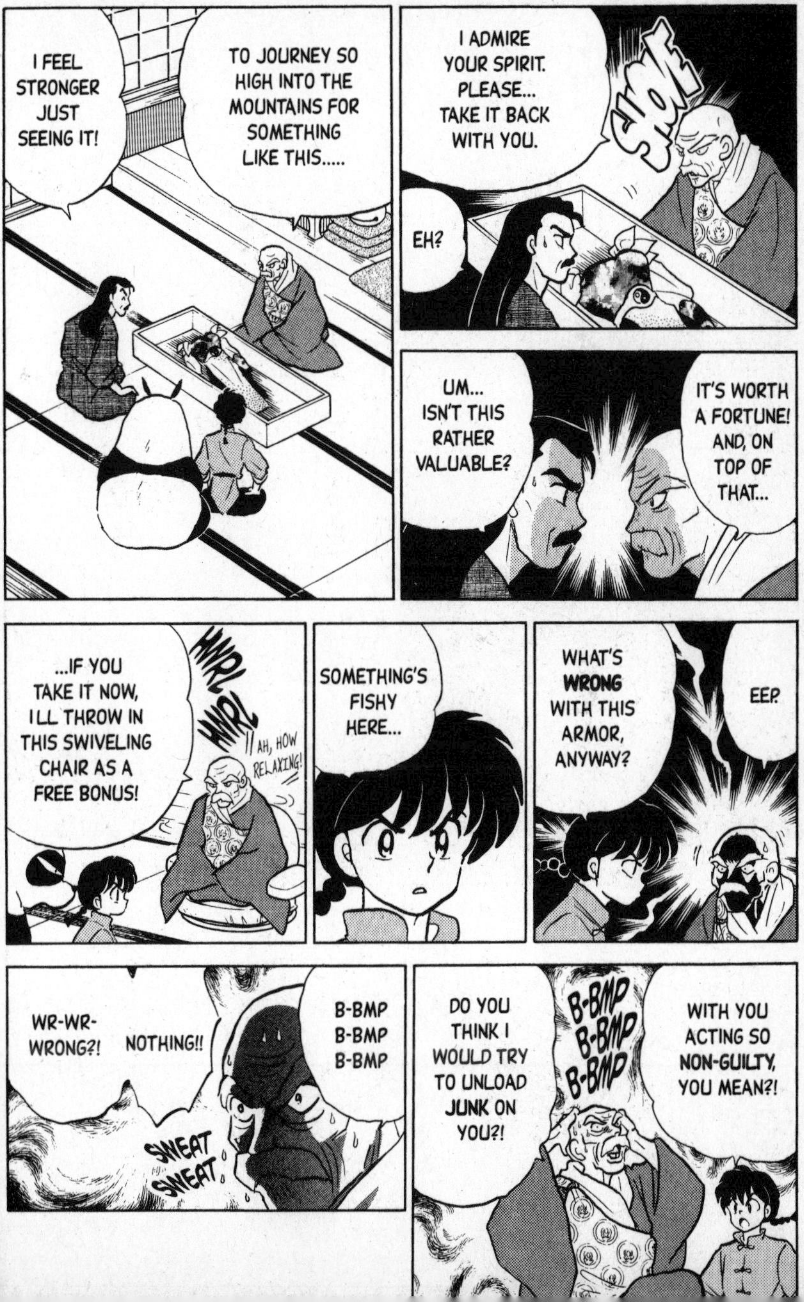
I FEEL STRONGER JUST SEEING IT!
TO JOURNEY SO HIGH INTO THE MOUNTAINS FOR SOMETHING LIKE THIS.....
I ADMIRE YOUR SPIRIT. PLEASE... TAKE IT BACK WITH YOU.
SHOVE
EH?
UM... ISN'T THIS RATHER VALUABLE?
IT'S WORTH A FORTUNE! AND, ON TOP OF THAT...
...IF YOU TAKE IT NOW, I'LL THROW IN THIS SWIVELING CHAIR AS A FREE BONUS!
HWRL HWRL
AH, HOW RELAXING!
SOMETHING'S FISHY HERE...
WHAT'S WRONG WITH THIS ARMOR, ANYWAY?
EEP.
WR-WR-WRONG?!
NOTHING!!
SWEAT SWEAT
B-BMP B-BMP B-BMP
DO YOU THINK I WOULD TRY TO UNLOAD JUNK ON YOU?!
B-BMP B-BMP B-BMP
WITH YOU ACTING SO NON-GUILTY, YOU MEAN?!

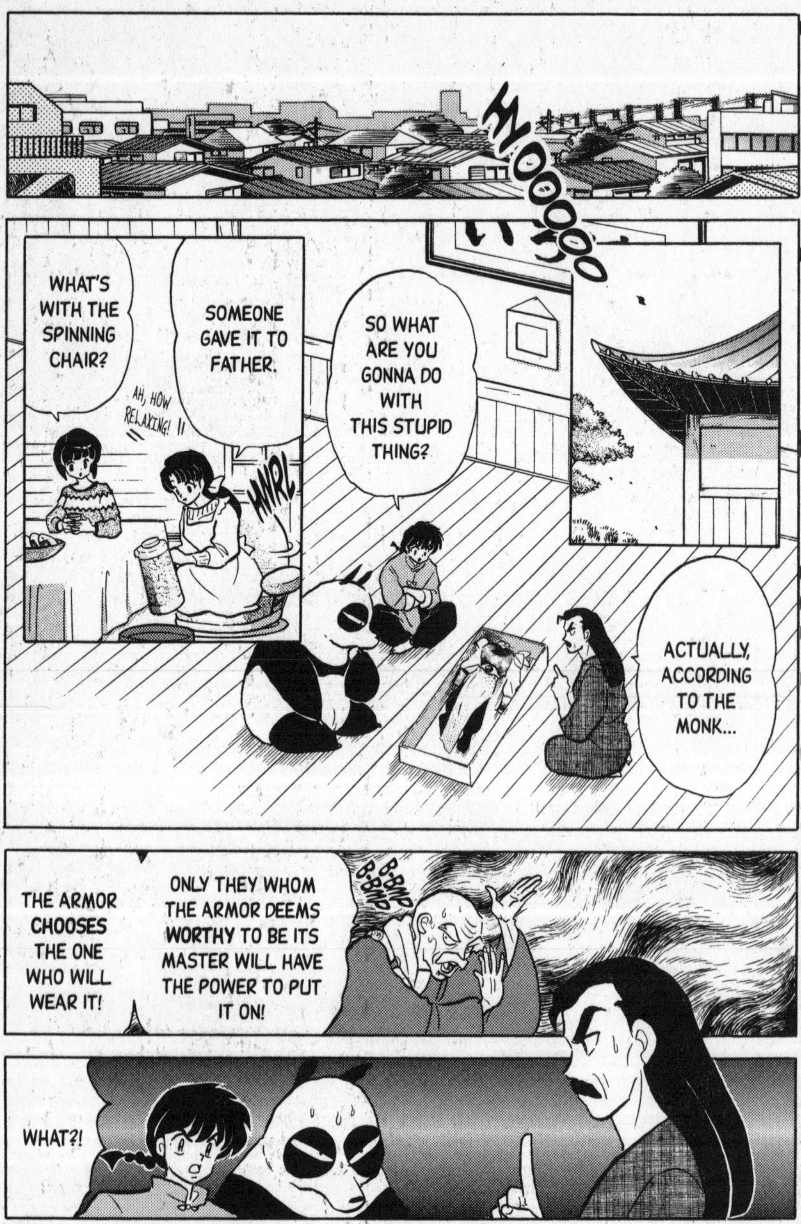
KYOOOOOO
WHAT'S WITH THE SPINNING CHAIR?
SOMEONE GAVE IT TO FATHER.
AH, HOW RELAXING!
WHIRL
SO WHAT ARE YOU GONNA DO WITH THIS STUPID THING?
ACTUALLY, ACCORDING TO THE MONK...
THE ARMOR CHOOSES THE ONE WHO WILL WEAR IT!
ONLY THEY WHOM THE ARMOR DEEMS WORTHY TO BE ITS MASTER WILL HAVE THE POWER TO PUT IT ON!
B-BMP B-BMP
WHAT?!

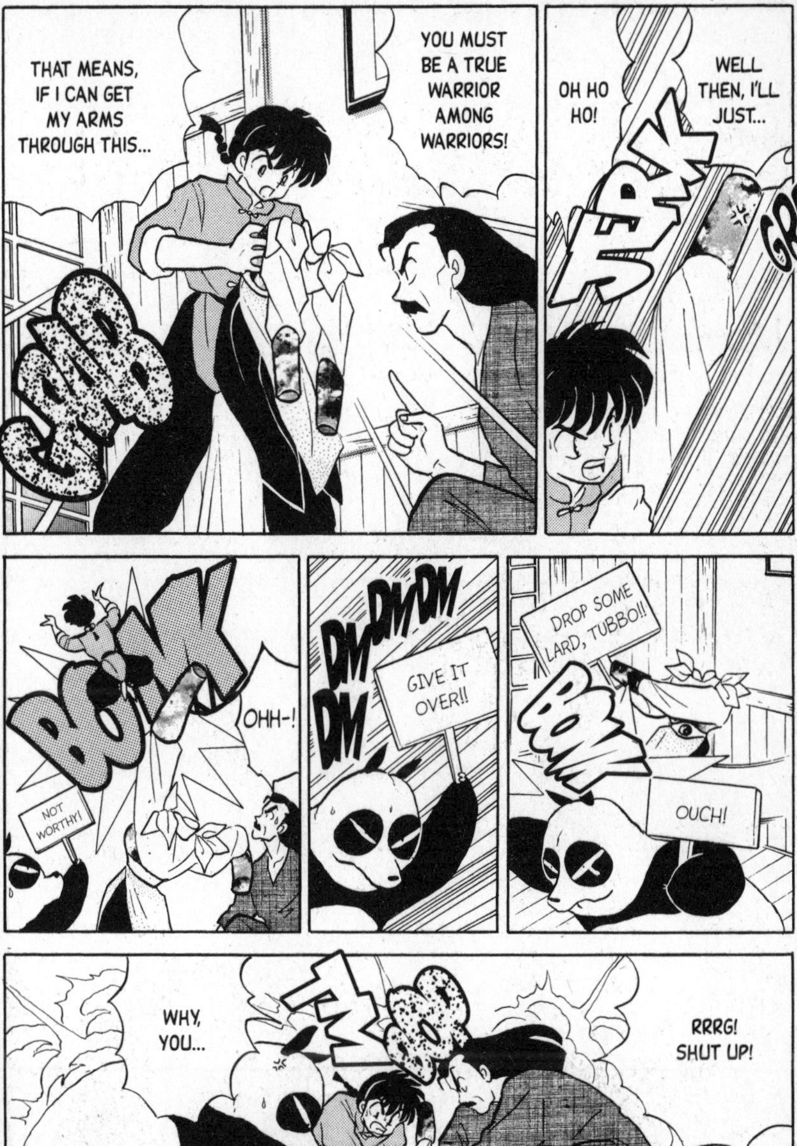
THAT MEANS, IF I CAN GET MY ARMS THROUGH THIS...
YOU MUST BE A TRUE WARRIOR AMONG WARRIORS!
OH HO HO!
WELL THEN, I'LL JUST...
JERK
GRR
BOINK
OHH-!
NOT WORTHY!
DM DM DM DM DM
GIVE IT OVER!!
DROP SOME LARD, TUBBO!!
BONK
OUCH!
WHY, YOU...
RRRG! SHUT UP!

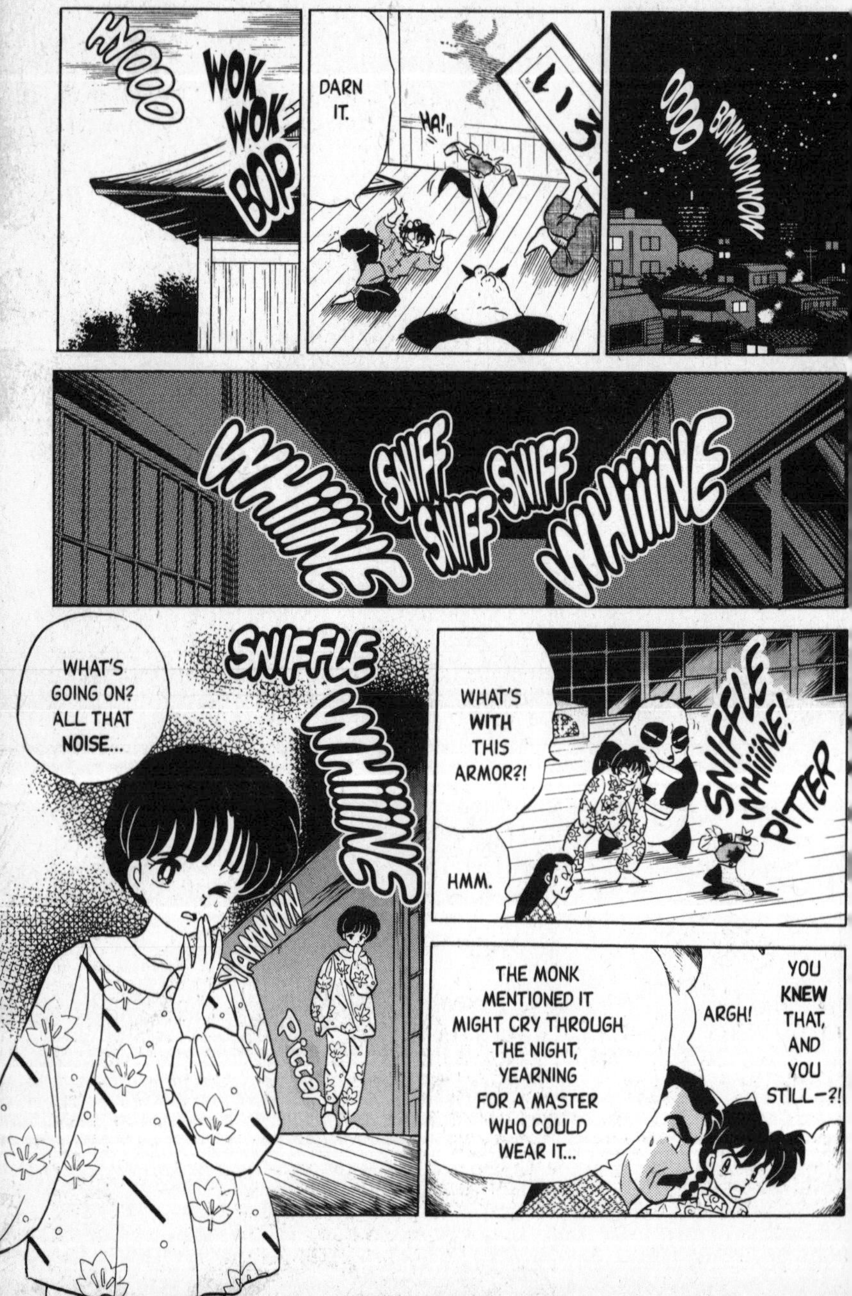
HYOOO
WOK WOK BOP
DARN IT.
HA!!
OOOO BOWWOWWOW
WHIIIINE
SNIFF SNIFF
SNIFF
WHIIINE
WHAT'S GOING ON? ALL THAT NOISE...
SNIFFLE
WHIIIINE
YAWWWN
Pitter
WHAT'S WITH THIS ARMOR?!
HMM.
SNIFFLE WHIIIINE! PITTER
THE MONK MENTIONED IT MIGHT CRY THROUGH THE NIGHT, YEARNING FOR A MASTER WHO COULD WEAR IT...
ARGH!
YOU KNEW THAT, AND YOU STILL-?!

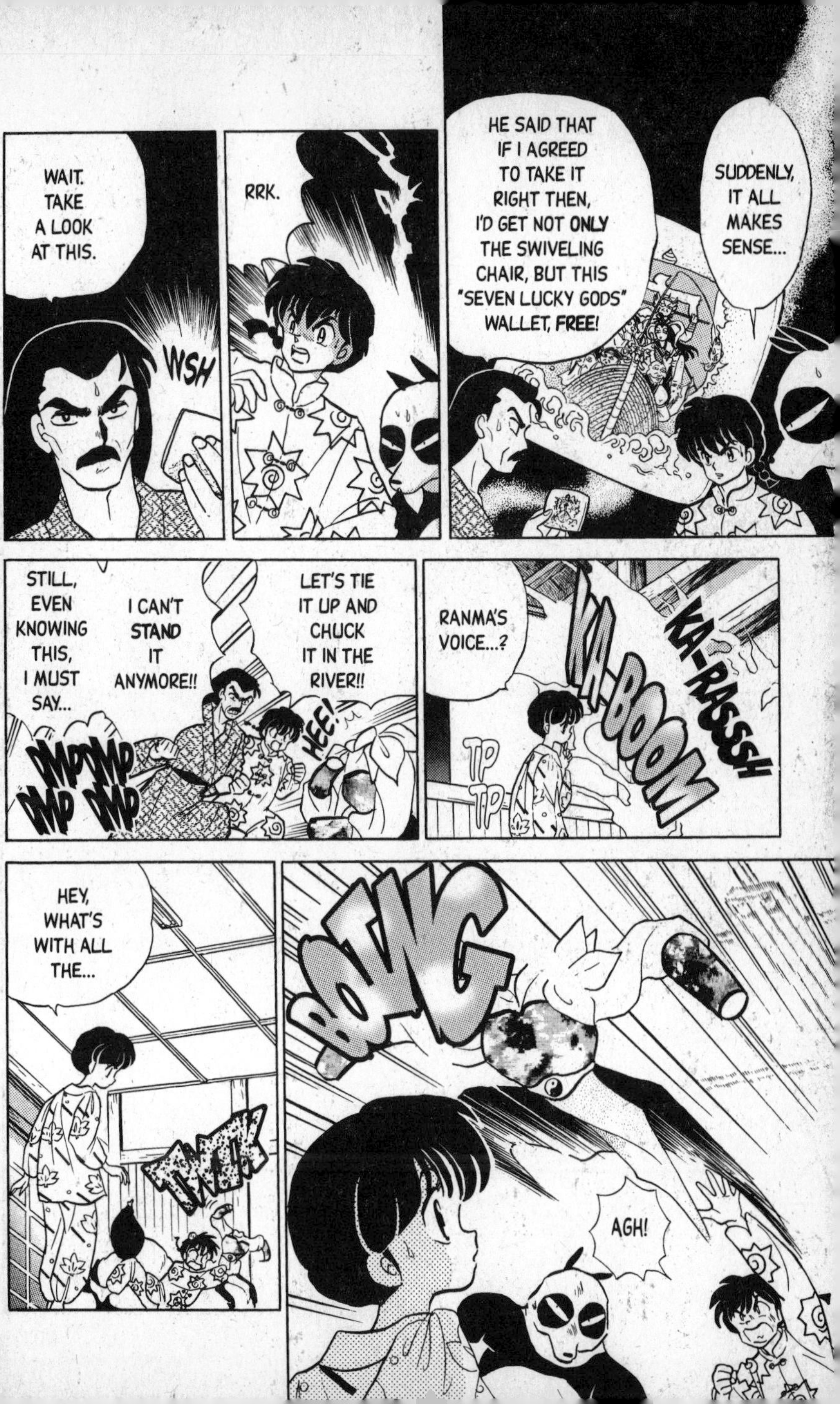
WAIT. TAKE A LOOK AT THIS.
WSH
RRK.
HE SAID THAT IF I AGREED TO TAKE IT RIGHT THEN, I'D GET NOT ONLY THE SWIVELING CHAIR, BUT THIS "SEVEN LUCKY GODS" WALLET, FREE!
SUDDENLY, IT ALL MAKES SENSE...
STILL, EVEN KNOWING THIS, I MUST SAY...
I CAN'T STAND IT ANYMORE!!
LET'S TIE IT UP AND CHUCK IT IN THE RIVER!!
HEE!
DMP DMP DMP DMP
RANMA'S VOICE...?
KA-RASSSH
KA-BOOM
TP TP
HEY, WHAT'S WITH ALL THE...
BOING
AGH!

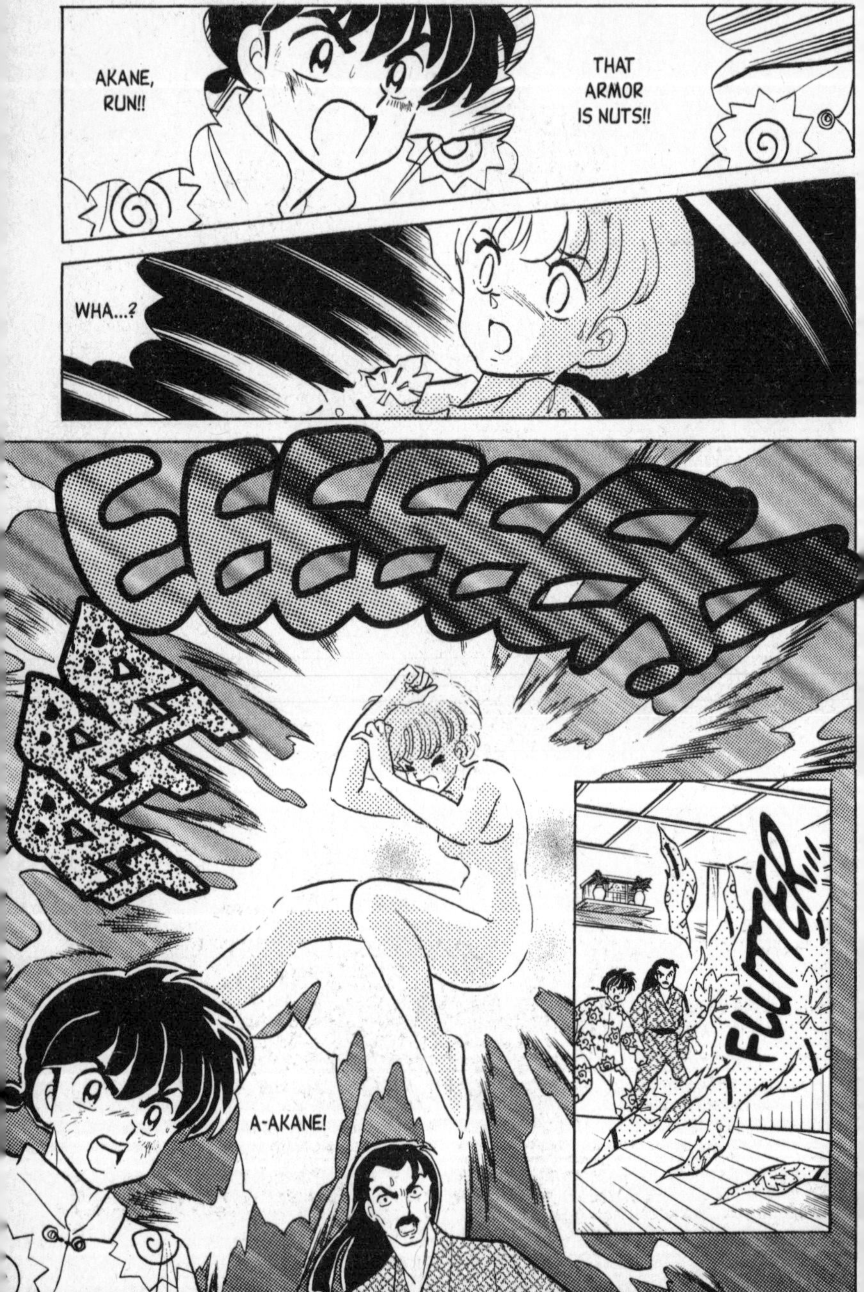
AKANE, RUN!!
THAT ARMOR IS NUTS!!
WHA...?
A-AKANE!
FLUTTER...!!

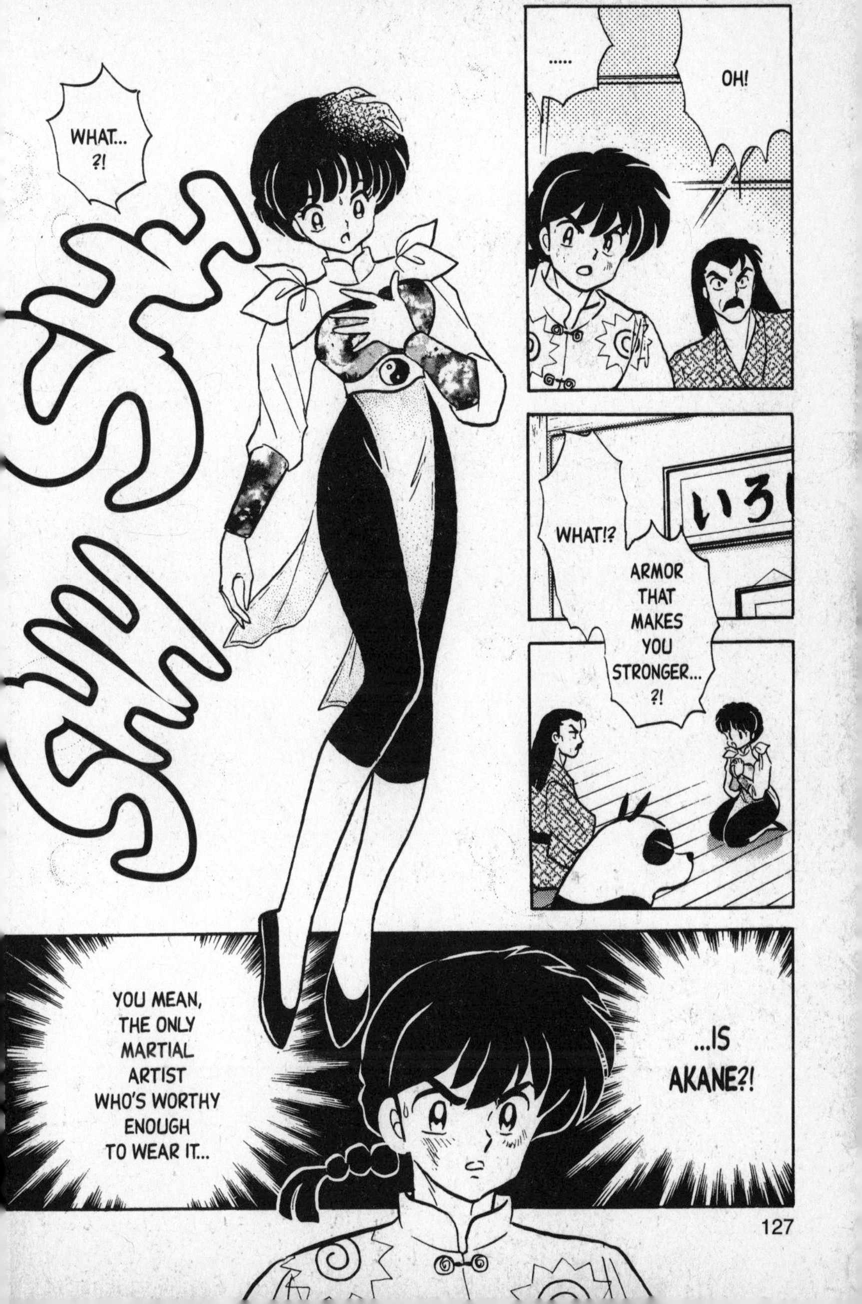
WHAT... ?!
.....
OH!
WHAT!?
ARMOR THAT MAKES YOU STRONGER... ?!
YOU MEAN, THE ONLY MARTIAL ARTIST WHO'S WORTHY ENOUGH TO WEAR IT...
...IS AKANE?!

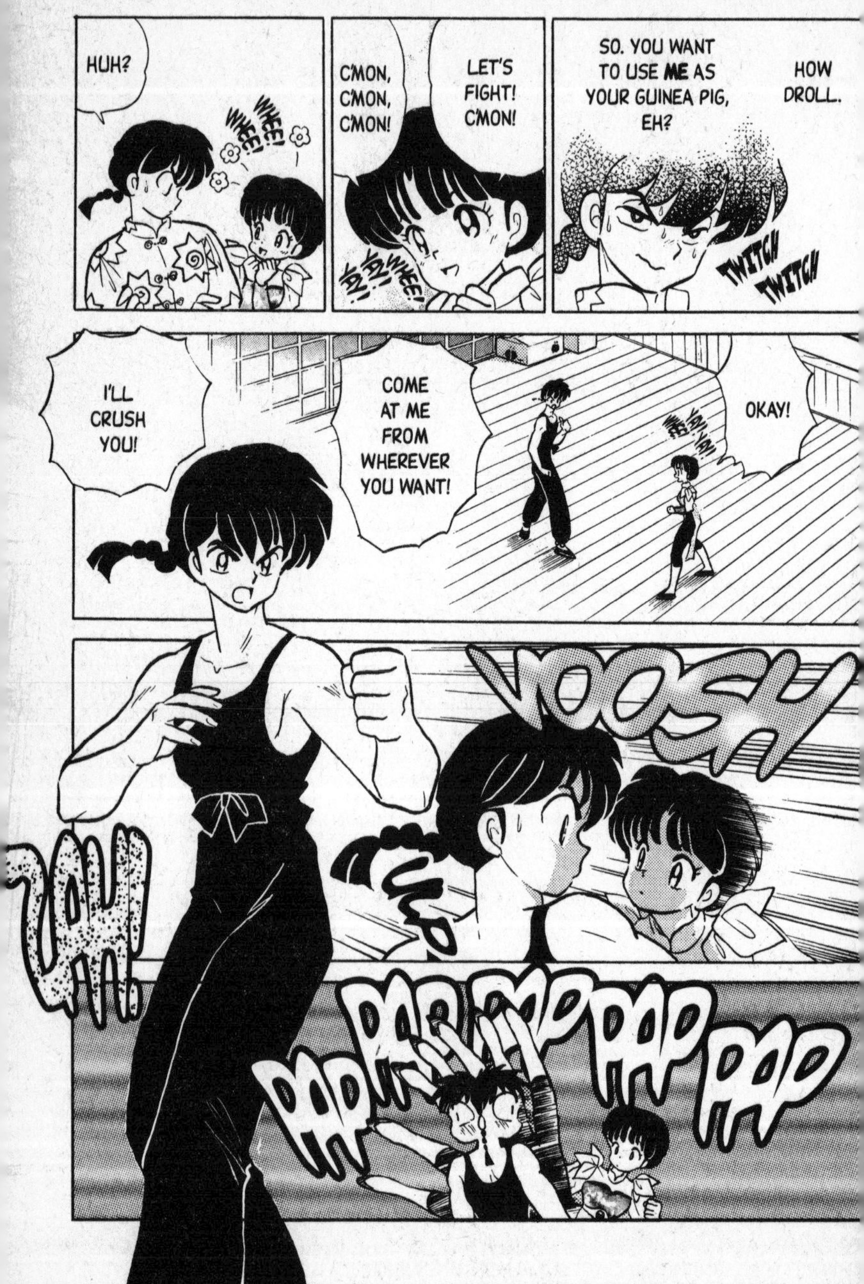
HUH?
WHEE! WHEE!
C'MON, C'MON, C'MON!
LET'S FIGHT! C'MON!
YAY! YAY! WHEE!
SO. YOU WANT TO USE **ME** AS YOUR GUINEA PIG, EH?
HOW DROLL.
TWITCH TWITCH
I'LL CRUSH YOU!
COME AT ME FROM WHEREVER YOU WANT!
OKAY!
WHEE! YAY! YAY!
VOOSH
YAH!!
ULP
PAP PAP PAP PAP PAP PAP PAP

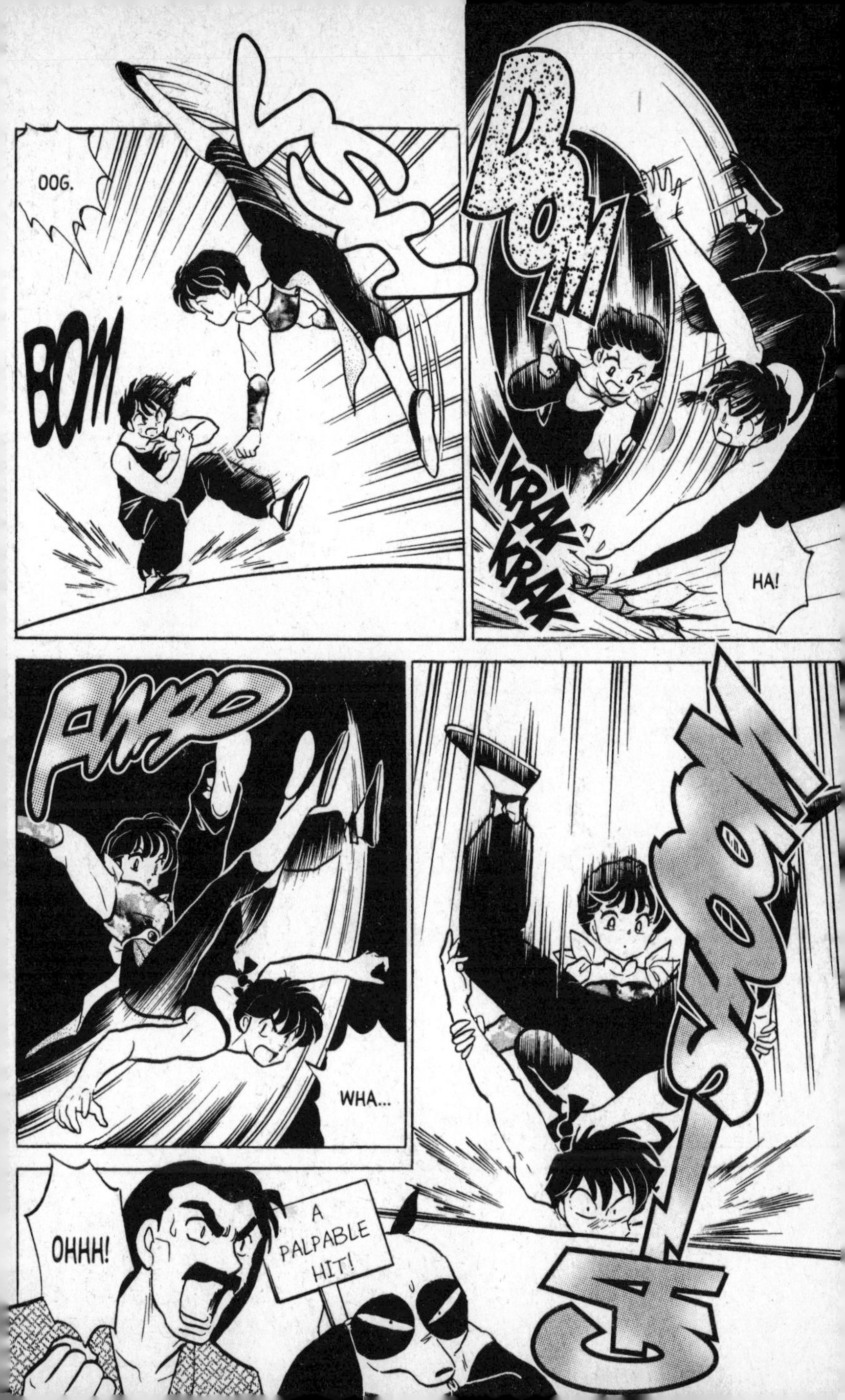
OOG.
BOM
KRAK KRAK
HA!
WHA...
OHHH!
A PALPABLE HIT!

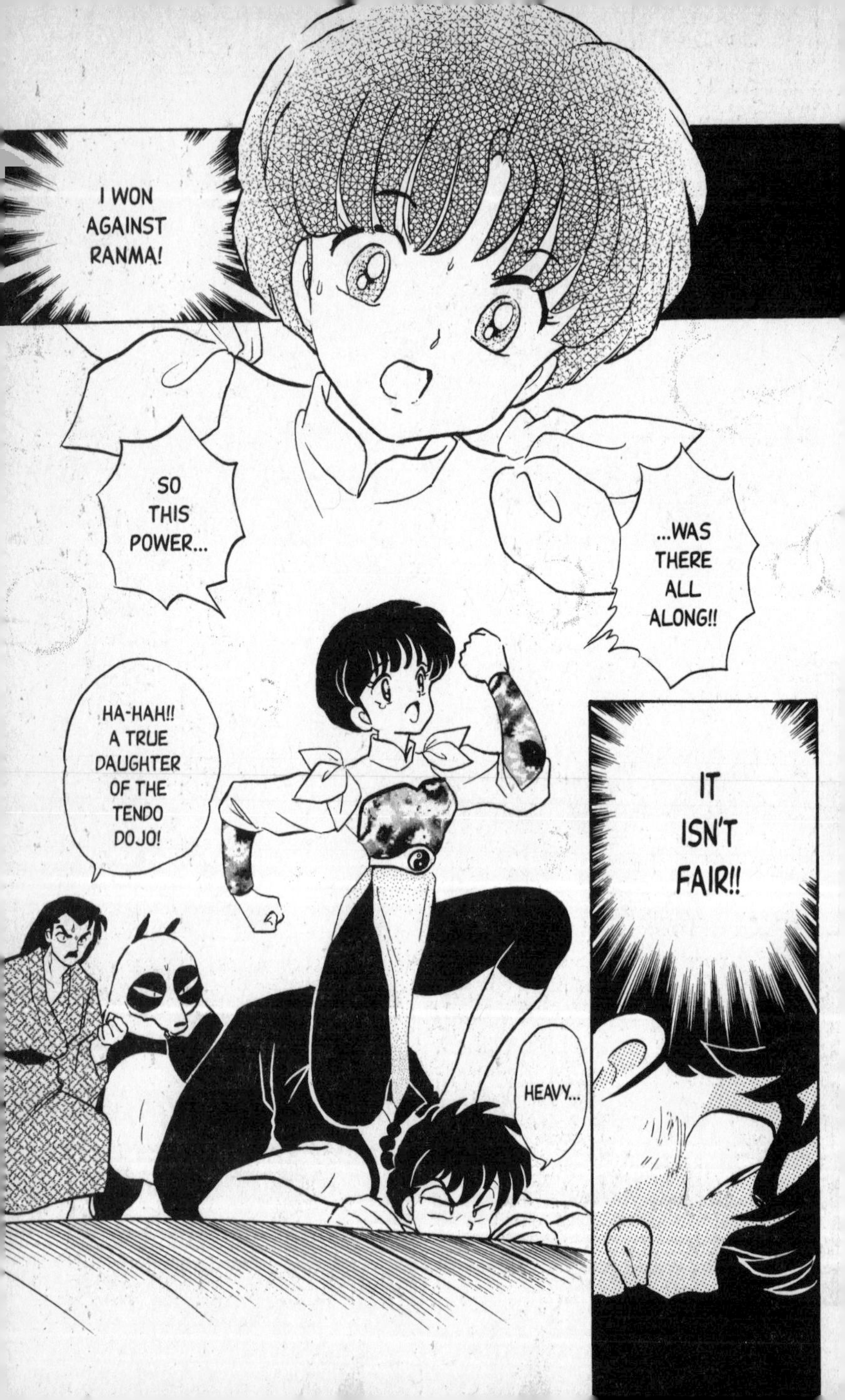
I WON AGAINST RANMA!
SO THIS POWER...
...WAS THERE ALL ALONG!!
HA-HAH!! A TRUE DAUGHTER OF THE TENDO DOJO!
HEAVY...
IT ISN'T FAIR!!

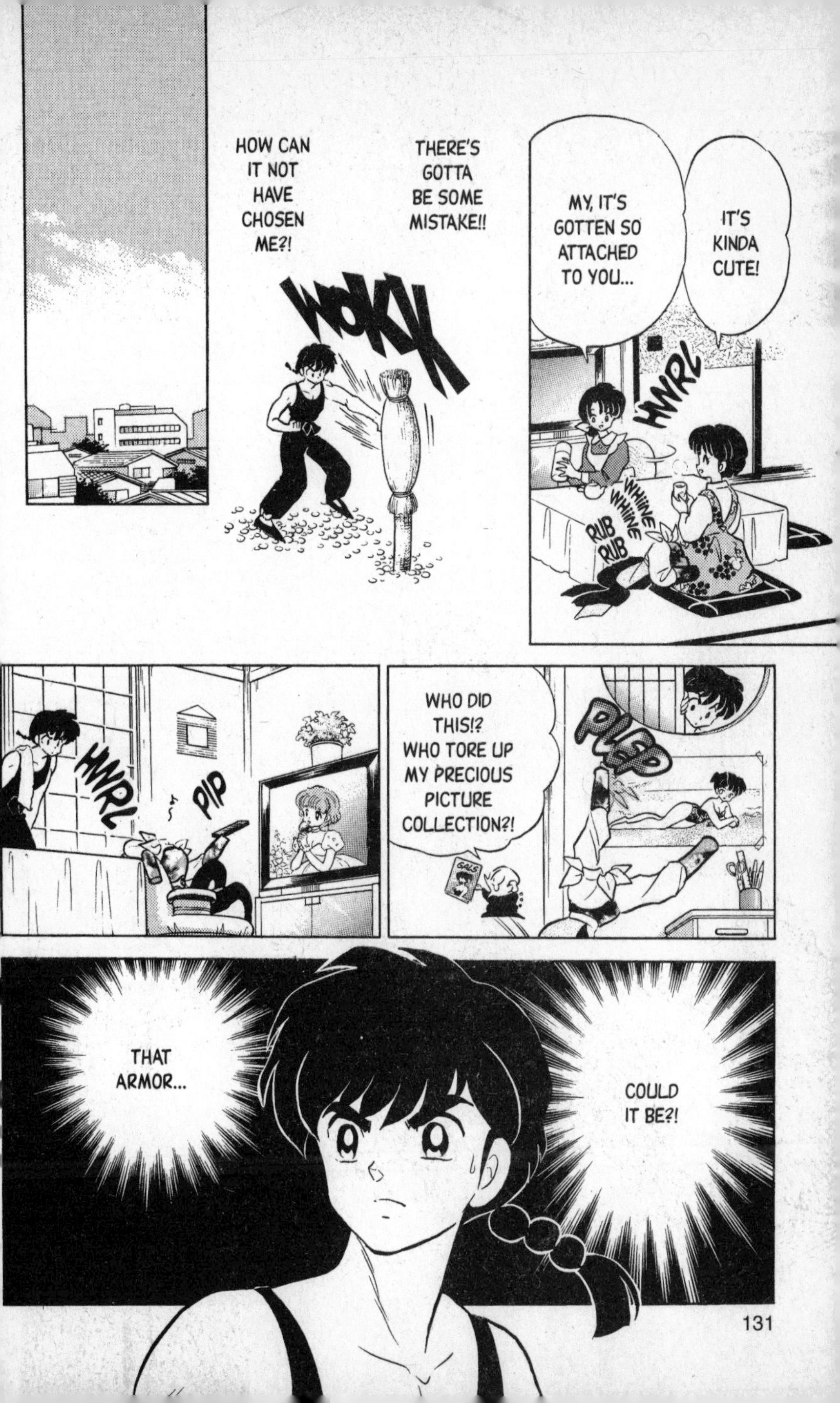

HOW CAN IT NOT HAVE CHOSEN ME?!
THERE'S GOTTA BE SOME MISTAKE!!
WOKK
MY, IT'S GOTTEN SO ATTACHED TO YOU...
IT'S KINDA CUTE!
HWRL
WHINE WHINE
RUB RUB
HWRL
PIP
WHO DID THIS!? WHO TORE UP MY PRECIOUS PICTURE COLLECTION?!
GALS
PLAP
THAT ARMOR...
COULD IT BE?!

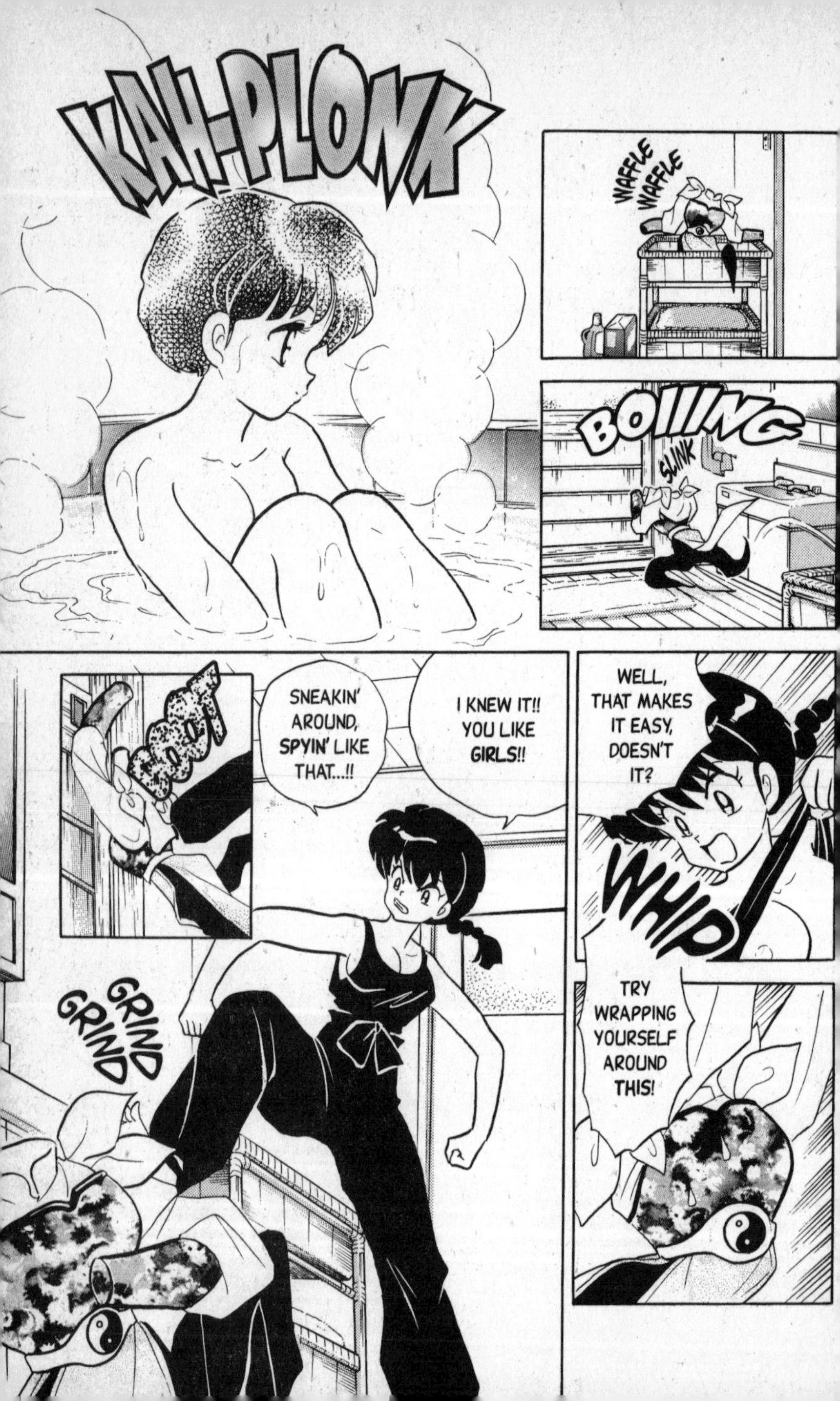
KAH-PLONK
WAFFLE WAFFLE
BOIIING
SLINK
SNEAKIN' AROUND, SPYIN' LIKE THAT...!!
I KNEW IT!! YOU LIKE GIRLS!!
GRIND GRIND
WELL, THAT MAKES IT EASY, DOESN'T IT?
WHIP
TRY WRAPPING YOURSELF AROUND THIS!

RRH!

TOO TIGHT... AROUND THE CHEST!!!

AND THE WAIST, IT'S SO LOOSE!!

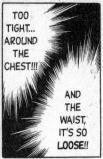

SKWEEE

YEAH...

IT REJECTED ME...

THAT MEANS...

YOU GOTTA BE **THICK-WAISTED** TO EVEN WEAR IT?!

PAT PAT

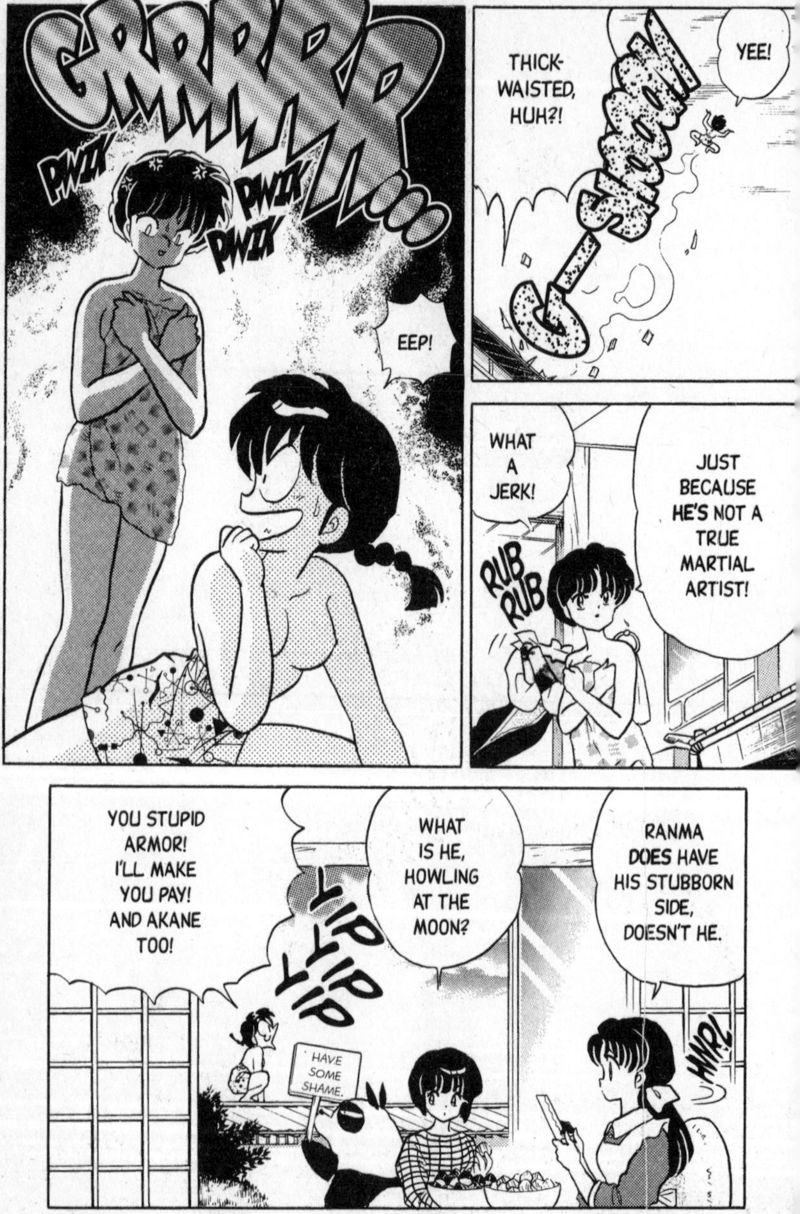
GRRRR...
PWIK
PWIK
PWIK
EEP!
THICK-WAISTED, HUH?!
YEE!
WHAT A JERK!
RUB RUB
JUST BECAUSE HE'S NOT A TRUE MARTIAL ARTIST!
YOU STUPID ARMOR! I'LL MAKE YOU PAY! AND AKANE TOO!
YIP YIP YIP
WHAT IS HE, HOWLING AT THE MOON?
HAVE SOME SHAME.
RANMA DOES HAVE HIS STUBBORN SIDE, DOESN'T HE.

PART 9
RANMA'S PLOT

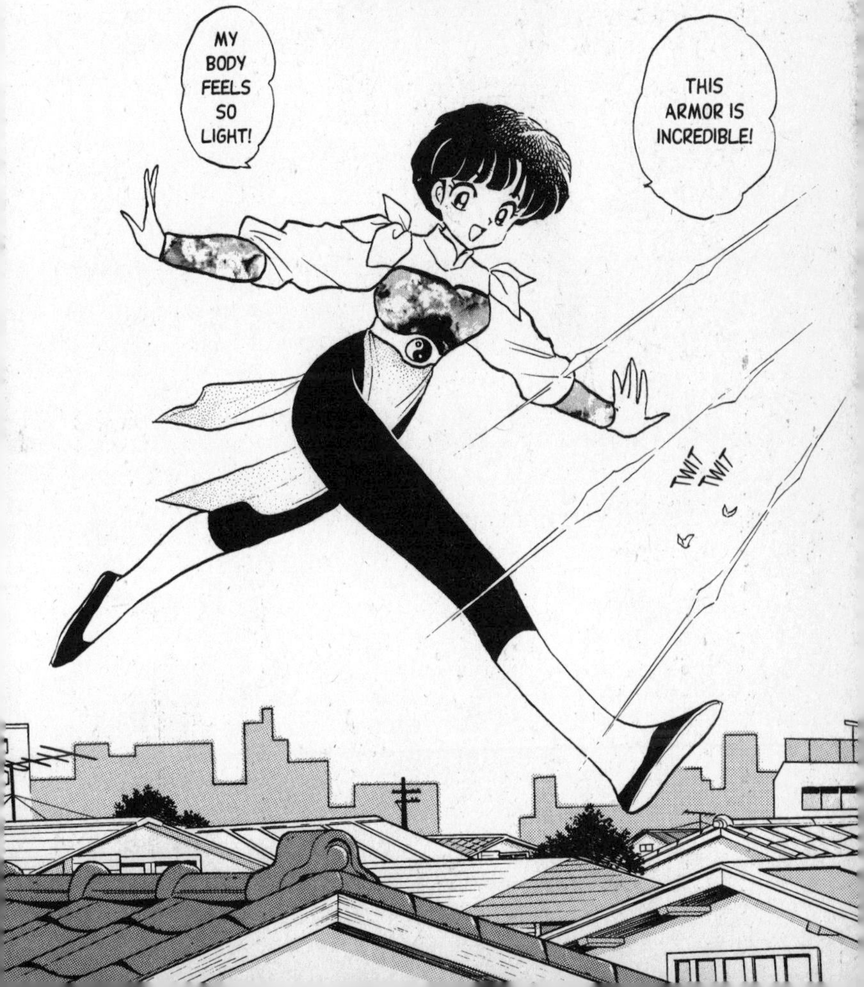
MY BODY FEELS SO LIGHT!
THIS ARMOR IS INCREDIBLE!
TWIT TWIT

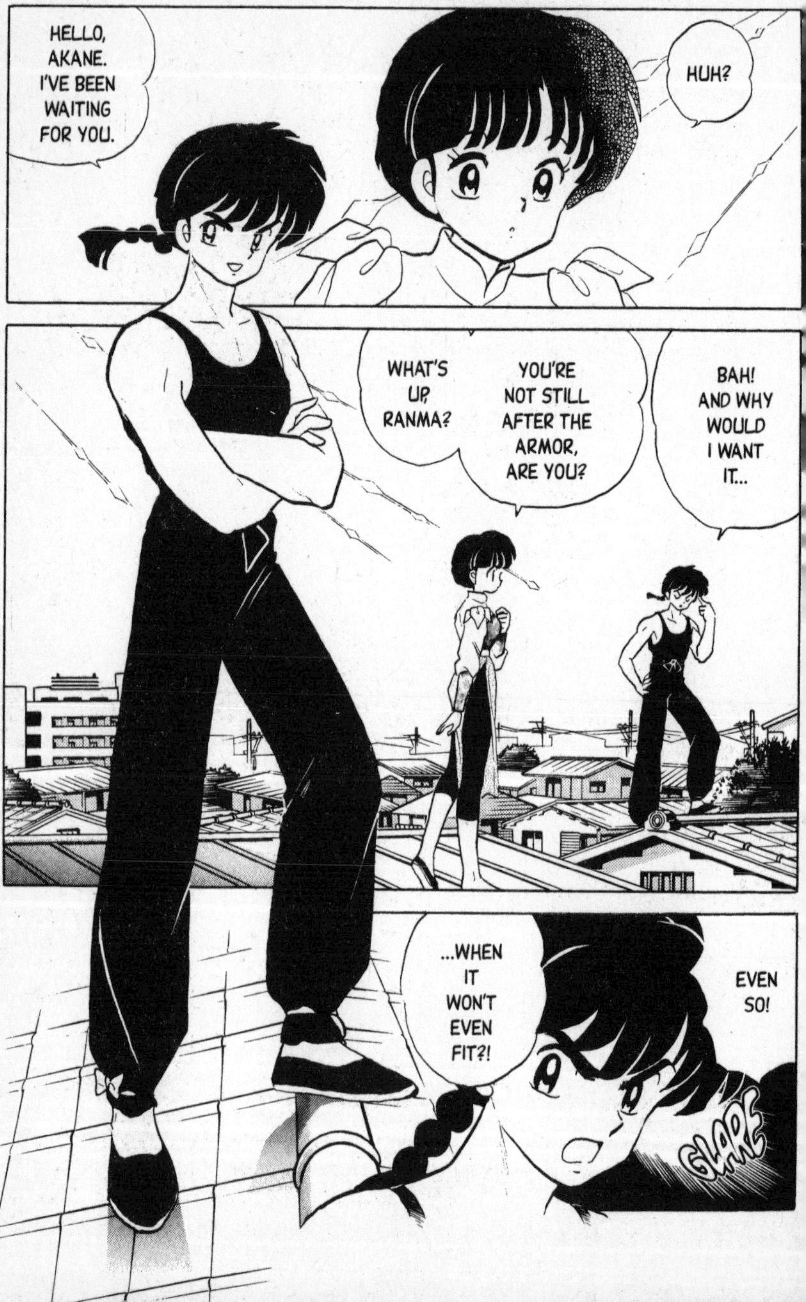
HELLO, AKANE. I'VE BEEN WAITING FOR YOU.
HUH?
WHAT'S UP, RANMA?
YOU'RE NOT STILL AFTER THE ARMOR, ARE YOU?
BAH! AND WHY WOULD I WANT IT...
...WHEN IT WON'T EVEN FIT?!
EVEN SO!
GLARE

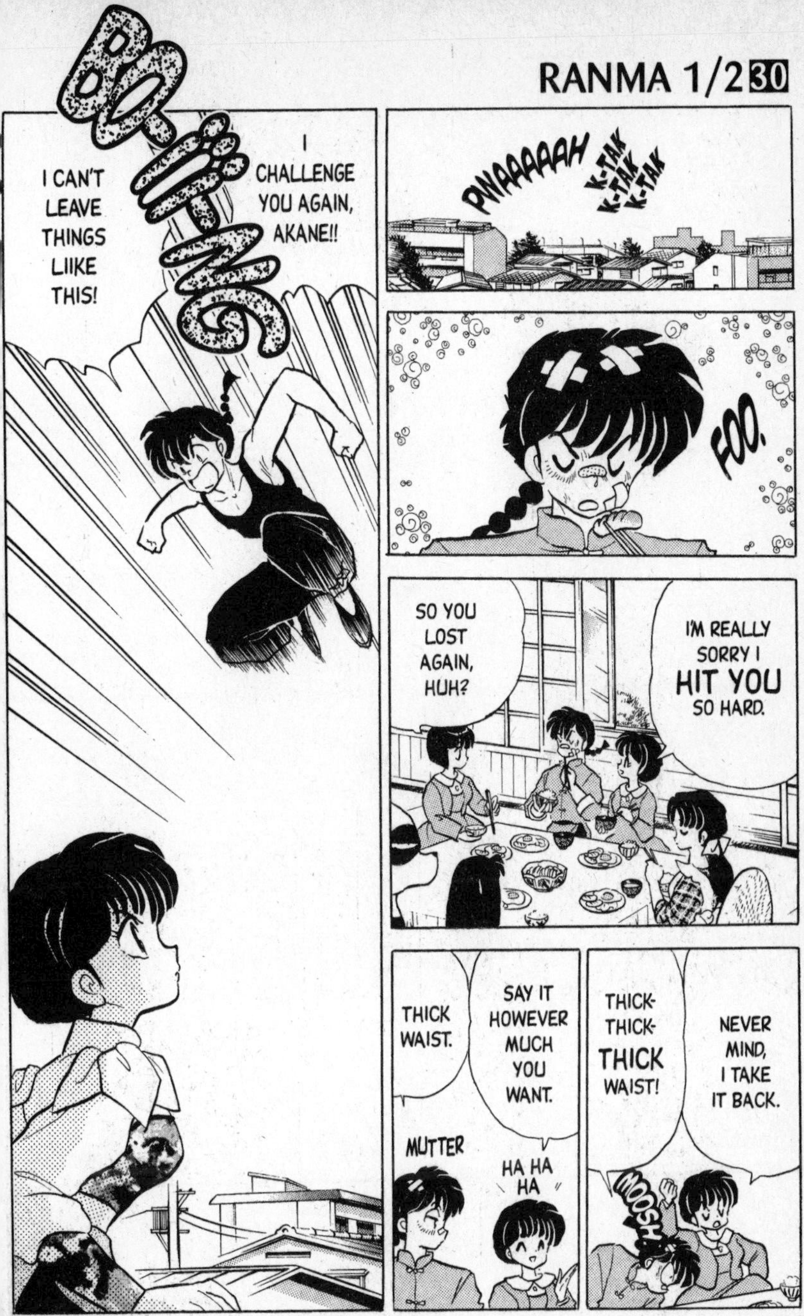
BOING
I CAN'T LEAVE THINGS LIIKE THIS!
I CHALLENGE YOU AGAIN, AKANE!!
PWAAAAAH
K-TAK K-TAK K-TAK
FOO.
SO YOU LOST AGAIN, HUH?
I'M REALLY SORRY I HIT YOU SO HARD.
THICK WAIST.
SAY IT HOWEVER MUCH YOU WANT.
MUTTER
HA HA HA
THICK- THICK- THICK WAIST!
NEVER MIND, I TAKE IT BACK.
WOOSH

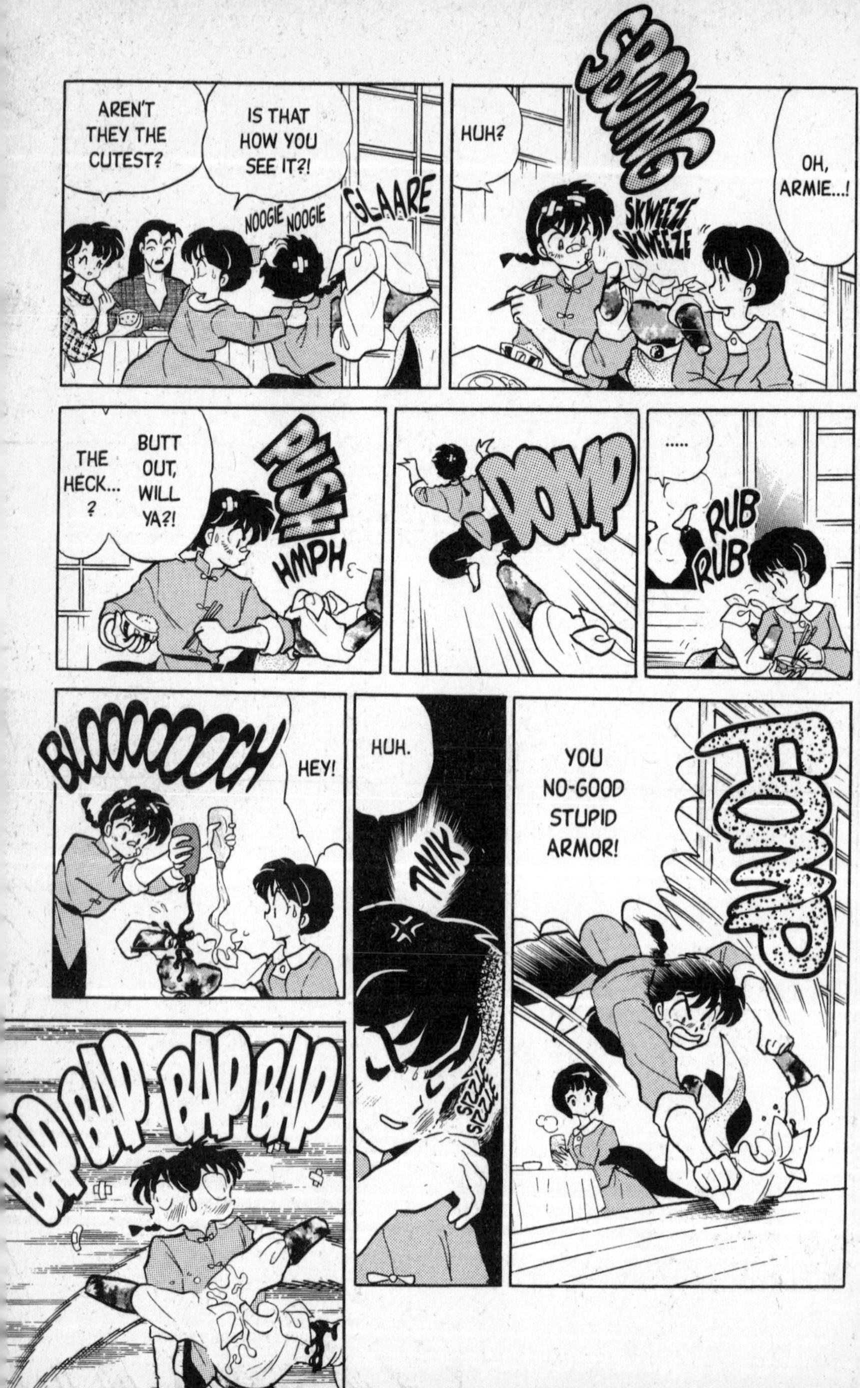
AREN'T THEY THE CUTEST?
IS THAT HOW YOU SEE IT?!
NOOGIE NOOGIE
GLAARE
SPROING
HUH?
SKWEEZE SKWEEZE
OH, ARMIE...!
THE HECK... ?
BUTT OUT, WILL YA?!
PUSH
HMPH
DOMP
.....
RUB RUB
BLOOOOOOCH
HEY!
BAP BAP BAP BAP
HUH.
TWIK
SIZZLE SIZZLE
YOU NO-GOOD STUPID ARMOR!
POMP

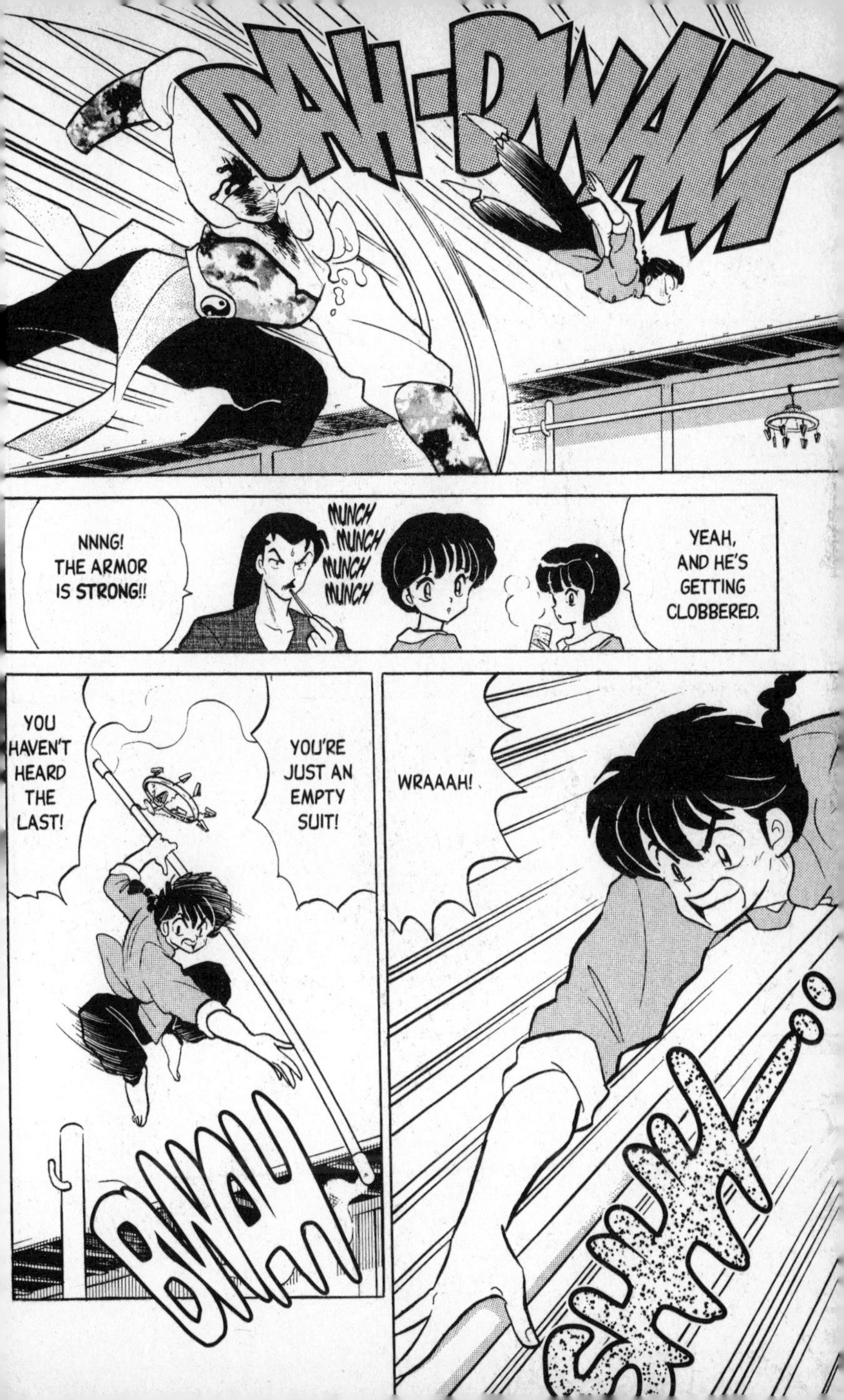
DAH-DWAK!
NNNG! THE ARMOR IS STRONG!!
MUNCH MUNCH MUNCH MUNCH
YEAH, AND HE'S GETTING CLOBBERED.
YOU HAVEN'T HEARD THE LAST!
YOU'RE JUST AN EMPTY SUIT!
WRAAAH!

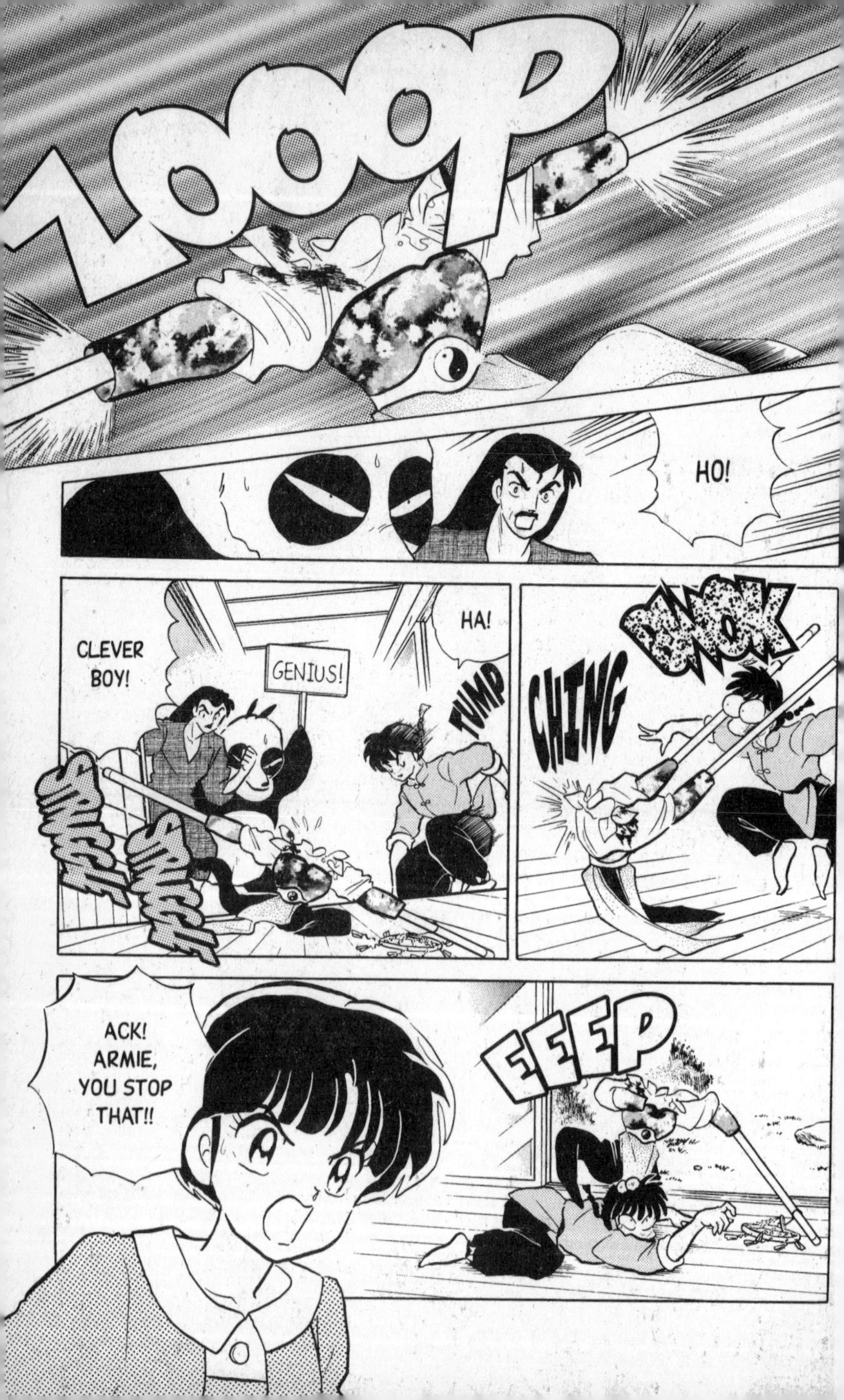
ZOOOP
HO!
CLEVER BOY!
GENIUS!
HA!
TUMP
CHING
ACK! ARMIE, YOU STOP THAT!!
EEEP

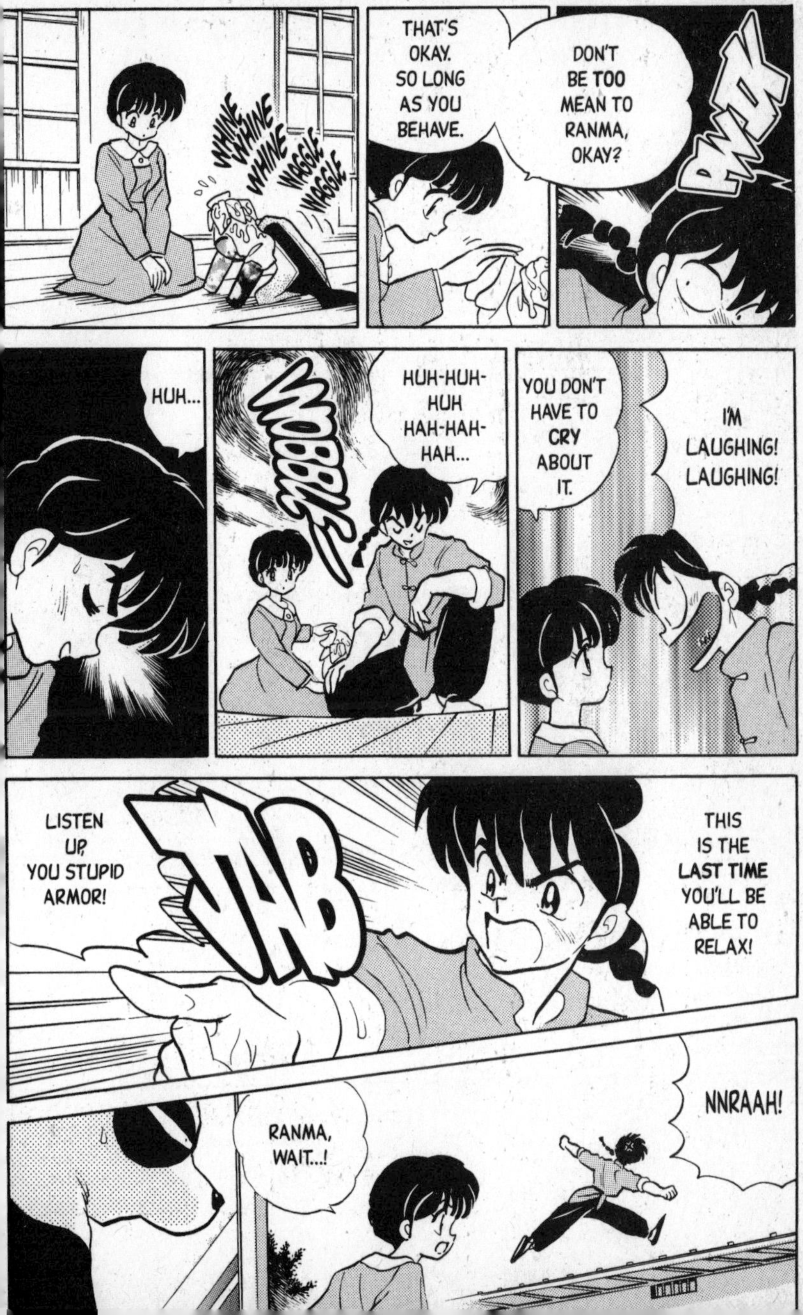
WHINE WHINE WHINE
WAGGLE WAGGLE
THAT'S OKAY. SO LONG AS YOU BEHAVE.
DON'T BE TOO MEAN TO RANMA, OKAY?
HUH...
WOBBLE
HUH-HUH-HUH HAH-HAH-HAH...
YOU DON'T HAVE TO CRY ABOUT IT.
I'M LAUGHING! LAUGHING!
LISTEN UP, YOU STUPID ARMOR!
JAB
THIS IS THE LAST TIME YOU'LL BE ABLE TO RELAX!
RANMA, WAIT...!
NNRAAH!

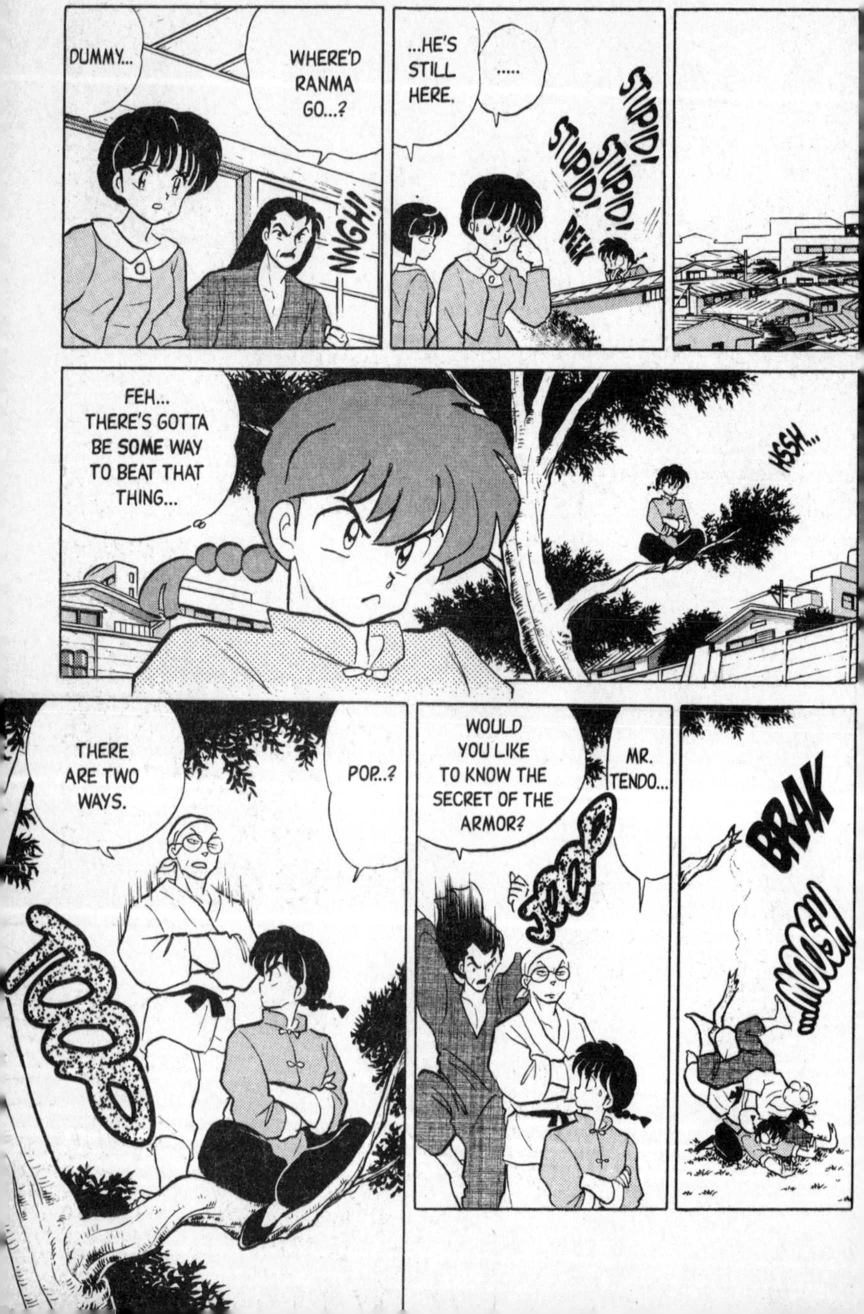
DUMMY...
WHERE'D RANMA GO...?
NNGH!
...HE'S STILL HERE.
.....
STUPID! STUPID! STUPID!
PEEK
FEH... THERE'S GOTTA BE SOME WAY TO BEAT THAT THING...
HSSH...
THERE ARE TWO WAYS.
POP...?
WOULD YOU LIKE TO KNOW THE SECRET OF THE ARMOR?
MR. TENDO...
BRAK
WHOOSH...

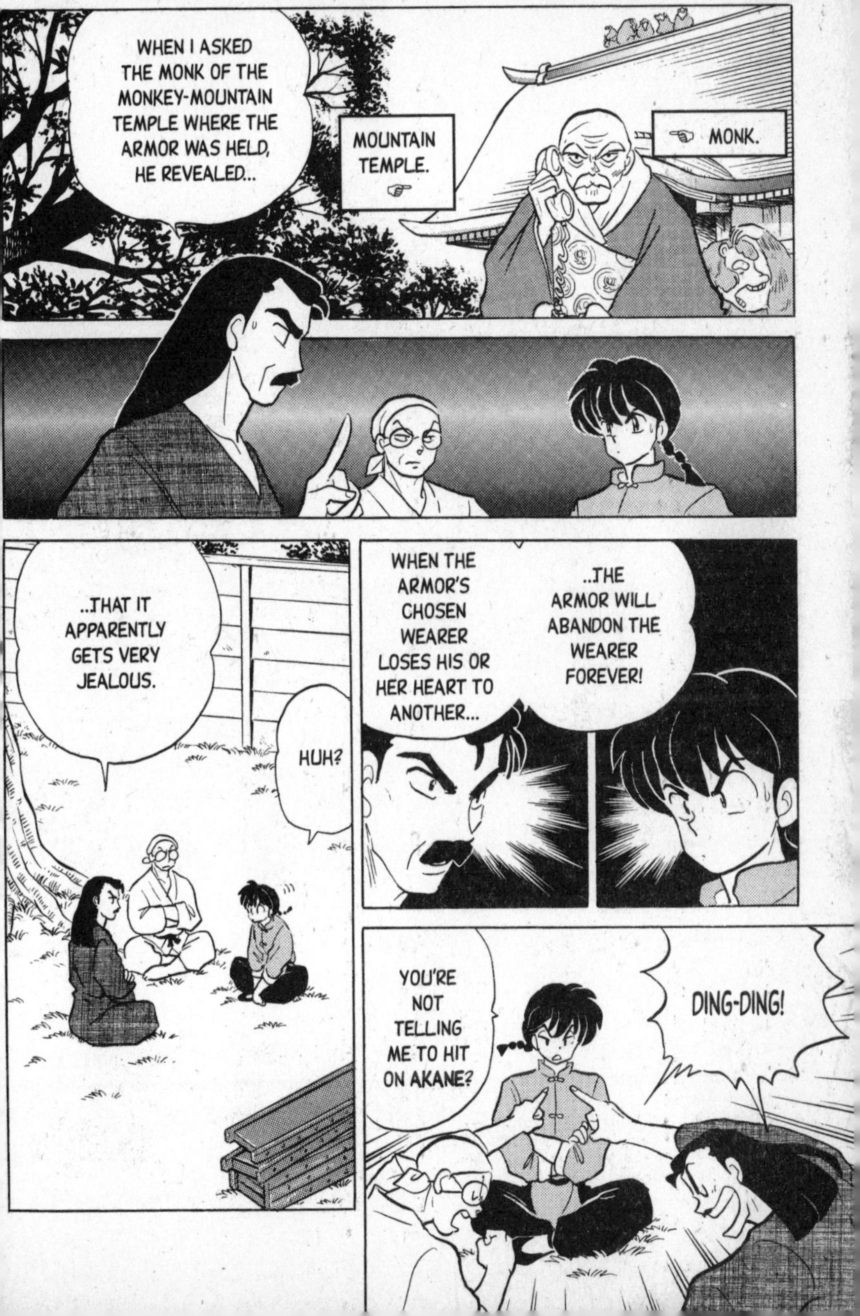
WHEN I ASKED THE MONK OF THE MONKEY-MOUNTAIN TEMPLE WHERE THE ARMOR WAS HELD, HE REVEALED...
MOUNTAIN TEMPLE.
MONK.
...THAT IT APPARENTLY GETS VERY JEALOUS.
HUH?
WHEN THE ARMOR'S CHOSEN WEARER LOSES HIS OR HER HEART TO ANOTHER...
...THE ARMOR WILL ABANDON THE WEARER FOREVER!
YOU'RE NOT TELLING ME TO HIT ON AKANE?
DING-DING!

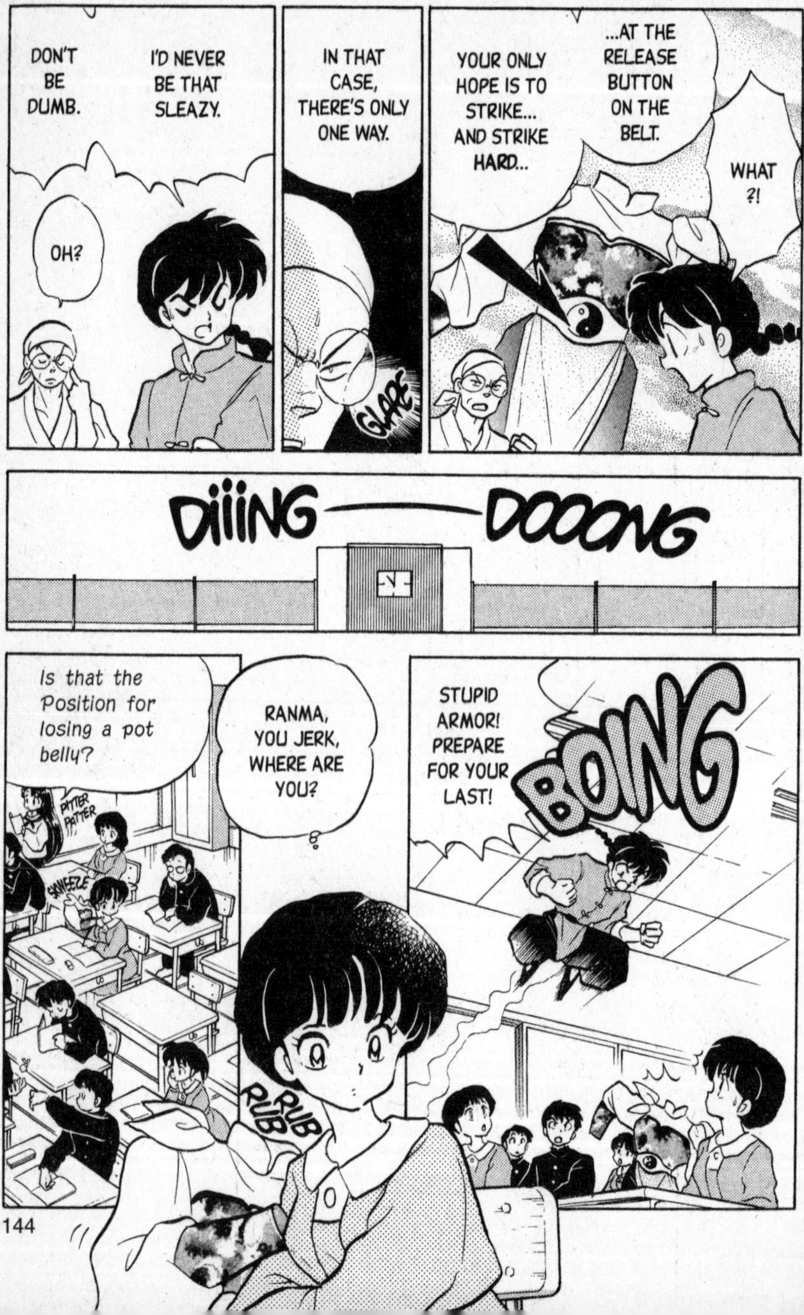
DON'T BE DUMB.
I'D NEVER BE THAT SLEAZY.
OH?
IN THAT CASE, THERE'S ONLY ONE WAY.
GLARE
YOUR ONLY HOPE IS TO STRIKE... AND STRIKE HARD...
...AT THE RELEASE BUTTON ON THE BELT.
WHAT ?!
DIIING——DOOONG
Is that the Position for losing a pot belly?
PITTER PATTER
SKWEEZE
RANMA, YOU JERK, WHERE ARE YOU?
RUB RUB
STUPID ARMOR! PREPARE FOR YOUR LAST!
BOING

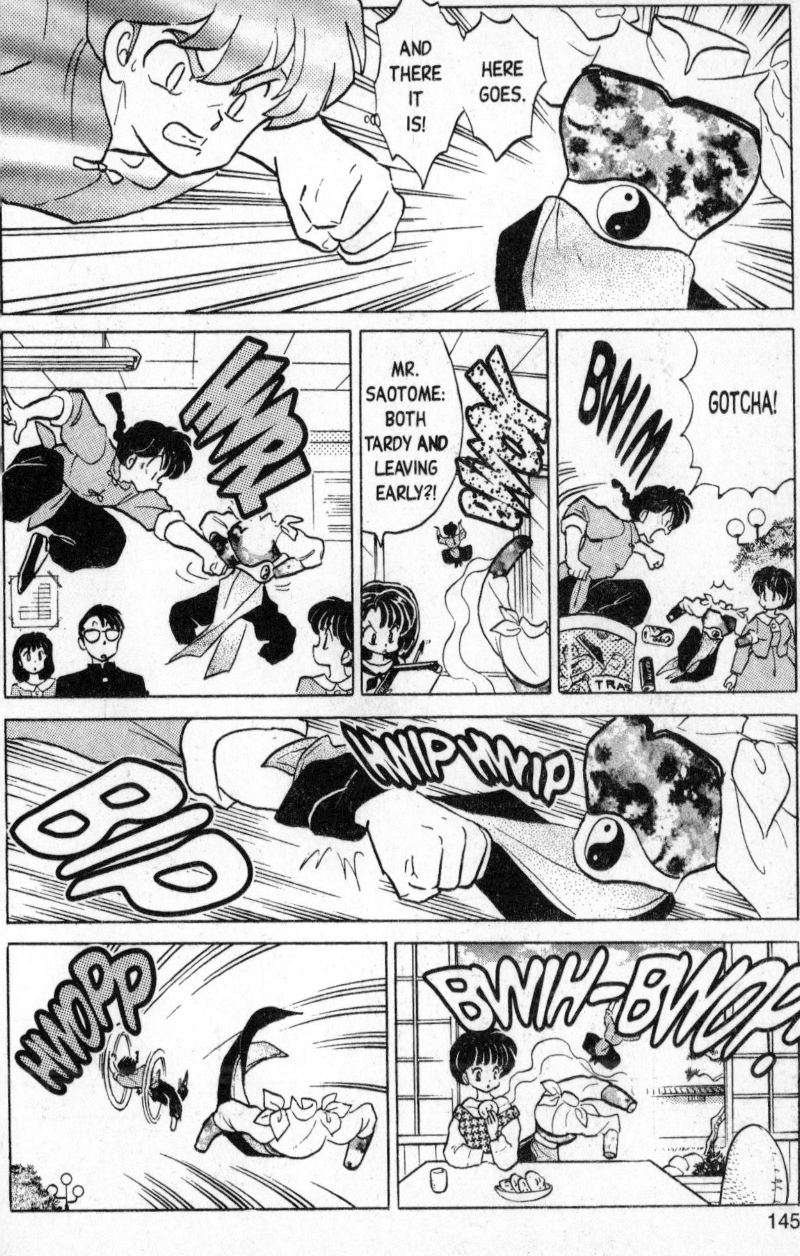
AND THERE IT IS!
HERE GOES.
MR. SAOTOME: BOTH TARDY AND LEAVING EARLY?!
BWIM
GOTCHA!
HWIP HWIP
BIP
HWOPP
BWIH-BWOP!

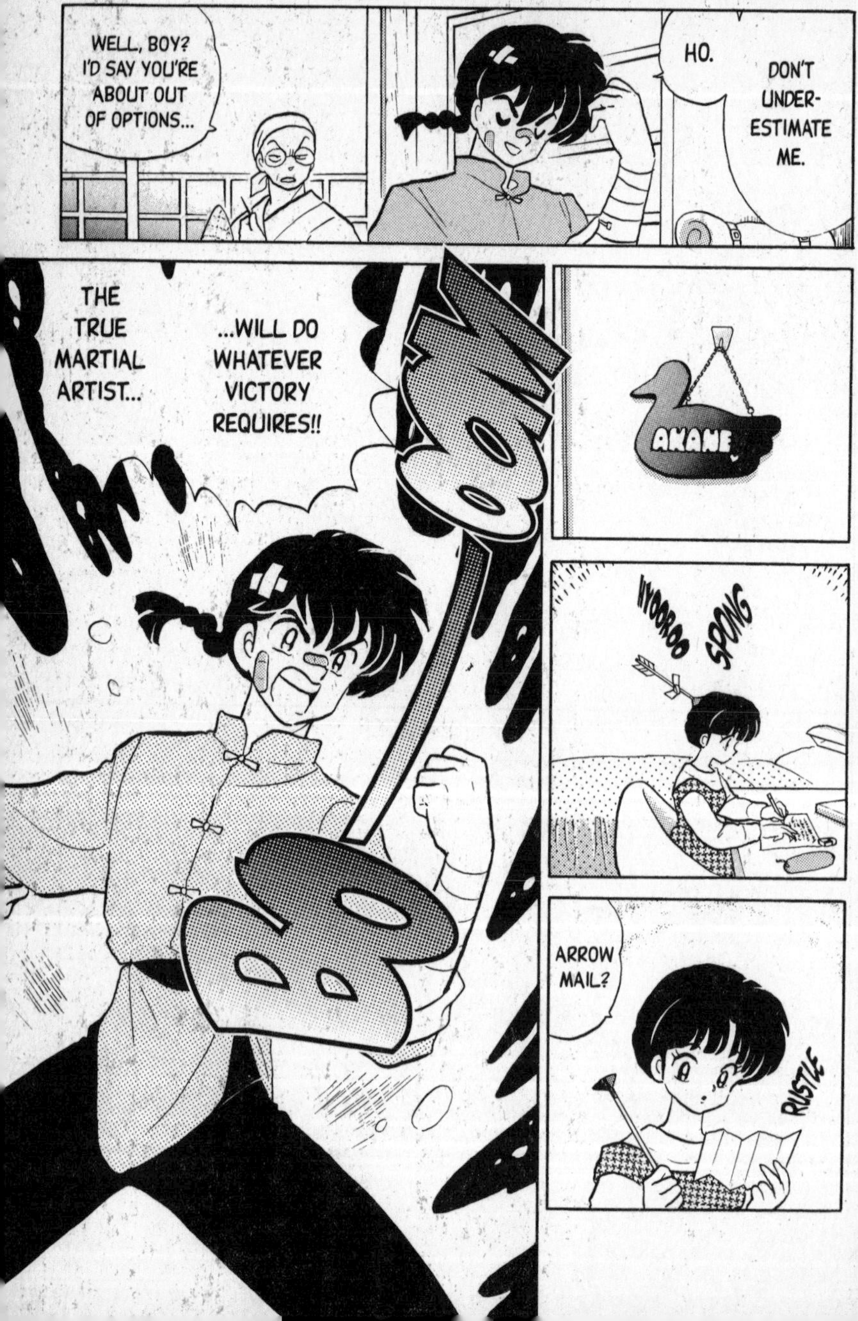
WELL, BOY? I'D SAY YOU'RE ABOUT OUT OF OPTIONS...
HO.
DON'T UNDER-ESTIMATE ME.
THE TRUE MARTIAL ARTIST...
...WILL DO WHATEVER VICTORY REQUIRES!!
AKANE
HYOOROO
SPONG
ARROW MAIL?
RUSTLE

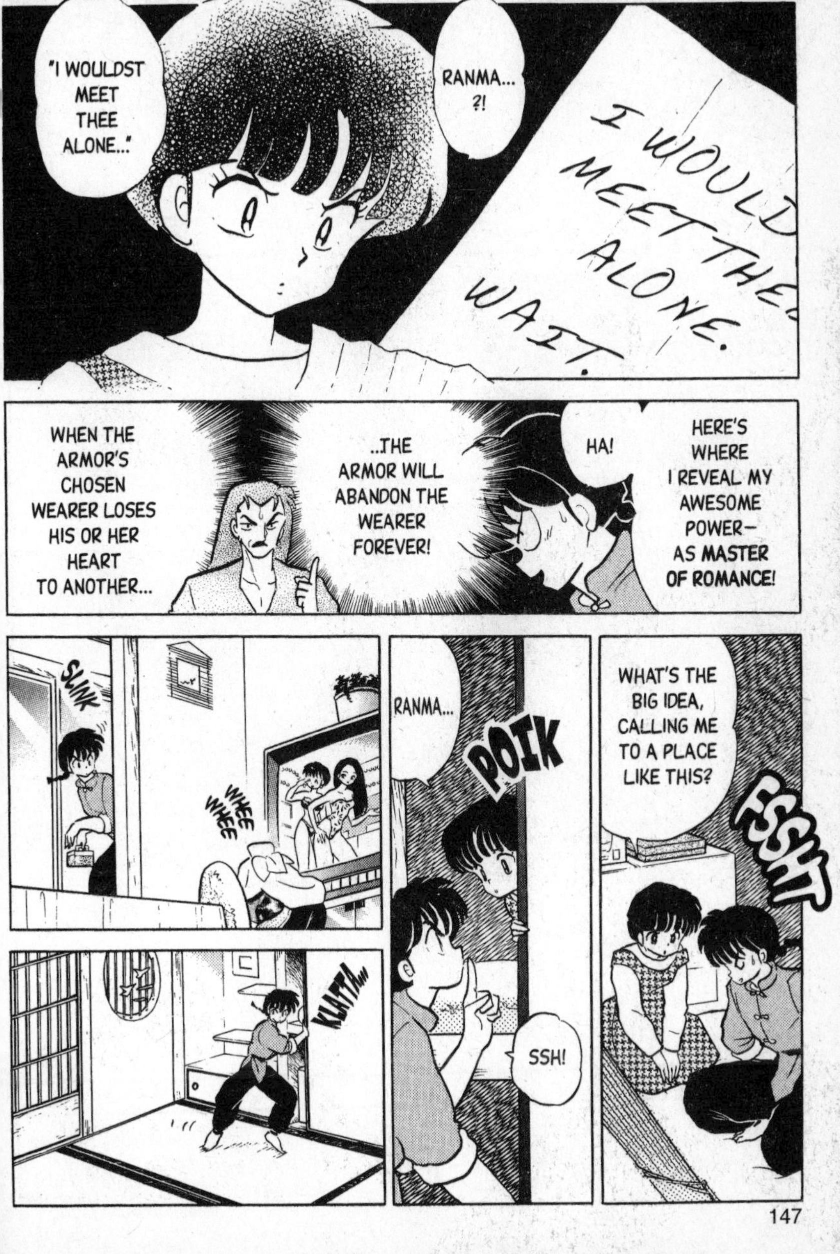
"I WOULDST MEET THEE ALONE..."
RANMA... ?!
I WOULD
MEET THE
ALONE.
WAIT.
WHEN THE ARMOR'S CHOSEN WEARER LOSES HIS OR HER HEART TO ANOTHER...
...THE ARMOR WILL ABANDON THE WEARER FOREVER!
HA!
HERE'S WHERE I REVEAL MY AWESOME POWER— AS MASTER OF ROMANCE!
SLINK
WHEE WHEE
KLATTA...
RANMA...
POIK
SSH!
WHAT'S THE BIG IDEA, CALLING ME TO A PLACE LIKE THIS?
FSSHT

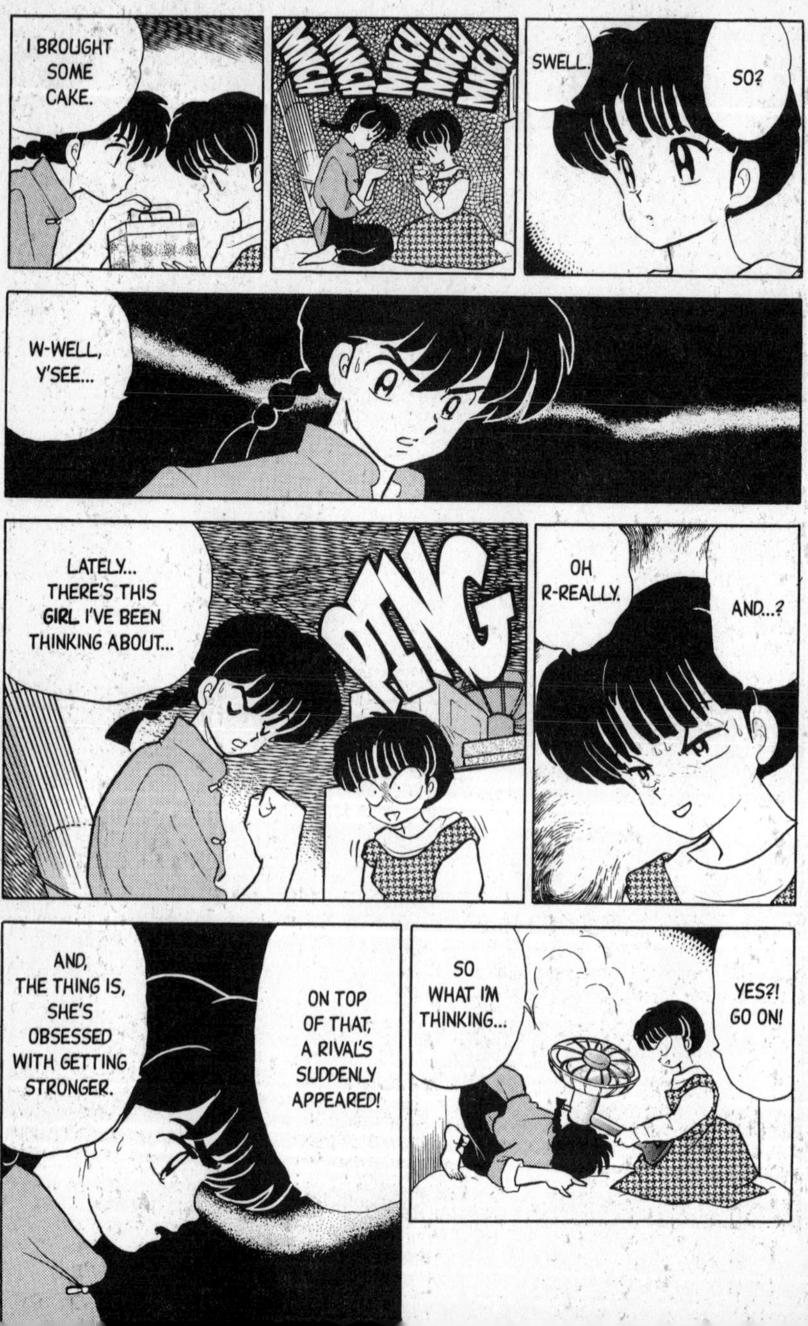
I BROUGHT SOME CAKE.
MNCH MNCH MNCH MNCH MNCH
SWELL.
SO?
W-WELL, Y'SEE...
LATELY... THERE'S THIS GIRL I'VE BEEN THINKING ABOUT...
PING
OH R-REALLY.
AND...?
AND, THE THING IS, SHE'S OBSESSED WITH GETTING STRONGER.
ON TOP OF THAT, A RIVAL'S SUDDENLY APPEARED!
SO WHAT I'M THINKING...
YES?! GO ON!

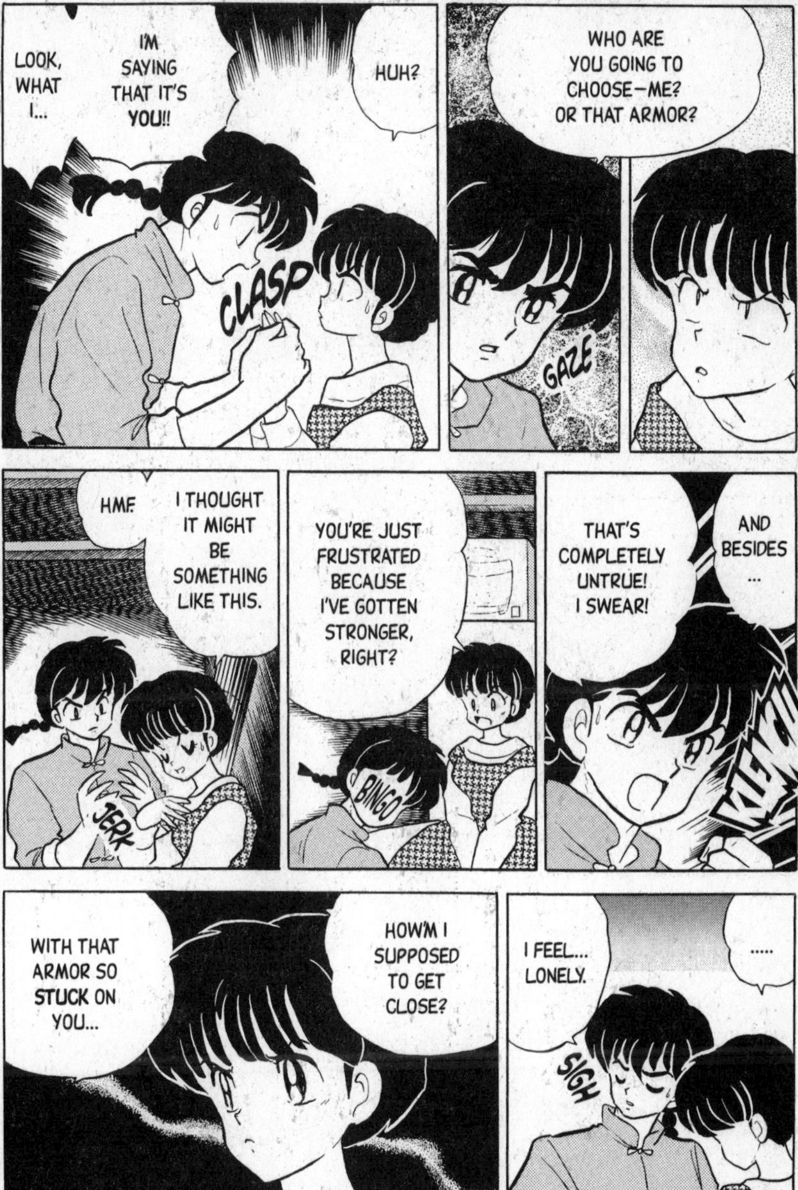
LOOK, WHAT I...
I'M SAYING THAT IT'S YOU!!
HUH?
CLASP
WHO ARE YOU GOING TO CHOOSE—ME? OR THAT ARMOR?
GAZE
HMF.
I THOUGHT IT MIGHT BE SOMETHING LIKE THIS.
JERK
YOU'RE JUST FRUSTRATED BECAUSE I'VE GOTTEN STRONGER, RIGHT?
BINGO
THAT'S COMPLETELY UNTRUE! I SWEAR!
AND BESIDES ...
WITH THAT ARMOR SO STUCK ON YOU...
HOW'M I SUPPOSED TO GET CLOSE?
I FEEL... LONELY.
.....
SIGH

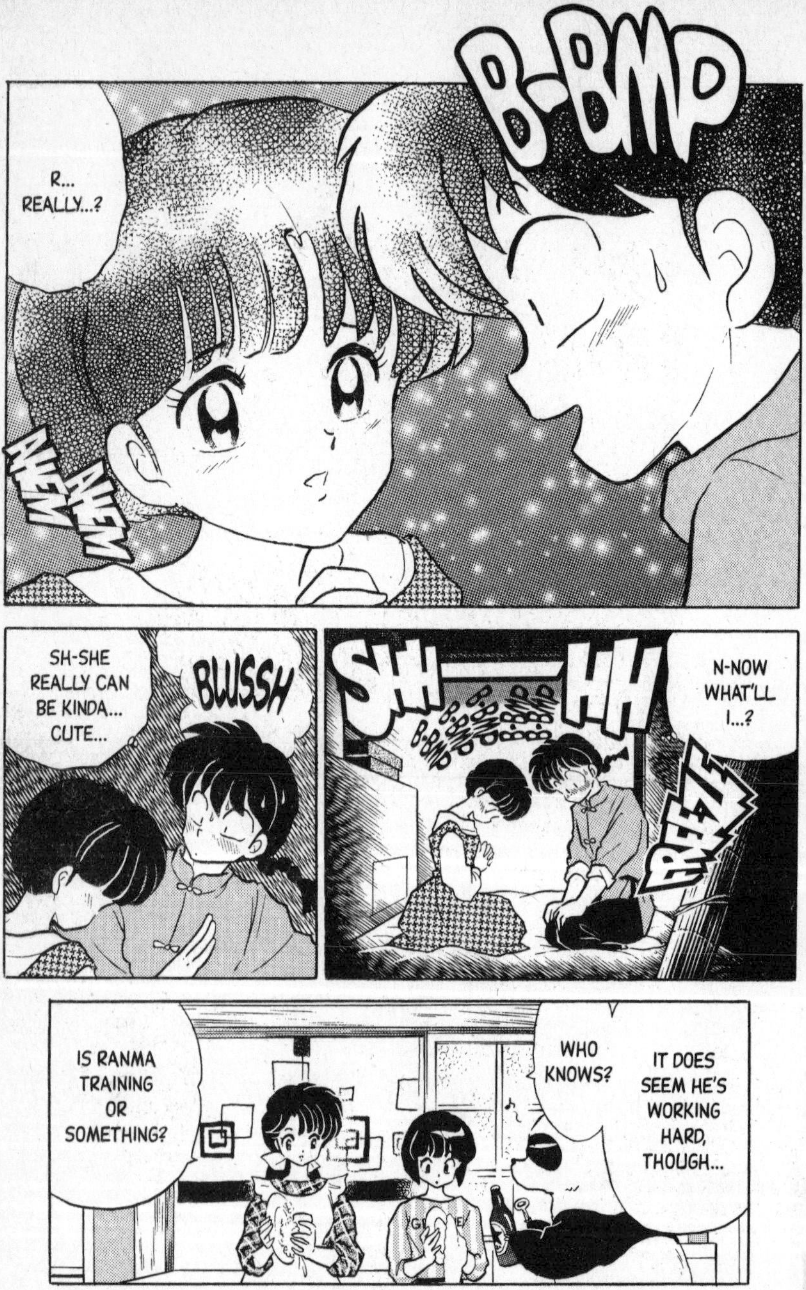
B-BMP
R... REALLY...?
AHEM AHEM AHEM
SH-SHE REALLY CAN BE KINDA... CUTE...
BLUSSH
SH—HH
B-BMP B-BMP B-BMP B-BMP
N-NOW WHAT'LL I...?
FREEZE
IS RANMA TRAINING OR SOMETHING?
WHO KNOWS?
IT DOES SEEM HE'S WORKING HARD, THOUGH...

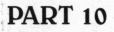

PART 10

THE FIRST TIME I SAID WHAT I FELT

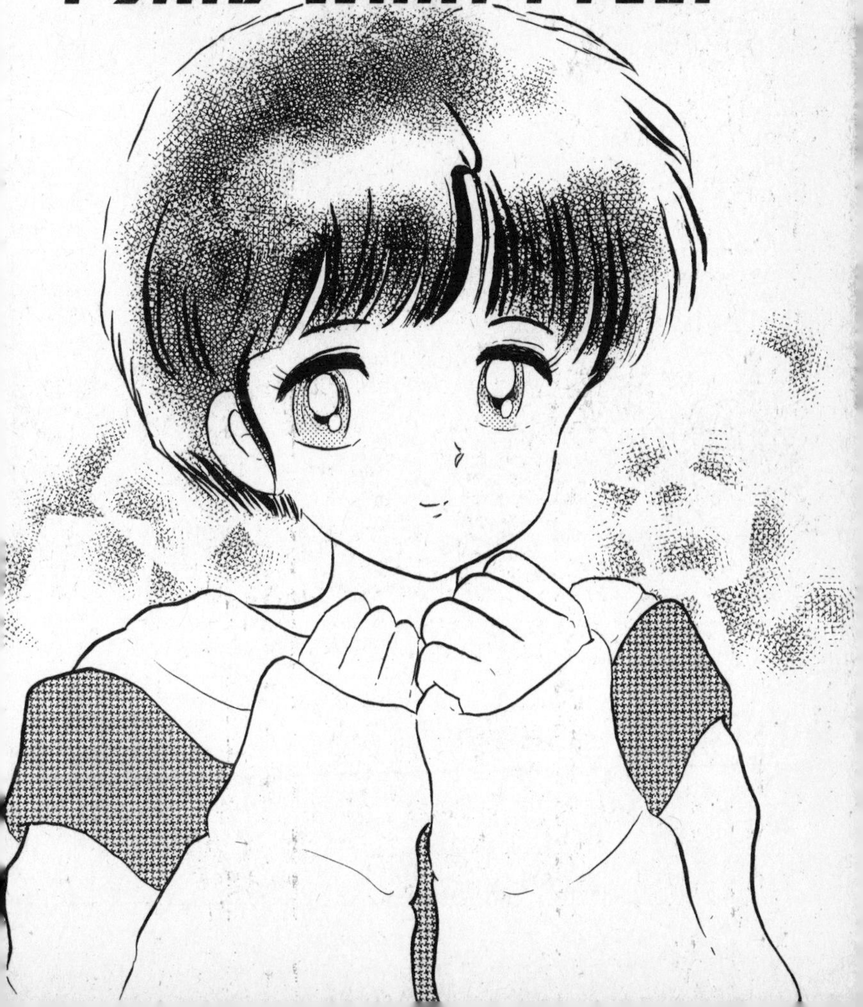

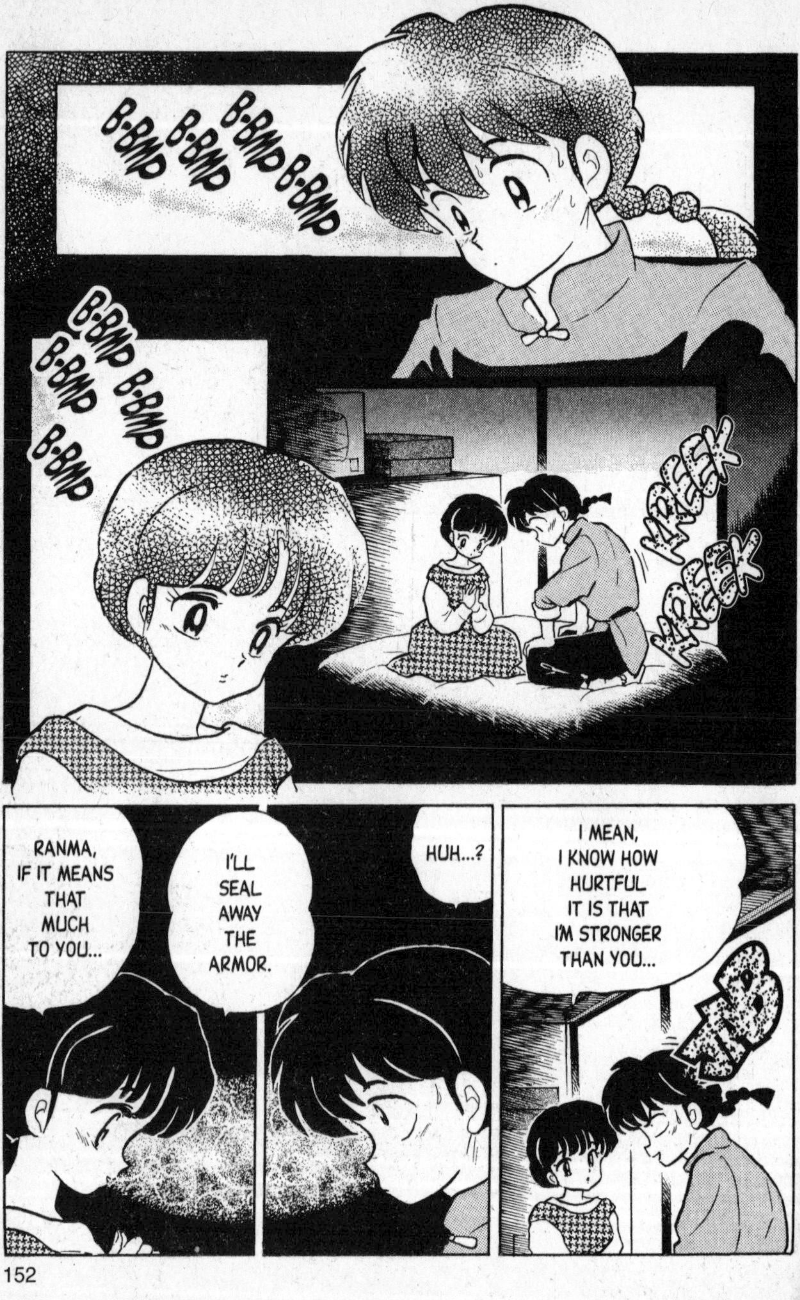
B-BMP B-BMP
B-BMP
B-BMP
B-BMP B-BMP
B-BMP
B-BMP
KREEK
KREEK
RANMA, IF IT MEANS THAT MUCH TO YOU...
I'LL SEAL AWAY THE ARMOR.
HUH...?
I MEAN, I KNOW HOW HURTFUL IT IS THAT I'M STRONGER THAN YOU...

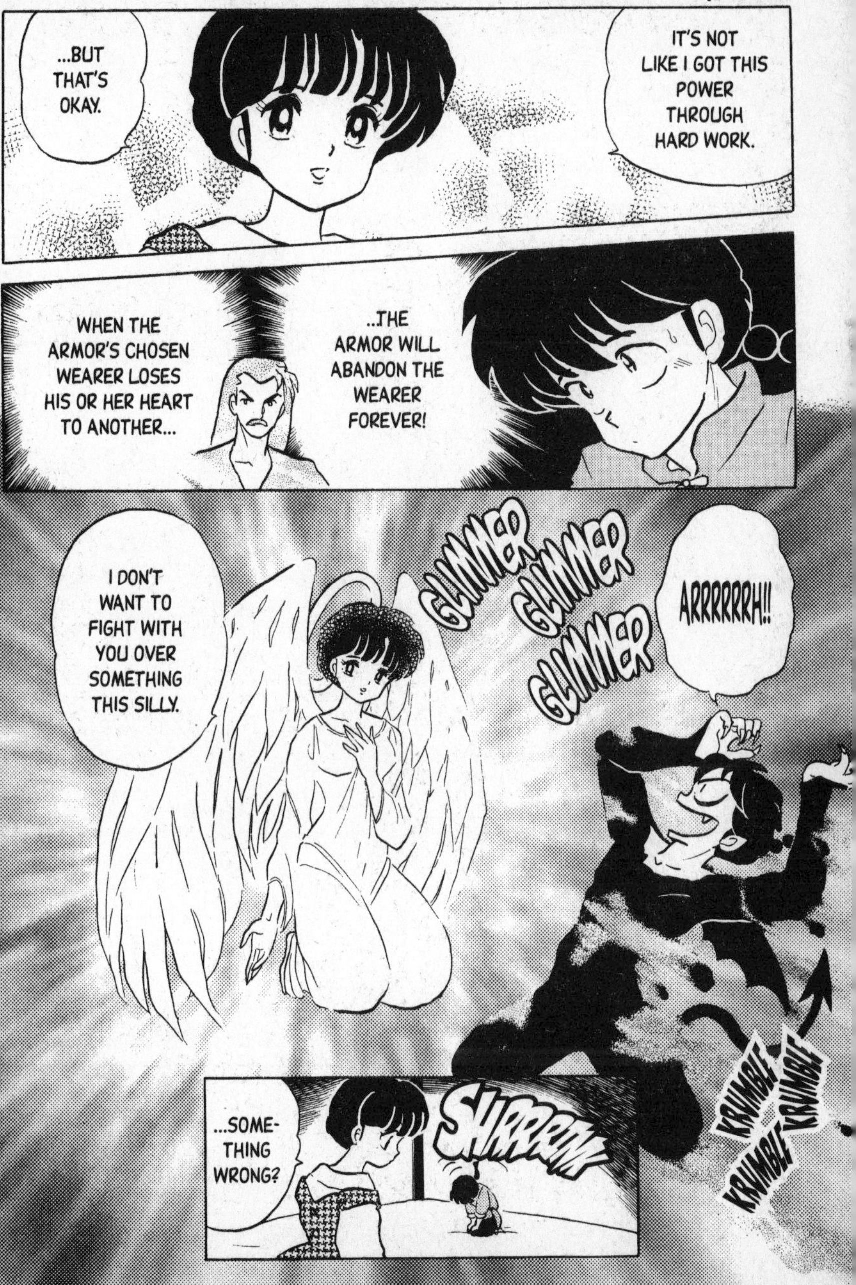
...BUT THAT'S OKAY.
IT'S NOT LIKE I GOT THIS POWER THROUGH HARD WORK.
WHEN THE ARMOR'S CHOSEN WEARER LOSES HIS OR HER HEART TO ANOTHER...
..THE ARMOR WILL ABANDON THE WEARER FOREVER!
I DON'T WANT TO FIGHT WITH YOU OVER SOMETHING THIS SILLY.
GLIMMER GLIMMER GLIMMER
ARRRRRRH!!
...SOME-THING WRONG?
SHRRINK
KRUMBLE KRUMBLE KRUMBLE

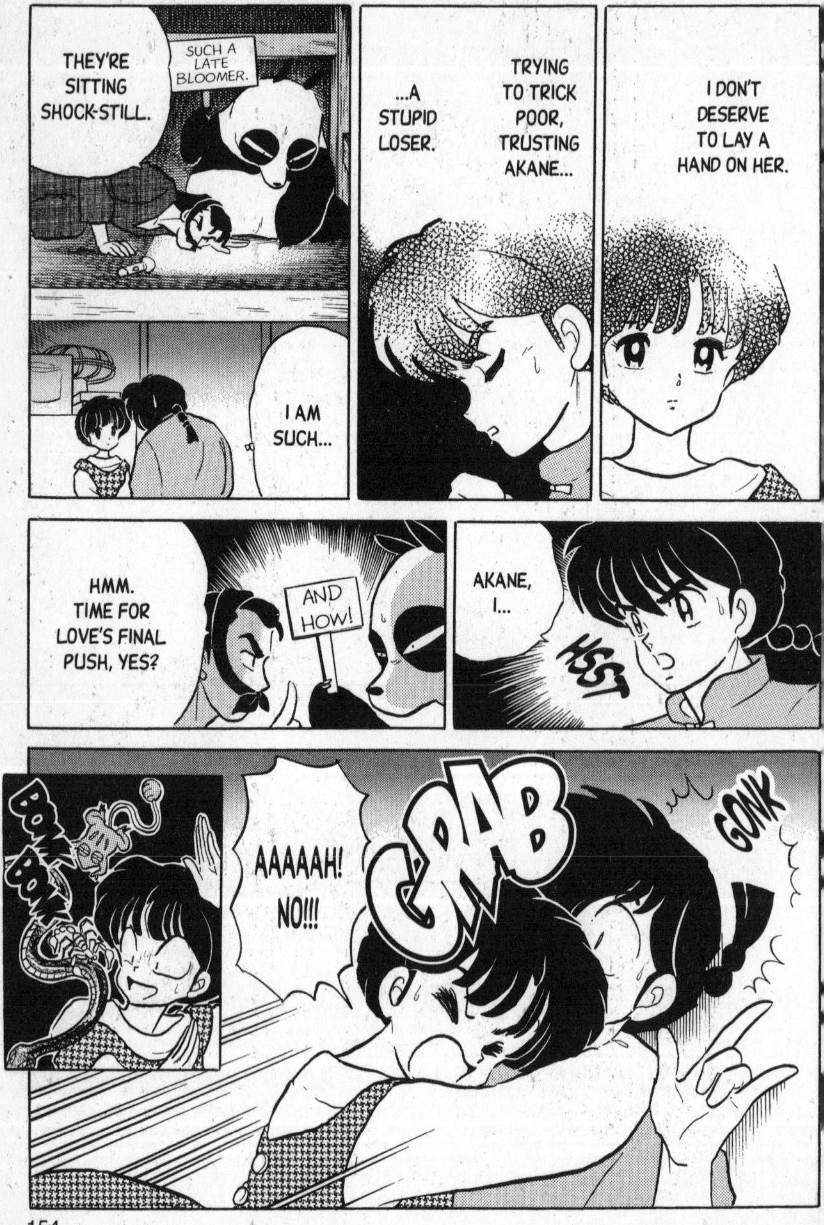
THEY'RE SITTING SHOCK-STILL.
SUCH A LATE BLOOMER.
I AM SUCH...
...A STUPID LOSER.
TRYING TO TRICK POOR, TRUSTING AKANE...
I DON'T DESERVE TO LAY A HAND ON HER.
HMM. TIME FOR LOVE'S FINAL PUSH, YES?
AND HOW!
AKANE, I...
HSST
BOINK
BOINK
AAAAAH! NO!!!
GRAB
GONK

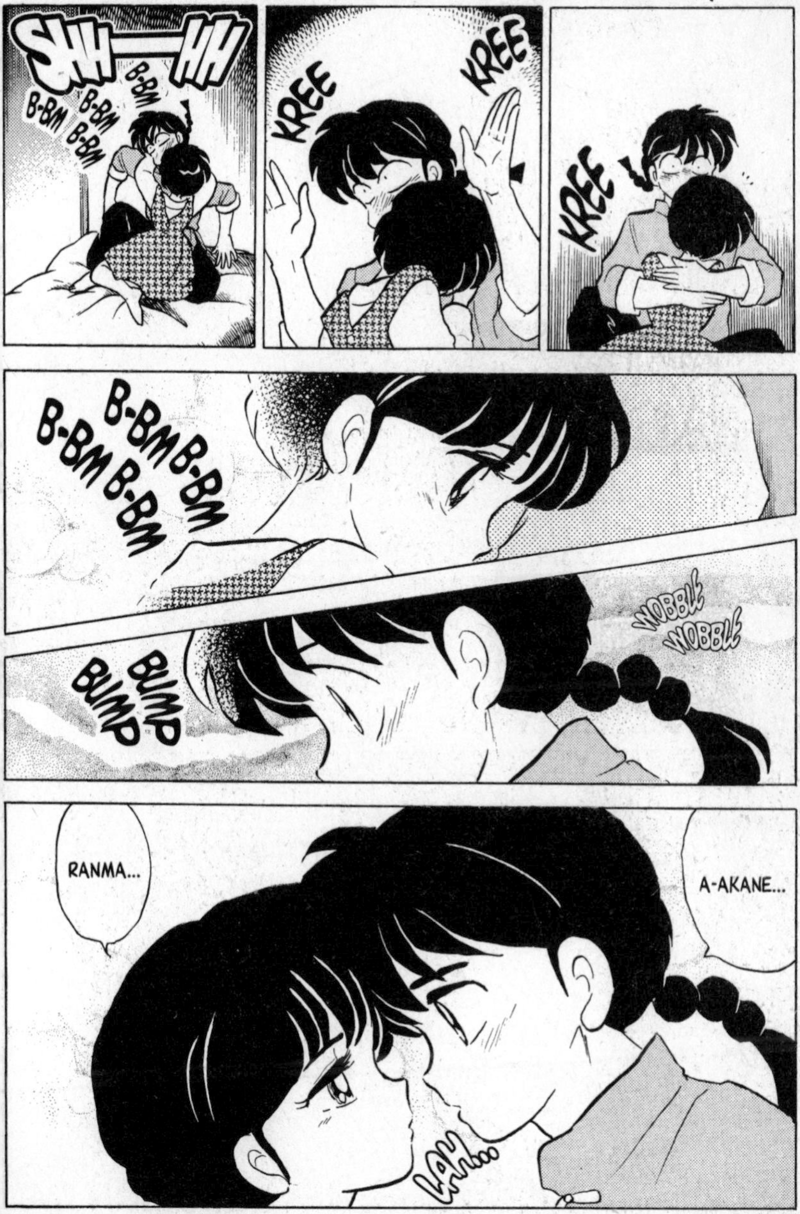
SHH—HH
B-BM
B-BM
B-BM
B-BM
KREE
KREE
KREE
B-BM B-BM
B-BM B-BM
BUMP
BUMP
WOBBLE
WOBBLE
RANMA...
A-AKANE...

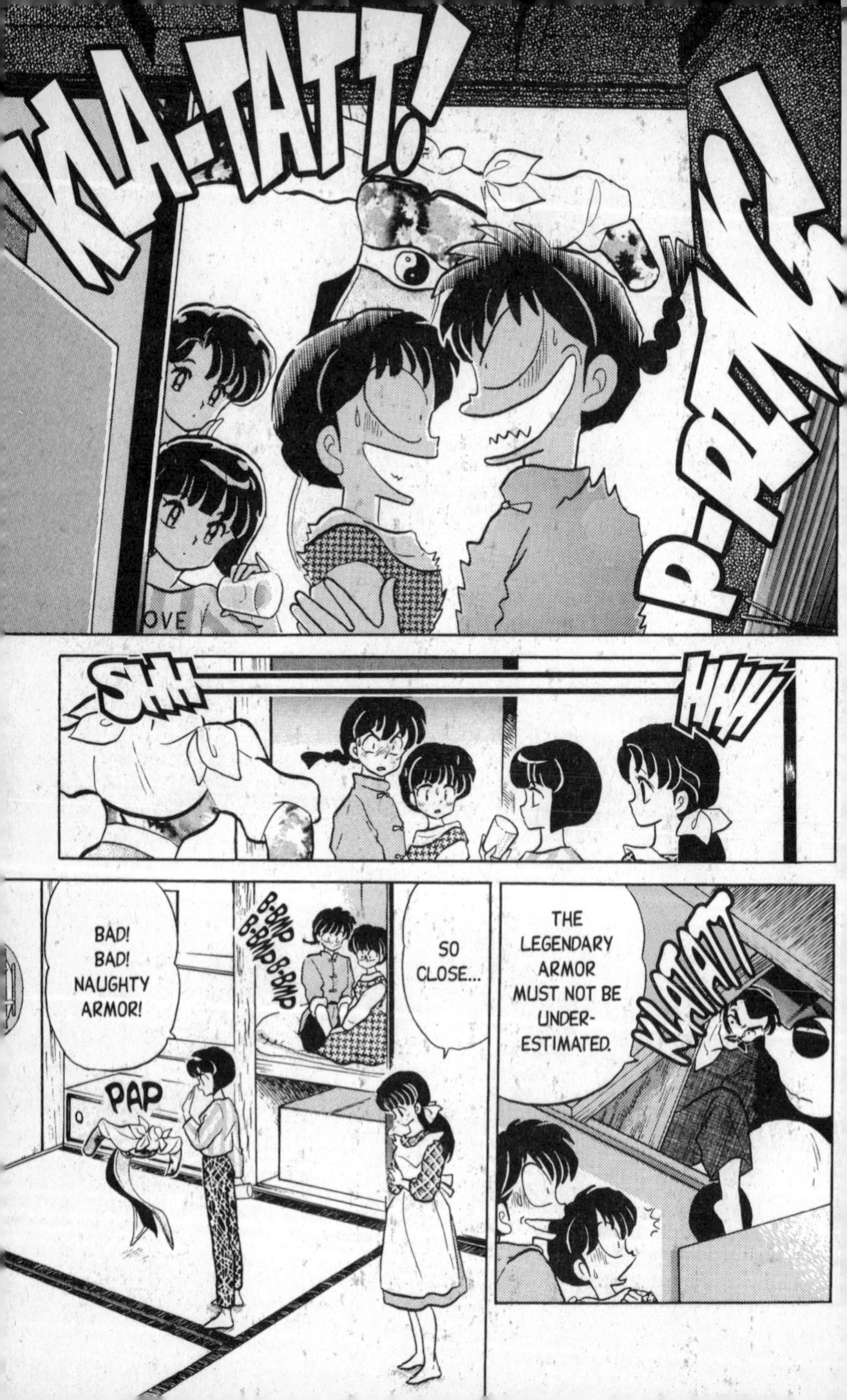
KLA-TATT!
D-PUNK
OVE
SHHHH
BAD! BAD! NAUGHTY ARMOR!
PAP
B-BMP B-BMP B-BMP
SO CLOSE...
THE LEGENDARY ARMOR MUST NOT BE UNDER-ESTIMATED.
KLATATT

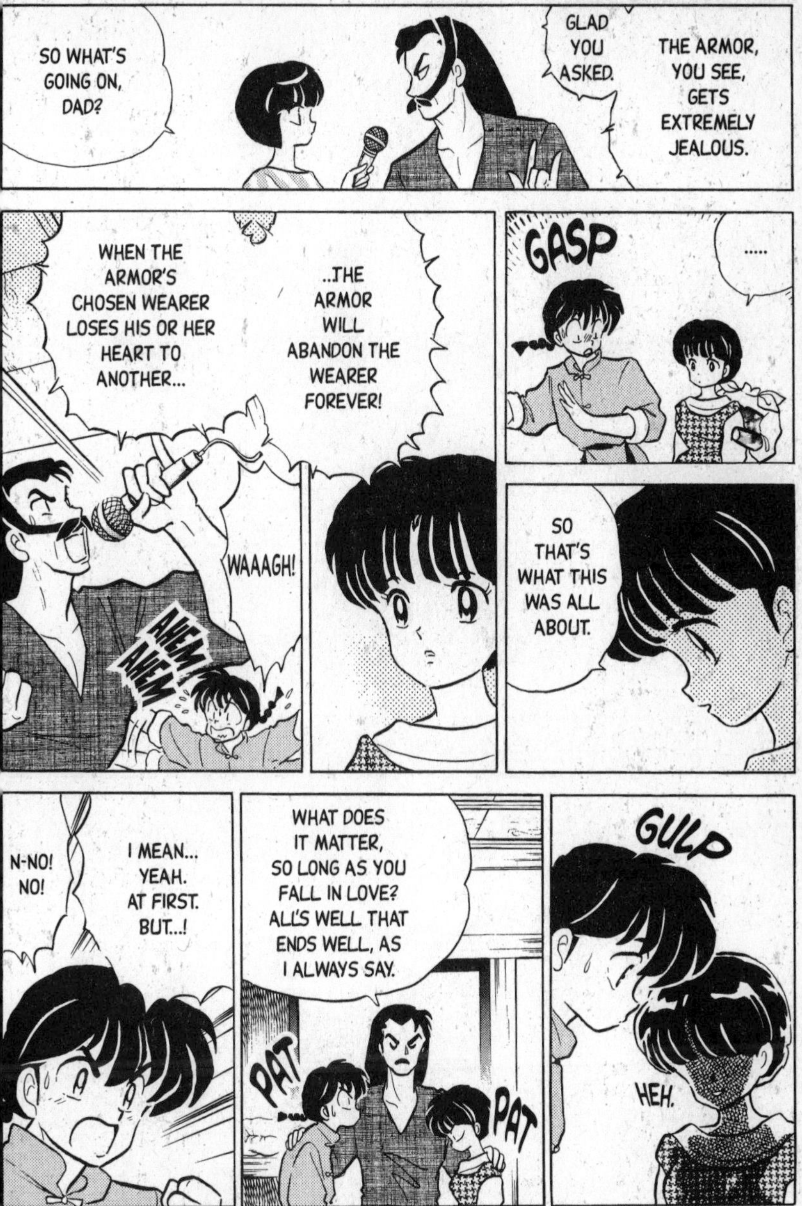
SO WHAT'S GOING ON, DAD?
GLAD YOU ASKED.
THE ARMOR, YOU SEE, GETS EXTREMELY JEALOUS.
WHEN THE ARMOR'S CHOSEN WEARER LOSES HIS OR HER HEART TO ANOTHER...
...THE ARMOR WILL ABANDON THE WEARER FOREVER!
WAAAGH!
AHEM AHEM
GASP
.....
SO THAT'S WHAT THIS WAS ALL ABOUT.
N-NO! NO!
I MEAN... YEAH. AT FIRST. BUT...!
WHAT DOES IT MATTER, SO LONG AS YOU FALL IN LOVE? ALL'S WELL THAT ENDS WELL, AS I ALWAYS SAY.
PAT
PAT
GULP
HEH.

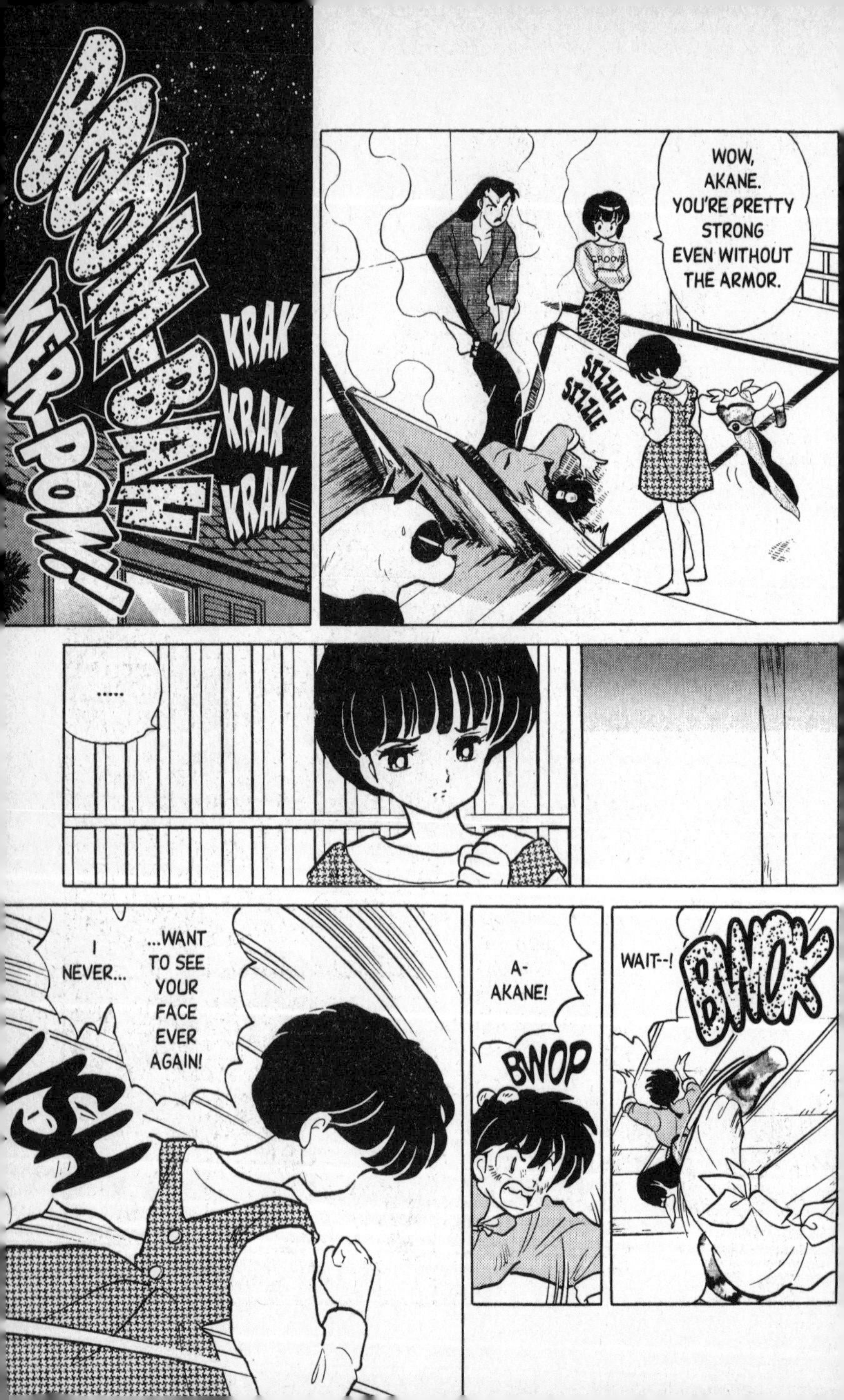
BOOM-BAH!
KER-POW!
KRAK KRAK KRAK
WOW, AKANE. YOU'RE PRETTY STRONG EVEN WITHOUT THE ARMOR.
SIZZLE SIZZLE
.....
I NEVER...
...WANT TO SEE YOUR FACE EVER AGAIN!
A- AKANE!
BWOP
WAIT--!
BWOK

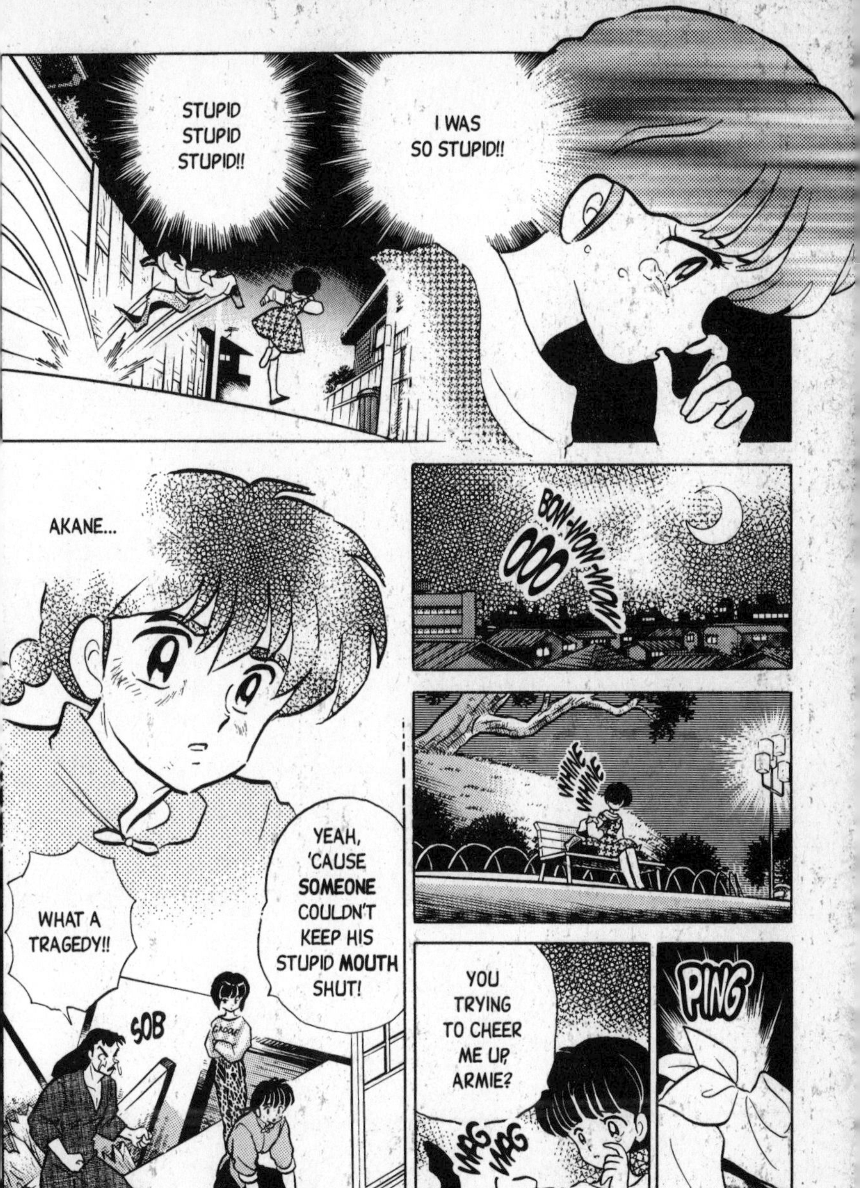
STUPID
STUPID
STUPID!!
I WAS
SO STUPID!!
AKANE...
WHAT A
TRAGEDY!!
SOB
YEAH,
'CAUSE
SOMEONE
COULDN'T
KEEP HIS
STUPID MOUTH
SHUT!
BOW-WOW-WOW
OOO
WHINE
WHINE
YOU
TRYING
TO CHEER
ME UP,
ARMIE?
WAG
WAG
PING

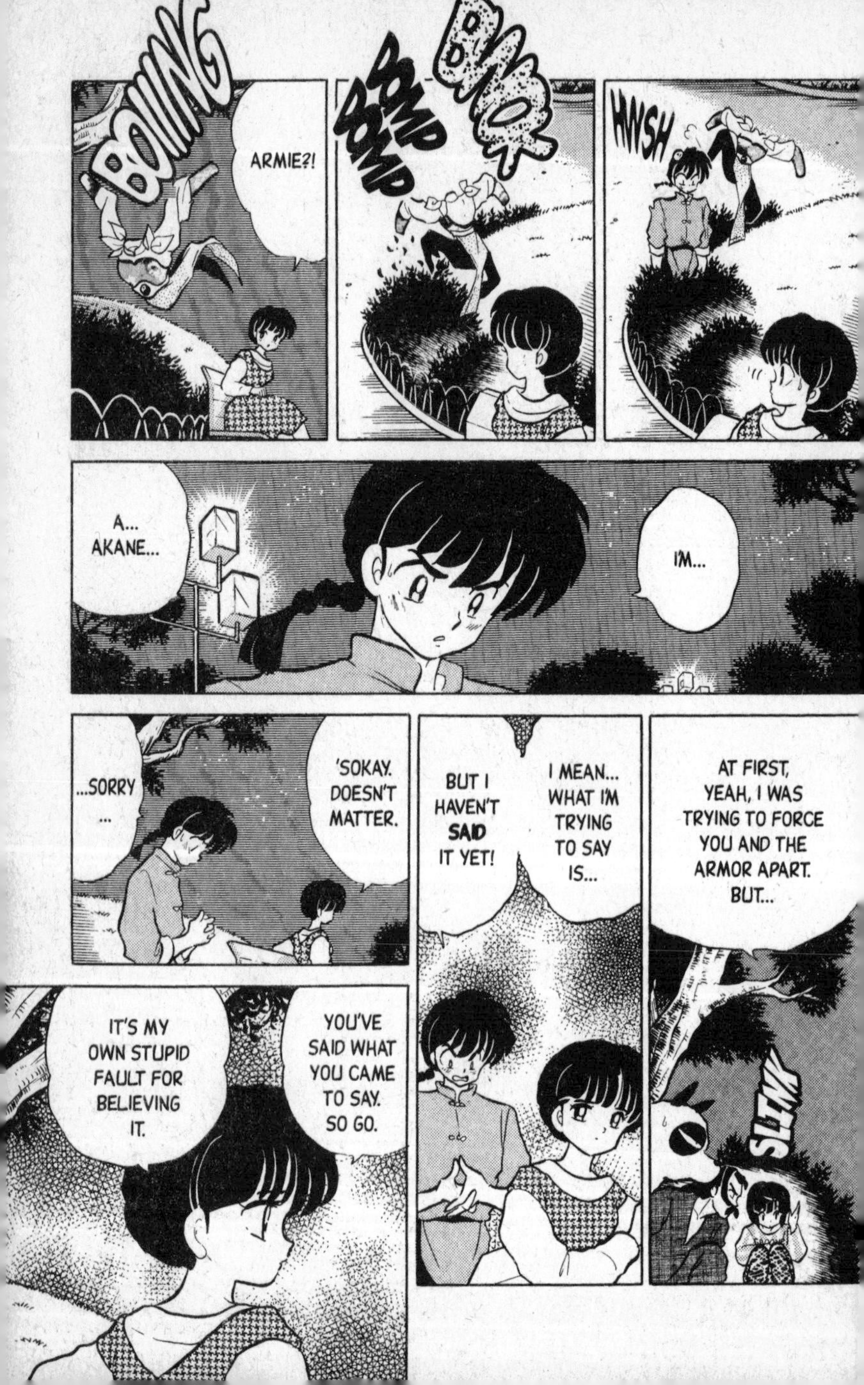
BOING
ARMIE?!
DOMP DOMP
DOMP
BONK
HNNSH
A... AKANE...
I'M...
...SORRY ...
'SOKAY. DOESN'T MATTER.
BUT I HAVEN'T **SAID** IT YET!
I MEAN... WHAT I'M TRYING TO SAY IS...
AT FIRST, YEAH, I WAS TRYING TO FORCE YOU AND THE ARMOR APART. BUT...
SLINK
IT'S MY OWN STUPID FAULT FOR BELIEVING IT.
YOU'VE SAID WHAT YOU CAME TO SAY. SO GO.

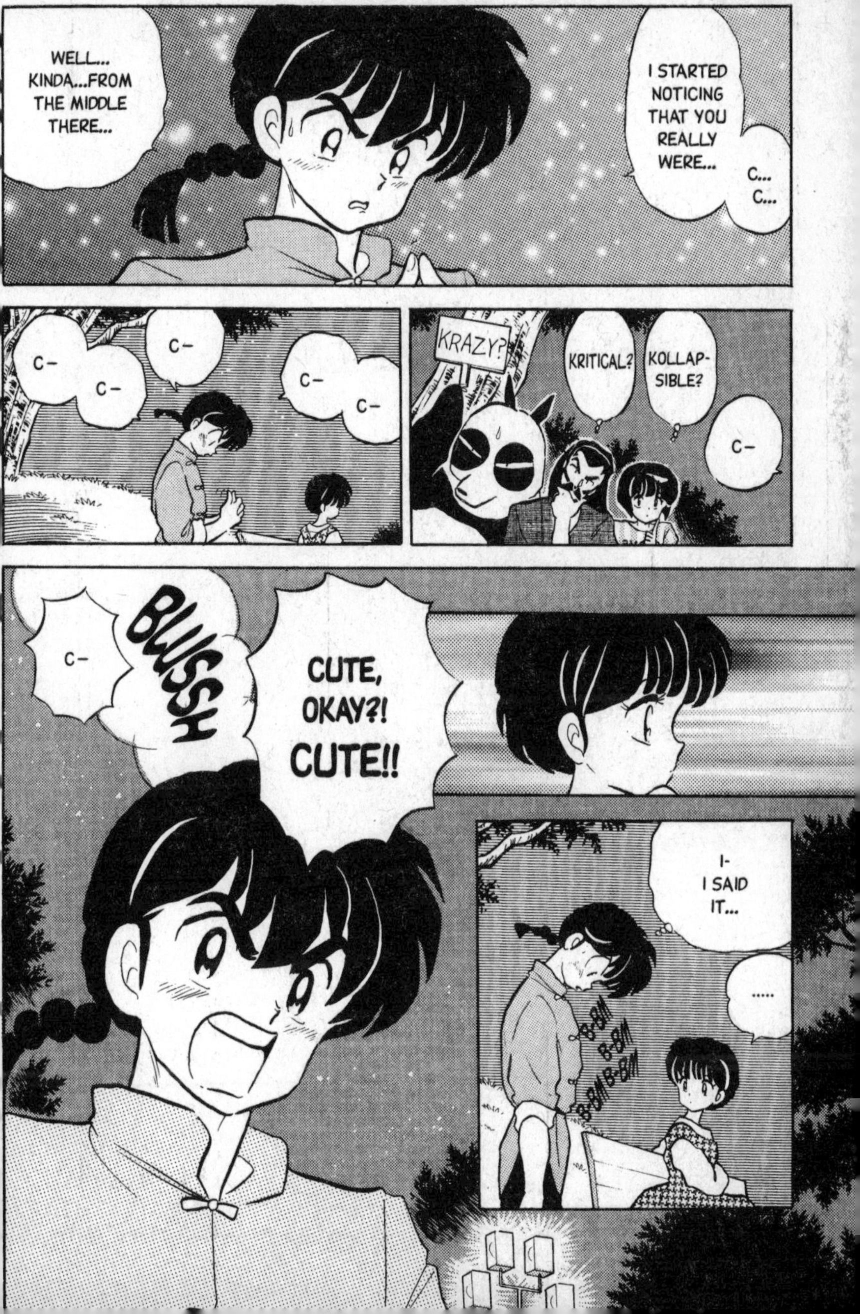
WELL... KINDA...FROM THE MIDDLE THERE...
I STARTED NOTICING THAT YOU REALLY WERE...
C... C...
C–
C–
C–
C–
C–
KRAZY?
KRITICAL?
KOLLAP-SIBLE?
C–
C–
BWSSH
CUTE, OKAY?! CUTE!!
I- I SAID IT...
.....
B-BM B-BM B-BM B-BM

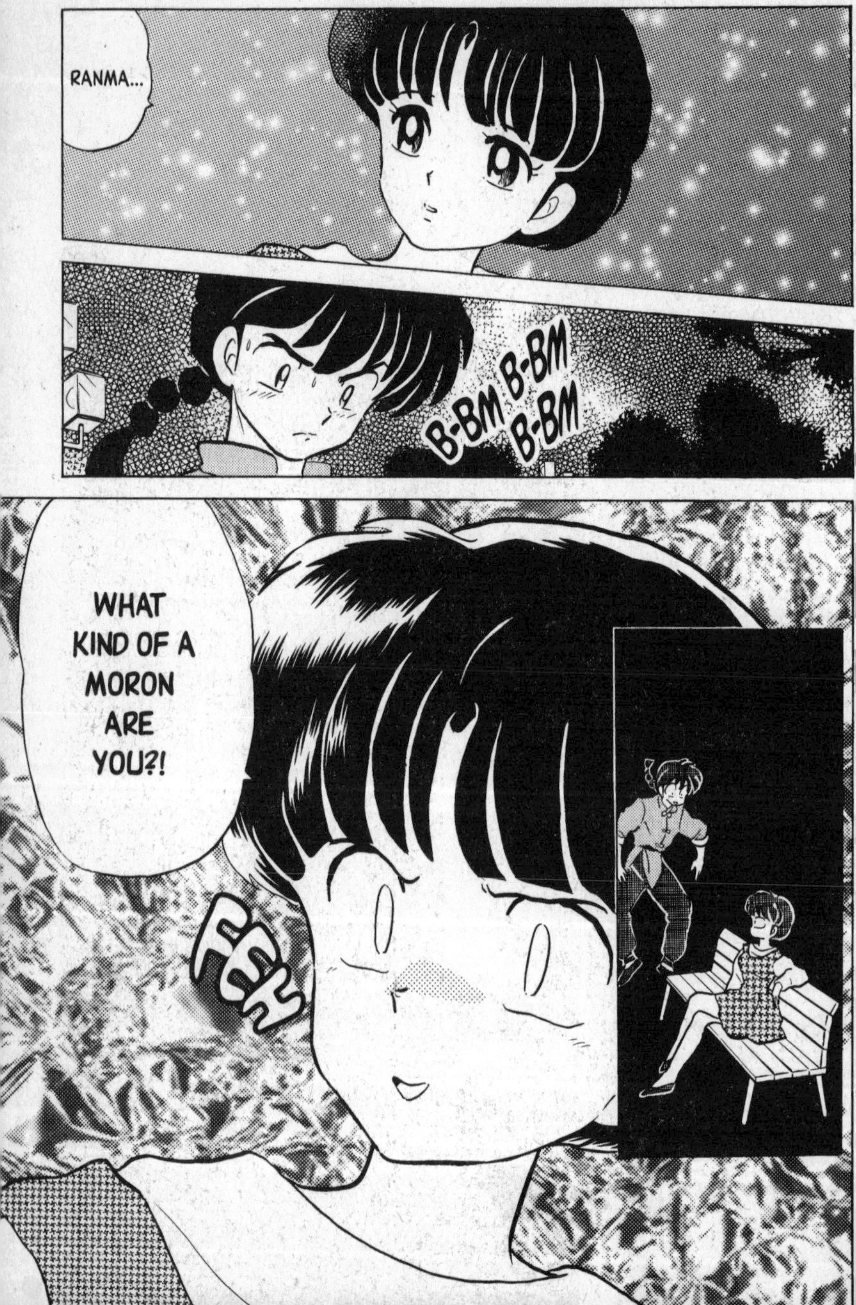
RANMA...
B-BM B-BM
B-BM B-BM
WHAT KIND OF A MORON ARE YOU?!
FEH

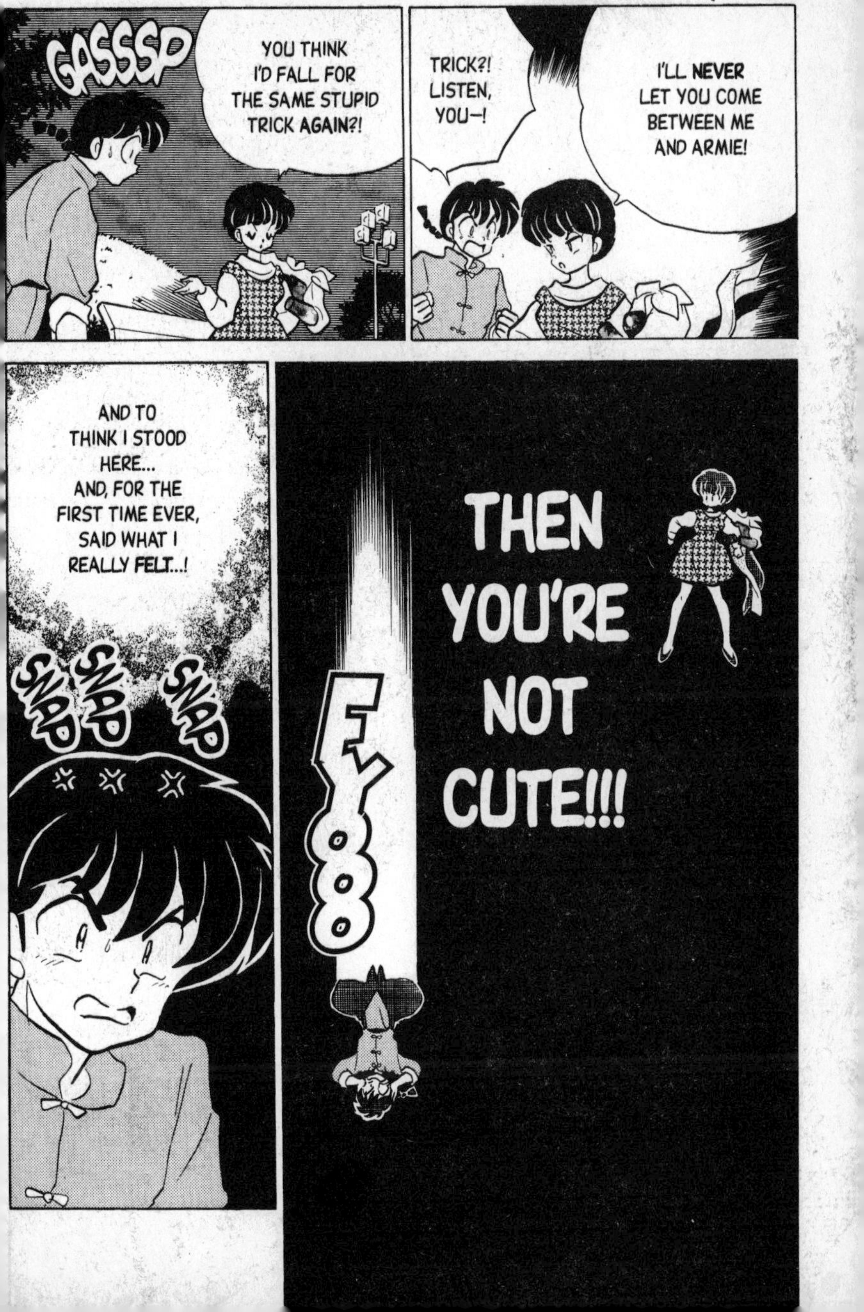
GASSSP
YOU THINK I'D FALL FOR THE SAME STUPID TRICK AGAIN?!
TRICK?! LISTEN, YOU—!
I'LL NEVER LET YOU COME BETWEEN ME AND ARMIE!
AND TO THINK I STOOD HERE... AND, FOR THE FIRST TIME EVER, SAID WHAT I REALLY FELT...!
SNAP SNAP SNAP
THEN YOU'RE NOT CUTE!!!
EYOOO

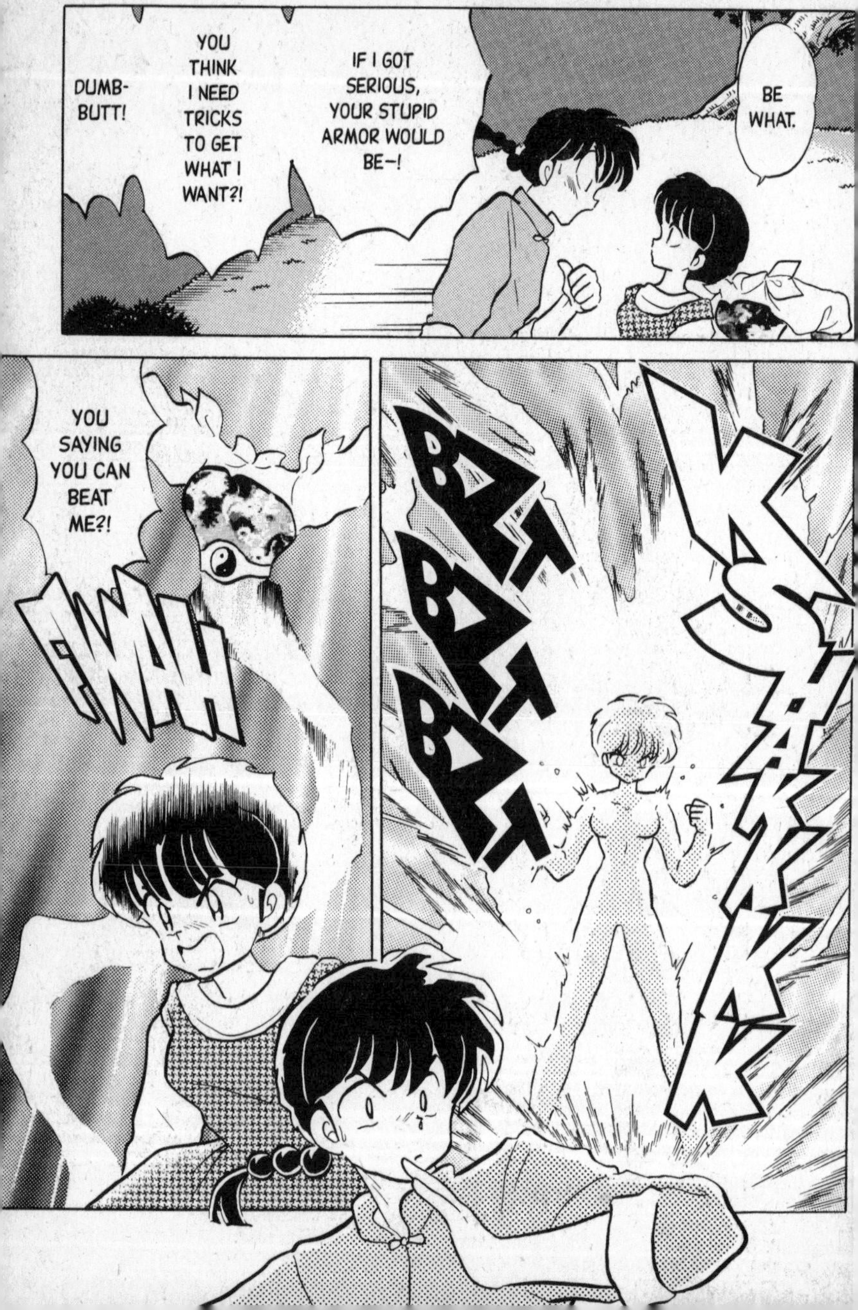
DUMB-BUTT!
YOU THINK I NEED TRICKS TO GET WHAT I WANT?!
IF I GOT SERIOUS, YOUR STUPID ARMOR WOULD BE--!
BE WHAT.
YOU SAYING YOU CAN BEAT ME?!
FWAH
BAT BAT BAT
KSHAKKKK

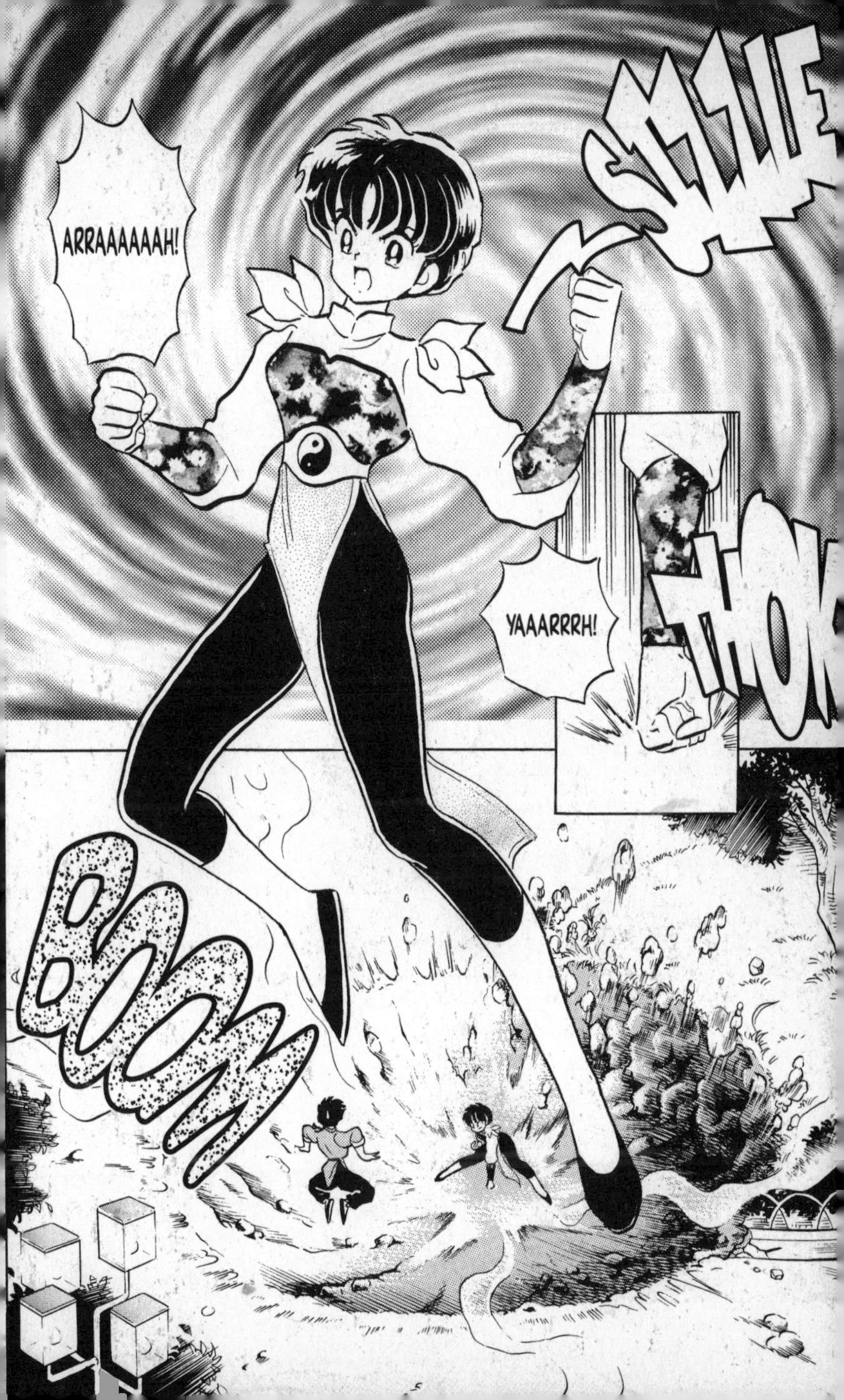
ARRAAAAAAH!
YAAARRRH!
BOOM

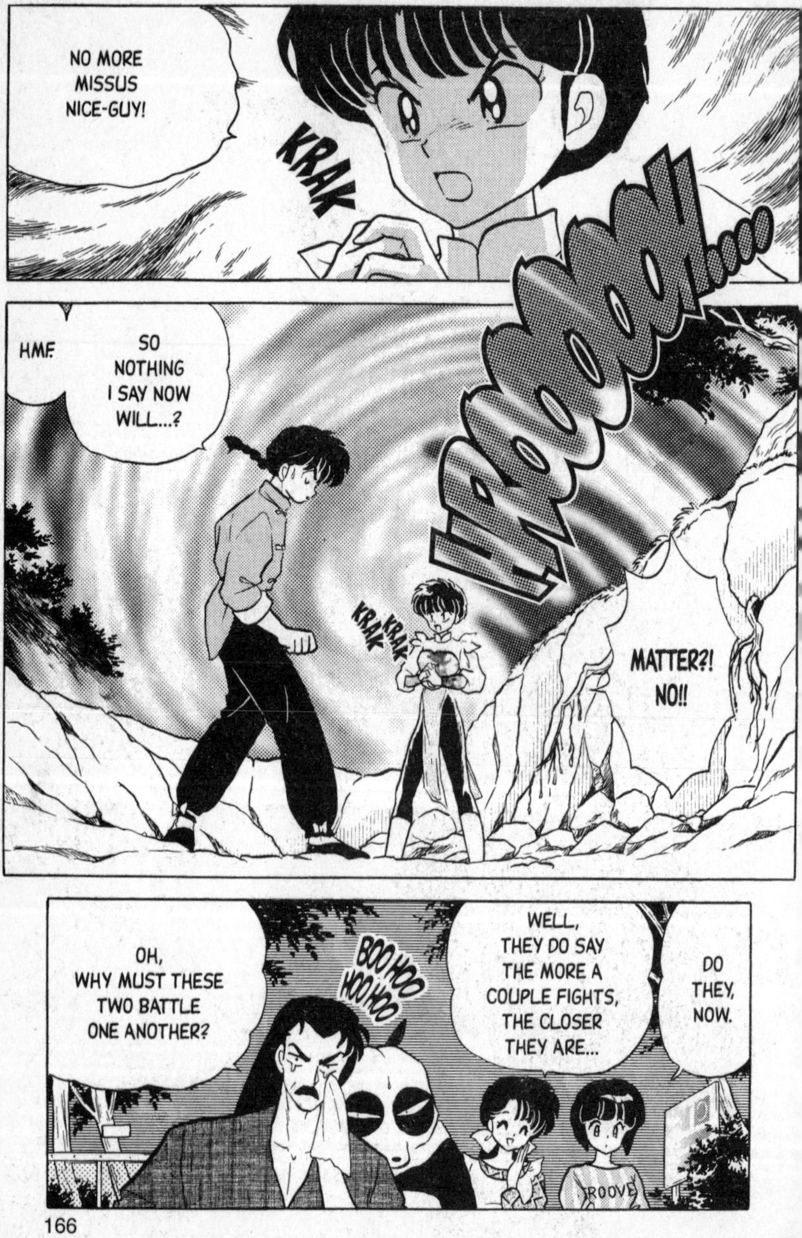
NO MORE MISSUS NICE-GUY!
KRAK
WROOOOOH.....
HMF.
SO NOTHING I SAY NOW WILL...?
KRAK KRAK
MATTER?! NO!!
OH, WHY MUST THESE TWO BATTLE ONE ANOTHER?
BOO HOO HOO HOO
WELL, THEY DO SAY THE MORE A COUPLE FIGHTS, THE CLOSER THEY ARE...
DO THEY, NOW.
ROOVE

PART 11
THE GREAT DIVIDE

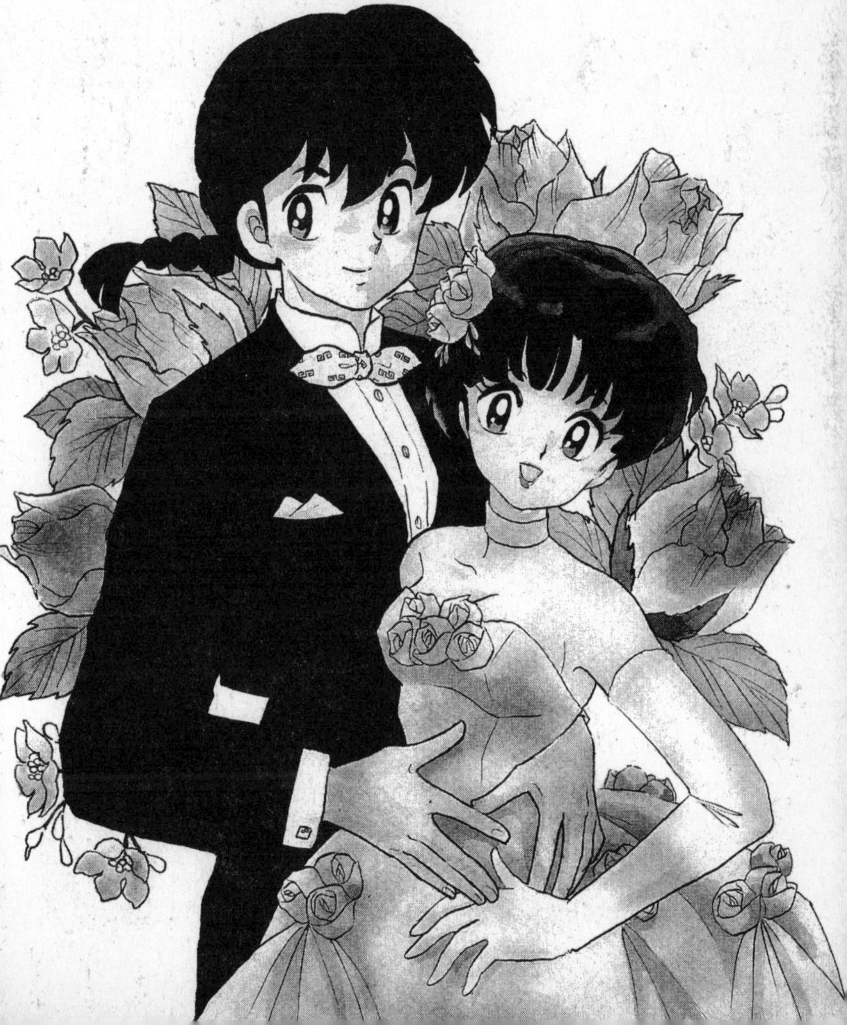

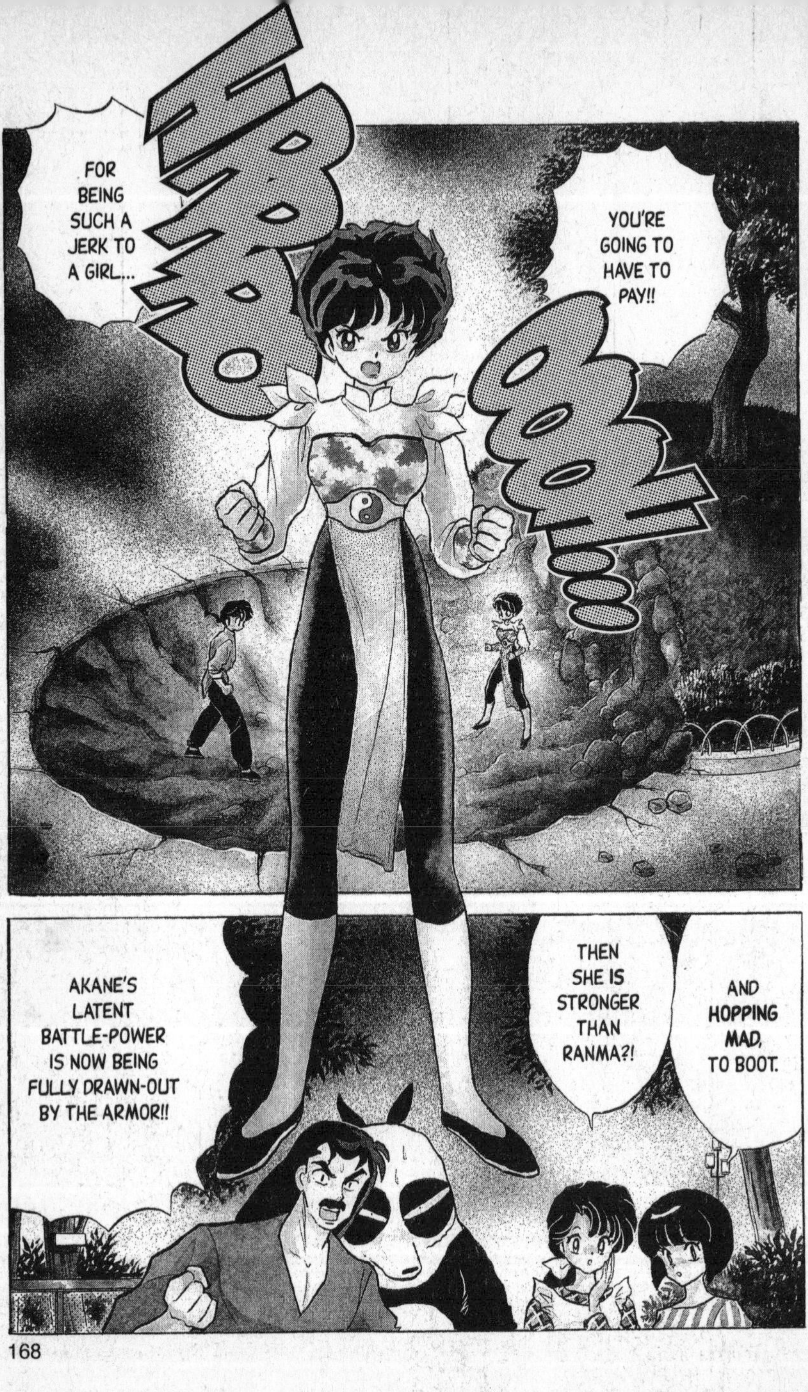
FOR BEING SUCH A JERK TO A GIRL...
YOU'RE GOING TO HAVE TO PAY!!
AKANE'S LATENT BATTLE-POWER IS NOW BEING FULLY DRAWN-OUT BY THE ARMOR!!
THEN SHE IS STRONGER THAN RANMA?!
AND HOPPING MAD, TO BOOT.

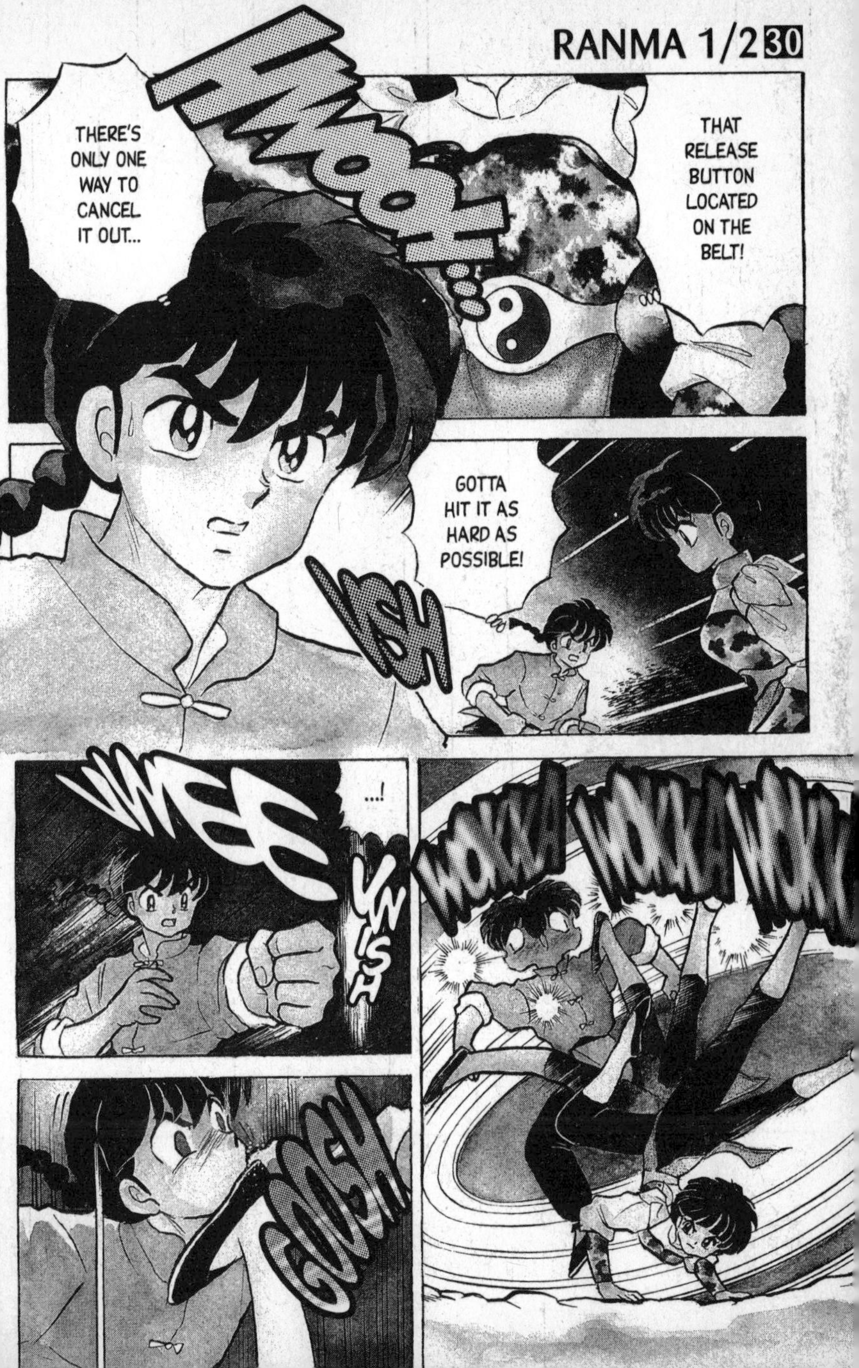
THERE'S ONLY ONE WAY TO CANCEL IT OUT...
THAT RELEASE BUTTON LOCATED ON THE BELT!
GOTTA HIT IT AS HARD AS POSSIBLE!
VISH
...!
VWISH
WOKKA

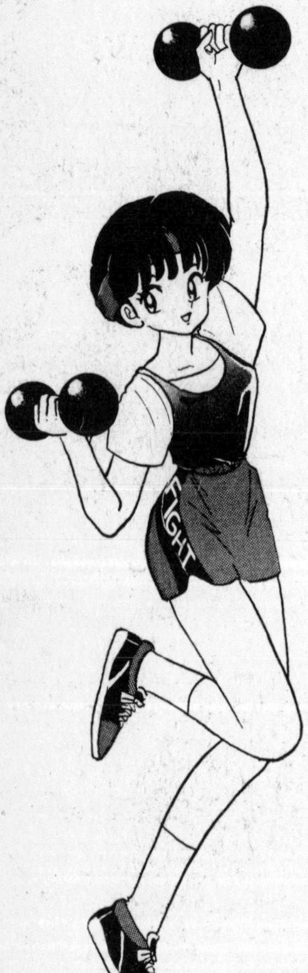
FIGHT

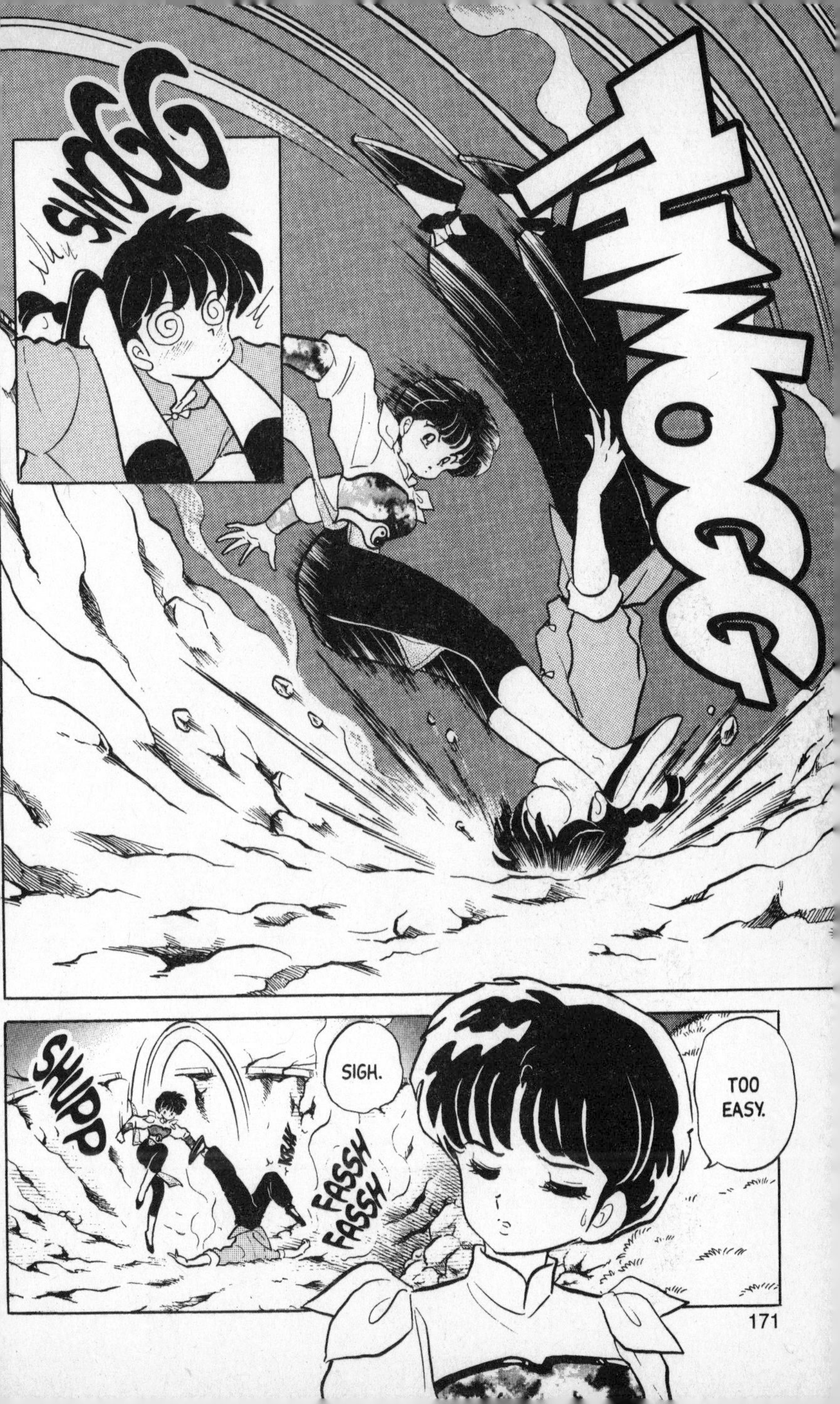
SWOGG
THWOGG
SHUPP
FASSH FASSH
SIGH.
TOO EASY.

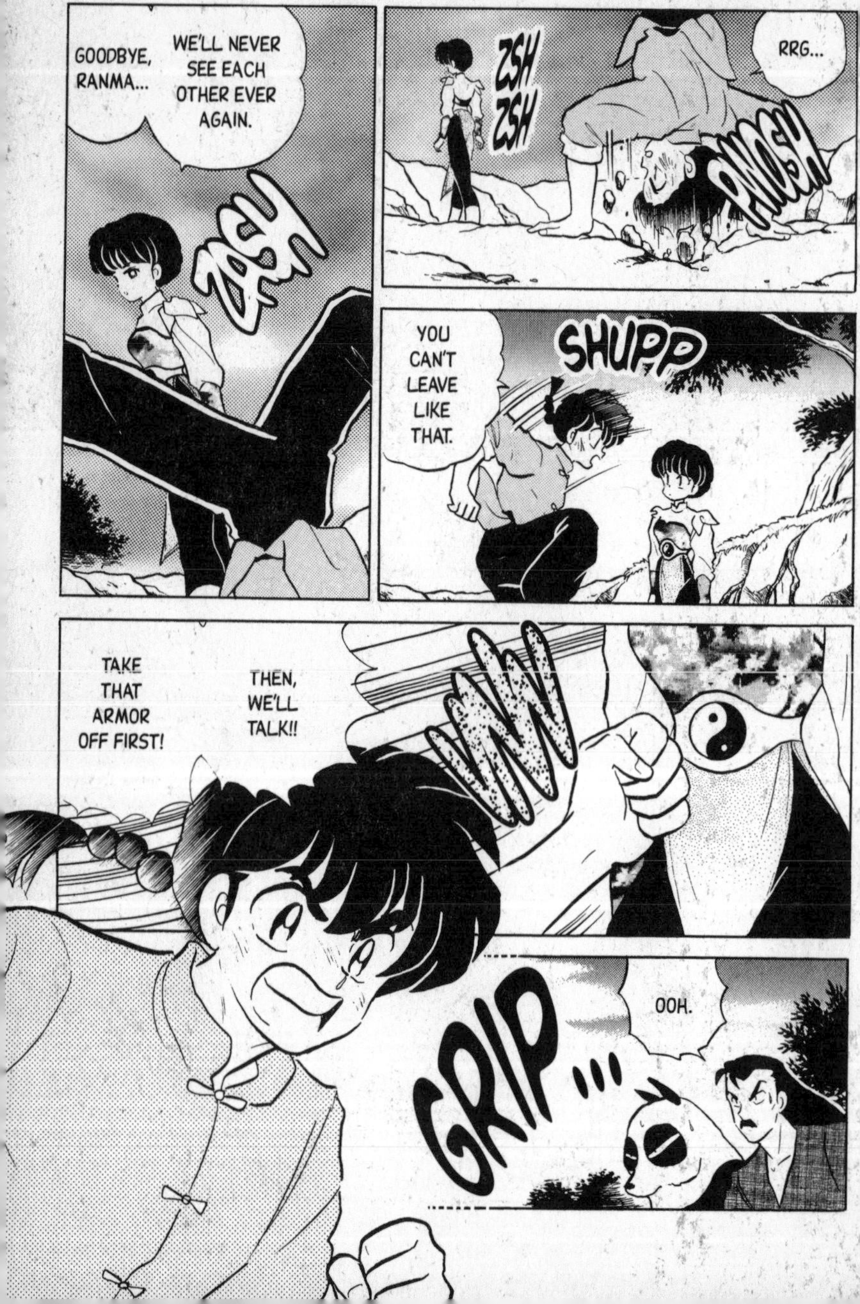
GOODBYE, RANMA...
WE'LL NEVER SEE EACH OTHER EVER AGAIN.
ZASH
ZSH ZSH
RRG...
DWOSH
YOU CAN'T LEAVE LIKE THAT.
SHUPP
TAKE THAT ARMOR OFF FIRST!
THEN, WE'LL TALK!!
GRIP...
OOH.

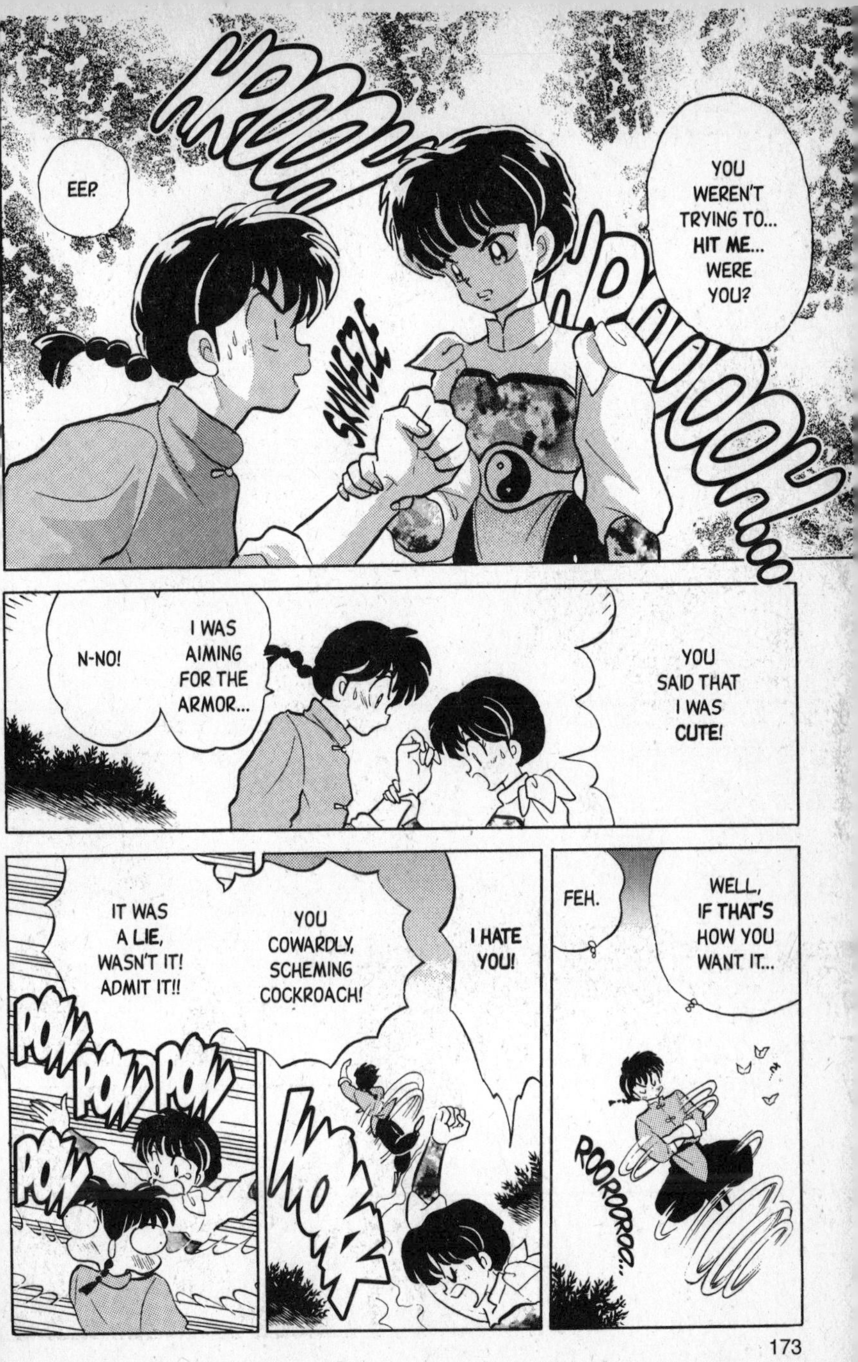
EEP.
SKWEEZE
YOU WEREN'T TRYING TO... HIT ME... WERE YOU?
N-NO!
I WAS AIMING FOR THE ARMOR...
YOU SAID THAT I WAS CUTE!
IT WAS A LIE, WASN'T IT! ADMIT IT!!
POW POW POW POW
YOU COWARDLY, SCHEMING COCKROACH!
I HATE YOU!
FEH.
WELL, IF THAT'S HOW YOU WANT IT...
ROOROOROO...

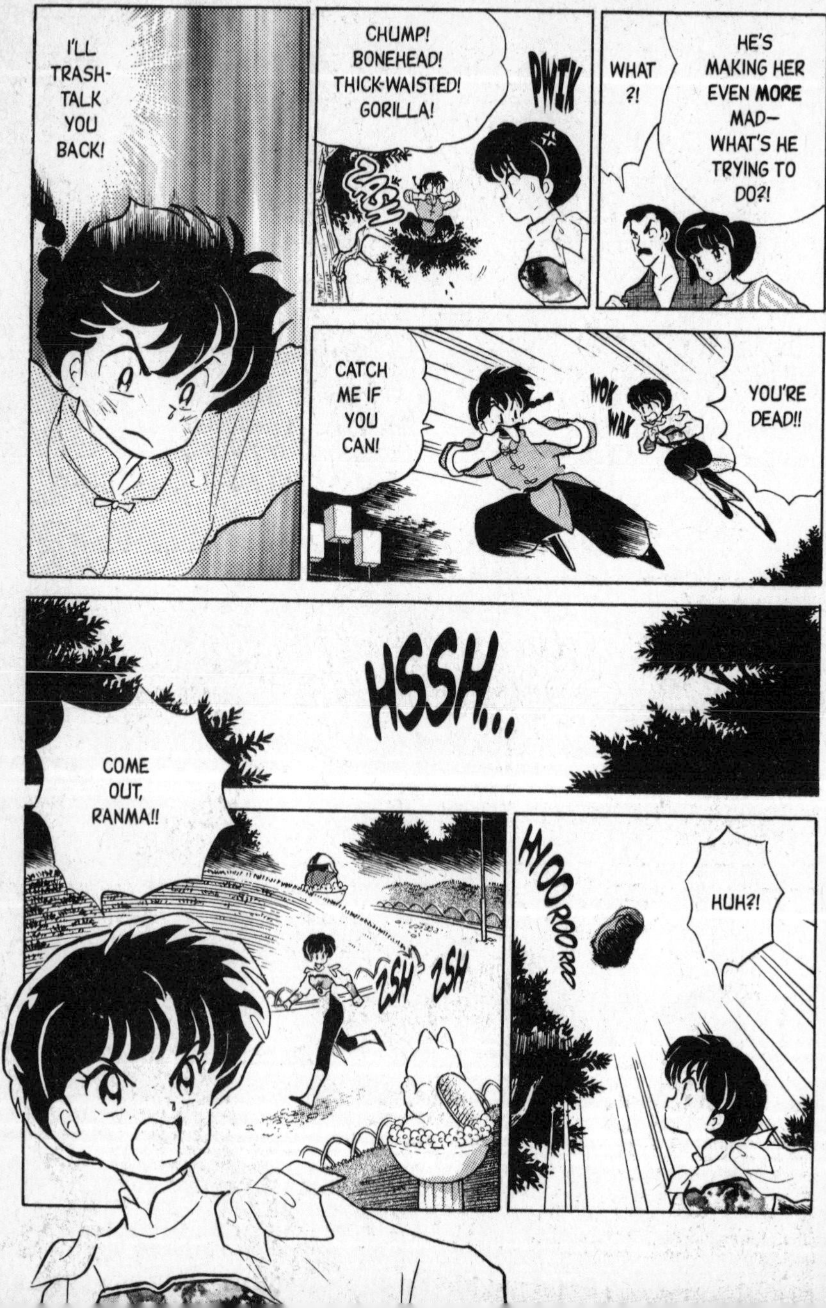
I'LL TRASH-TALK YOU BACK!
CHUMP! BONEHEAD! THICK-WAISTED! GORILLA!
PWIK
ZASH
WHAT ?!
HE'S MAKING HER EVEN MORE MAD— WHAT'S HE TRYING TO DO?!
CATCH ME IF YOU CAN!
WOK WAK
YOU'RE DEAD!!
HSSH...
COME OUT, RANMA!!
ZSH ZSH
HYOOROOROOROO
HUH?!

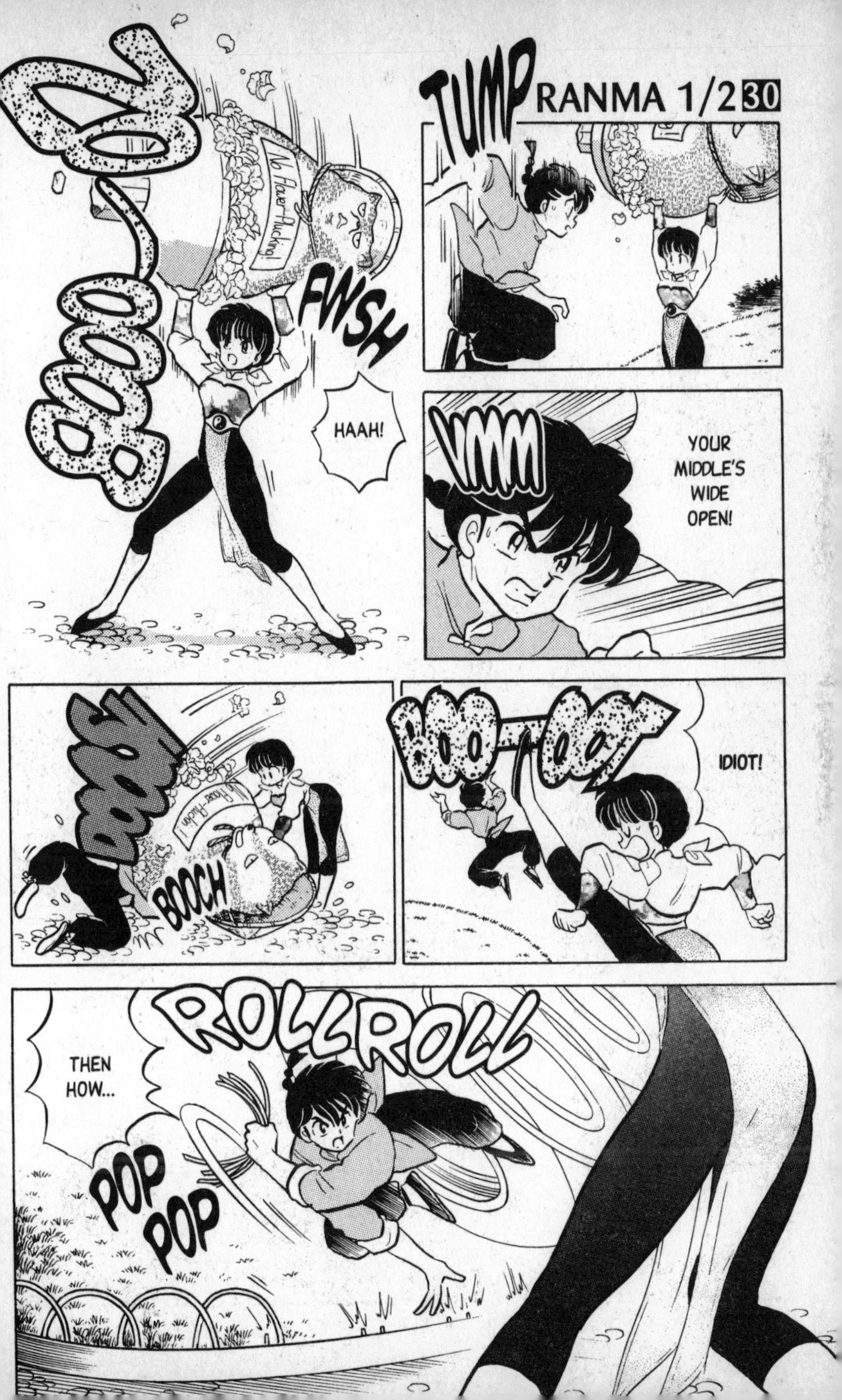
BOOO-OOM
No Flower Plucking!
FWSH
HAAH!
TUMP
VMMM
YOUR MIDDLE'S WIDE OPEN!
BOOSH
BOOCH
BOO-OOT
IDIOT!
ROLLROLL
THEN HOW...
POP POP

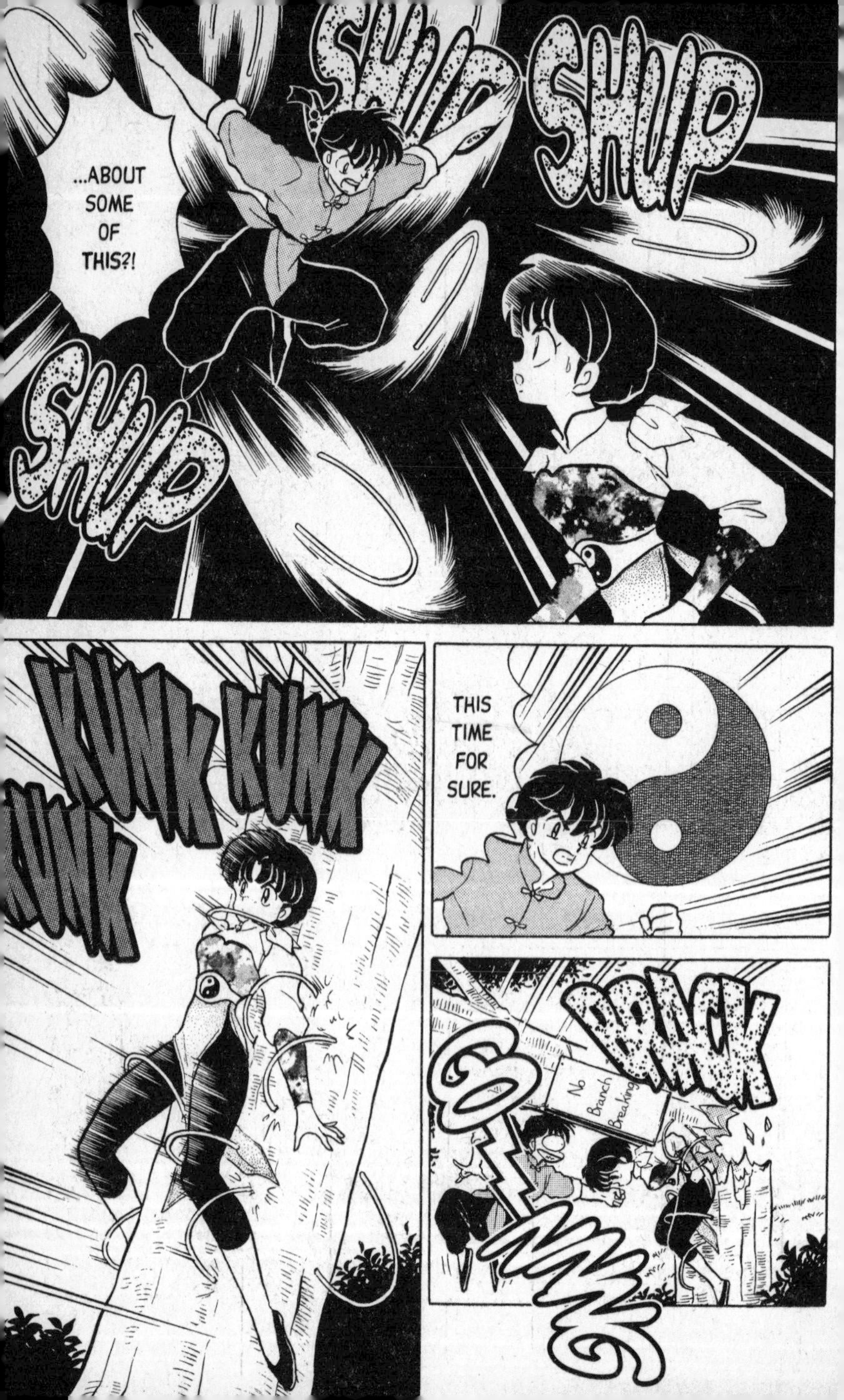

...ABOUT SOME OF THIS?!
SHUP SHUP
SHUP
KUNK KUNK
THIS TIME FOR SURE.
No Branch Breaking

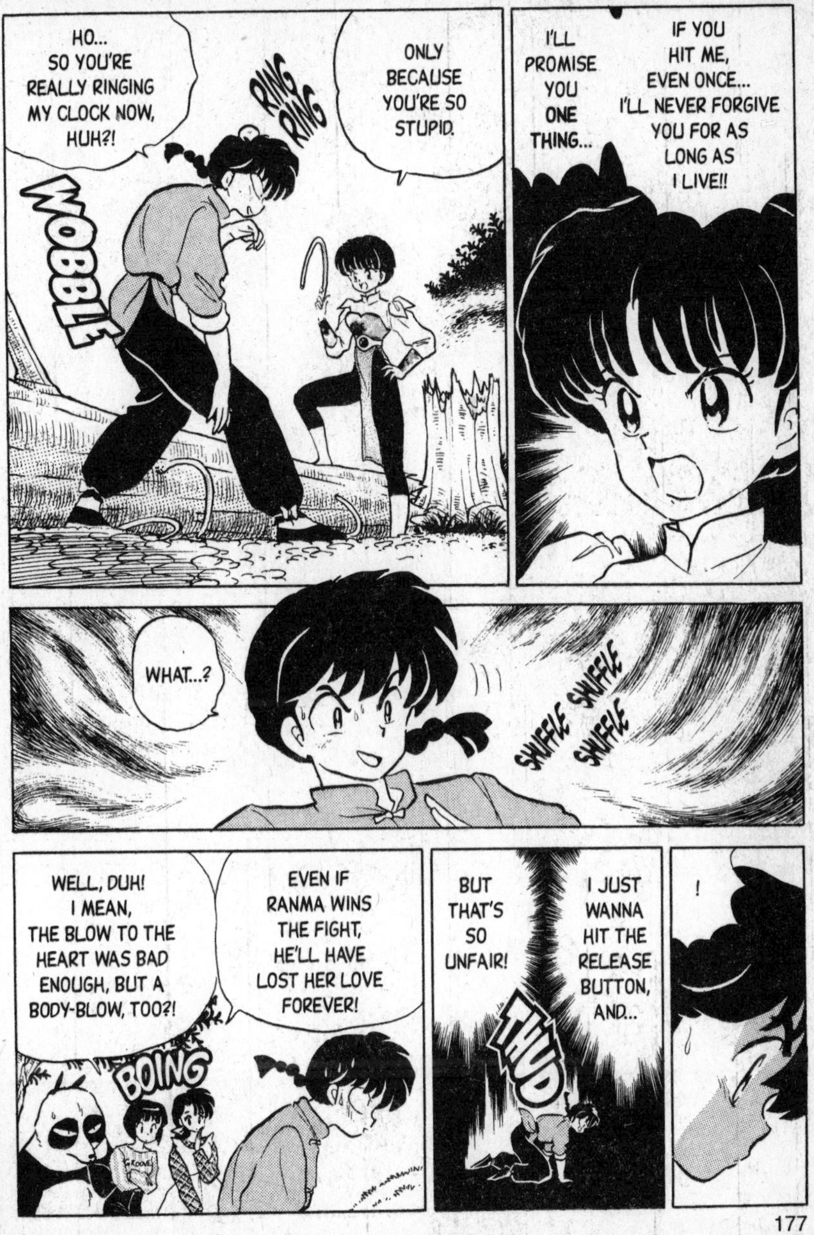
HO... SO YOU'RE REALLY RINGING MY CLOCK NOW, HUH?!
WOBBLE
RING RING
ONLY BECAUSE YOU'RE SO STUPID.
I'LL PROMISE YOU ONE THING...
IF YOU HIT ME, EVEN ONCE... I'LL NEVER FORGIVE YOU FOR AS LONG AS I LIVE!!
WHAT...?
SHUFFLE SHUFFLE SHUFFLE SHUFFLE
WELL, DUH! I MEAN, THE BLOW TO THE HEART WAS BAD ENOUGH, BUT A BODY-BLOW, TOO?!
EVEN IF RANMA WINS THE FIGHT, HE'LL HAVE LOST HER LOVE FOREVER!
BOING
BUT THAT'S SO UNFAIR!
I JUST WANNA HIT THE RELEASE BUTTON, AND...
THUD
!

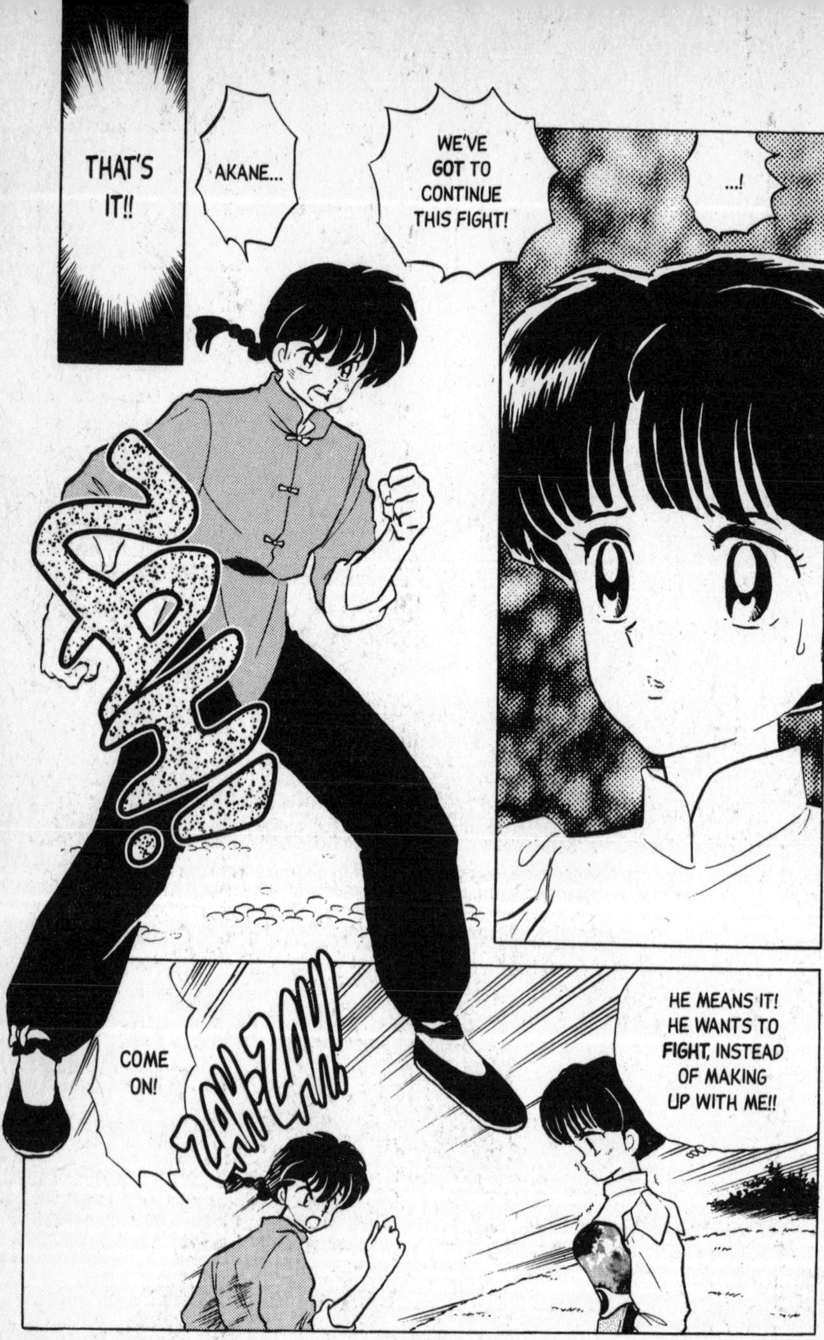
THAT'S IT!!
AKANE...
WE'VE GOT TO CONTINUE THIS FIGHT!
...!
COME ON!
HE MEANS IT! HE WANTS TO FIGHT, INSTEAD OF MAKING UP WITH ME!!
...

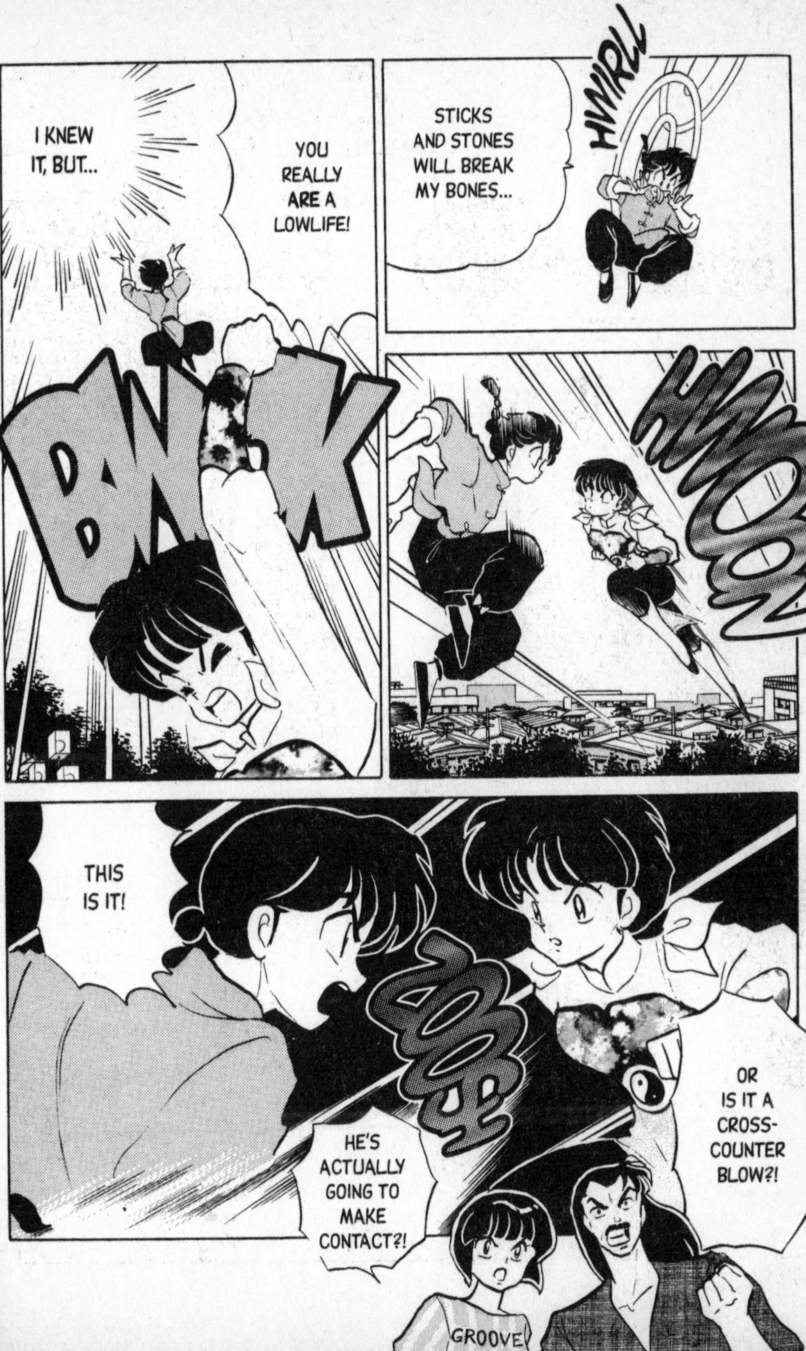
I KNEW IT, BUT...
YOU REALLY ARE A LOWLIFE!
BAMK
STICKS AND STONES WILL BREAK MY BONES...
HWIRLL
HWOOOM
THIS IS IT!
ZOOM
HE'S ACTUALLY GOING TO MAKE CONTACT?!
OR IS IT A CROSS-COUNTER BLOW?!
GROOVE

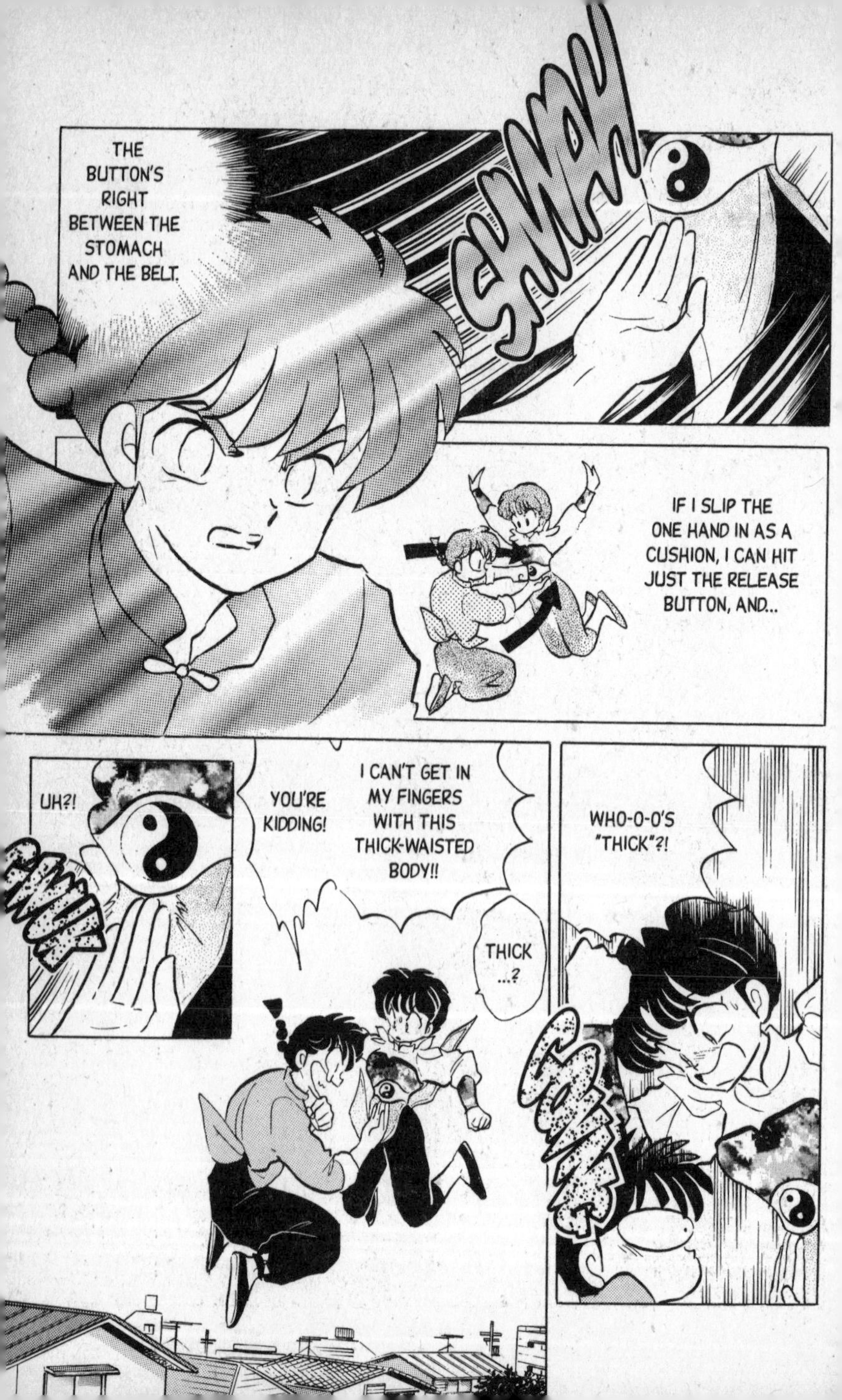

THE BUTTON'S RIGHT BETWEEN THE STOMACH AND THE BELT.
IF I SLIP THE ONE HAND IN AS A CUSHION, I CAN HIT JUST THE RELEASE BUTTON, AND...
UH?!
YOU'RE KIDDING!
I CAN'T GET IN MY FINGERS WITH THIS THICK-WAISTED BODY!!
THICK ...?
WHO-O-O'S "THICK"?!

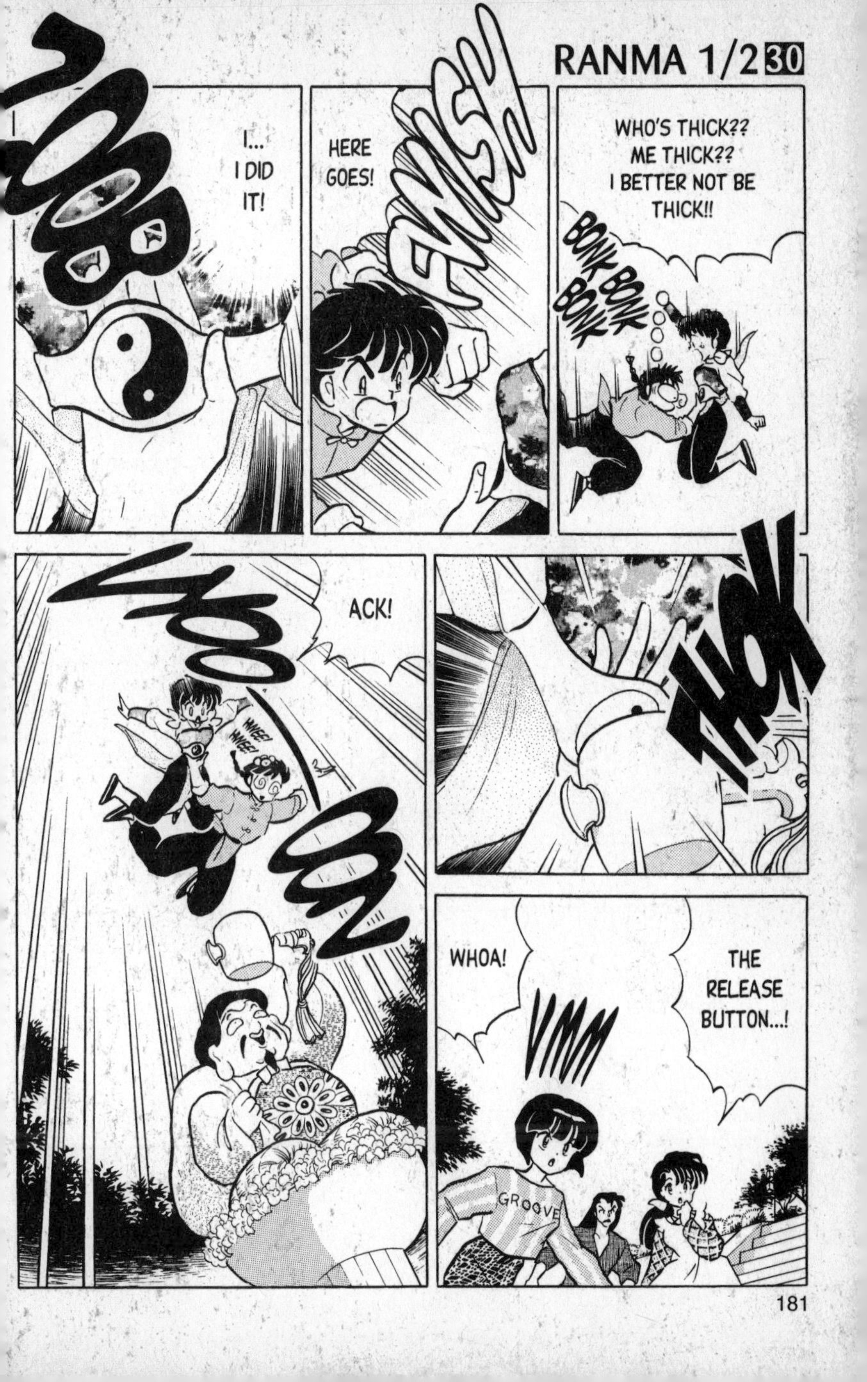
I... I DID IT!
HERE GOES!
WHO'S THICK?? ME THICK?? I BETTER NOT BE THICK!!
BONK BONK BONK
ACK!
THOK
WHOA!
THE RELEASE BUTTON...!
GROOVE

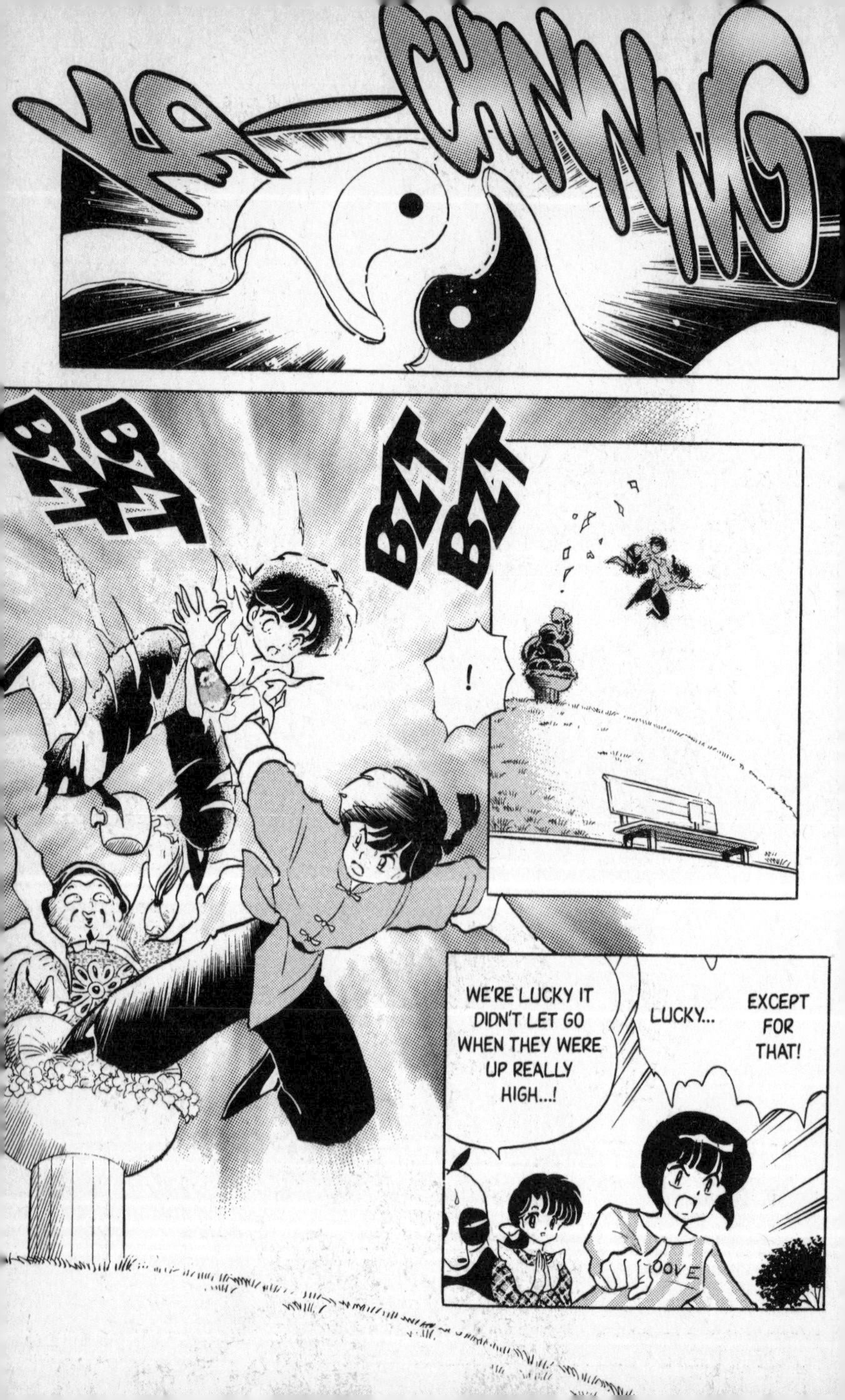
KA-CHINNNG
BZZT BZZT
BZZT BZZT
!
WE'RE LUCKY IT DIDN'T LET GO WHEN THEY WERE UP REALLY HIGH...!
LUCKY...
EXCEPT FOR THAT!

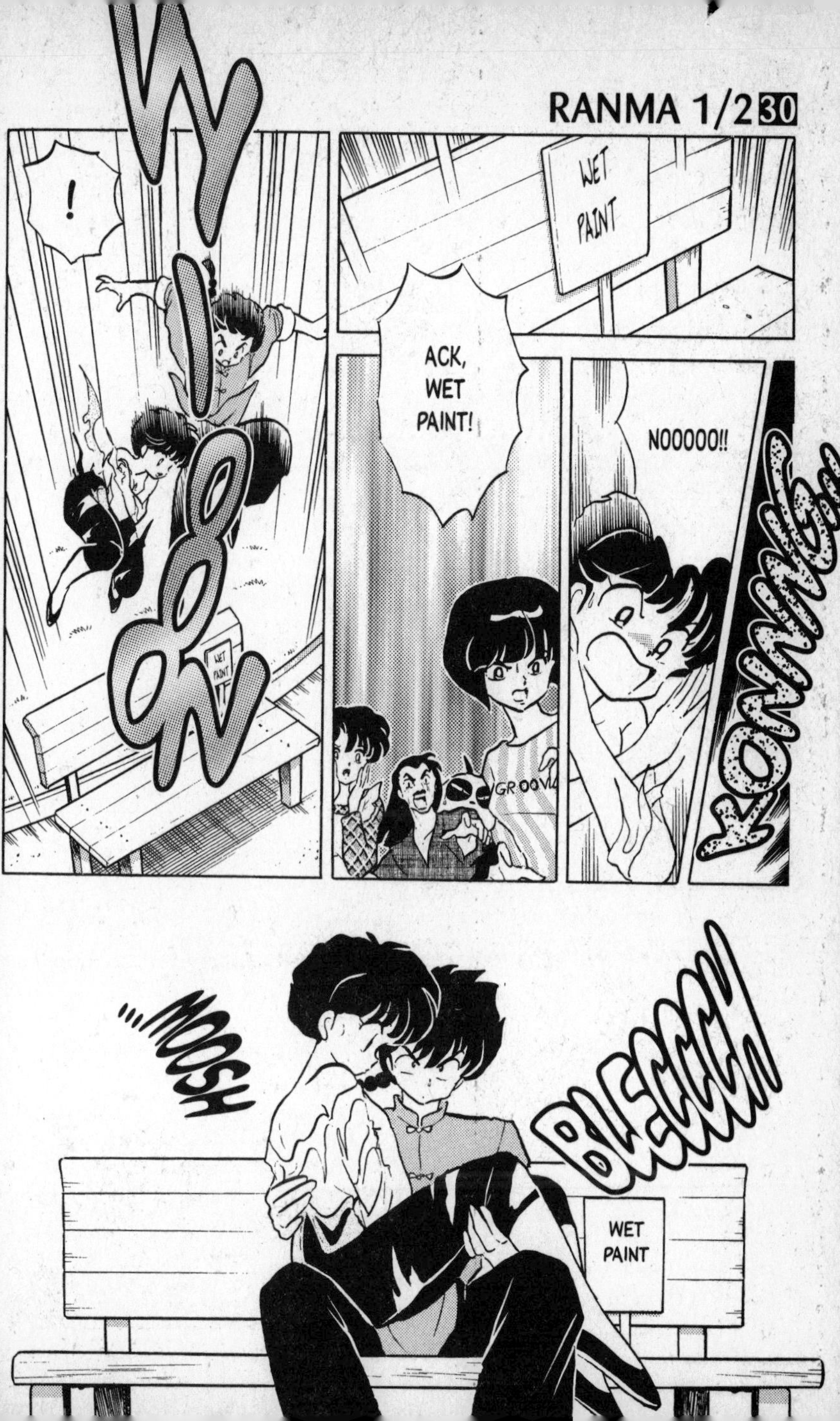
!
WET PAINT
WET PAINT
ACK, WET PAINT!
GROOV
NOOOOO!!
...MOOSH
BLECCCH!
WET PAINT

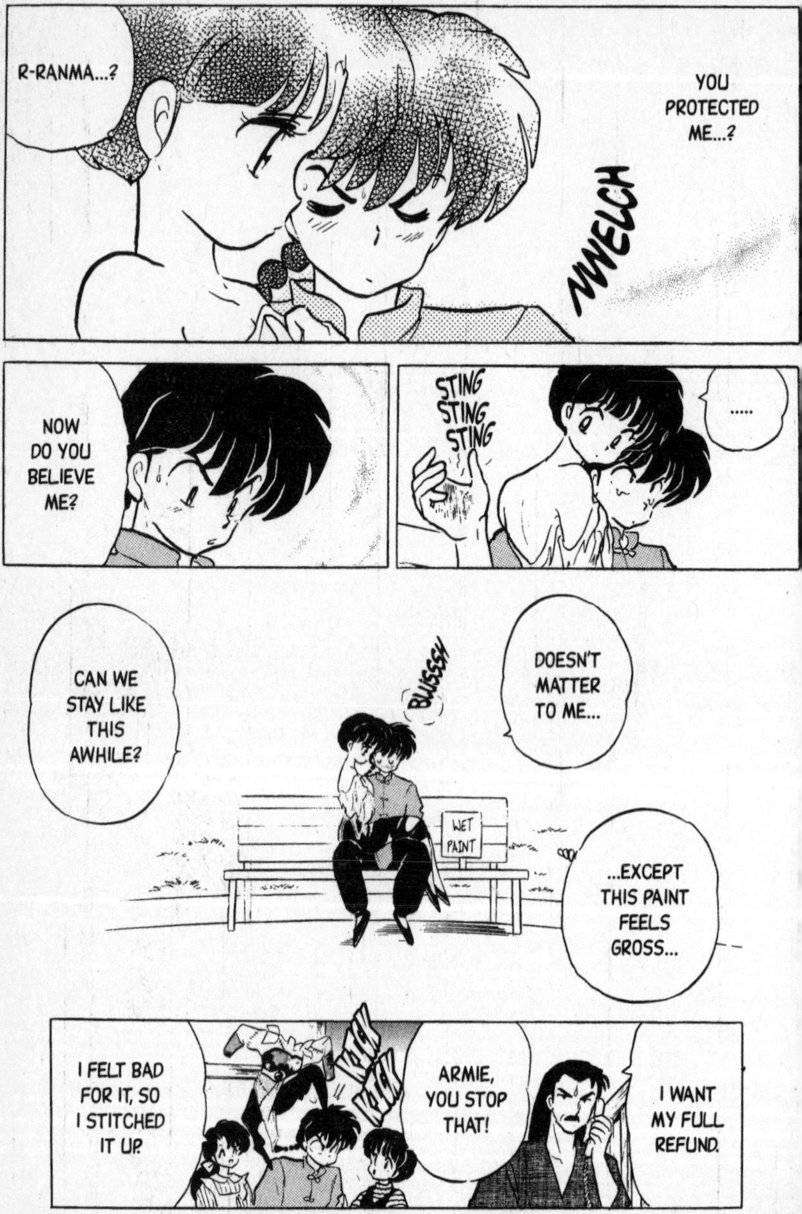
R-RANMA...?
YOU PROTECTED ME...?
NWELCH
NOW DO YOU BELIEVE ME?
STING STING STING
.....
CAN WE STAY LIKE THIS AWHILE?
BLUSSSH
DOESN'T MATTER TO ME...
WET PAINT
...EXCEPT THIS PAINT FEELS GROSS...
I FELT BAD FOR IT, SO I STITCHED IT UP.
ARMIE, YOU STOP THAT!
I WANT MY FULL REFUND.

EDITOR'S RECOMMENDATIONS

If you enjoyed this volume of Ranma 1/2, then here is some more manga you might be interested in:

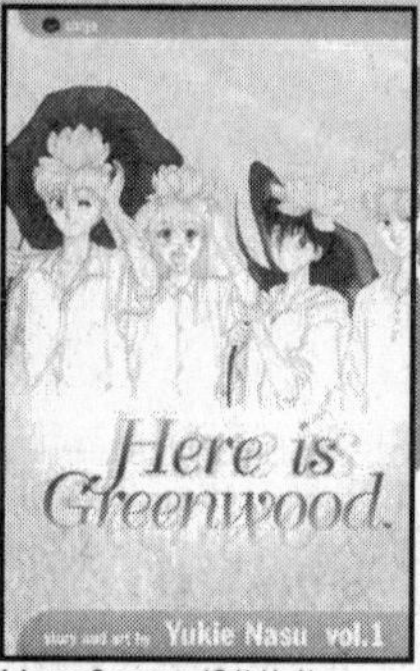

Here is Greenwood
Yukie Nasu vol.1

HERE IS GREENWOOD

Perhaps written for a slightly older audience than most of Rumiko Takahashi's work, Yukie Nasu's *Here is Greenwood* is exactly like *Ranma 1/2*, except for the martial arts (none), the wacky hijinks (almost none), and the occasional depiction of the adult relationships among its students. Okay, aside from the fact that they both have male high school students in them, they have nothing in common. But they're both cool!

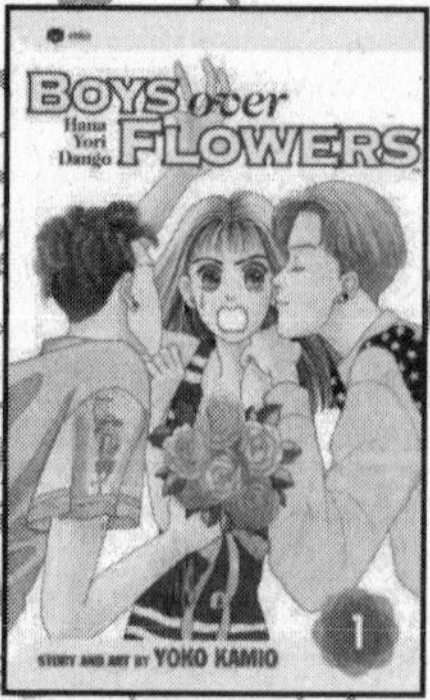

BOYS over FLOWERS
Hana Yori Dango
1
STORY AND ART BY YOKO KAMIO

BOYS OVER FLOWERS (HANA YORI DANGO)

Another tale of high-school life in Japan, *Boys Over Flowers* (or "HanaDan" to most of its fans) is not without its serious side, but overall tends to fall into the "rabu-kome" or "love-comedy" genre.

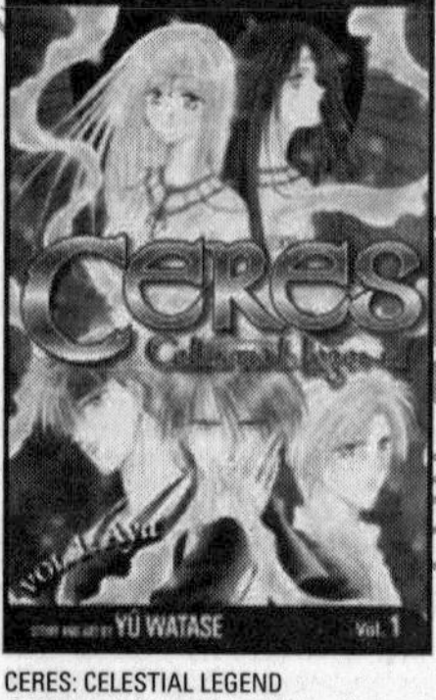

Ceres
YÛ WATASE
Vol. 1

CERES CELESTIAL LEGEND

Aya Mikage is a trendy Tokyo teen with not much else on her mind but fashion, karaoke, and boys. But a terrible family secret involving an ancient family "curse" is about to make things a lot more difficult.

About Rumiko Takahashi

Born in 1957 in Niigata, Japan, Rumiko Takahashi attended women's college in Tokyo, where she began studying comics with Kazuo Koike, author of CRYING FREEMAN. She later became an assistant to horror-manga artist Kazuo Umezu (OROCHI). In 1978, she won a prize in Shogakukan's annual "New Comic Artist Contest," and in that same year her boy-meets-alien comedy series URUSEI YATSURA began appearing in the weekly manga magazine SHÔNEN SUNDAY. This phenomenally successful series ran for nine years and sold over 22 million copies. Takahashi's later RANMA 1/2 series enjoyed even greater popularity.

Takahashi is considered by many to be one of the world's most popular manga artists. With the publication of Volume 34 of her RANMA 1/2 series in Japan, Takahashi's total sales passed one hundred million copies of her compiled works.

Takahashi's serial titles include URUSEI YATSURA, RANMA 1/2, ONE-POUND GOSPEL, MAISON IKKOKU and INUYASHA. Additionally, Takahashi has drawn many short stories which have been published in America under the title "Rumic Theater," and several installments of a saga known as her "Mermaid" series. Most of Takahashi's major stories have also been animated and are widely available in translation worldwide. INUYASHA is her most recent serial story, first published in SHÔNEN SUNDAY in 1996.

COMPLETE OUR SURVEY AND LET
US KNOW WHAT YOU THINK!

☐ Please do NOT send me information about VIZ products, news and events, special offers, or other information.

☐ Please do NOT send me information from VIZ's trusted business partners.

Name: _____

Address: _____

City: _____ **State:** _____ **Zip:** _____

E-mail: _____

☐ **Male** ☐ **Female** **Date of Birth** (mm/dd/yyyy): ___ / ___ / _____ (Under 13? Parental consent required)

What race/ethnicity do you consider yourself? (please check one)

☐ Asian/Pacific Islander   ☐ Black/African American   ☐ Hispanic/Latino

☐ Native American/Alaskan Native   ☐ White/Caucasian   ☐ Other: _____

What VIZ product did you purchase? (check all that apply and indicate title purchased)

☐ DVD/VHS _____

☐ Graphic Novel _____

☐ Magazines _____

☐ Merchandise _____

Reason for purchase: (check all that apply)

☐ Special offer   ☐ Favorite title   ☐ Gift

☐ Recommendation   ☐ Other _____

Where did you make your purchase? (please check one)

☐ Comic store   ☐ Bookstore   ☐ Mass/Grocery Store

☐ Newsstand   ☐ Video/Video Game Store   ☐ Other: _____

☐ Online (site: _____)

What other VIZ properties have you purchased/own? _____

_____

How many anime and/or manga titles have you purchased in the last year? How many were VIZ titles? (please check one from each column)

ANIME	MANGA	VIZ
☐ None	☐ None	☐ None
☐ 1-4	☐ 1-4	☐ 1-4
☐ 5-10	☐ 5-10	☐ 5-10
☐ 11+	☐ 11+	☐ 11+

I find the pricing of VIZ products to be: (please check one)

☐ Cheap   ☐ Reasonable   ☐ Expensive

What genre of manga and anime would you like to see from VIZ? (please check two)

☐ Adventure   ☐ Comic Strip   ☐ Science Fiction   ☐ Fighting

☐ Horror   ☐ Romance   ☐ Fantasy   ☐ Sports

What do you think of VIZ's new look?

☐ Love It   ☐ It's OK   ☐ Hate It   ☐ Didn't Notice   ☐ No Opinion

Which do you prefer? (please check one)

☐ Reading right-to-left

☐ Reading left-to-right

Which do you prefer? (please check one)

☐ Sound effects in English

☐ Sound effects in Japanese with English captions

☐ Sound effects in Japanese only with a glossary at the back

THANK YOU! Please send the completed form to:

ARAM PUBLIC LIBRARY
DELAVAN, WI

NJW Research
42 Catharine St.
Poughkeepsie, NY 12601

All information provided will be used for internal purposes only. We promise not to sell or otherwise divulge your information.